**Studia Fennica**
Anthropologica 4

# Dwelling in Political Landscapes

Contemporary Anthropological Perspectives

Edited by Anu Lounela, Eeva Berglund and Timo Kallinen

Finnish Literature Society · SKS · Helsinki · 2019

**STUDIA FENNICA ANTHROPOLOGICA 4**

The publication has undergone a peer review.

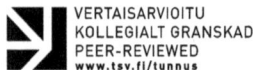

VERTAISARVIOITU
KOLLEGIALT GRANSKAD
PEER-REVIEWED
www.tsv.fi/tunnus

© 2019 Anu Lounela, Eeva Berglund, Timo Kallinen and SKS
License CC-BY-NC-ND 4.0 International

Cover Design: Timo Numminen
EPUB: Tero Salmén

ISBN 978-951-858-087-7 (Print)
ISBN978-951-858-114-0 (PDF)
ISBN 978-951-858-113-3 (EPUB)

ISSN 0085-6835 (Studia Fennica)
ISSN 1796-8208 (Studia Fennica Anthropologica)

DOI: https://doi.org/10.21435/sfa.4

A free open access version of the book is available at https://doi.org/10.21435/sfa.4
or by scanning this QR code with your mobile device.

BoD – Books on Demand, Norderstedt, Germany 2019

# Contents

# Acknowledgements

Producing a book is a collective affair, and we have many people to thank. Above all, we thank the authors and the countless people around the world at fieldsites, research meetings and domestic spaces, without whose input the chapters would never have been produced. We also wish to thank the organisers of the Biennial Conference of the Finnish Anthropological Society on the topic of "Landscapes, sociality and materiality" in Helsinki in 2015: Katja Uusihakala, Tuomas Tammisto, Heikki Wilenius and Hilja Aunela, and the various people at Helsinki's wonderful House of Science and Letters who helped things to run smoothly.

For financial support we wish to thank the Finnish Cultural Foundation who not only supported the production of the manuscript text but made it possible to continue the conversation at a separate workshop held in Helsinki in September 2016.

We are grateful to Anna Tsing and Philippe Descola who not only provided inspiration with their talks in Helsinki, but allowed us to publish their texts as part of this book. We also thank *Suomen Antropologi - Journal of the Finnish Anthropological Society* for permission to reproduce their lectures.

Finally, our thanks go to the production staff at the Finnish Literature Society and the board of its Studia Fennica book series. We are particularly grateful to Kenneth Sillander whose critique and encouragement have helped along the process, as did the constructive feedback of the two anonymous reviewers of the manuscript. Thanks also go to Eija Hukka for her valuable work in the design and copyediting process.

Helsinki 2019
*Anu Lounela, Eeva Berglund, Timo Kallinen*

Eeva Berglund
https://orcid.org/0000-0003-0269-562X

Anu Lounela
https://orcid.org/0000-0002-8903-1983

Timo Kallinen
https://orcid.org/0000-0001-7916-6203

# Landscape is not what it used to be: Anthropology and the politics of environmental change

Our epoch is one of significant shifts in how relations among societies and natures are formed, maintained and lived. We suggest that new anthropological perspectives on landscape have great potential to address the resulting conundrums. People all over the globe are experiencing new hazards and unprecedented situations as their environments change at speeds never before experienced. Massive species loss is just one transformation affecting life forms and their interactions, climate change another, and there are many more rapid and sometimes profound material and social changes that anthropologists working around the world attend to and document. That said, alongside these changes, there are also significant continuities.

Through exploring how the material and conceptual are entangled in and as landscapes, this book takes up the invitation posed by such emerging situations, to open up the potentials in anthropology and related fields, for understanding life when 'things are not what they used to be'. Complex entanglements of seemingly disconnected processes and the recent sense of crisis concerning environment, movements of people, climate change and other planetary transformations, raise questions over the role of anthropology and about appropriate methodologies for studying these developments.

The book's origins are in the Biennial Conference of the Finnish Anthropological Society 'Landscapes, Sociality and Materiality' (2015)[1] much of which touched upon questions of how materialities and social

1 The Biennial Conference of the Finnish Anthropological Society 2015, 'Landscapes, sociality and materiality' was held in Helsinki in October, 2015. Katja Uusihakala and Anu Lounela acted as the principal organisers, but Jenni Mölkänen, Tuomas Tammisto and Heikki Wilenius contributed just as importantly in conceptualising and organising the event. The conference sought to discuss how the concept of landscape works as a tool of anthropological inquiry when we are looking at how forms of materiality and sociality connect in the production of places and spaces. The fifteen panels covered a wide range of topics such as multispecies ethnography and the Anthropocene, memory, sacred landscapes, globalisation, politics of nature and urban landscape, and more.

formations are entangled in the production of specific landscapes. During the conference, it turned out that many anthropologists are adopting and adapting Tim Ingold's work, which offers promising ways to make sense of ethnographic encounters in places where novel human and nonhuman configurations are emerging. Particularly, the dwelling perspective, which Ingold has developed in many texts (e.g. Ingold 2000), points to environments as outcomes of continuous human and nonhuman entanglements. He conceives landscapes as moments in constantly shifting relations of dwelling, where dwelling is understood as immersion in the flow of life in general. Importantly for Ingold, humans are like all animals in that they develop in movement and action, simultaneously sensing and impacting on their surroundings as they do so, even if this is denied by the conventions of modern (Western) thought (2000: 186). From such ingredients, Ingold has built up a highly influential anthropology of nature, which foregrounds landscapes as something that humans produce, and in which they actively participate, even as landscapes furnish us with both the material resources and meanings we need to survive. Landscape thus understood is neither social nor natural but socionatural.

However, as many authors of the book note, this phenomenological approach offers few tools to analyse how profound transformations in landscapes alter meanings and value relations. Thus, there seem to be limits to how far we can go with this approach and its privileging of the sensory. When new and old configurations of political power are transforming places and experiences of landscapes, even having effects on intimate knowledge people gain when they move within them, Ingold's broadly phenomenological contribution feels insufficient and risks appearing apolitical.

Noticing this gap and the emergence of rapid environmental changes around the globe, the book discusses human and nonhuman entanglements mostly within transformed landscapes. As it is, all humans today live in global as well as local situations wherein, following the 1970s post-gold, free market era and the financial crisis of 2008, economic policies and conditions have resulted in the increasing intensification of capitalism, neoliberalisation and a growing gap between the poor and rich, as well as new polarisations between divergent worldviews and practices (Gregory 1997; Ortner 2016). Increasingly, large-scale projects are transforming material flows and inter-species relations, in processes that extend even to previously intimate landscapes, while in some places, even access to land has become severely restricted. 'Land grabbing' by private corporations, conservation organisations or states, whether to gain wealth or gain power, has become a focus of scholarly interest too. There is a long history of connections between competition for land and processes of wealth accumulation, even in places where rights to land have been characteristically overlapping rather than exclusive (Polanyi 1944; Peluso and Watts 2001; Hansen and Stepputat 2006), but our contributors suggest that land grabbing should be understood as more than a territorial issue (see also Árnason et al. 2012). What is increasingly at issue are landscapes as meaningful social and material entanglements and relations extending to spirits, ancestors, winds, daylight and so on. In the examples in the chapters, landscapes are often forms of remembrance of past generations; tampering with them can equal collective violence.

These developments take place not only in the Global South, but also in the North, and they touch upon people anywhere, rural, urban and other. In some parts of the globe, rural landscapes are transformed as people migrate out, emptying the landscape especially of young people. As immigrants head for the cities, these come under pressure from overcrowding and from capital as it materialises in ever larger building projects. The connections between these geographically distant processes have become important also for anthropological landscape research, with one result being that the concept of landscape has been freed of its usually rural co-ordinates: the term is equally fruitful for the study of urban life and its dynamics. A composite or configuration of features of different kinds, landscape as concept connects different spatial processes and so helps make visible links between places – and indeed landscapes – separated by distance, such as unsustainable resource extraction in one place and seemingly unstoppable acceleration of urbanisation in another. When it comes to changing urban landscapes, generalising across the globe is foolhardy, but it is fair to say that cities everywhere increasingly feature commodity-led transnational imagery and offer homogenised experiences (Julier 2008; Easterling 2016). But if dispossession and dislocation follow, so does collective creativity that results in renewed landscapes. Efforts to create meaningful futures still produce places to dwell, in auto-constructed favelas or displaced persons' camps as much as in more middle-class projects (Immonen, Berglund, this volume). So in cities too, movement and landscape go together, with mobility and connectivity articulating inequality and its production. This more dynamic approach, which does not reduce cities to nodes in some larger network, knits together urban and rural or non-urban processes, and it complements the more holistic and notionally apolitical emphasis on dwelling (McFarlane 2011). Undoubtedly modern cities are very much the products of the need for movement and rhythmic patterns of coming and going established by industrial systems of labour, as Ingold has argued (2000: 323–338). But despite such urban experiences usually being presented as alienating and therefore not really 'dwelling', anthropologists know that cities are also places of dwelling.

Wherever changes in the surroundings and conditions of life are relevant to people, they constitute 'environmental issues' that go well beyond what that meant in twentieth-century debate. If that focussed on the relationship between human activity and healthy bio or ecosystems, or parts of them (Harvey 1993: 2), in current struggles brought about by broadly neoliberal place-politics, people create counter movements and alternative forms of knowledge. These may manifest in muted ways, such as humour or quiet resistance (Plaan, this volume), but may also lead to producing maps that seek to show – with mixed success and contradictory results – socially valued features that official representations overlook (Peluso 2012; Lounela, this volume). These movements may target the state or business, or even challenge a social order based on economic growth (Berglund, this volume), but they may also target social groups and foster racist or nationalist discourses that completely disavow the histories of today's environments, shaped as they are, by powers close by and far away.

Furthermore, climate-related environmental hazards such as floods, fires and droughts have intensified in recent years, affecting landscapes in many novel ways. While we were writing this chapter in the summer of 2018, fires destroyed large areas of forest in Sweden, and weeks of soaring temperatures put climate onto the public agenda across the Northern hemisphere as never before. Fires and floods, draughts and other extreme weather conditions have for a long time taken place in the Global South, as anthropologists know, but in the most parts of the wealthy North it was easy, until recently, to belittle such things. Now sensory experience, gatherings of different beings and marks of memorable pasts – landscapes in fact – are increasingly understood as not the same as they used to be.

With such unprecedented transformations under way, landscape studies have extended to what some anthropologists have called "anthropology on the edge" (Hastrup 2014) with the suggestion that researchers should search for new methods. Doing fieldwork around the world has for some time brought anthropology closer with dramatic landscape transformation and drawn attention to how spaces of consumption get constructed in one place while extraction and exploitation change worlds elsewhere. A focus on this darker side of global social life is not new in anthropology, as Sherry Ortner spelled out in her historical survey of anthropology's encounters with the "problematic conditions of the real world under neoliberalism" (2016: 50), conditions that some disciplines fail to spot let alone analyse. At play are systemic landscape-altering dynamics, including "the removal of government regulations on business; the reduction of the power of labor to make demands; the downsizing of the labor force itself; the privatization of many public goods and institutions; and the radical reduction of programs of social assistance for poor people" (ibid.: 52). Many of the authors here also point at the 'dark side' of the capitalist processes that affect landscapes and change lives. Drawing from the conference panels, their texts push the anthropological study of landscapes in different ways: combining social and natural sciences to examine materialities and socialities in 'disturbed landscapes'; considering movements of people, non-human and other agents; touching on climate change and multispecies anthropology; problematising how rapid change impacts on identities; engaging with sacred and ritual spaces in the making of meaningful landscapes. First, however, we review how anthropology has thus far broached the topic.

## Landscape studies: Politics and experiences

Interest in landscape studies has grown among anthropologists especially since the 1990s. Prior to that, landscape featured in the ecological anthropology or cultural ecology that emerged in the 1950s as an effort to bring ecosystems and cultures into one theoretical loop. Ecosystems were proposed as biophysical entities that interact with human society, the environment as an ecosystem that humans adapt to (Steward 1955;

Geertz 1963; Rappaport 1968). Gradually, as a response to studies that kept culture and sociality separated from nature, a more concerted anthropology of landscape emerged, which sought to avoid the idea that environment determines human livelihood systems or meaningful practices. Many anthropologists stressed the importance of *place* in the making of meaningful genealogies and topologies (Hirsh and O'Hanlon 1995; Feld and Basso 1996; Fox 2006), while others focussed on ways to overcome to the dualisms that persistently dogged analyses of the human place in nature (Descola and Pálsson 1996; Ingold 2000; Strathern 1980; MacCormack and Strathern 1980).

Thus, the anthropology of landscape has progressed as a study of the spatial dimensions of social and material encounters and meanings, where landscape was discussed as an object and as the background for life in a specific community (Malinowski 1984 [1922]). In this tradition, landscape is an object of the human gaze, stable, unchanging and outside human control. In another tradition landscape was discussed more as a process of meaningful interaction between humans and their surroundings (Keesing 1982; Bender 1993; Hirsch and O'Hanlon 1995). These studies often connected places, that is, landscapes to identity formation where "landscape refers to the perceived settings that frame people's senses of place and community" (Stewart and Strathern 2003: 4).

The later discussion on landscape dovetailed with a wider scholarly concern with humans and nature. Landscape has multiple roles here: as visual representation, active agency, materiality (Tilley and Cameron-Daum 2017). This phenomenological approach, associated particularly with Tim Ingold, points to landscape as eternally under construction, never complete (1993: 162). The Ingoldian approach also suggests understanding "being in the world" as something that embodies memories. This so-called dwelling perspective posits landscape or environment as endlessly becoming part of the human organism and vice versa, with Ingold stringently arguing against notions of humans transcending or controlling their surroundings. More recently, Ingold has integrated the study of landscape with approaches that draw from the arts. He has put special emphasis on imagination and perception, leading to the suggestion that we should find: "a way that would reunite perception and imagination while yet acknowledging the human condition, [...], to be that of a being whose knowledge of the world, far from being shaped by operations of mind upon the deliverances of the senses, grows from the very soil of an existential involvement *in* the sensible world" (Ingold 2012: 3). He stresses that landscapes are both imagined and sensed, and researching them should also involve the flow of material and sensory awareness. Mind is not severed from matter in his view, which makes landscapes important vehicles of memories of the past and imagining the future, as is also suggested in many places in this book (Järvi, Lounela, Uusihakala).

The empirical case studies in this book, however, show how markings of people's past experiences in specific places are being erased and remade with new intensity and speed. New markings are either obscuring once meaningful features of the surroundings or leaving them open to new meanings and assemblages, including as "weedy places" (Tsing 2015). Some of the contributors even describe how transformations in the landscape make it difficult to recognise specific places. They fail to embody memories (see Lounela, Mölkänen, this volume), rather raising the question of what futures can emerge out of these profound changes, and so making new imaginaries possible. Anthropological encounters make it clear that these transformations are often the result of power dynamics, and so many of the authors suggest that the politics of landscape has to be integrated into our analysis and theoretical discussion. For instance, the chapters by Lounela and Zanotelli and Tallè explicitly argue that the phenomenological approach in the anthropology of landscape needs to be reconciled with the issue of process and power. Further, the concept of landscape needs to specify the peculiarities and hierarchy of meanings and materiality in the location under scrutiny, perhaps extending also from land as such to air (Zanotelli and Tallè, this volume) or sea (Plaan).

Similar omissions in the literature were recognised in Barbara Bender's edited volume, titled *Landscape: Politics and Perspectives* (1993), which was also concerned with the political dimensions of landscape. A landmark work in critiques of elite conceptions of landscape, the book assembles (to use a twenty-first century word) an impressive cross-disciplinary range of analyses where political relations extend from status, class, religious sectarianism and gender to colonial relations familiar in anthropology. Its case studies demonstrate that politics inheres in landscapes and in discussions of them. Later, Bender and Winer (2001) further criticised the idea that places and landscapes are always familiar, suggesting that there is a need for a "stronger sense of movement within enlarged worlds" that would go beyond movement and travel in terms of Nomadology (Deleuze and Guattari 1981, cited in Bender and Winer 2001: 8). They suggest approaching it in terms of locations and dislocations; how places connect to other places either through narratives or practices, and propose to study places through narratives and experiences of people on the move, for instance, migrants and refugees.

Another angle is offered by Steven Emery and Michael Carrithers (2016), and anthropologists such as Arnar Árnason et al. (2012) and Jo Vergunst (Vergunst and Árnason 2012), for whom the phenomenological approach within landscape studies is important, but not sufficient. Emery and Carrtihers (2016) suggest that narratives and representations are at the core of the politics of landscape, but point out that not only the ruling class but also those working the land, such as farmers, contribute in their struggles for power through narratives and representations, which in turn contribute to the politics of landscape.

Yet another discussion on the politics of landscape invokes an old Northern European landscape discourse. This discussion owes much to Kenneth Olwig, well known Danish geographer, who explored the early history of Danish landscape and drew attention to the significance of the polity and its laws as part of it:

> The concept of Landschaft as used in Renaissance Europe referred to a particular notion of polity rather than territory of a particular size [...] The root of the word *Landschaft* is *Land*, and the two terms were sometimes used interchangeably [...] The link between the ideas of customary law, the institutions that embody law, and the people enfranchised to participate in the making and administration of law is of fundamental importance to the meaning of the root *Land* in Landschaft (2002: 16–17).

Thus the Northern European landscape concept refers to something human-made; it is a polity rather than a natural, material or aesthetic aspect of the land. The polity defines how the physical environment is shaped in any specific place, hence "[p]hysical environment was a reflection of the political landscape" (2002: 21). However, here the distinction or dualism of people and nature becomes a problem, since it leads to the clearly flawed argument that humans determine and are separated from the material characteristics of landscape. This problem of the human-nature dualism and human dominance has recently been tackled by Anna Tsing, who proposes a multispecies approach where landscapes are understood as "places for patchy assemblages, that is, for moots that include both human and nonhuman participants" (2015: 304), importantly, not forgetting capitalist processes. We return to this below.

As we show in the following, many ways have already been proposed to overcome the opposition between a political-economic analysis in territorial terms on the one hand, and a phenomenological approach where sensorial experience, materiality and language are central, on the other. Guiding our efforts here has been a premise that as a concept, landscape is most fully appreciated when it is placed within the social dynamics of contemporary political history. We suggest that this also leads to more intimate and culturally specific understandings of how landscapes are also imbrications of individual and collective choices. We further suggest that a focus on transformation and disturbed or disturbing landscape could fruitfully bring together the political and phenomenological approaches.

### Transformations: Disturbed and disturbing landscapes

Most of the focus in this book is on landscape change. Economic anthropologists have argued that landscape transformation actually started when people practicing hunting and gathering shifted to agriculture; domestication of plants and animals demanded new institutions, and new technologies transformed nature on an ever bigger scale. Thus, change was both social and material (see Cliggett and Pool 2008; Crothers 2008: 135). While foragers lived in abundance, of time and often food (Sahlins 1972), and were mobile (Woodburn 1982; Lounela 2017), shifting cultivators were forced to transform the landscape. But even there the landscape is left to revert as there is normally no need for a social group to return to the same place for several years. Careful observation would show that even when such a landscape is not significantly transformed, it is still social and political.

In efforts to include politics in the analysis, history, time and temporality emerge as key issues. This was noted already by cultural historian Fred Inglis for whom "landscape is the most solid appearance in which a history can declare itself" (1977: 489), and therefore to "say anything about a landscape, you must consider the practice of its production" (1977: 490). Ingold's anthropology also engages time, for instance in the essay 'The temporality of the landscape' from 1993, and again in the book *Making: Anthropology, archaeology, art and architecture*, from 2013. However, he suggests that as anthropologists interested in the human condition, we should not preoccupy ourselves with the same questions as historians of art, but with the lifeworld of "wriggling, zigzag lines" (2013: 137) inside of which, as inhabitants, we necessarily find ourselves and find our ways into the future. Landscapes are not just apprehended as lived experience but materialised over time through that. This does actually suggest questions about choices and their implications, which means that Ingold's anthropology, too, can address politics.

Elsewhere Ingold has discussed transformation by picking up on the nineteenth-century work of Friedrich Engels. He too discussed it in terms of the domestication of land and animals contrasting this with collecting, hunting and gathering, which do not transform nature (Ingold 2000: 78). In Ingold's view, Western thinking has positioned people outside of nature and attributed the power of thought to them only: "History itself comes to be seen as a process wherein human producers, through their transforming reaction on nature, have literally constructed an environment of their own making" (Ingold 2000: 215). In his analysis, European modernity presents nature as something out there, separated, manageable and to be transformed. Objecting to this understanding, Ingold suggests that transformation is not something people do from above or outside, rather objects and materialities, as well as humans, "grow from the mutual involvement of people and materials in an environment" (ibid.: 347). Hence his helpful focus on human entanglements with landscapes over time. Pitching analysis at the level of human experience and practice though, easily makes bigger socio-economic transformations dissolve from view. Although politics somehow remains, discussion of how politics and human experience relate, let alone of the violent change that anthropology increasingly documents, is difficult to discern in his work.

Anna Tsing takes the "ruins of capitalism", the Anthropocene, and multispecies scholarship as her points of departure (2015) to generate quite a different style of landscape anthropology. Drawing on assemblage as a conceptual tool, she argues that early modern capitalism was a starting point for the "long-distance destruction of landscapes and ecologies" (2015: 19), and that capitalism has made possible the new era of human influence on the earth – the Anthropocene. Capitalism brings destruction and profound changes in multispecies relations, but something new always emerges. Our analysis may show transformation to be destructive but also open up the landscape for new possibilities. For instance, an already destroyed landscape may become a place for new species interactions and gatherings. As Tsing argues, "Industrial transformations turned out to be a bubble of promise followed by lost livelihoods and damaged landscapes. [...] If we end the story with decay, we abandon all hope – or turn our attention to other sites of promise and ruin, promise and ruin" (2015: 18). Thus, even the weedy places gather new actors and elements, giving hope for the future.

Disturbances are at the core of Tsing's approach. These may be caused by humans or natural forces; they may be initiated by industrial activities, small scale agriculture or natural forces and forms of disturbance such as fire, floods or something similar. As Tsing notes, "[d]isturbance is a change in environmental conditions that causes a pronounced change in an ecosystem" (2015: 160). Multispecies relations or human-nature encounters within damaged landscapes offer Tsing a particular lens through which to discuss sociomaterial change. Wherever there is disturbance, it is multi-species interactions that give rise to new assemblages, or what she calls gatherings and moots. Over time these produce landscapes. This approach allows Tsing to claim that decision-making processes and powerful persons are not the most important subjects of analysis, rather, we should look at the encounters and collaborations constituting the assemblages from which future landscapes emerge (2015: 29).

The disturbance concept is borrowed from ecology, but it seems to work well in anthropology to highlight how landscapes are heterogeneous, changing and always in the process of being shaped and shaping. For Tsing the concept helps to understand how capitalism as accumulation (of wealth to the few), alienation (of people from nature or things), and objectification (of nature and people) transform nature and people, and multispecies relations within a landscape. These changes may be small or large. Thus disturbance is also about scale. If the form of disturbance is huge, it causes more devastation and change (Tsing 2015: 160–161). What is so exceptional in this analysis is how it explores what emerges in the disturbed landscapes in the course of the transformation, not forgetting humans from the multi-species analysis. However, the task is demanding, and not everybody is able or willing to do the multispecies study and collaborative research process. The approach also raises the question of whether stressing change, multi-species and assemblage, also threatens to dissolve questions of structural power. Further, as anthropologists understand places, social relations and their historical underpinnings, they also appreciate that not all landscapes are understood or experienced and analysed as transformed entities.

Bruno Latour, for instance, offers tools for landscape anthropology that keep this question open. He uses the idiom of assemblages as well as Actor Network Theory (ANT) to insert the social into the material. For him the social is "a very peculiar movement or re-association and reassembling" (2005: 7). Rather compatible with Ingold's and Tsing's work, Latour's work also shifts the analytical focus to movement and action. This allows agency and social structure to appear together, and makes it possible to account for relations and connections that are simultaneously material and semiotic. It also makes non-humans into actors (or co-dwellers) rather than symbolic or passive projections of human meanings. With Latour's background in studying technoscience, these vocabularies turn out to be particularly helpful in studying the technology-intensive context of urban landscapes, which we discuss below.

Another set of helpful tools to think with have been Arjun Appadurai's 'scapes'. Taking issue with the anthropological tendency to create representations of bounded communities with their particular 'cultures', Appadurai took inspiration from the concept of landscape to help deal analytically with globalisation. He proposed to explore disjunctures between economy, culture and politics by looking at five dimensions of global cultural flow: ethnoscapes, mediascapes, technoscapes, financescapes and ideoscapes. These all "point to the fluid, irregular shapes", which are historical, personal, contextual and global (1990: 7). Global scale processes have also been central in the field of political ecology as developed within geography and anthropology. That discourse is more implicit than explicit in this book, but is equally a useful starting point for tracing disturbances in landscapes (cf. Neumann 2011).

## Landscape and the visual

These elaborations necessarily build on legacies of European thought that were never straightforward. The Northern European variant of the concept of landscape, with its etymological origins in German *Landschaft*, referred to a polity. By contrast, the Dutch notion of *landschap* had visual and artistic implications. This had to do with the genre of landscape art, which originated in fifteenth and sixteenth century Italy, but which later developed and gained great popularity in the Netherlands. It is through the Dutch route that the word probably made its way into the modern English lexicon (Wylie 2011: 302). This rather old understanding of landscape as a visual representation of a scene or a view has underpinned many critical approaches since the 1980s. They have also been a major source of theoretical inspiration for several chapters in this book.

The work of cultural geographer Denis Cosgrove (1985; 2008; Cosgrove and Daniels 1988) was seminal. For him it was Renaissance Italy where landscape first emerged as a way of seeing. The invention of a painting technique known as 'linear perspective' meant a radical departure from ealier understandings of visual art. This new technique, based on geometry, allowed the painter to produce representations of three-dimensional space on a flat canvas. Thus natural environments, buildings, and people could be reproduced on the canvas so that they appeared 'realistic' but at the same time provided an illusion of order (Cosgrove 1985; see also Pálsson 1996: 65–66). To quote anthropologist Gísli Pálsson (1995: 3), the painter's canvas was no longer "decorative space for the glorification of finite orders and godly designs" and art started to focus on "cognitive and spatial research, the representation of human activities and their place in nature and history." Accordingly, the human observer was detached from space, which in turn became an object of her/his gaze (Cosgrove 1985: 49).

However, this was not merely an artistic or intellectual revolution, as landscape was closely tied to the practical appropriation of space. As pointed out by Cosgrove, the perspective of landscape painting applied the same geometrical rules as, for example, navigation, mapping, land surveying and artillery warfare. Just like its more practical contemporaries, landscape as a way of seeing sought to achieve "the control and domination over space as an absolute, objective entity, its transformation into the property of individual or state" (ibid.: 46). Consequently, for Cosgrove the study of landscape entailed the interrogation of the politics and regimes of power that try to determine and regulate how the world should be seen (Wylie 2011: 307). Even though the understandings of landscape as a way of seeing have been strongly criticised in landscape studies informed by phenomenology (e.g. Ingold 1993; Olwig 1996), it is precisely the political aspect that the authors of this volume have sought to adopt and combine productively with other approaches.

Connections between visibility, pictorial representations of landscapes, and political power, especially in the context of modern nation states, have been explored further by political scientist and anthropologist James C. Scott in his highly influential book *Seeing Like a State* (1998). In order to achieve greater control of environment and society, modern states adopted a narrow way of seeing, according to Scott, that brought into "sharp focus certain limited aspects of an otherwise far more complex and unwieldy reality" (ibid.: 11). For Scott the key example of how states "see" things is the cadastral map. Maps depicted the state's terrain and its people only in regard to those aspects that were in the interest of the state, measuring and cataloguing, for instance, the accessible natural resources and property relations of a given area for taxation purposes, and ignoring all culturally specific local knowledge. Thus cadastral maps stood in opposition to customary maps that recorded those features of the landscape that would, for example, help secure subsistence or have ritual importance (ibid.: 11–47). In this respect, if indirectly, Scott's work aligns with studies of the importance of landscapes for Western imperialism and colonisation, especially in altering or erasing indigenous presence and perspectives (e.g. W. J. T. Mitchell 2002; also Järvi, Lounela, Mölkänen, Uusihakala in this volume).

Scott calls the ideology behind this vision "high-modernism". It puts its trust in the possibility of endless economic growth and technological progress (1998: 4). However, the most radical aspect of Scott's proposition is not that the state's gaze is focused on objects that it can manipulate for its own ends. It is rather that the state also strives to modify reality so that it would become more "legible". According to Scott (ibid.: 82), modern statecraft has been "a project of internal colonization" since the state-builders do "not merely describe, observe, and map", they also "shape a people and landscape that will fit their techniques of observation." Endeavours such as nationwide land reforms, villagisation policies, centralised urban planning and literacy campaigns are all instances of the inclination to streamline a complicated reality. Although Scott is decidedly critical of the high-modernist agenda, he points out that often it has been drawn to serve progressive goals and hence meant to implement positive changes in the lives of the citizens. Given how often it has met with rejection and resistance, the question is rather where and why did it go wrong.

The thesis has attracted pertinent critiques (e.g., H. West 2001; Ferguson 2005; Li 2005), but Scott's critical assertiveness and theoretical vocabulary could be and have been appreciated by those who study the political side of landscapes. In this book, the chapters by Lounela and Mölkänen do analyse developments that serve as examples of the high-modernist gaze whose miscalculations are reflected negatively in the landscape. Writing of the aftermath of massive forestry and agricultural schemes, Lounela, for instance, shows how administrative mapmaking, whether for extractive or restorative projects, is complicit in obliterating memories about the social meaning of landscape in rural Indonesia. Mölkänen describes how conservation agencies and scientists view a Malagasy rainforest as if from a distance, as an abstract entity, a habitat of rare and endangered species. This differs radically from the perceptions of those who live off the forest.

A completely different approach, which nonetheless takes its cue from landscape as visual representation, comes from structuralist anthropology. Philippe Descola (2013: 57–63) has discussed the significance of the linear perspective of landscape painting for the emergence of the modern concept of nature. For him landscape painting was the artistic expression of an ideology, where nature is considered an autonomous object separable from humanity and on which the human spectator can project meanings. According to Descola, this "way of representing the human environment in all its exteriority was of course indissociable from the movement to mathematize space that in this same period was promoted by geometry, physics, and optics" (ibid.: 61). Tracing this historical development forms an important part of his powerful critique on the assumed universality of Western "naturalistic cosmology", which has also stimulated the authors of this volume (e.g. Brown).

In Descola's more recent work (2016 [or this volume]), focused on Amazonia, landscape has become 'transfiguration'. In relation to a place, transfiguration is understood as a "deliberate conversion of a piece of land into a global iconic sign which highlights some features of the site previously not emphasized" (ibid.: 12). Descola's illustration are swidden horticulturalists in Amazonia. Here the difference between the forest and the garden is not conceived as an opposition along the lines of nature and culture or wild and domesticated, as in Western thinking. Rather, a structural continuum exists between the two. From a human perspective, the work of cultivation turns forests into gardens, while abandoned gardens revert back to forests. From the point of view of spirits or animals, considered the 'cultivators' of the forest, fallows left behind by humans turn back to gardens again. Both types of landscapes are signs representing each other but are also merging into each other, even if as people describe and understand the relations between communities of different living beings, they invoke these differences. Descola's insights inspire Tammisto's chapter on swidden horticulturalists in Papua New Guinea: cultivations and fallows are signs and indexes of social relationships and activities.

## Designed urban landscapes and representational politics

Thus far anthropological vocabularies about landscapes and dwelling have rarely been applied in urban or other technology-rich settings. Cities, whether fast-growing or shrinking, are usually associated with alienating lives and spectacular shows of modern progress (and more recently, decline, see Ringel 2018). Paradigmatically technological and thus artificial, cities are also often discussed as exemplars of a political economy of appearances. Martin Heidegger has been an important inspiration for this work as he has for Ingold. And Timothy Mitchell has drawn on Heidegger's famous essay on the 'Age of the World Picture' (1938) to great effect to discuss the rise of the exhibition as part of colonial and capitalist order (1988). Jean Baudrillard's (1994) insights about images and simulation in the hyperreal world of commodities, are another inspiration in accounts of capitalism's perverse effects on biotic systems (including human systems) and even on ideas of truth and reality. One easy-to-grasp empirical reference has been the garish artificiality of mid-twentieth-century American landscapes. Since then, social life has also been shown to be built not just of bricks and mortar (or sand, see Immonen, this volume) but of imagery, with critical scholars in many disciplines (Carrier and Miller 1998; Julier 2008) drawing important attention to the power of images and power-point presentations circulated by representatives of government, real estate, finance and increasingly also green technologies (see Mölkänen, Zanotelli and Tallè, this volume) who travel the world selling their goods and ideas.

In contrast, the insights of landscape research built on the dwelling perspective are paradigmatically applied not in cities, but in hunting and gathering contexts, or in connection with craft and art (Ingold 2013). They do show up in work on making and repair, for instance the builder-dwellers of Earthship homes studied by Rachel Harkness (2011) and other manual building experts studied by anthropologists (Marchand 2008), and in the immediacy of activities like repair and craft whose popularity is on the rise. Typically, skilful engagements between actors and their surroundings are taken to need highlighting as important processes producing lived landscapes. The small scale is privileged, as is the human body. This has the effect of re-connecting things that modern epistemology separated with such negative consequences, as Ingold, Haraway and many others argue. More problematically, it also has the effect of excluding the majority of humanity that inhabits towns and other technologically saturated environments, from analysis. In architecture and design literatures, dwelling on dwelling (as it were) and foregrounding the processual rather than fixed nature of built environments enlightens, but it can seem rather beside the point when set against gargantuan projects of landscape change co-ordinated through global capital.

One approach has been to use infrastructure as a descriptive and analytically useful concept, particularly in contexts of obviously systematic technological intervention. Since pioneering work by Geoff Bowker and Susan Leigh Star (1999), social science interest in infrastructure has spread (Simone 2004; Larkin 2013), whilst in anthropology infrastructural systems appear as elements of material politics that connect and disconnect across multiple locations and scales, always within situated contexts that offer no guarantees of their working as their creators intended them to. A good example might be efforts to manage solid waste as for instance Penny Harvey (2014) has shown. Besides material stuff, infrastructures impact lives as rules, protocols and standards (Bowker and Star 1999; Easterling 2016), not least those implicated in global finance.

With intensifying material exchange around the globe and attendant struggles over environments, built and unbuilt, lively inter-disciplinary and normatively driven research is emerging on how urban landscapes in particular are changing (Dovey et al. 2017). With accelerating urbanisation, the fate of biotic life in built up areas has also fuelled new research as well as policy. Similarly urban ecosystems are newly visible as sources of food and other valued goods (Charnley et al. 2018; also Berglund, this volume). The landscape concept does varied work in this research, sometimes less connected with people sometimes more, but often with bureaucratic and technological dimensions as well as intimate and embodied ones included. As Fran Tonkiss so clearly puts it, cities are where the body politic and the body social are enacted with particular intensity in power-laden spatial configurations, and they are sites where the 'virtual' and the 'actual' (immediately apparent to the senses) are experienced, which makes cities significant for producing belonging, politically and subjectively (Tonkiss 2013: 175). To echo Olwig's insights about polity (above), cities are landscapes.

A parallel and sometimes intersecting research vocabulary on environmental change is so-called assemblage urbanism (McFarlane 2011). Going beyond the obvious point that cities are made up of many different kinds of things, technical, cultural, biotic and what have you, it draws attention to the togetherness (or thrown-togetherness, Massey 2005) and consequent relationality of how cities are assembled. Here ontologically and phenomenologically distinct features combine to make meaning and future possibility. In an ethnographically driven perspective that takes global resource flows seriously, assemblages make a nonsense, in fact, of any residual boundaries between urban and rural, refusing (or at least claiming to) pregiven notions of either globalisation or neoliberalism (Ong and Collier 2005), and rather questioning these rhetorically strong but analytically blunt terms. Some critics argue that the horizontal logics of assemblage and actor-network approaches deconstruct nature too far (Pollini 2013) and that they lend themselves to analyses that in fact parallel neoliberal ideology, ignore political and cultural hierarchies and weaken critique (Fortun 2014). However, when dwelling and assembling approaches are brought together in specific contexts, the more disturbing aspects of socio-technical change can be productively critiqued (McFarlane 2011; Dovey et al. 2017).

Invoking assemblages in social science – by Anna Tsing or Donna Haraway for example – has multiple intellectual genealogies (e.g. Gilles Deleuze, Manuel deLanda, Jane Bennett, Bruno Latour), but it does importantly also decentre the human, and highlight multiple and contingent relations in ways that align well with studies of landscapes. In this reckoning, landscapes are similar but not identical to assemblages. They are, as the chapters here attest, in flux and vague in their extent, and their constituent parts are not significant in themselves but as part of a larger whole. Notwithstanding this complexity, the concept of landscape itself remains powerful. It is meaningful across audiences and yet can do analytical work in exploring people's varied and constantly changing capacities to make meaningful lives for themselves.

## Landscapes, power and consumption

As both political and geological formations are being changed in a quest for raw materials and energy, the volume needed to satisfy society's dependence on cheap fossil fuels is nothing less than staggering: already at the end of the last millennium organic matter equivalent to the planet's entire production of plant and animal life for 400 years was needed to produce the fossil fuels consumed in a single year (T. Mitchell 2009: 402). The looming exhaustion of non-renewable resources has moved the exploration and production activities to areas previously not considered rich enough for industrial scale extraction (e.g. Willow and Wylie 2014). Many of the chapters of this book present cases from so-called frontier landscapes, where rapid and aggressive extraction has caused disturbing changes in the landscape that would have been unimaginable in the recent past (e.g. Lounela), but also cases where different methods of modern resource extraction form a continuum over several generations and hence are a part of the local landscape and history (e.g. Moffitt).

If considered to bring jobs and other economic opportunities, resource extraction projects are often viewed positively in marginalised and vulnerable places (e.g. Fajans 1998). However, negative landscape change caused by large-scale extraction today, especially mining, defies the imagination. As anthropologist Stuart Kirsch (2014: 6) puts it, the environmental impact can be so invasive "that people come to question their fundamental assumption about the natural world." Worse still, with environmental degradation as much about relationships between people as about relationships between people and environment (Willow 2014: 241), the impact on cultural meanings and social relations drastically transforms life, as Lounela's (this volume) study in Central Kalimantan shows.

Such crises easily go unnoticed. The unequal relationships formed through global commodity chains also allow decision-makers and consumers to dissociate themselves from the consequences of their way of life both geographically and politically (Willow 2014: 241). Global urban growth has been directly dependent on changing rural landscapes into extractive resource pools, as noted in Berglund (this volume). Thus are spectacular cityscapes made possible by upheavals elsewhere. These are spectacular in a different way, for example, massive clearcuttings in rural Indonesia (Lounela), mega-size wind farms in the lagoon landscapes of coastal Mexico (Zanotelli and Tallè), or fracking in northern Canada (Moffitt). The specificities of these connections often remain vague except to a few specialists: urbanites do not know exactly where the raw materials for their built environment or daily provisions originate, while the inhabitants of the production areas can only speculate on what happens to the resources that are being extracted and exported from their environment (e.g. Walsh 2004). Little wonder social movements promoting new awareness have emerged, but still the poles of commodity chains remain far apart (Lyons and Moberg 2010; P. West 2012).

The unsustainable nature of the way of life carried out and promoted by the Global North has not gone unnoticed. Even more severe than the exhaustion of natural resources is the crisis of global warming. This has forced the extractive industries to look into the sustainability of their techniques and products – or at least claim to do so (Kirsch 2010). More importantly perhaps, it has also led to the invention and development of so-called green technology. However, rolling out such technologies, wind farms for instance, can have surprisingly similar effects on landscapes as conventional extraction schemes (see Zanotelli and Tallè, Moffitt, this volume). In addition to green technology, the climate change era has also seen the proliferation of new forms of commodification, for instance, ecotourism and emissions trading, designed to protect and enhance the position of vulnerable populations, species and landscapes (see Lounela). They are also problematic in the same ways as the older ways of appropriating nature (e.g. Büscher and Davidov 2013). In addition to the disconnect between centres of consumption and peripheral production, startling disconnects are also apparent in new forms of commodification of nature. Mölkänen (this volume) explains how the Malagasy horticulturalists who work as guides in a national park speculate on the motivations of scientists and ecotourists who visit the park in order to study endangered species. Furthermore, just as in the case of 'sustainable' extraction, schemes like ecotourism displace other possible responses with narrowly conceived 'market-based solutions'.

To conclude, we introduce the chapters of the book, highlighting how the issue of power in all its meanings runs through them in different ways.

In the opening chapter, 'The buck, the bull, and the dream of the stag: some unexpected weeds of the Anthropocene', Anna Tsing discusses weedy landscapes, in other words, places where human disturbance has profoundly altered ecosystems, perhaps after mining, timber cutting or some similar activity. Adapted from the keynote lecture, the chapter presents landscape as humanly disturbed or damaged, yet always assembling itself into something new, perhaps into 'weedy' landscapes entangled in the lives of human and nonhuman species. This novel approach is also treated in her monograph, *The Mushroom at the End of the World* (2015), where she focuses on how nature and humans are intertwined as part of the Anthropocene but also entangled within longer standing phenomena, like capitalism and environmentalism. Tsing tells how a Danish brown-coal mining site is taken over by red deer after the mine is abandoned. What is interesting is that the 'wild' (deer, wild grass and so forth) in the densely populated and intensively agro-industrialised county like Denmark can be found at the site of the abandoned mine – an example of what she calls "sites of human-made ruin". These are also places where humans form new contacts with animals, such as the red deer hunted by Danes. Human-disturbed landscapes are thus reassemblings of different weeds, or as she calls it, places of rewilding. She suggests that anthropologists, together with scholars from other disciplines, should look at the heterogeneity and histories of the world-making projects in weedy landscapes at different scales of time and place. Here she invokes the Anthropocene. Her actor-oriented, but historically informed ethnographic account of the Anthropocene through the lens of the Danish human-disturbed landscape offers a true alternative to research still grounded in a masculine gaze and stable image of landscape. From this analysis she is able to argue that there is hope, even in the weediness.

Anu Lounela's chapter explores landscapes in Central Kalimantan that are prone to accelerated changes following environmental, industrial and development projects. These create and destroy landscapes at the same time, bringing with them new settlements, deforestation, canal digging, oil palm and other estates, and conservation areas. The indigenous population, Ngaju Dayaks who have long dwelt along the Kahayan River, have taken part in these transformations and have seen (and contributed to) how the changes have removed markings and now threaten to erase place-based memories. However, at the same time Ngaju Dayaks imagine future landscapes through drawing maps. Lounela describes ruptures with past dwelling experiences – illegal logging, mining, new estates and natural disasters here and there – making everything in the landscape appear to be on the move. Using the concept of landscape, however, she points to constant negotiations between agents and activities that through both immersive experience and new representation, like mapping, produce new futures.

Joonas Plaan focuses on changing political, ecological and cultural conditions in the Baltic Sea. The analysis extends and develops the anthropological concept of landscape to capture the constant adaptation and impermanent fluidity of the waters that connect people around the world. As visual representation of landscape was once contrasted with the transformational practices of everyday life, so seascape can be both a visual thing out there and a holistic experience. In contrast to landscapes, however, the seascape does not allow for permanent markings, which may partly account for the relative lack of attention in the literature to marine environments. But just as with analysing landscapes, where emphasising skills and pre-modern characteristics leaves questions about politics and power unanswered, so with seascapes. Plaan's account of the fascinating political transformations in and around Kihnu Island, not least the Soviet period that many people still remember, and the often disastrous ways these were coupled with marine-based economic practices, offers a window onto interesting adaptations in the way people relate to their immediate environment. At the same time, he draws attention to the politics of knowledge, particularly those dynamics that made scientific or official knowledge become weak politically. In that sense, this example from a small community in a small sea belonging to a small country, Estonia, in fact offers an intriguing account of an increasingly common condition everywhere, as changing environments put pressure on everyone to be experimental.

Jenni Mölkänen takes us to Madagascar, where state-supported neoliberal policies transform landscapes as they fuel extractive resource use on one hand and fix and preserve threatened nature, on the other. Conservation agencies work with capitalist logics that affect the way local populations, Tsimihety, not only look at natural landscape but become aware of themselves. Tsimihety cultivate rice and vanilla while hunting and gathering on the borders of a large national park, which has brought with it environmental scientists, state officials, new regulations and money for instance through ecotourism. Mölkänen describes how knowledge is gained through walking and subsistence practices, and building marks such as tombs. Out of movement, narratives, sharing and marking, a landscape has emerged. With the national park and ecotourism, not only the physical landscape but also Tsimihety understandings of the role and value of lemurs, state and environment have started to shift. People have become aware that there is something in the landscape they do not know, and they realise that they are marginal in world economics; they now look and make sense of their landscape differently.

Francesco Zanotelli and Cristiano Tallè transport readers to the state of Oaxaca in southern Mexico, where historical tensions take on specific dynamics as communities of lagoon-based fishermen and peasants reject an initially virtuous looking project, a large-scale wind power scheme. They describe compellingly the all-too-familiar threats to the economies and ecologies of the region, but add a fascinating account of how landscape extends to the air and the waters that, together with human and animal agents, are known to have transformative agency. Conceptually, their example pays particular attention to the construction of meaning through linguistic as well as material processes. Above all the authors focus on how agency lies in weather, both at human and geological timescales. The agents are also made to appear in cosmological memory, myths, personal biographies and everyday conversations as well as in place names. Environmental information is available, as anthropologists have recently begun to emphasise (e.g. Kohn 2013), in both material and semiotic forms, should one have the skills to pay attention to it. Alert, however, to the politics of 21st-century 'clean' energy policy, the authors find that it is the local language of myth that allows people to make sense of the different powers battling it out in their environment. This articulates an understanding or appreciation of conflicting forces distributed around them, allowing people to elaborate moral as well as practical guidelines for dwelling.

Especially where extractive industries go back a long time, technologies of landscape transformation and industrial development are part of local history. Such narratives help people figure out their past and imagine their future. Morgan Moffit describes how the politics of hydrocarbon and extraction has figured in the making of Sahtu landscapes in the Nothwest Territories of Canada, imagined as a frontier since the 1920s. Northern landscapes are prone to profound transformations due to climate change that has brought along melting of permanent sea-ice. These climatic changes, with significant effects on the indigenous populations of the region, have developed new forms of activism and resistance. Countering the image of the 'northern frontier', the Dene and Métis people living in Tulít'a understand landscapes through their family histories. This clashes with the idea of the resource frontier produced by politicians or non-local Euro-Canadians. The historicised narratives on extractive activities in the making of landscape, as told by the indigenous populations, make for a strong anthropological account of how material and semiotic histories are entangled in the landscape.

Tiina Järvi's chapter focuses on the politics of history, memory and re or displacing populations in the process of nation building in Israel. Marking landscape is central, as the Israeli government erases (traces of) Palestinian occupation and transforms place by rebuilding new natures, notably imported pine trees, in the national park of Mount Carmel. The chapter illustrates vividly how landscape transformation may completely erase the traces of local social relations and histories leaving only imaginaries and competing narratives. Grounding her argument on Tim Ingold and Mitch Rose's notion of dwelling and landscape formation, she argues that marking and claiming is a spatial and temporal process reordering the landscape that then becomes a materialization of 'Zionist imaginary'. While here erased memories and displaced populations are not the result of neoliberal policies as such, they are part of the capitalist and nation-building processes, which have effects on social material formations of the landscape. In this vein, 'traces of absence' and new natures or replanted pine tree forests become markers of lost and rebuilt identities and possibilities in the national landscape formation.

Moral meanings also come to the fore in the chapter by Jasmin Immonen, based on recent fieldwork in Peru, where rapid urbanisation together with the creative adoption of new technologies such as smart phones among local youth, give rise to contested and unexpected meanings becoming embedded in the landscape. Put differently, the story she recounts tells of how young people make a place for themselves in a society in-the-making, against pressures of globalism and the now-fading aspirations of older forms of citizenship in post-development Peru. They inhabit fast-growing settlements were a lack of collective history is compensated for by a pervasive demand to 'move forward'. Many locals respond to this demand in often festive work parties that literally transform the previously sandy desert environment into an urban, technologically connected one. In fact, Immonen even suggests that in these landscapes of social media that partake of the local street together with global digital platforms like Facebook, there is emerging a new class of people that cannot adequately be described as working-class or middle-class. Here the precarious physical landscape has an analogy in the economic condition of precariousness now so common around the world: fickle forces animated by faraway powers impose their own layered shapes, particularly in urban and other landscapes built according to the understandings and specifications of mobile capital.

Similar understandings of the economic importance of technological apparatuses come to the fore in Eeva Berglund's chapter. She uses Helsinki to illustrate the contrasting aspirations of real estate investors and their supporters in municipal governments around the world on the one hand, and small scale, low capital and often green tinged and/or socially motivated grassroots initiatives such as urban gardens, maker spaces, sharing schemes and so on in cities both north and south, on the other. As in the Peruvian case, the urban landscape is obviously also a technological, and in this particular case, scientifically apprehended, world, even as it is dwelt in the sense that Ingold has elaborated. The chapter argues for introducing the anthropological landscape concept more forcefully into urban studies, where new vocabularies drawing on concepts like assemblages or actor networks have been understandably popular in recent years. Weaving an argument from illustrations of urban activism, Berglund argues that grassroots activists' practical engagements orient them towards creating relationships with others in a particular place as well as towards a conception of ordinary social life as facing limits. In practice this implies both the need and a moral imperative towards some level of local self-sufficiency, a refusal to be a place that just processes goods extracted from elsewhere to be returned to some other elsewhere as waste.

If dreams of future cities are animated by a kind of nostalgia for a golden future, it is of course more likely for communities to identify and look for nostalgic forms of comfort in the past. Katja Uusihakala shows how narratives of homeland have animated and continue to inform how former 'Rhodesians' make claims to land they have left behind and yet which, as the personal stories she recounts so vividly recall, have left such strong imprints. Here to the contrasts between the modern and anti-modern, the urban and the rural, the moral and the chaotic are shown to combine and flip as they link together places and memories. In addition to shaping diasporic subjectivities, intensely recalled landscape experiences partake of a quasi-religious character. As moving as these accounts are, Uusihakala traces the way they are shaped in a narrative form using nature/culture concepts with deep and tenacious roots in Western thinking. Her intention is however, to show that despite these powerful tropes, whatever it might have been over time, the European landscape imaginary has itself never been a simple thing. Learning new skills, embedding the moral and political layers of landscape in both story and terrain, all produced a way of life even as they were part of a colonial impulse. Reflecting on the landscape of collective imagination can thus sustain a romance as much as a way of life.

Philippe Descola's contribution is based on his Edward Westermarck Memorial Lecture, which he presented in association with the Finnish Anthropological Society to coincide with the Landscape conference. The perspective he develops is highly ethnographic yet also theoretical, taking Amerindian forests and gardens as its empirical referent. Coming from a structuralist school of thought, Descola stresses visual perception and imitation, and highlights continuities between these domains usually identified as separate and different, suggesting that gardens both represent and index forests. Considering landscape within anthropology, Descola identifies two distinct traditions of thought: first, where landscape has been produced through human labour; and second, where landscape is a human representation. Here he suggests a third approach, using the concept of "transfiguration": landscape is the outcome of the processes by which material objects are composed into something in a place (*in situ*). At the same time it is also a change in appearance: Landscape ends up becoming something different than before when it is transfigured, becoming a sign and expressing itself in codes, scale models and so forth (*in visu*). Like Tsing in her chapter, Descola suggests that the landscape concept is a way to overcome an old Western human-nature dualism. He stresses, however, the visual and the representational, arguing that landscape is a material composition but also that it is sign and representation.

Tuomas Tammisto's account describes how, among the Mengen of Papua New Guinea, food, or acts of giving and feeding, like gardens, are important media for working out social relations. In this vein, the Mengen garden landscape is a historically and temporally meaningful index of social relations produced through work as Descola (2016) has argued. Mengen people also have intimate knowledge, in Ingold's terms, of their landscape, forests, and gardens, suitable species to be planted, which is expressed in their tree or village calendar; this knowledge is passed on through visits to and narratives about the landscape. However, this temporal landscape is also vulnerable to tensions, since it might "remember too much", for which reason people sometimes erase their or other's traces within the landscape. This happens especially when they wish to avoid competing claims to the territory. Referring to Descola's ideas, the detailed ethnographic account shows how visual structures of landscape are produced through work and related dwelling experiences, thus embodying social relations.

How are epistemological and ontological questions related to landscape conceptualisations and formations? Jason M. Brown takes up these question in his theoretical contribution to the book. Criticising Western sciences for their epistemological misreading of indigenous (landscape) ontologies, he suggests that, unlike many other scientists, some anthropologists have already suggested novel approaches to natural resource management and understanding of landscapes. In his view, the ontological and phenomenological turns in anthropology (Latour 1993; 2004; Descola 1996; 2013; Ingold 2000; Kohn 2013), albeit somewhat different discussions, contribute to new 'anthropology of life' through which the nature-people dualism is dissolved in different ways. For instance, Eduardo Kohn explores human and non-human semiosis, while Descola proposes four ontological typologies classifying Western/modern and non-Western human relations to non-humans. Further, Bruno Latour suggests a science of things or new political ecology that bring things (non-humans) into the same analytical framework with humans. According to Brown, this kind of anthropology of life proposes that indigenous ontologies are not only metaphors of landscapes, to be represented as such in the literature or in natural resource management projects, but rather that there is one ontological landscape – anthropologists should take seriously the constituencies of landscape as actors and show that the World in itself is experiential and we should not make it an epistemological question.

Taken together, these ethnographic analyses show the continuing usefulness of anthropology's experience-near modes of investigation, of moving and dwelling through landscapes, remembering and caring for them. At the same time, they take on board the unprecedented conditions under which people everywhere are having to make sense and forge relationships to the worlds they inhabit. Since landscapes are not what they used to be, neither can anthropology be.

# References

Appadurai, Arjun 1990. Disjuncture and Difference in the Global Cultural Economy. *Public Culture* 2 (2): 1–24.

Árnason, Arnar, Nicolas Ellison, Jo Vergunst and Andrew Whitehouse (eds) 2012. *Landscapes Beyond Land: Routes, Aesthetics, Narratives.* New Yor: Berghahn.

Bender, Barbara (ed.) 1993. *Landscape: politics and perspectives.* Providence, Berg.

Bender, Barbara and Margot Winer (eds) 2001. *Contested landscapes: Movement, exile and place.* Berg.

Bowker Geoffrey C. and Susan Leigh Star. 1999. *Sorting Things Out: Classification and Its Consequences.* Cambridge (Mass.): MIT Press.

Büscher, Bram and Veronica Davidov (eds) 2013. *The Ecotourism-Extraction Nexus Political Economies and Rural Realities of (un)Comfortable Bedfellows.* London: Routledge.

Charnley, Susan, Rebecca J. McLain and Melissa R. Poe 2018. Natural Resource Access Rights and Wrongs: Nontimber Forest Products Gathering in Urban Environments. *Society & Natural Resources* 31 (6): 734–750.

Cligget, Lisa and Christopher A. Pool (eds) 2008. *Economies and the transformation of landscape.* Alham: Altamira Presss.

Cosgrove, Denis 1985. Prospect, Perspective and the Evolution of the Landscape Idea. *Transactions of the Institute of British Geographers* 10 (1): 45–62.

Cosgrove, Denis 2008. *Geography and vision: seeing, imagining and representing the world.* London: I.B. Tauris.

Cosgrove, Denis and Stephen Daniels (eds) 1988. *The Iconography of Landscape: Essays on the Symbolic Representation, Design and Use of Past Environments.* Cambridge: Cambridge University Press.

Crothers, George M. 2008. From foraging to farming: The emergence of exclusive property rights in Kentucky prehistory. In Lisa Cligget and Christopher A. Pool (eds), 2008, *Economies and the transformation of landscape.* Alham: Altamira Press.

Descola, Philippe 1996. Constructing Natures: Symbolic ecology and social practice. In Philippe Descola and Gísli Pálsson (eds), 1996, *Nature and Society: Anthropological Perspectives.* New York: Routledge.

Descola, Philippe 2013. *Beyond Culture and Nature.* Chicago, IL: University of Chicago Press.

Descola, Philippe 2016. Landscape as Transfiguration. Edward Westermarck Memorial Lecture, October 2015. *Suomen Antropologi: Journal of the Finnish Anthropological Society* 41 (1): 3–14.

Descola, Philippe and Gísli Pálsson (eds) 1996. *Nature and society: Anthropological perspectives.* New York: Routledge.

Dovey, Kim, Fujie Rao and Elek Pafka 2017. Agglomeration and assemblage: Deterritorialising urban theory. *Urban Studies* 55 (2): 1–11.

Easterling, Keller 2016. *Extrastatecraft: The power of infrastructure space.* London: Verso.

Emery, Steven and Michael Carrithers 2016. From lived experience to political representation: Rhetoric and landscape in the North York Moors. *Ethnography* 17 (3): 388–410.

Fajans, Jane 1998. Transforming Nature, Making Culture: Why the Baining are not environmentalists. *Social Analysis* 42 (3): 12–27.

Feld, Steven and Keith H. Basso (eds) 1996. *Senses of place.* Santa Fe: School of American Research Press.

Ferguson, James 2005. Seeing Like an Oil Company: Space, security, and global capital in neoliberal Africa. *American Anthropologist* 107 (3):377–382

Fortun Kim 2014. From Latour to late industrialism. *HAU: Journal of Ethnographic Theory* 4 (1): 309–329.

Fox, James J. (ed.) 2006. *The poetic power of place: Comparative perspectives on Austronesian ideas of locality.* Canberra: ANU Press.

Geertz, Clifford 1970. *Agricultural Involution: The processes of ecological change in Indonesia.* Berkeley: Association of Asian Studies by University of California Press.

Gregory, Chris 1997. *Savage money: The anthropology and politics of commodity exchange.* Amsterdam: Harwood Academic.

Hansen, Thomas Blom and Finn Stepputat. 2006. Sovereignty revisited. *Annual Review of Anthropology Annual* 35: 295–315.

Harkness, Rachel 2011. Earthships: The Homes That Trash Built. *Anthropology Now* 3 (1): 54–65.

Harvey, David 1993. The Nature of the Environment: The dialectics of social and environmental change. *Socialist Register* 29: 1–51.

Hirsch Eric and Michael O'Hanlon (eds) 1995. *The anthropology of landscape: Perspectives on place and space.* Oxrford: Clanderon.

Inglis, Fred 1977. Nation and Community: A Landscape and its Morality. *The Sociological Review* 25 (3): 489–514.

Ingold, Tim 1993. Temporality of the landscape. *World Archaelogy* 25 (2): 152–174.

Ingold, Tim 2000. *The Perception of the Environment: Essays in livelihood, dwelling and skill.* London: Routledge.

Ingold, Tim 2013. *Making: Anthropology, archaeology, art and architecture.* London: Routledge.

Jacobs, Jane 1965. *The Death and Life of Great American Cities.* Harmondsworth: Penguin Books in association with Jonathan Cape.

Julier, Guy 2008. *The Culture of Design.* 2nd Edition. London: SAGE Publications.

Keesing, Roger 1982. *Kwaio Religion: The living and the dead in a Solomon Island society.* New York: Columbia University Press.

Kirsch, Stuart 2010. Sustainable Mining. *Dialectical Anthropology* 34 (1): 87–93.

Kirsch, Stuart 2014. *Mining Capitalism: The Relationship between Corporations and Their Critics.* Oakland: University of California Press.

Kohn, Eduardo 2013. *How forests think: Toward anthropology beyond human.* Berkeley: University of California Press.

Larkin, Brian 2013. The Politics and Poetics of Infrastructure. *Annual Review of Anthropology* 42: 327–343.

Latour, Bruno 2005. *Reassembling the social: An introduction to actor-network-theory.* Oxford; New York: Oxford University Press.

Latour, Bruno 1993. *We Have Never Been Modern.* Cambridge, MA: Harvard University Press.

Latour Bruno 2005. *The Politics of Nature: How to Bring the Sciences into Democracy.* Cambridge, MA: Harvard University Press.

Li, Tania Murray 2005. Beyond "the State" and Failed Schemes. *American Anthropologist* 107 (3): 383–394.

Lounela, Anu 2017. Continuity and Change in Central Kalimantan: Climate Change, Monetization of Nature, and its Bearing on Value Orientations. In Cathrin Arenz, Michaela Haug, Stefan Seitz and Oliver Venz (eds), *Continuity under change in Dayak societies.* Wiesbaden: Springer.

Lyon, Sarah and Mark Moberg (eds) 2010. *Fair Trade and Social Justice: Global Ethnographies.* New York: New York University Press.

MacCormack Carol P. and Marilyn Strathern (eds) 1980. *Nature, Culture and Gender.* Cambridge: Cambridge University Press.

Malinowski, Bronislaw 1984 [1922]. *Argonauts of the Western Pacific: An account of native enterprise and adventure in the archipelagos of Melanesian New Guinea.* Long Grove: Waveland Press.

Marchand, Trevor H. J. 2008. Muscles, Morals and Mind: Craft Apprenticeship and the Formation of Person. *British Journal of Educational Studies* 56 (3): 245–271.

Massey, Doreen 2005. *For Space*. London, Thousand Oaks, New Delhi: SAGE Publications.

McFarlane, Colin 2011. The city as assemblage: Dwelling and urban space. *Environment and Planning D: Society and Space*, 29: 649–671.

Mitchell, Timothy 1988. *Colonising Egypt*. Cambridge: Cambridge University Press.

Mitchell, Timothy 2009. Carbon Democracy. *Economy and Society* 38 (3): 399–432.

Mitchell, W. J. T. 2002. Imperial landscape. In W. J. T. Mitchell (ed.), *Landscape and Power* (Second Edition). Chicago: University of Chicago Press.

Neumann, Roderick P. 2011. Political Ecology III: Theorizing landscape – progress report. *Progress in Human Geography*, 35(6): 843–850.

Olwig, Kenneth R. 1996. Recovering the Substantive Nature of Landscape. *Annals of the Association of American Geographers* 86 (4): 630–653.

Olwig, Kenneth R. 2002. *Landscape, nature, and the body politic: From Britain's renaissance to America's new world*. Madison: University of Wisconsin Press.

Ong, Aihwa and Stephen J. Collier (eds) 2005. *Global assemblages: technology, politics, and ethics as anthropological problems*. Malden, MA, Blackwell Publishers.

Ortner, Sherry B. 2016. Dark anthropology and its others: Theory since the Eighties. *HAU: Journal of Ethnographic Theory* 6 (1): 47–73.

Pálsson, Gísli 1995. *The Textual Life of Savants: Ethnography, Iceland, and the Linguistic Turn*. London: Routledge.

Pálsson, Gísli 1996. Human-environmental relations: Orientalism, paternalism and Communalism. In Philippe Descola and Gísli Pálsson (eds), 1996, *Nature and Society: Anthropological Perspectives*. New York: Routledge.

Peluso Nancy P. 2012. What's nature got to do with it? A situated historical perspective on socio-natural commodities. *Development and Change* 43 (1): 79–104.

Peluso, Nancy P. and Michael Watts (eds) 2001. *Violent environments*. Ithaca: Cornell University Press.

Polanyi, Karl 1944. *The Great Transformation*. Boston: Beacon Press.

Pollini, Jacques 2013. Bruno Latour and the Ontological Dissolution of Nature in the Social Sciences: A Critical Review. *Environmental Values* 22 (1): 25–42.

Rappaport, Roy A. 1967. Ritual Regulation of Environmental Relations among a New Guinea People. *Ethnology* 6 (1): 17–30.

Rappaport, Roy A. 1968. *Pigs for the ancestors: Ritual in the ecology of a New Guinea people*. New Haven: Yale University Press.

Ringel, Felix 2018. *Back to the Future: An ethnography of Germany's fastest-shrinking city*. New York Berghahn.

Sahlins, Marshall 1972. *Stone Age Economics*. New York: De Gruyter.

Simone, AbdouMaliq 2004. People as Infrastructure: Intersecting Fragments in Johannesburg. *Public Culture* 16 (3): 407–429.

Scott, James 1998. *Seeing Like a State: How certain schemes to improve the human condition have failed*. New Haven: Yale University Press.

Steward, Julian 1955. *Theory of cultural change: The methodology of multilinear evolution*. Urbana: Univeristy of Illinois Press.

Stewart, Pamela J. and Andrew Strathern. 2003. *Landscape, memory and history: Anthropological perspectives*. London: Pluto Press.

Strathern, Marilyn 1980. No Nature, No Culture: The Hagen case. In Carol P. MacCormack and Marilyn Strathern (eds), *Nature, Culture and Gender*. Cambridge: Cambridge University Press.

Tilley, Christopher 1997. *A Phenomenology of Landscape: Places, Paths and Monuments*. Oxford: Berg.

Tilley, Christopher and Kate Cameron-Daum. 2008. *An Anthropology of Landscape*. London: UCL Press.

Tonkiss, Fran 2013 *Cities by Design: The social life of urban form*. Cambridge: Polity Press.

Tsing, Anna 2015. *The mushroom at the end of the world: On the possibility of life in capitalist ruins*. Princeton: Princeton University Press.

Vergunst, Jo and Arnar Árnason. 2012. Introduction: Routing landscape: Ethnographic studies of movement and journeying. *Landscape studies* 37 (2): 147–154.

Walsh, Andrew 2004. In the Wake of Things: Speculating in and about sapphires in northern Madagascar. *American Anthropologist* 106 (2): 225–237.

West, Harry 2001. Sorcery of construction and socialist modernization: Ways of understanding power in postcolonial Mozambique *American Ethnologist* 28 (1): 119–150.

West, Paige 2012. *From Modern Production to Imagined Primitive: The Social World of Coffee from Papua New Guinea*. Duke University Press.

Willow, Anna J. 2014. The New Politics of Environmental Degradation: Un/Expected Landscapes of Disempowerment and Vulnerability. *Journal of Political Ecology* 21 (1): 237–257.

Willow, Anna J. and Sara Wylie 2014. Politics, ecology, and the new anthropology of energy: Exploring the emerging frontiers of hydraulic fracking. *Journal of Political Ecology* 21 (19: 222–236.

Woodburn, James 1982. Egalitarian societies. *Man* (NS) 17 (3): 431–451.

Wylie, John 2011. Landscape. In John A. Agnew and David N. Livingstone (eds), *The SAGE Handbook of Geographical Knowledge*. Los Angeles: SAGE.

ANNA TSING

http://orcid.org/0000-0002-0411-959X

# The buck, the bull, and the dream of the stag: Some unexpected weeds of the Anthropocene[1]

We live in a world of weeds – a world of human ecological disturbance that stretches around the planet. Yet scholars know too little about weeds, by which I mean the organisms that take over after human disturbance. New anthropologies of landscape can offer assistance here by showing how to entwine human and nonhuman histories. With hopes to invigorate emerging forms, this essay offers an excursion into some collaborative transdisciplinary fieldwork on a former brown-coal mining site in Denmark.[2] After mining was discontinued, animals wandered in, and recreational hunters bought up much of the area. It's a 'wild' place by Danish standards. It's also a place to know weedy landscapes – the kinds of places that characterise the Anthropocene, our time of industrial ruin.

One of the weeds in my story is red deer, a species once common in Denmark, but wiped out, except in game parks, in the 18th century. The red deer in our field site are descendants of escapees from those enclosures: maroons, survivors – and now, too, aggressive weeds. Scholars don't

---

1   This lecture was originally published in *Suomen Antropologi: Journal of the Finnish Anthropological Society* 42 (1): 3–21. It is reprinted with the permission of the author and publisher.

2   I am grateful to the Aarhus University Research on the Anthropocene (AURA) team for the collaborative research on which this article is based. Mathilde Højrup deserves special gratitude for helping me understand the social history of central Jutland and translating Danish research on this issue. Thanks to Anu Lounela and the Finnish Anthropological Society for soliciting this essay for their special concern with landscape. The fieldsite, located in central Jutland, is Søby Brunkulslejerne; it is the focus for AURA's collaborative fieldwork, which promotes collaborations between humanists and natural scientists. Anthropologists work here together with biologists, ecologists, science-studies scholars, and artists. To date, AURA research at this site has been conducted by Filippo Bertoni, Nathalia Brichet, Nils Bubandt, Thiago Cardoso, Rachel Cypher, Maria Dahm, Pierre Du Plessis, Natalie Forssman, Peter Funch, Frida Hastrup, Maria Henriksen, Colin Hoag, Mathilde Højrup, Agata Konczai, Thomas Kristensen, Katy Overstreet, Julia Poerting, Meredith Root-Bernstein, Jens-Christian Svenning, Heather Swanson, Line Thorsen, and Stine Vestbo, as well as myself. My paper draws from all their research. Master's theses from this research include Dahm 2014 and Højrup 2015. A special issue of articles from this research is in preparation.

*Figure 1. Adolf Henrik Mackeprang (1833–1911). Kronhjort ved en sø, morgendis. Oil on canvas. 122 x 90 cm. Courtesy of Ribe Kunstmuseum.*

ordinarily think of deer as weeds, but that lens, I'll argue, draws us into storytelling practices in which landscapes come to life in the conjunctures of many trajectories, human and nonhuman.

My story begins with a painting, Adolf Henrik Mackeprang's 'Red deer by a lake, morning mist' (Figure 1). It's not exceptional: it is one of many Mackeprang stag paintings.[3] While Danish, it evokes similar paintings from other parts of northern Europe and, while 19th century in origin, one sees copies of such paintings today everywhere from wall decoration to real estate brochures. It's not exceptional, but it tells a persistent story.

The image shows a proud but vulnerable masculine authority. It lures viewers to the chase. One might call that lure 'the dream of the stag,' and, while not the whole topic of this essay, it will be its guiding trope. Two purposes for the dream of the stag are set out here, interwoven. First, there are material stags and hunters, which help me understand weedy landscapes. Coordinations across human and nonhuman projects, I argue, make landscape assemblages coalesce.[4] Weeds, which shout challenges to stability,

---

3   I would have preferred Mackeprang's 'Roaring stag standing by a lake', the more iconic treatment, seen in many reproductions (http://www.plentyofpaintings.com/Adolf-Henrik-Mackeprang/Roaring-Stag-Standing-By-A-Lake-oil-painting.html) and forms of homage (e.g., http://hp-comic.com/roaring-stag-standing-by-a-lake/). However, I was unable to obtain permission for that painting.

4   For further discussion of this point, see Gan and Tsing, n.d.a.; Tsing, n.d.

show us transformations in which landscape assemblages come together and fall apart.

Second, there is the *dream* of the stag. The dream mesmerises, causing viewers to focus on the wild enchantments of interior self-making. Interior wildness, in turn, makes landscape histories disappear. Landscapes appear without history, and with the completeness and coherence of a theater backdrop. This is no way to know landscapes – especially the weedy landscapes we share with red deer stags. But first let me show you the dream of the stag in action.

## Follow me

Look over my shoulder; but please be quiet. I am walking as silently as I can along a forest path. My companion is a hunter, a landowner, a financial genius in the Danish garment business. He has gained and lost more money in a few minutes than farmers make in most of a lifetime. I'll call him 'Bull' to mark his barrel chest, his aristocratic aspirations, and his continuing search not just for game but also for rising markets, the ones we call 'bull'. As the evening approaches, we reach a hunting high seat and climb up. In Denmark, individual hunting is done from high seats so that a hunter can safely aim for the ground at the end of the shot. American-style stalking is illegal. Furthermore, high seats must not have roofing or too-comfortable seats. The Bull and I perch precariously on a board and, protected from view, peer over the side. We are looking onto a large grassy meadow, surrounded by dense plantation groves of pine and spruce. The red deer hide in the forest during the day, but at dusk they come out to feed. Shooting is only allowed until sunset, so we have a short window of time. We peer anxiously into the evening.

This time, we don't have long to wait. A hind peeks out from the forest, looks around, and leads her two companions into the meadow. One is another hind; the third is a young buck, perhaps two or three years old. It is late October, and hinds are already pregnant. They have spread out without contest by the stags; only this, I'm told, allows this young buck to hang out with hinds. They eat peacefully, too far away for a shot. Our watching, too, is relaxed and peaceful.

Then an older hind enters from the other side of the open space. She is leading a large group of hinds and calves – and a big stag with a rack of antlers. The Bull is riveted, his grip ready as he stares at the stag through the sight of his gun. It's much too far to shoot, but that doesn't stop his fascination. The other riveted one is the young buck. He stares; he approaches with his head high. The stag looks up from eating. The buck is less than a third of his size, hardly a threat. The stag waves his antlers for a moment and then goes back to eating. But young buck is mesmerized. He stands; he raises his head; he eases back a step but then urges himself to step forward again. And Bull too: mesmerized. He does not want to shoot hinds and calves. It is the stag that draws him. Or perhaps, in both cases, the dream of the stag.

I'm interested in these asymmetrical gazes. The stag does not look at either buck or Bull, and buck and Bull do not look at each other. Each

*Figure 2. Red deer at Søby Brunkulslejerne. The lake is an abandoned mining hole. Wildlife camera photograph used by permission of Michael Hauge.*

stares at the stag. What are they seeing and not seeing? And how does the entanglement of their respective non-entanglements shape the landscape? Both things interest me: their non-engagement with each other, and the emergent landscape assemblage that's made possible despite that. The coordination between these two non-meeting stares – the unintentional work of the dream of the stag – is key to the weedy dynamics of this place.

The presence of red deer here is already strange. As mentioned above, free-roaming red deer were exterminated in 18th century Jutland. Furthermore, Jutland has become more and more tame, especially since 19th- and 20th-century industrial techniques allowed the conversion of moorland into modern farms. Other than road verges and hedgerows, one can hardly find a square metre of non-agro-industrial space. The trees are plantation crops; the soils are augmented with fertilizers. It takes an abandoned mine to host a scene of wildness. That's why the place is interesting for the Aarhus University Research on the Anthropocene (AURA) research team, whose collaborative research underlies my thinking here.[5] Many nature reserves and parks across northern Europe are abandoned mines or other sites of human-made ruin. But our field site is not a park. Red deer wandered in by themselves along with an array of surprising guests, including invasive nonnatives such as raccoon dogs as well as the deeply prohibited wild boar and, most recently, the frightening and thrilling: wolves. What a diverse menagerie to have assembled itself!

One might think of this kind of reassemblage as auto-rewilding. 'Rewilding' refers to the placement of animals in human-disturbed landscapes, whether to aid ecosystems services or merely to enhance biodiversity. Auto-rewilding, then, would be the rewilding activities of animals themselves, and I would include plants and other organisms as auto-re-wilders too. Auto-rewilding is one of the most important processes for making our human-disturbed world today. Without auto-rewilding, our

5   See anthropocene.au.dk for more information on this program.

disturbed landscapes would be thin and bare, devoid of organisms except those we put there. But auto-rewilding offers ambivalent futures. On the one hand, we owe the richness of our feral landscapes to auto-rewilding. On the other hand, auto-rewilders often kill the chances of other, less aggressive and disturbance-loving species. Auto-rewilders are bold. They are weedy. Like us, they do not play well with others. They help us make the Anthropocene, the proposed epoch of outsized human disturbance.

## We ought to know something about landscapes of auto-rewilders

Anthropocene scholars have been more interested in feats of human engineering than in weeds. The problem is not the dream of the stag; in fact, it's something like its converse, the lure of universal history, which denies the presence of diverse landscapes altogether. Climate scientists and geologists introduced the term Anthropocene; global and universal time is their gift from the Enlightenment, and they are not about to give it up.[6] For anthropologists, in contrast, heterogeneity matters. Anthropocene gains traction only when we introduce inequality, history and cultural specificity. Landscapes are useful for such analysis. Landscapes can show us weedy configurations: the gathering of human and nonhuman trajectories. I turn to landscape, then, as a tool that might vitalize Anthropocene discussions – and bring us back to auto-rewilding.

An argument about landscape's genealogy has stifled the term *landscape*'s potential in anthropology. Cultural geographers made us wary by showing us a genealogy that takes us into Dutch landscape painting, the picturesque and the reification of nature as an object of Enlightenment vision (e.g., Cosgrove 1985). From the perspective of that genealogy, to study landscape is to flatten our perspectives to notice only the distant view. Although phenomenological approaches to landscape have continued to thrive (Ingold 2011), the term's genealogical taint blocked the array of other approaches – materialist, ecological, historical, etc. – that otherwise might have blossomed around the term. I am grateful to geographer Kenneth Olwig (1996) for taking us beyond this impasse. Olwig argues that an earlier and more pertinent genealogy of landscape in Germanic Europe is that place in which political moots could be gathered to discuss *things*, that is, issues of importance. A landscape is a gathering in the making. This definition lends itself to analysis of many of the problems which landscape studies can address. Landscapes are both imaginative and material; they encompass physical geographies, phenomenologies, and cultural and political commitments.

The definition can be extended, too, to encompass multispecies gatherings in the making (Tsing 2015). My landscapes are moots in which many living beings – and non-vital things as well, such as rocks and water – take part. They come together to negotiate collaborative survival, the 'who lives and who dies' and the 'who stays and who goes' enactments of the landscape.

6   Bonneuil and Fressoz (2015) offer a useful introduction to the history of Anthropocene discussions.

They may not acknowledge each other directly. They may ignore each other, as with the buck and the Bull. But each declines or flourishes in the effects of the world-making projects initiated and maintained by the others.

Landscapes, then, are gatherings of ways of being in the making. As ecologists argue, they are units of heterogeneity: a landscape can exist at any scale as long as it encompasses heterogeneous patches. There are landscapes on a leaf and on a continent. The so-called 'landscape scale' of GIS is only one of many scales for landscapes worth exploring. And ways of being? Ways of being are historically shifting enactments. Species is relevant, but hardly fully determinate. A farmer and a financier have different human enactments; so too a racehorse and a plow horse have different horse enactments. Rocks and water also have historically shifting ways of being. In landscape moots, ways of being emerge – and shape what's possible for all the others.

Landscapes are historical, and they allow us to think across a variety of scales, from deep time to current events. Such shifting scales of time are the focus of discussion about the Anthropocene, a term that continues to be contested – and thus still open. How might we bring landscape into discussions of the Anthropocene? In the next section, my challenge is to let landscape interrupt Anthropocene universal histories – both by taking those time lines seriously and by showing how they look different when used to peep at particular landscapes. Landscapes interrupt History; this allows me to come back later to let history interrupt landscapes – or at least the kind that arise in the spell of the stag.

## Timelines are high seats for watching shifting landscapes

What are we to do with Anthropocene timelines? Timelines need not propose epochal shifts; they can also offer points from which to watch for something new. Think of them, perhaps, like a hunting high seat: they are sites, moments, and events from which our awareness of landscape transformations might be heightened. Consider, for example, the key dates currently in play for the beginning of the Anthropocene. These dates are competing entries – but here I make them points for noticing landscape change. Some archaeologists have suggested that the Anthropocene should begin with the very first plant and animal domestications, a date that could make Anthropocene and Holocene coterminous (Smith and Zeder 2013). Some geographers argue for 1610, a global $CO_2$ drop that can be explained by the genocide of Native Americans by European-introduced diseases (Lewis and Maslin 2015). Genocide encouraged forest regrowth in the New World, lowering global $CO_2$ and perhaps explaining the latter half of the Little Ice Age in Europe. Climate scientists first promoted 1784 as the start date for the Anthropocene because of the invention of the steam engine, a marker for the industrial revolution (Crutzen and Stoermer 2000). Now many have turned their attention to 1945, the first atom bomb, with its clear radioactive signature in sediments around the world, and the 'great acceleration' of human population and industrial disturbance (Steffen et. al. 2015).

If these dates are high seats from which to notice human innovations, they are also high seats from which to notice new kinds of weeds. Consider the weediness brought into the world by each of the innovations noticed by Anthropocene scholars. The domestication of plants and animals brings weeds of crops and livestock, from rats to the plants that hide in the grain, as barley did in wheat. There are weeds too of disturbed field edges, plants and animals that thrive with human disturbance. There are new diseases for humans and their domestic animals, as pathogens pass back and forth in the crowded conditions of domestic life. Measles and smallpox are examples. These forms of weediness come into the world and stay with us.

The European conquest of the New World offers a whole other catalogue of weeds. Historian Virginia Anderson (2006) offers the term 'creatures of empire', by which she means the livestock brought by European settlers, which, through their wandering, eating, and property status, helped destroy Native Americans, human and nonhuman. The term might be extended to consider that whole suite of species that travels with conquering humans. First, there are those one might call 'shock troops', that is, those that help human invaders do their bloody work. In the New World, European pathogens did that first work; livestock followed them. But there were also one might describe as 'camp followers', the suite of intentionally and non-intentionally introduced organisms that made life more difficult for natives, human and not human.[7] Think of starlings, first introduced to the US to commemorate Shakespeare's birds, now spread across the continent displacing native birds. These are creatures of human invasions.

Beginning in the late 18th century, the industrial revolution rationalized landscapes for capitalist asset-making. Several kinds of weediness were born from this rationalization. Pests and pathogens, for example, proliferated and emerged in new, more virulent kinds from the crowded monocrops of rationalized farming. Wetlands were drained, and fertilizers destroyed specialized ecologies; such losses empowered certain kinds of weeds. These are feral landscapes from inside agricultural and industrial rationalization. At its side, however, there were survivors, such as the remnant American prairie grasses described by historian William Cronon (1992); these grasses came to live only on railroad verges, where sparks lit fires and no one regulated the results. Weediness reaches to embrace both terrifying and hopeful ecologies.

The post-World War II 'great acceleration' has also been an acceleration of feral landscapes. Industrial capitalism moves to the most remote spots on earth to use and then quickly abandon them as sites for asset-production. Feral landscapes replace not just the last wilderness areas but also the last peasant ecologies, with their comparatively long-term accommodations between humans and nonhumans. The massive use of fertilizer runs off into waterways, ruining them for fish and water plants. Meanwhile, toxins proliferate, and slow-degrading anthropogenic substances, including plastics, scatter everywhere.

---

7   The term originates from Crosby (2004); I am indebted to his analysis here.

**Table 1. Unexpected weeds of the Anthropocene**

**Onset date 1.** 10,000 BP: domestication
* Crop and livestock companions (e.g., rats; barley)
* Weeds of disturbed verges
* Zoonoses (diseases transmitted between humans and domestic animals)

**Onset date 2.** 1610: creatures of empire
* 'Shock troops' kill natives directly, e.g., livestock, pathogens
* 'Camp followers,' e.g., weedy invaders, lessen the life chances of natives

**Onset date 3.** 1784: industrialization
* Agro-industrial weeds, pests, and pathogens
* Native survivors in non-rationalized edge space

**Onset date 4.** 1945: Great Acceleration
* Toxic landscapes (e.g., radioactivity and chemical contamination)
* Eutrophication and dead zones
* Acceleration of industrial use and abandonment

How do these forms of weediness combine and layer upon each other? Every feral landscape dynamic layers forms of weediness brought into being at varied historical moments. Take auto-rewilding, which combines all the forms of weediness I have mentioned. Auto-rewilders are disturbance-loving and disturbance-making; the weeds of crops and livestock are talented auto-rewilders. Auto-rewilders are weedy invaders, drawing agilities from both ancient and modern conquests. Auto-rewilders are survivors in non-rationalized edge spaces; an abandoned industrial site is an edge made large. Auto-rewilders make use of the acceleration of industrial use and abandonment.

**Table 2. Auto-rewilding's historically layered agilities**

* Auto-rewilders are disturbance-loving and disturbance-making (cf 10,000BP)
* Auto-rewilders are weedy invaders (cf 1610)
* Auto-rewilders are survivors in non-rationalized edge spaces (cf 1745)
* Auto-rewilders make use of the acceleration of industrial use and abandonment (cf 1945)

The numbing speed of capital's mobility makes auto-rewilding the best agility we have for survival – as well as a terrifying mess. By *agilities* I mean ways of being that emerge from historical opportunities.[8] Where earlier thinkers imagined only mechanical repetition among nonhumans, I'm looking for emerging talents. Auto-rewilders have lots. Even where auto-rewilders are blocked, they may be lying in wait to seize the time.

---

8   I take the term 'agility' from Donna Haraway (2007), who uses it to describe a game in which people and dogs learn each other's capacities. The term here refers to many kinds of historically acquired abilities, across species.

Because of these layered agilities, the high seats I've identified for noticing weedy developments do not tell a historical story in themselves. Instead, they call out for stories of particular landscapes, told at multiple time-and-space scales. In those stories, we can watch agilities, which, though they emerge from different times and places, assemble for a definitive effect in the friction of landscape. In the next section of this essay, I offer a thumbnail history of the Søby brown coal beds – not of the coal, which comes much earlier, but of human habitation since the end of the last Ice Age. Several kinds of auto-rewilding agilities have developed on this multiply disturbed anthropogenic landscape. I narrate three landscape assemblages, each of which condenses human and nonhuman histories in an emergent cohesion of the multispecies moot: the moor, the mine, and the mess. Such histories are the Anthropocene in action, time lines interrupted by landscape – and landscapes radically transformed by histories at multiple scales.

## The moor, the mine, and the mess: time lines interrupted by landscape

First, the moor: already a feral landscape, emerging from human burning and grazing. It was never a landscape of full control, although people used and guided it, but rather a gathering of sheep, fire, heather, farmers, mud, sand, gravel, and, not far below, an iron hardpan, itself a historical development of human-nonhuman relations.[9] The moor emerged from these entanglements, exceeding any singular purpose.

The Søby brown coal fields inherited its sand and gravel from the glaciers. Eastern Denmark was glaciated, but a sliver of southwest Denmark – including this site – remained free of glaciers. Instead, however, it was completely covered with glacial outwash, the result of glacial movement without being of the glacier.

Trees followed the retreating glaciers, and particularly birch, lime and oak. Humans, too, moved north as the glaciers receded. Jutland is known

---

9 The story of the making of hardpan-lined moors is a wonderful model for noticing the unintentional interplay between humans and geology, so central to the Anthropocene. Here is how archaeologist Karl Butzer (1982: 125–126) tells the consequences of Mesolithic deforestation in northern Europe: 'In cool wet environments with low-nutrient soils, removal of forest reduces plant evapotranspiration and raises the already high water table; furthermore, deforestation reduces soil biota, increases soil acidity, and thus favors leaching of soil nutrients. As a consequence, acid tolerant plants, such as spruce, heather, and mosses expand, reinforcing the trend toward acid soils in which 'raw' humus accumulates. Seasonal dehydration of exposed soil leads to irreversible dehydration of iron and aluminum oxides, favoring subsoil hardpan formation and further impeding proper internal soil drainage. Eventually, infertile and waterlogged cultural podsols, peats, and heath soils are generated, creating soils that are marginal or unsuitable for agriculture, while favoring an acidic vegetation of little grazing value. In this way, extensive cultural wastelands (moors and heaths) were formed in northwestern and northern Europe, particularly in montane environments and on sandy substrates.'

41

*Figure 3. Frederik Vermehren (1823–1910), A Jutland Shepherd on the Moors, 1855, 59.5 x 80 cm, National Gallery of Denmark (right: detail).*

for its comparatively late Neolithic, but eventually humans cut down those trees, and since they were growing on sandy glacial outwash, they did not spring back. In their slowness, they were overtaken by another landscape assemblage: the moor, a place of heather, sheep and shepherds.

Figure 3, a well-known Danish landscape painting, shows the 19th century, a time of grazing intensification; for the earlier period, imagine it as a patch. What's missing in the image is fire, another participant in this gathering of ways of being. Without burning and grazing, trees come back. The moor is a feral landscape gathering historical agilities of humans, sheep, heather and fire.

This painting also shows knitting, a long-standing livelihood activity of the peasants who lived on the moor – and one that, through the twists and turns of fiber, led to the continuing importance of the textile and garment industry in central Jutland. Here, then, my stories must enter the intertwined histories of textiles, on the one hand, and Jutland ecologies, on the other. It is not fortuitous that my character Bull is a garment industry king. Changes in the organization of textile and garment production go a long way in shaping the varied weedy landscapes that have congealed in Søby. But let me continue to climb each Anthropocene high seat, one by one.

Back when peasants occupied the moor, every shepherd had his wool knitting, and knitted garments became not just a local specialty but also an item of trade. By the 17th century, wool traders from central Jutland were selling their products in Copenhagen, and, when Copenhagen traders complained, the king even gave them special licenses (Klitmøller 1998). The year1610 is my second Anthropocene vantage point from which to survey weedy ecologies. What do we see? Despite advances in the wool trade, the Jutland moors were reeling toward the peripheries – sinking in their mud, as it were.

Two 17th-century retreats associated with human-sponsored global environmental change emerge in the records. First, the Little Ice Age left

Jutland cold and damp; agriculture dwindled, and sheep died from diseases (Hansen 1983: 398). Lewis and Maslin (2015) argue that European cooling during this period is an effect of New World genocide. Second, the transfer of organisms associated with European conquest disadvantaged European wool production as other textiles became available.

Scholars have paid considerable attention to the asymmetrical ecological effects of 16th- and 17th-century European conquests (Crosby 2004; Grove 1996). Compared to Americans, Europeans were lucky; the flow of invasive species at that time was going mainly the other way. Consider, however, the spread of European attention toward Asia. The whole point of funding exploration – both west and east – was to position European traders to get Indian cottons and Chinese silks without the mediation of Muslims, whom Christian Europeans had learned to despise. In 1600 and 1602, respectively, the British and Dutch East India Companies were formed, with their gunboats and wealthy investors. By 1610, Europeans had a presence in the Asian trade. In 1664 alone, the British East India Company imported over a quarter of a million pieces of calico and chintz (Wells 2007: 26). The result in Jutland? Wool was no longer exciting to urban elites, who could now buy colorful cotton and silk. Jutland's moors dozed unmolested and mixed with oak scrub as European metropoles looked elsewhere for their riches. Slavery, colonialism, and the industrial revolution – the dynamic developments of Europe – came into being through the search for cotton, not wool (Beckert 2014). The sustainability of the moor's weedy ecology was a side effect of the trade in cotton and silk, which allowed wool production to molder in backwaters such as central Jutland. Only later would wool production be modernized.

The industrial revolution is my next high seat, and, indeed, central Jutland landscapes were transformed. In the important sheep counties, the sheep population more than doubled between 1837 and 1871 (Hansen 1983: 388). By 1847, an estimated 25,000 people were occupied in knitting, and while most knitting was done by individual peasants, workshops emerged in the Herning area, which imported wool from surrounding, poorer districts (Hansen 1983: 386).

In the last part of the 19th century, the meaning of 'progress' changed. After Denmark lost its most fertile farmlands to Prussia in 1864, Danes dedicated themselves to turning Jutland's moors into modern farms, saying, 'what was lost without must be regained within' (Olwig 1984: 58). Artificial fertilizers and machines that could break the moor's iron hardpan made it possible to plant crops and tree plantations and to raise dairy cattle and pigs. Sheep rearing declined as moors disappeared. Yet the emerging Herning-Ikast-Brande textile triangle was an exception; already a center for wool production, wool remained the center of modernization efforts. Small factories sprung up, and travelling wool-sellers increased (Klitmøller 1998). Wool merchants introduced knitting machines and a putting-out system for wool garments. Knitting scaled up, no longer left in the hands of peasants. Serious money could be made, enough to become capital. By the early 20th century, textile and garment entrepreneurs were importing cotton to add to their businesses; the decline of Jutland sheep herding would no longer form an impediment to textile production.[10] By the mid-20th century, one hundred and fifty factories produced textiles and clothing, much of it for export (Hansen 1983:385).

Note that Danish, like English, uses the French word entrepreneur to praise businessmen as those who make things happen. From the first, these garment and textile entrepreneurs were a close-knit group, tied by kinship, marriage, and personal favors (Illeris 1983; 1992). They were also what we now call 'flexible': they moved capital around from one business sector to another.

This is one way to understand why some invested in brown coal during World War II. The Damgaard family, for example, had three notable brothers, raised in textiles: Aage, Mads, and Knud. When World War II came along, it was Knud who moved back and forth from brown coal mining at Søby to textile production. He also continued to work closely with his textile-industry brothers, starting a textile high school among other things.[11] Not all the investment in brown coal mining came from the regional textile and garment industry; entrepreneurs arrived from all over Denmark. But the regional commitments of this industry have laid continuing sediments on the landscape, even in its disruptions.

We have arrived at World War II, my next high seat for weedy landscapes, and the Søby mines. What a time it was: everything was turned upside down in the most literal sense. The war cut Denmark off from its British coal supplies; some politicians tried to protect Danes from being conscripted into Germany; poor moor farmers were delighted to sell their land to entrepreneurs.[12] The net result of this conjuncture was a make-work program of shoveling for one of the world's most inefficient and dirty fuels, brown coal. Great holes were dug and drained; sand piles and acid lakes were left behind. This is a good landscape to think about auto-rewilding precisely because the former ecosystem was wiped out. Thus the 'mess'.

After 1958, brown coal companies were required to put funds in a landscape rehabilitation fund, and it was used for tree replanting, particularly with fast-growing exotic conifers such as American lodgepole pine. Lodgepole turned out to be an accomplished auto-rewilder; it took off across the landscape, and now landowners battle, unsuccessfully, to cut it down (Gan and Tsing n.d.b.). It also invited all kinds of animals, including red deer, who showed up for the first time in 1985. That brought hunters, who bought up the land and fought against development, citing the instability of the sand piles left by mining, with their proneness to sudden collapse. With management for hunting, other animals moved in; daring auto-rewilders took over. Fed by the hunters, red deer proliferated like proverbial rabbits.

10  See http://www.visitherning.com/ln-int/herning/textile-city-herning
11  See http://www.kulturarv.dk/1001fortaellinger/en_GB/herning-folk-high-school
12  As British and German coal were gobbled up for war mobilizations, Denmark began looking for energy sources. With German occupation of Denmark in 1940, coal imports from the United Kingdom were fully closed. For discussions of early policy decisions that led to brown coal mining by hand, see Nielsen 1982; Kristensen 2009. Mathilda Højrup's interviews established that many farmers were eager to leave (Højrup 2015).

Meanwhile, after the war, the textile and garment industry rationalized and boomed. Then came the end of the Cold War; former Soviet states became much cheaper places to make textiles and garments (Illeris 1992). Our entrepreneurs were ready with their flexibility. They outsourced all production and specialized in design and innovation – and amassing capital. Their textile workers lost their jobs. But business analysts think of them as great models (Illeris n.d.). They have lots of money and lots of time. They invest in modern art – and hunting. They push others out of their hunting grounds, thus encouraging the red deer. Red deer suppress the plants, making the landscape useless for farms or tree plantations. Together, hunters and red deer create a particular kind of weediness.

## This is country for the dream of the stag

These histories help me read how the dream of the stag enchants at Søby. For the Bull, hunting has something to do with playing with money: each tests his mettle; each develops his drive. Hunting also draws government ministers and CEOs into his network; he invites them to his hunts, thus augmenting financial flexibility, another kind of freedom. As he explained, he isn't interested in shooting for meat. If he kills, he lets someone else do the butchering. Besides, the autumn stags he prefers are so rank that no one wants to eat them. It's his confrontation with the great male that is at stake. So too for the buck, who looks at the stag with the urge to fight. The buck, like the Bull, is a historical figure, a bundle of congealed agilities in this moment of auto-rewilding. He stands there in preparation; he is grooming himself to steal the herd and to inseminate the hinds. While the hinds can be said to lead the herd, they lead for food and safety. The bucks, in contrast, are masters of reproduction and expansion. In this protected zone, the landscape assemblage I've called the mess, there is room for male pretension and fighting, more than in a stable ecology. Herds can spread and reproduce; males search for wild corners. Just as for the Bull, for the buck this is a historical time for freedom and ferocity.

The dream of the stag thus acts as an axis of coordination between the projects of the buck and the Bull. Without much notice between the two, they find themselves with overlapping projects of world-making. Through such overlaps, a landscape emerges. Lots of other organisms, as well as non-vital things, occupy this landscape. But every time even a small coordination emerges, a moment of friction if you will (Tsing 2005), it has landscape-making effects. It gives the assemblage at least a momentary trajectory. The feral menagerie of the Søby brown coal fields – from wolves to lodgepole pines – owes a lot to a moment of coordination between the projects of red deer, on the one hand, and financial entrepreneurs, on the other. All landscapes are made in such moments of friction. This is why we need both human and nonhuman histories to know them.

The coordination between red deer and hunters encourages a particular kind of weedy landscape; it also blocks out others. This is the message of nature writer George Monbiot's recent book *Feral*, an exploration of the possibilities of rewilding (Monbiot 2015). Several chapters take readers to Scotland, a good analog for the central Jutland site I've been describing. Red deer hunters own huge tracts of land there, and red deer and hunters together encourage a particular landscape. (Mathilde Højrup's research followed the central Jutland nexus there: one landowner is a central Jutland garment magnate, and he brings Jutland-style hunting to Scotland.[13]) Monbiot doesn't like the landscape of red deer and hunter landowners. He sees another weedy landscape waiting at the gates, excluded. If you fence even a small area so that deer can't get at it, he shows, a forest begins to emerge. Oaks and pines are auto-rewilders just waiting for a different set of coordinations to allow them to return. Monbiot argues for the advantage of this set of weeds, in waiting. They encourage a much larger suite of animals; they restore some of the floral richness of the place. Every landscape coordination blocks out other coordinations. Every weed that takes over excludes others. This is a useful caution. Without calling it by name, Monbiot ties exclusion to the dream of the stag. He mentions the British painting, 'Monarch of the Glen', which shows a Scottish red-deer stag with vague wild mountains behind him. Landscape details cannot be in focus – because the hunting coordination disallows it. Monbiot condemns the dream of the stag for blocking the richness of other coordinations.

The dream of the stag is a form of self-absorption in which other enabling engagements are forgotten. One coordination mesmerizes; other landscape assemblages disappear. What if we take this insight into theoretical territory? There is an irony here I want to probe. To be enchanted by the dream of the stag is to care about nonhumans – but only to be caught in the erasure of landscape assemblage. How can our very best thinkers about multispecies relations yet return again and again to human exceptionalism and landscapes made entirely by human dreams and schemes?

## One place to begin is with unrepentant human exceptionalism

My reading of the dream of the stag makes me sympathetic, even as I disagree. Human exceptionalism excludes nonhumans as outside the charmed circle of world-making. Here other humans take the place of the stag; the theorist is mesmerized by the dream of the human. In limiting focus to this one enchanting antagonist, then, other entanglements are erased. Human self-making rather than multispecies' coordination takes over the analysis. The enhanced agilities of the viewer, caught in the dream of the human, block out the lifeworld histories that make the dream possible.

From here, it is easy to alight on philosopher Martin Heidegger, that astonishing thinker about language, being and dwelling as agilities of humans. In his focus on the dream of the human, however, he excludes all others, although at least he has the courage to say so. Consider his famous claim that animals are poor in world (Heidegger 1995 [1929–30]: 185). This statement would reduce my buck's gaze to instinct; as an animal, to

13  Mathilde Højrup, personal communication, October 2015.

Heidegger, the buck has only its inherited sensory sphere. It cannot develop agilities or make worlds; humans alone are world makers. Yet consider how this is a reflex of how Heidegger defines 'world', which for him requires language as logos, a particular human proclivity. If we defined world from a deer's proclivities, humans would be poor in world. Heidegger is focused on the human; the animal is collateral damage. But watch how this blocks the history of landscape assemblages. The animal is instinctive, that is, mechanical; it has no history, for history, to Heidegger, is made in the meaning space of language.[14] The animal is ahistorical because it does not live with language. Thus animals have no historical projects to coordinate with humans; the *mise en scene* of human life, the landscape, must be entirely human made. Heidegger offers an exceptionally clear statement of the dream of the human, which catches us in its enchantments, blinding us to others. Indeed, late in life, Heidegger moved away from this stance, thus making his earlier position even clearer. It is as if my buck was there. In 'Language in the poem', Heidegger (1971 [1959]) shows us the gaze of a deer, albeit a deer in a poem; the lines between human and deer blur in the face of their common mortality (see Mitchell 2011). The dream of the deer, ironically, releases Heidegger from the dream of the human.[15]

From here, it is not too large a step to anthropologists working on alternative ontologies. Consider those with the strongest critiques of the West, that is, theorists of radically different ways to do worlds (e.g., Mignolo 2011; Escobar 2011; Viveiros de Castro 2015). I am full of excitement and respect for this move, which has woken anthropology from a long doze. And yet – isn't it a branch of human exceptionalism? This might be a shocking claim. Lots of nonhumans are key figures of concern, from jaguars to shamans' snuff bottles.[16] Yet these nonhumans do not have their own ontologies; they are brought into being by humans. Only humans have ontologies; only humans make worlds. Only humans make landscapes.[17]

I tend to agree that only humans have ontologies. Ontologies are philosophies of being, and it's not clear to me that any organisms other than humans bother with philosophy. Yet perhaps the situation changes when we consider Helen Verran's term 'ontics' (Verran 2001). Ontics are not philosophies but practices in which modes of being are enacted. Anyone can

14 Aho (2007:10) explains this point as follows: '*Logos*, on [Heidegger's] view, articulates the unfolding historical space of meaning, making it possible for us to be attuned to things. The animal is not tuned in this way because it is held captive within its environment by instinctual responses.... The animal's way of being...is 'ahistorical...'"

15 'The stranger's footstep/ rings through the silver night./ Would a blue deer remember his path?' (Trakl 1915). On the twilit paths of spiritual transition, rememberance moves between human and deer. The blue deer is *Wild*, a game animal and a beast, but both human and animal are transformed by the twilight into witnesses of movement and death. Mitchell (2011) guides my reading here.

16 For jaguars, see Viveiros de Castro (2004); for snuff bottles, see Pedersen (2012).

17 The major exception of which I am aware is Eduardo Kohn's *How Forests Think* (2013), although even Kohn makes communication the *sine qua non* of being, an almost Heideggerian move.

do ontics, whether or not they are interested in philosophy. A deer, a plant, a stone: all have ontics, even if they don't have ontologies. Furthermore, ontics are humbler than ontologies; they don't demand to take up all the space. Most thinkers about ontology divide the world into contrasts. There is Ontology A and Ontology B, and ne'er the twain shall meet. Ontics, in contrast, touch, overlap, work around each other, layer, and mutate in each other's presence. There are axes of coordination as well as refusals. Looking at landscape emergence is a matter of ontics. It is the coordination between the ontics of the buck and the Bull, rather than their coherence in a single cosmology, which offers a powerful trajectory to landscape history. Landscape assemblages arise in the juxtaposition of varied modes of making worlds; no single cosmology can order a landscape alone.

## So why has it been so easy to ignore this point?

The dream of the stag, or the jaguar, or the West, enchants viewers to enhance their own agilities in the chase while neglecting the coordinations that make this possible. The landscape blurs and the only nonhumans that can be seen are those that occupy the space of the dream, the space of the chase.

This argument is not a plug for a more scientific storytelling. When it comes to the dream of the stag, scientistic stories can be just as bad as cosmological stories. Let me return to Monbiot's *Feral* (2015) as exemplar. When I first read that book, I couldn't get to the ecological insights because I was so disturbed by the frame. The premise of the book is that rewilding begins in the heart of the self, and while masculinity is never mentioned directly, it is clear that this is what is intended. Rewilding, to Monbiot, means putting oneself into dangerous situations on purpose in order to cultivate an imagined intimacy with wild animals and primitive people. By 'imagined' here, I mean fantasized. Monbiot's intimacy with these Others is limited by the fact that this is a project for building the self; it is the wild interiority of the masculine self that best promotes the feral, he tells us. This is not about relationships or coordinations but about individuals who find their feral selves. As Monbiot puts it, describing how good it feels to shoulder a dead deer he found in the woods, '[c]ivilization slid off as easily as a bathrobe' (2015: 33). One is left with one's inner animal. Despite Monbiot's dislike of red deer hunting, this is the dream of the stag. Monbiot's immersion in multispecies landscapes is eclipsed by self-making, which erases other agendas.

Again, the dream of the stag helps me be sympathetic, even as I disagree. It helps me put Monbiot's chase in the context of his antagonists, the ones he calls 'civilization'. Consider the public intellectuals of Anthropocene discussion. A powerful group has grown up to advocate the 'good Anthropocene', that is, the one that can be controlled and exploited by familiar civilizational tools. I think of these voices as the 'inheriting sons' of Anthropocene thought. They are 'ecomodernists' who use the master's tools to refurbish the master's house. Their tools are capitalism, elite technology and canonical philosophy.

*Figure 4.*
*Adolf Henrik*
*Mackeprang*
*(1833–1911).*
*Kronhjort.*
*Oil on canvas.*
*76.2 × 56.4 cm.*
*ARoS Aarhus*
*Kunstmuseum.*

(See, for example, Breakthrough Institute 2015; Ellis and Ramankutty 2008; Purdy 2015). They tell us that these tools can fix what's broken; they don't worry about weeds. Like other social engineers before them, they tell us that nothing will go wrong with their plans. They are not lured by the dream of the stag; they just want to inherit the property.

In contrast, Monbiot is a rebellious son. He sees the problem of civilization; he develops his will to resist the mandate of the father. Here he joins other rebellious sons: heroes, pirates, loners. (See, for example, Abbey 1968; Watson 1980; Krakauer 1996). They immerse themselves in wild places to sop up their wildness. They hope that the sheer strength of their newly established selfhood will defeat civilization. Yet they are limited by the dream of the stag. They don't notice the entanglements and coordinations that take them there. It's hard not to imagine that they are escaping from the wife and kids. If we want to take the Anthropocene seriously, even through description, we must do better than either of these two masculine alternatives, inheritors and rebels.

*The Anthropocene is an invitation to pay attention to weeds*

So many of us are Anthropocene weeds. Weeds are creatures of disturbance; we make use of opportunities, climb over others and form collaborations with those who allow us to proliferate. The key task is to figure out which kinds of weediness allow landscapes of more-than-human livability. This requires history at many scales. Thus the field site I have described, an unremarkable ruined place in the boring center of Denmark: any ruined place can provoke stories of weedy assemblage for the last 10,000 years – and the last 10 years.

Through attention to the coordinations that allow particular weedy assemblages, landscape can be a research object that shows us the heterogeneity of world-making projects. To watch the dream of the stag, and yet attend to coordinations that hunters ignore, we need to make histories of landscapes that involve all kinds of beings, human and not human. Thus, too, we can take up a central analytic challenge of thinking Anthropocene: how to combine landscape and history such that difference and possibility remain in sight.

What can varied approaches to landscape do? In this essay I have addressed this question by throwing many different kinds of materials together. Perhaps this can open further conversation about the more-than-human social worlds around us – and the challenge of surviving the Anthropocene.

# References

Abbey, Edward 1968. *Desert Solitaire: A Season in the Wilderness*. New York: McGraw-Hill.

Aho, Kevin 2007. Logos and the Poverty of Animals: Rethinking Heidegger's Humanism. *The New Yearbook for Phenomenology and Phenomenological Philosophy* 7: 1–18.

Anderson, Virginia 2006. *Creatures of Empire: How Domestic Animals Transformed Early America*. Oxford: Oxford University Press.

Beckert, Sven 2014. *Empire of Cotton: A Global History*. New York: Knopf.

Bonneuil, Christophe and Jean-Baptiste Fressoz 2015. *The Shock of the Anthropocene*. London: Verso.

Breakthrough Institute 2015. *Ecomodernist Manifesto*. http://www.ecomodernism.org/manifesto-english/ <accessed 13 June 2017>

Butzer, Karl 1982. *Archaeology as Human Ecology: Method and Theory for a Contextual Approach*. Cambridge: Cambridge University Press.

Cosgrove, Denis 1985. Prospect, Perspective and the Evolution of the Landscape Idea. *Transactions of the Institute of British Geographers* 10 (1): 45–62.

Cronon, William 1992. *Nature's Metropolis: Chicago and the Great West*. New York: W.W. Norton.

Crosby, Alfred 2004. *Ecological Imperialism: The Biological Expansion of Europe*. 900–1900. Cambridge: Cambridge University Press.

Crutzen, Paul and Eugene Stoermer 2000. 'The 'Anthropocene'. *Global Change Newsletter* 41: 17–18.

Dahm, Maria 2014. Habitat Selection by Red Deer (*Cervus elaphus*) at a Former Brown-coal Mining Area. Master's thesis, Section for Ecoinformatics and Biodiversity, Aarhus University.

Ellis, Erle and Navin Ramankutty 2008. Putting People in the Map: Anthropogenic Biomes of the World. *Frontiers in Ecology and the Environment* 6 (8): 439–447.

Escobar, Arturo 2011. Sustainabity: Design for the Pluriverse. *Development* 54 (2): 137–140.

Gan, Elaine and Anna Tsing n.d.a. How Things Hold: A Diagram of Coordination in a Satoyama Forest. Manuscript in progress.

Gan, Elaine and Anna Tsing n.d.b. How Weeds are Made, or, Does *Paxillus involutus* Aid Succession to Lodgepole Brush on Sandy Brown-coal Overburden? Manuscript in progress.

Grove, Richard 1996. *Green Imperialism: Colonial Expansion, Tropical Island Edens, and the Origins of Environmentalism, 1600–1860.* Cambridge: Cambridge University Press.

Hansen, Viggo 1983. The Danish Hosiery Industry: A Specific Rural Industry in Central Jutland. In Brian Roberts and Robin Glasscock (eds). *Villages, Fields and Frontiers: Studies in European Rural Settlement in the Medieval and Early Modern Periods.* Oxford: British Archaeological Reports (International Series 185).

Haraway, Donna 2007. *When Species Meet.* Minneapolis: University of Minnesota Press.

Heidegger, Martin 1971 [1959]. Language in the Poem: A Discussion of Georg Trakl's Poetic Work. In *On the Way to Language.* Translated by Peter Hertz. New York: Harper and Row.

Heidegger, Martin 1995 [1929–30]. *The Fundamental Concepts of Metaphysics: World, Finitude, Solitude.* Translated by William McNeill and Nicholas Walker. Bloomington: Indiana University Press.

Højrup, Mathilde 2015. An Unstable Landscape: A Multispecies Ethnography of Landslides, Shifting Discourses of Belonging, and Changing Practices of Nature Management in a Former Danish Brown Coal Mining Area. Master's thesis, Aarhus University, Department of Anthropology.

Illeris, Sven 1983. Adapting to Foreign Competition: The Textile and Clothing Industry in the Herning-Ikast Area of Jutland, Denmark. In Peter Schaeffer and Scott Loveridge (eds). *Small Town and Rural Economic Development.* Westport: Greenwood Publishing.

Illeris, Sven 1992. The Herning-Ikast Textile Industry: An Industrial District in West Jutland. *Entrepreneurship and Regional Development* 4 (2): 73–84.

Illeris, Sven n.d. Outsourcing of Textile and Clothing Industry from Denmark to Baltic Transition Countries. http://www.geo.ut.ee/nbc/paper/illeris.html <accessed 13 June 2017>

Ingold, Tim 2011. *Perception of the Environment: Essays in Livelihood, Dwelling and Skill.* London: Routledge.

Klitmøller, Linda 1998. Fra hosebindende hedebonde til maskinstrikkende husmand: Om samspillet mellem trikotageproduktion og landbrug i Hammerum herred i tre hundrede år,' *Bol og by* 2: 64–99.

Kohn, Eduardo 2013. *How Forests Think: Toward an Anthropology Beyond the Human.* Berkeley: University of California Press.

Krakauer, John 1996. *Into the Wild.* New York: Random House.

Kristensen, Finn J. 2009. Søby Klondike. *Geografisk Orientering* 3: 174–178.

Lewis, Simon and Mark Maslin 2015. Defining the Anthropocene. *Nature* 519: 171–180.

Mignolo, Walter 2011. *The Darker Side of Western Modernity: Global Futures, Decolonial Options.* Durham: Duke University Press.

Mitchell, Andrew 2011. Heidegger's Later Thinking of Animality: The End of World Poverty. *Gatherings: The Heidegger Circle Annual* 1: 74–85.

Monbiot, George 2015. *Feral: Rewilding the Land, the Sea, and Human Life.* Chicago: University of Chicago Press.

Nielsen, Arne V. 1982. *Ringkøbing Amt: Geologi og Landskab.* Holstebro: Historisk Samfund for Ringkøbing Amt, Hardsyssel-håndbog 1.

Olwig, Kenneth 1984. *Nature's Ideological Landscape.* London: Unwin Hyman.

Olwig, Kenneth 1996. Recovering the Substantive Nature of Landscape. *Annals of the Association of American Geographers* 86 (4): 630–653.

Pedersen, Morten 2014. Islands of Nature: Insular Objects and Frozen Spirits in Northern Mongolia. In Kirsten Hastrup (ed). *Anthropology and Nature.* London: Routledge.

Purdy, Jedidiah 2015. *After Nature.* Cambridge: Harvard University Press.

Smith, Bruce and Melinda Zeder 2013. The Onset of the Anthropocene. *Anthropocene* 4: 8–13.

Steffen, Will, Wendy Broadgate, Lisa Deutsch, Owen Gaffney and Cornelia Ludwig 2015. The Trajectory of the Anthropocene: The Great Acceleration. *Anthropocene Review* 2 (1): 81–98.

Trakl, Georg 1915. *Sebastian im Traum.* Translated by Jim Doss and Werner Schmitt. Leipzig: Kurt Wolff Verlag. http://www.literaturnische.de/Trakl/seb.htm <accessed 13 June 2017>

Tsing, Anna Lowenhaupt 2005. *Friction: An Ethnography of Global Connection.* Princeton: Princeton University Press.

Tsing, Anna Lowenhaupt 2015. *The Mushroom at the End of The World: On the Possibility of Life in Capitalist Ruins.* Princeton: Princeton University Press.

Tsing, Anna n.d. When the Things We Study Respond to Each Other: Tools for Unpacking 'the Material'. In Knut Nustad and Penny Harvey (eds). *Anthropos and the Material.*

Verran, Helen 2001. *Science and an African Logic.* Chicago: University of Chicago Press.

Viveiros de Castro, Eduardo 2004. Perspectival Anthropology and the Method of Controlled Equivocation. *Tipití* 2 (1): 3–22.

Viveiros de Castro, Eduardo 2015. *The Relative Native: Essays on Indigenous Conceptual Worlds.* Chicago: University of Chicago Press.

Watson, Paul 1980. *Sea Shepherd: My Fight for Whales and Seals.* New York: W. W. Norton.

Wells, Troth 2007. *T-shirt.* Oxford: New Internationalist.

ANU LOUNELA
https://orcid.org/0000-0002-8903-1983

# Erasing memories and commodifying futures within the Central Kalimantan landscape

Profound changes in socio-natural environments are taking place at an accelerating rate around the world, affecting the ways people dwell within the landscape, relate to place and imagine the future. This chapter focuses on relationship between dwelling and politics by looking at a landscape that has changed to such an extent that previously familiar places have become almost unrecognisable to the local population. Hence, dwelling in these landscapes is considered so challenging that people are starting to avoid them or relating to them through new technologies. To be more precise, I will explore the politics involved when landscapes are (re)made through new technologies and representations as contrasted with dwelling, that is, as a way to *live in* emerging landscapes. I argue for incorporating a phenomenological understanding of landscape into understanding the politics of environmental transformation (political ecology) by exploring multi-scalar experiences and representations in relation to profoundly transformed landscapes.

The village of Buntoi in Central Kalimantan is located in what Anna Tsing would call a "disturbed landscape" (Tsing 2015). Large-scale timber logging started here in the 1960–1970s, when timber corporations accessed the land and began cutting down large trees. In the 1990s, a paved road was constructed to ease transportation; in 1996, the Mega Rice Project (henceforth MRP), through which President Suharto intended to transform 1.4 million hectares of swamp forest into rice fields, was extended to the vicinity of the village, transforming previous dwelling places into something entirely different. These changes in the landscape are felt both in terms of experience and livelihoods; for instance, since deforestation resulted in dry peat soils, fires regularly erupt (see Galudra et al. 2010).[1] Disturbance in the landscape means profound ecological change, which in turn opens up the landscape to the new (eco-social) assemblages, gazes, and relations (Tsing 2015), including to climate change mitigation schemes, conservation projects and also new species and humans (Lounela 2015; 2017; forthcoming).

---

1 Between 2000 and 2008, Central Kalimantan lost about 0.9 million hectares of forest and still has a high rate of forest loss. The reasons have to do with changes in national and local policies (decentralisation) and institutional, social and ecological change (Suwarno and Sumarga 2015: 78). The recent large forest fires (esp. 2015) and spread of oil palm have added to the problem.

In 2010, Central Kalimantan was nominated as a climate change pilot province by the central government and President Susilo Bambang Yudhoyono.[2] Consequently, Central Kalimantan and many villages like Buntoi, became the site of climate change mitigation activities, especially REDD+, the acronym for the UN programme on Reducing Emissions from Deforestation and Degradation plus. Initially, REDD aimed at reforestation and forest conservation through result-based payments and carbon trade (Howell 2014: 1), later integrating social dimensions and questions of livelihood into REDD + schemes. These climate change mitigation projects have been initiated by international donors and local NGOs in collaboration with state agencies, and implemented in specific *places,* using specific techniques.[3] They produce maps to show land use plans and property rights, in an effort to stabilise and transform socio-natural relations.

James Scott (1998) has famously argued that states produce abstract knowledge through maps, which tend to simplify or even misrepresent local (complicated) knowledges and practices. Nancy Peluso, among the others, has noted that the mapping of forest resources is a political act, and for the last couple of decades a counter-mapping movement has resisted the state appropriation of 'customary' lands through drawing their own maps (Peluso 1995: 383–384). However, as noted by Stuart Kirsch (2006: 202), counter-maps too may displace the embodied knowledge normally gained through local practices and dwelling. While state maps typically indicate property boundaries and mark land rights, increasingly NGOs and indigenous people's groups, supported also by international organisations, such as those coordinating climate change mitigation schemes, also produce maps representing use rights, high-value species and local knowledge.

This article shows that maps are political representations of the landscape that may structure how local populations will experience dwelling in the future. Maps are produced both by external specialists who stress the visual and the abstract, who "know by seeing" and make landscapes legible from the distance (Scott 1998), and by local populations, who attach cultural

2    REDD+ mitigation projects have become widespread in Indonesia since the COP13 (Conference of the Parties) meeting in 2007 in Bali: the number of pilot projects on the ground has varied as they have been stopped, restarted and continued. After negotiations that could be traced back to the meeting in 2007, the government of Norway and Indonesian President Susilo Bambang Yudhoyno signed a Letter of Intent, which led to Central Kalimantan being declared a climate change pilot province on 23 December 2010.

3    In the beginning, REDD+ pilot projects operated together with the Payment for Ecosystem Services (PES) or other carbon trading schemes and trials aiming to contribute to the UN-initiated climate change treaty (Angelsen and McNeill 2008). When the COP 21 Paris Agreement to limit temperature increase to less than two degrees Celsius was signed, REDD+ was mentioned. It was thus officially recognised as a performance-based payment mechanism to reduce emissions. However, no carbon trade mechanism is directly mentioned. The agreement has been criticised for not achieving enough and for playing fossil fuels and deforestation against each other (see Lang 2015).

values and meaning to landscape on basis of their "knowing from within" (Emery and Carrithers 2016: 394).

This opens up four important questions. How do people, living in Buntoi, live and dwell in a place that is being transformed so profoundly and that is constantly under threat? What kind of future do they imagine for these places? Who are the dwellers and how do they experience the landscape? What kinds of new assemblages and representations are being formed through their encounters?

Like the rest of this book, this chapter is informed by a long history of debate over structural and phenomenological approaches in landscape studies. Some cultural geographers, such as Denis Cosgrove, proposed radical cultural geography that combined Marxist materialist and symbolic approaches in the analysis of the spatial formations of landscapes (Cosgrove 1983: 10). Anthropologist Christopher Tilley rejected Cosgrove's notion of structured landscapes and, building on Tim Ingold's dwelling perspective (see Introduction, this volume), argued that landscape instead constitutes a "physical and visual form of the earth as an environment and as a setting in which locales occur and in dialectical relation to which meanings are created, reproduced and transformed" (1994: 25). In a similar vein, Steven Emery and Michael Carrithers (2016) explore seemingly oppositional approaches to landscape, namely the Ingoldian dwelling phenomenology and Cosgrove's cultural geography, which focus on political representations of the landscape, and argue that recent ethnographic writings on landscape do not sufficiently theorise the relationship between dwelling and politics (2016: 393; see also Árnason et al. 2012). In order to overcome this limitation in ethnographic research on landscape, they borrow from rhetoric culture theory in an effort to combine both representation and dwelling perspectives into a single framework. In other words, they explore "how landscapes are used to make stories, arguments and moral positions both plausible and appealing" (Emery and Carrithers 2016: 395) in rhetorical situations.

Scholars have argued that landscapes are produced through processes of dwelling and engaging in specific encounters, through which the landscape is opened up to new socio-natural gatherings and relations (Ingold 2011; Tsing 2015). This phenomenological approach stresses the importance of organisms (animals and humans), experience, movement, emergence, imagination and perception:

> It is to join with a world in which things do not so much exist as occur, each along its own trajectory of becoming. In the life of imagination, the landscape is a bundle of such trajectories, forever ravelling here and unravelling there (Ingold 2012: 14).

Ingold's 'dwelling perspective' implies that "landscape is constituted as an enduring record of – and testimony to – the lives and works of past generations who have dwelt within it, and in so doing, have left there something of themselves" (Ibid.: 189). However, it is not only the experiences and marks of human dwelling and living within the landscape that matter, but also the material elements, plants, trees and animals and their interaction between humans and non-humans that contribute to processes of constituting a landscape: "the perspective of dwelling, [represents] a way to overcome the entrenched division between the 'two worlds' of nature and society, and to re-embed human being and becoming within the continuum of the lifeworld" (Ingold 2011: 4; see also Bird-David 1992; Descola and Pálsson 1996; Descola 2013). In this worldview, humans do not construct or build nature; rather, they come into being in relation to, and through engagement with, the material and non-humans around them while at the same time producing intimate knowledge (Ingold 2000: 47, 112). Allerton, following Ingold, notes that there is no built and unbuilt environment; landscape is an enlivened and lived-in environment; Southeast Asian landscapes, such as the one in Buntoi, are often animate, that is, inhabited by ancestors and spirits in addition to humans, animals, plants and other natural elements (Allerton 2013: 5, 97).

In certain respects, this case study provides challenges to the phenomenological approach to landscape. Being bound up with state formation and global capitalist processes, especially frontier making, Buntoi landscape has long been profoundly transformed. From an ecological and social standpoint, it has long been experiencing severe disturbances. This concept, disturbance, has been introduced from the natural sciences into ethnographic research by Anna Tsing (2015):

> Disturbance is a change in environmental conditions that causes a pronounced change in an ecosystem. Floods and fires are forms of disturbance; humans and other living things can also cause disturbance. Disturbance can renew ecologies as well as destroy them. How terrible a disturbance is depends on many things, including scale (Tsing 2015: 160).

For instance, large forest fires may alter an entire ecosystem. However, disturbance is not always destructive, rather it may also produce new human-plant-animal-spirit assemblages: "The disturbed landscape is socially transformed eco-social gathering. [...] Disturbance opens the terrain for transformative encounters, making new landscape assemblages possible" (2015: 160). The disturbed landscape raises questions around the phenomenological approach to landscape. How does a profoundly disturbed landscape relate to intimate knowledge and memories of dwelling places? What happens when familiar marks in the landscape have been wiped out, erasing or changing the mnemonic devices that bind the memories of the local populations and their lived experiences to each other? What's more, severely disturbed landscapes have increasingly become targets of environmental interventions: conservation agencies, climate change pilot projects, and so forth, invite local populations to imagine their future by reproducing the landscapes through visual and managerial techniques, and introducing environmental restoration efforts.

Anthropological debates concerning the separation of landscape studies into political versus dwelling perspectives have invited various responses. This chapter suggests that these approaches can be fruitfully combined through ethnographic research, specifically by focussing on experiences of dwelling in a severely disturbed landscape where people make great effort to try to take hold of the landscape through (simplifying) representations such as maps. Hence, this chapter explores landscape of political experience through an ethnographic case study among the Ngaju people in the village of Buntoi, Central Kalimantan.[4]

## Buntoi: It is not only a capitalist landscape

The village of Buntoi is about two hours' drive with motor vehicle along the asphalt road that leads to Bahaur, on the southern coast. It is located in the district of Pulang Pisau, along the Kahayan River. The village elders claim that the village dates back to 1670, when it was called Lewuk Dalam Betawi. According to the villagers, it has been a trading port for the Batawian people (today known as the native Jakartans) since the 17th century, during Dutch colonial rule. The first missionaries arrived in the area in the first half of the 19th century. The Ngaju have practiced hunting, gathering and shifting cultivation, but also engaged in barter and trade in forest products along the rivers. Since the 1940s, after the Second World War, they began to trade rubber and plant cassava for trading purposes; in this period of time, capitalist relations became embedded within the Ngaju landscape (see Lounela 2017).

Today, Buntoi is one of eleven villages in the sub-district of Kahayan Hilir. During fieldwork the population was about 2,700,[5] many of whom are immigrants (Banjar, Javanese, Madurese) who either married villagers or moved there for work, mainly as rubber tappers. The Ngaju obtain their livelihoods mainly from rubber tapping, in combination with shifting cultivation, collecting forest products, hunting and fishing, various precarious jobs or working as state officials. Several decades ago the economy was based on swidden rice cultivation, mostly understood as a collective or family activity that did not involve money – groups of men and women went, in rotation, out to the village fields. Recently, however, much slash-and-burn rice cultivation involved monetary transactions, with many Ngaju paying others to do the work for them. In the rubber economy, initially the Ngaju collected rubber from the local latex trees, such as *jelutung* (*Dyera costulata*)

4   The chapter is based on ethnographic fieldwork conducted in three 1.5–3 month periods in Buntoi and the Central Kalimantan province capital city of Palangkaraya between 2014 and 2016, and two short research periods in the Central Kalimantan district of Kapuas and village of Mentangai Hulu in 2012–2013. I acknowledge funding by the Kone Foundation in 2012–2013, and the Academy of Finland for 2014–2016. I wish to thank Dr Pujo Semedi and Angela Iban from the University of Gadjah Mada, Oeban and other people in POKKER, and Alina (names of the villagers are pseudonyms), my companion throughout fieldwork in Buntoi. The chapter is dedicated to Pak Nambang who passed away far too early in 2018. I also wish to thank the editors of the book, Eeva Berglund and Timo Kallinen, and the workshop participants, as well as Isabell Herrmans and Kenneth Sillander for their valuable comments. The content of the chapter is solely on my responsibility.
5   Perencanaan penggunaan lahan desa Buntoi, Kecamatan Kahayan Hilir Kabupaten Pulang Pisau, Tahun 2014–2024. Public Document 2014.

in the swamp forests. After Indonesian independence (1945), people planted industrial rubber trees (*Hevea brasiliensis*) in gardens along the banks of the canals (called *handel*) in plantation-type styles (see Lounela 2017).

The indigenous religion of the Ngaju people is Kaharingan, which divides the cosmos into the upper and lower world, equated with upriver and downriver. The upper world has its own deity, called Mahatara or Mahatala, indicating the Hindu influence on Kaharingan, and the underworld deity is called Tambon – a mythical water snake – or *jata* in the everyday language (Schärer 1963: 12–15).[6] Even though numerous Ngaju have converted to Christianity or Islam, some Ngaju still hold beliefs related to Kaharingan. According to the man known as the customary head of the religion, only eight Kaharingan-practicing families are left in Buntoi. He blamed the Christian religion (rather than Islam) for the decline of Kaharingan, and noted that mostly only old people (including himself) still practiced Kaharingan customs, like giving offerings to the spirits. However, I witnessed several situations in which offerings were given to spirits or ancestors, indicating that human-nature-spirit-ancestor exchange relations are still embedded within the landscape.[7]

Various spirits have specific locations that indicate their position in the cosmos; so-called higher spirits – deceased people of higher status – live in the upper world, while the lower world is inhabited by female spirits, although both worlds are inhabited by good and bad spirits (Schärer 1963: 16–19). After death, humans may also turn into animals, reside within the landscape, and communicate with people. These spirit animals may also take the form of humans and appear in specific situations in the human world. For example, a crocodile living in the Kahayan River may be an ancestor as well as the founder and protector of the settlement. Deceased humans may be defined as "transformed ancestors" among the many Dayak groups, including the Ngaju (see Béquet 2012; Couderc 2012: 169–176).

One morning, during fieldwork in Buntoi, I went fishing (*merempa*) together with an elderly couple from the village. We were out for many hours under a hot and humid sun; our trip consisted of sitting first in a little boat, and then walking on the sand and collecting shrimp and catching fish along the shores of the Kahayan River. As we waited for low tide in the little boat, I asked if there were any crocodiles in the river. "Yes, there are", the woman replied, "but they will not disturb us, one has to let them know first, then they will not disturb us. Ancestors [*datu*] are everywhere, deep in the water, close to that big island." It was at this point that I realised she talked about

---

6     See Hans Schärer (1963), *Ngaju religion: the conception of God among a South Borneo people*. Schärer did missionary work among the Ngaju in South Borneo in the 1930s and was later trained in anthropology. His work offers a good comparative reference for contemporary ethnographic material, but should only be regarded as such.

7     Catherine Allerton has noted that in Flores, spirits and ancestors often became blurred; spirits could be understood as ancestors of the land (2013: 110). Among the Ngaju in Buntoi, some ancestors were named and not regarded as spirits, but sometimes the ancestors seemed to be perceived as spirits too. This I think is the case with spirit animals, which are considered ancestors.

ancestors who sometimes take the form of a crocodile (*jata*) and who live deep down in the river.

She held the view that the ancestors could turn the *kampong* (settlement) invisible and dark to protect it from outsiders wanting to harm the village, who would then see only trees in the darkness; this was the ancestor's way of protecting the *kampong*. In her view, nothing bad had happened to Buntoi, which good fortune was a result of powerful ancestors inhabiting the river and a nearby island.

Clearly the landscape of Buntoi is constituted by social relations, and sustained through exchange relations between living people, ancestors and living spirit beings and animals and plants. In order to be able to engage in these exchange relations, one should know who resides in this landscape. However, one can only achieve such intimate knowledge through dwelling in it. I had seen tiny houses and large yellow flags on an island in front of the settlement, along the rivers and also in the village. These were the houses of the spirits and ancestors. They are connected to ancestral lineages of the villagers. If the ancestors are not visited and given gifts, they might then ask for gifts through dreams – they might appear not only to the persons in question, but also to other people with whom they could communicate and who could deliver the message to the persons concerned. The villagers should perform rituals, offering gifts to the ancestors and asking them to protect or assist them in achieving some particular objective. Spirits inhabit certain trees in the forests; one should ask permission from them (*roh gaib*) before felling large trees. However, people should also (and the same goes for foreigners) ask permission before entering an ancestral place; ancestors are known to "possess" those places (see Robbins 2003), and only spirits may grant access to humans.

The local customary head of the Kaharingan religion explained that when people practice slash-and-burn rice cultivation, they must first give part of the rice seeds to the spirit of the rice. They must then give part of the harvest first to the spirits of the stones (who make the tools sharp). They may also ask the kings (*raja*) of the monkeys and mice not to disturb their cultivation by giving them their share (*bagian*) through a specific offering. In this way, spirits will not disturb their slash-and-burn cultivation or other efforts in the forests. In this way, everybody will receive their just share without the spirits becoming angry.

Documentation of local forest types, gathered by the local customary leaders and others in the village, clarifies that the spirits inhabit several types of places: *bahu* is land that is cultivated using slash-and-burn methods, which means it is periodically left fallow. It can return to forest in due time, and be planted with fruit trees or similar. *Kaleka* refers to abandoned spaces in small settlements (of perhaps one family) where fruit trees often grow; *Sahep* is deep peat soil, and sometimes a place for hunting and placing traps that are called *sahepan*; finally, there are forests that should not be disturbed by humans at all, called pukung *pahewan* (also *leka uluh*).[8]

---

8   Dokumen prencanaan penggunaan lahan desa Buntoi, kecamatan Kahayan Hilir Kabupaten Pulang Pisau tahun 2014–2024. Public document.

Against this background of elaborate understandings of the local surroundings, it is curious why the Ngaju began cutting down trees when corporations entered the area in the 1960s. Nevertheless, a logging company built a factory just opposite the village along the Kahayan River, and a large-scale logging operation started in the forests behind the village: most of the large trees were cut down and small canals were cut across the peat land to transport the logs to the Kahayan River. In the 1990s, an asphalt road was built across the village, which reduced river transportation dramatically but also increased access to the cities and the flow of goods and money to the village. In 1995, President Suharto inaugurated the Mega Rice Project (MRP), which led to the destruction of almost all the forests across the 1.4 million hectares of peat land. The project aimed to transform the area into rice fields in Central Kalimantan. The scheme failed, and what was left in its place was something I would call a naked, deforested and wounded landscape of canals that was, furthermore, vulnerable to fires. The local men who took part in the cutting down of the forests referred to it as cleansing (*pembersihan*): not only large trees, but also small trees, were cut down and canals grew in size enormously as the machines dug into the land. Further still, during my fieldwork, construction began on a new coal power plant along the banks of the Kahayan River opposite the settlement.

Such frontier development is one reason why the Ngaju have started to engage in exchange relations with the state or corporations rather than with spirits. Eilenberg has discussed frontier as a distinct aspect of a border. He, as well as other geographers and anthropologists, defines frontier as a "discourse of state imaginaries of opportunistic wilderness and infinite unexploited resources" (2014: 161). In the Indonesian context, frontier landscape has mostly been discussed as an open space with respect to capitalist claims and corporate and market demands: changes are rapid; nature is being converted into natural resources and extracted in a violent manner; new property regimes are being formed with new actors (Tsing 2005; Peluso and Lund 2011; McCarthy 2013; Lounela 2017). Illuminating comparisons abound elsewhere. For instance, Joel Robbins has argued that among the Urapmin of Papua New Guinea, "possession", understood in Hegelian terms as mutual recognition, is an inherent part of exchange. Urapmins are ready to give their land away to mining companies in order to become recognised by the modern state and become modern citizens (moving into the city), and they might well consider this a form of exchange (2003: 21). Similarly among the Ngaju, people in Buntoi are increasingly engaging in exchange relations with the state and transnational agencies rather than with spirits. Frontier development, the impact of Christian hostility towards Kaharingan beliefs, and the erosion of local knowledge (*ilmu*), all had a role in how the state and other agencies were able to capitalise upon as they sought to appropriate natural resources. The resulting shift in exchange relations became especially clear to me, when I took a journey through a disturbed landscape together with some villagers and NGO activists.

## Walking through a disturbed landscape: Encounters

I had heard that in the newly formed and legally recognised village forest area (*hutan desa*), which I describe in more detail below, it was still possible to find natural forest (*hutan alam*) – but I had never seen or visited such forest even though I had often expressed my wish to do so. When I expressed my wish to visit this natural forest, though it was inside the village forest area, many villagers told me that it was very difficult to visit; it was too far away. Finally, one day, I was able to join two NGO workers, one from South Kalimantan, the other a Ngaju from a village along the Kapuas River, who wanted to see the forest, together with a middle-aged man and woman from the village who had also never visited it. Alina, a villager in her thirties, was especially happy to join us. This, her first visit to the forest, was now possible because in me she now had a female companion and could travel together with the men. We were led by Karli, a young half Madurese and half Ngaju man who lived far away, within the village but on the border of the forest. Karli and his brother Parli often spent time in the forest hunting, patrolling and serving as guides for local groups that needed to go to the forest, consultants, state officials, NGOs or donors.

The idea had been to leave at sunrise, but it was 9 a.m. before we left the village with two boats. It was obviously late, considering that we were to walk about six kilometres from the riverside deep into the forests, and this after about nine kilometres by boat along the river. The trip was supposed to take two days and one night. We were late because we had had a debate about how to go into the forest: Karli had been of the opinion that we should take boats and travel through the canals and rivers passing the neighbouring village, and then enter the forest there, which would mean not having to walk for too long. However, my host forbade us from doing so for three reasons: we could not enter the neighbouring village without permission, secondly, there was illegal logging going on nearby (and loggers may carry guns) and, thirdly, it was not safe for me as a western white person as I could be mistaken for someone on a mission to investigate local natural resources for economic or other interests.

During our boat trip on the large canal, for about the first two kilometres from the village we saw old rubber trees growing amongst rattan and bamboo and some fruit trees, after which a number of relatively young rubber tree plantations spread along the banks. Alina told me that the rubber trees were planted there some time after the big fires that followed the MRP in 1997. The further from the village we went, the more obvious it became that there had been profound disturbances: the land here had burned at least once, but more probably two or three times, since 1997. After traveling nine kilometres by boat, the canal became so narrow that we could not continue. We pulled up the boats and left them in the bushes, took drinking water with us, and started to walk.

Where we landed, I found no traces of the 'pristine' forest, or even relatively old anthropogenic (human-modified) forest (Descola 2016). What I saw was an ecosystem that had emerged out of recent forest fires, not swiddens made by locals.[9] *Kelakai* (*Stenochlaena palustris*) bushes and grass spread high (sometimes reaching my head) along the banks of the canal and made walking very difficult.[10] The peat soil was soft and wet and the vegetation was sharp. Sometimes water reached up to my waist, and it was full of biting ants. Some isolated trees about ten years old grew here and there. It seemed to me that it would take years before the forest would regenerate. After about three kilometres more, we reached more dense and regenerating forest, though it was still quite young. But the walk thus far had taken a long time: it was already afternoon and raining, and the heat was almost unbearable. Karli suggested that we turn back because soon it would be dark, and we would not be able to reach the pristine forest that day.

A young mapping expert named Dung, who was helping an NGO located in the capital city of Central Kalimantan, was traveling with us. He used a GPS to establish our coordinates and figure out where we were, and how many kilometres we had walked so far. Karli laughed at him for his ridiculous technology: his own feeling was that we were about three kilometres away from the forest. "Feeling", replied Dung, with irony. Karli explained the forest is a place where there is no seniority. Once he himself had saved a mapping expert who had become lost in the forest. Although the expert had claimed seniority and superior knowledge of the forests, by the time Karli found him, he was wounded and in a bad state. Karli had not gone to school maybe, but he knew the forest. Knowing and feeling the forest in the intimate way Karli did was related to how he had been dwelling in it. In contrast, Dung was used to calculating distances using modern technology and orienting himself with that knowledge (see Emery and Carrithers 2016).

This was a curious encounter and point of debate: in Buntoi village, Karli is considered an expert in matters to do with the forest. It is his job to stop illegal loggers and hunters as well as prevent forest fires. He is half Madurese and half Ngaju; one villager told me that his Madurese smell had been washed away to make him 'local'.[11] He was living six kilometres away from

9   Philippe Descola (see also this volume) suggests that landscape should be understood in terms of transfiguration *in situ* (in the practices of the place) and *in visu* (the representational view), which he explores through Amazonian subsistence gardens (resembling, by the way, many Southeast Asian gardens) and which "render patently visible the relationship between cultivate vegetation and the forest cover it replaces" (2016: 7); there is a continuum between the forest and garden in terms of their similar ecological principles.

10  Kelakai is an edible plant and is a part of the Ngaju diet. However, in a forest with few trees it totally takes over until the trees are high again.

11  There is a long history of Madurese (immigrants from east Java) presence in Buntoi and Central Kalimantan (see also Lounela 2017). Tensions between the Dayaks and Madurese have been high in recent decades for many reasons I am not able to discuss here. However, violent conflicts between the groups occurred in 1996–1997, 1999 and 2001, which was the worst one. In 2001 conflict 150, 000 Madurese were displaced, with Madurese deaths reportedly between 431 to 3000, depending on the source (Smith 2005: 1).

the village centre, on the edge of the forest[12] in a neighbourhood built up, according to some stories, in the seventies, when loggers had built huts (later houses) there, to live in while they were in the forest. Karli continuously hunted, walked through and patrolled the forest area, but I never heard him talking about the forest spirits. During our walk, he did not point out any specific places or trees, although like his brother Parli he could navigate his way through the forest better than most people from the village. Karli had intimate knowledge of this specific landscape, but he could not relate so easily traditional Ngaju beliefs concerning the forest.

In Buntoi, many Ngaju had started to avoid going into the forest: "it is dangerous, because one could die", as the son of the customary head told me when describing getting lost there with a group of men some years earlier. He explained that they had been afraid of dying from thirst and hunger before finally being found. Thus, the forest was no longer familiar even to young Ngaju living in the village centre. On the other hand, new encounters included the NGO staff, consultants, donors, biologists and social scientists, and state officials, who explored the landscape through new techniques with no social memories. But all these people were concerned about the destructive changes to the landscape, thus partaking in unexpected collaborations and encounters (Tsing 2005). Following Anna Tsing (2015), I would propose that this kind of severely disturbed landscape is open to transformative encounters and assemblages; things and relations dissolve and gather again in such a landscape. Disturbance does not only refer to permanent changes in ecosystem, but to profound changes in social relations. Further below I will discuss other aspects of such encounters, for example those that resulted in the mapmaking and subsequent legalisation of the forest village area in 2013.

## Climate change mitigation and new representations of landscape

Stuart Kirsch has nicely described how the Yonggom of Papua New Guinea continue to "emphasize relations to place" despite the landscape destruction caused by mining companies (2006: 201). In their struggle to maintain and renew their relationships with places that have histories, they have turned to mapmaking. Likewise, in Buntoi people have been involved in mapmaking since at least 2011. Their mapmaking practices have mainly been supported by transnational climate change mitigation projects. In this section, I will argue that this kind of mapmaking produces a particular landscape along with the ways in which people dwell within it – and will continue to do so in the future.

---

12 Since the village law 1979 the villages all over Indonesia have been structured so that the Village is divided into units: village; hamlet *(dusun)* and neighbourhood *(rukun tetangga)*.

Already in 2009, the Partnership for Governance Reform programme[13] had begun promoting climate change mitigation projects and REDD+ programmes at the government and local community levels: Buntoi village was part of these programmes, notably of forest governance reform (decentralisation through the village forest programme – *hutan desa*).[14] After 2010 the Partnership programme, UNORCID (United Nations Office for REDD+ Coordination in Indonesia) and USAID IFACS (Indonesia Forest and Climate Support: Reducing Emissions through sustainable forest management) supported different kinds of projects in Buntoi village.

POKKER SHK, an NGO located in the regional capital city of Palangkaraya, in Central Kalimantan, was given funding to facilitate the formation of a village forest area unit (*hutan desa*), which would help conserve 7,025 hectares inside the village area in collaboration with three other villages (altogether 16,000 hectares in the district of Pulang Pisau). The main idea seemed to be that legalisation of the village area could enhance forest restoration efforts and stop illegal logging and forest fires. As it stands, most of the land in the Pulang Pisau district has been designated state forest land.[15] This village forest area unit was the same forest through which I had walked together with Karli and the others in our search for pristine forest.

The legalisation and mapping of the forest village area went as follows: the village forest area in Buntoi was mapped for the first time by POKKER in 2011, and a proposal to set aside a village forest area was made to the governor of Central Kalimantan and the Ministry of Forestry. The Ministry of Forestry verified the proposed village forest area, and after that in 2012, issued a Decision Letter (SK) to establish a village forest area within the state-protected forest.[16] The governor of Central Kalimantan further issued the SK to implement the management of the village forest area (*Rencana Kelola Hutan Desa*) permit in 2013. The permit is for 35 years, but it can be extended, and the management of the forest should be evaluated every five years.[17] After the legalisation process was complete, USAID IFACS supported strengthening the management of the village forest through POKKER SHK,

13  The partnership programme dates back to the 1990s. It was established in 2000 as a United Nations Programme (UNDP) to enhance good governance and respond to the economic and social crisis at that time: it "is a multi-stakeholder organization established to promote governance reform. It works hand-in-hand with government agencies, CSOs, the private sector, and international development partners in Indonesia to bring about reform at both the national and local levels. The Partnership builds crucial links between all levels of government and civil society to sustainably promote good governance in Indonesia." Retrieved from http://www.kemitraan.or.id/our-history (28.9.2015).

14  http://www.kemitraan.or.id/sites/default/files/Kalteng%20-Kemitraan%20 Closing%20Paper.pdf, pages 30–31.

15  The state forest land, which has been divided into different categories, covers 82 per cent of the total 1,035,910,740 ha of land in the district. *Ringkasan eksekutif. Kajian Lingkungan Hidup Strategis (KHLS) RTRW, Kabupaten Pulang Pisau.* 15.7.2014.

16  Keputusan Menteri Kehutanan No: SK.586/Menhut-II/2012 tentang Penetapan Kawasan Hutan Lindung sebagai Areal Kerja Hutan Desa Buntoi seluas 7.025 hektar di Kec. Kahayan, Kab. Pulang Pisau, Kalimantan Tengah.

17  PP No 6 Tahun 2008.

which supported the capacity building of the Village Forest Management Organization (*Lembaga Pengelolaan Hutan Desa*) in the village.[18] USAID IFACS took a "landscape approach" in its climate change mitigation program. The strengthening of the village forest fit well with it:

> The IFACS Katingan Landscape covers 1.7 million hectares, largely consisting of deep peatland, and comprises Sebangau National Park and provides critical habitat for orangutan and other wildlife. The landscape includes parts of two districts–Katingan and Pulang Pisau–and the municipality of Palangkaraya. Central Kalimantan Province is still 59% forested (according to Ministry of Forestry data), but it suffers the highest rate of deforestation in Indonesia, after Riau Province in Sumatra. [...] MSFs [Multi-Stakeholder Forum] in this landscape have an increasingly strong and vibrant membership, especially in Palangka Raya where they continue to focus on five thematic areas – green open space; implementation of SEA [Strategic Environmental Assessment], and GIS [Geographical Information System] forum and capacity; environmental journalism; community forestry; non-timber forest products; and livelihoods. IFACS will continue to support MSF programs especially for fire prevention and monitoring, shifting focus to Pulang Pisau District in the final work plan period. SDI [Spatial Data Infrastructure] network development will increase capacity of stakeholders in using accurate spatial data in Palangka Raya municipality and Pulang Pisau District (USAID-IFACS final report 2015: 126).

The village forest area in Buntoi is part of the so-called Kalawa forest area, which includes four villages. The Kalawa forest was understood to be communal forest, legally under the control of the state, but it is also a 'traditional' forest that includes the so-called *pukung pahewan* area – a sacred forest that should not be exploited that is guarded by the spirits and ancestors. People have been collecting forest products, hunting and fishing in this forest area for a long time. Ideally then, conserving it would benefit the local people, who would then continue to have access to it and to non-timber products, though hunting is now forbidden.

In April 2014, two young workers at POKKER SHK from Palangkaraya, conducted another mapping project, now outside of the village forest area. This time around, the NGO focused on the canals that crossed the peat lands bordering the village forest area. I travelled with them along the three different canals and took part in the mapping together with Alina and some other villagers. The core village settlement, made up of five main neighbourhoods together with a longhouse now preserved as a museum, and old family homes, is located along the Kahayan River. Behind the houses spread the gardens, with a mix of rattan, fruit and rubber trees, and other plants mirroring the forest. A paved road cuts through the gardens approximately 100 metres behind the houses, after which the old rubber gardens extend about two kilometres along the canals towards the village forest area. Then new rubber plantations mostly spread along the canals until the so-called *kolektor*, a small canal that runs horizontally past the

---

18  USAID IFACS terminated its activities in 2016, but a new programme called USAID LESTARI was to take over some of the earlier programmes.

main canals, and which the villagers understand as marking the boundary between their land use area and state forest categorised as protected forest. On another map, the *kolektor* was marked as a resettlement area in the event that the coal power plant being constructed nearby should pollute the surrounding area too much.[19]

This map (see Figure 1) was supposed to indicate zones of rights to land – especially the state categories - and rivers that have been transformed into canals. As in cartography generally, on the map made by POKKER SHK, imagining the future involves processes of visual zoning by an external gaze and producing abstract space. Colours on a map show different zones of land use. The white represents the settlement and cultivated rubber and fruit or rattan gardens area, which is most often understood to be under private ownership. The red line is asphalt road. The yellow section indicates the area categorised as state forest used for (industrial) production, but which the villagers may access so long as they do not cut down trees and so long as government has licensed other uses. The green represents state forest land and protected forest area (*kawasan hutan lindung*), where only limited activities are allowed.

One interesting point about this map is how it recreates property rights at the same time as it conceals social traces. There are no markings showing sacred sites, family homes, the longhouse, graves and so forth. As Kirsch, following Scott (1998), notes, a map legible to the state "bears the risk of displacing other, embodied ways of knowing one's land" (2006: 202; see also Lounela 2009). Indeed, the Ngaju have gained an intimate knowledge of the landscape through family practices – with parents and some of the children or grandparents practicing shifting cultivation, fishing, engaging in rubber tapping, collecting fruits and so forth. They dwelled within the landscape while getting to know it and transmitting this knowledge. The new maps represent a different kind of reality and future, a view from above, one without social traces, but with new boundaries (Kirsch 2006: 203).

On our walk to the forest, Karli seemed to be sceptical about the maps. Why waste so much money on those maps? What use do they have? Are they being sold to someone? When I returned the village in 2016, two years later state officials had erected cement pillars designating state boundaries on land that villagers considered their own. When I looked at the NGO map later, I could see the marked boundaries between the protected state forest area, and state land allocated for other uses, and land under the heading of private property. But when walking with the villagers within the landscape, we only noticed people's gardens, planted rubber, human-made canals and young trees in the protected forest area (on the maps, now also part of the

---

19  When I arrived in the village in April 2016, state officials were in the process of marking the state forest area with cement pillars, which they were erecting on land that the villagers considered their own and which they in turn had marked with rubber trees. The dispute soon became heated. Some villagers felt that beyond the *kolektor* there was a two kilometer-wide zone of adjustment. There is no room to elaborate here, but it does show how maps can also be 'insecure' proof of the claims to land.

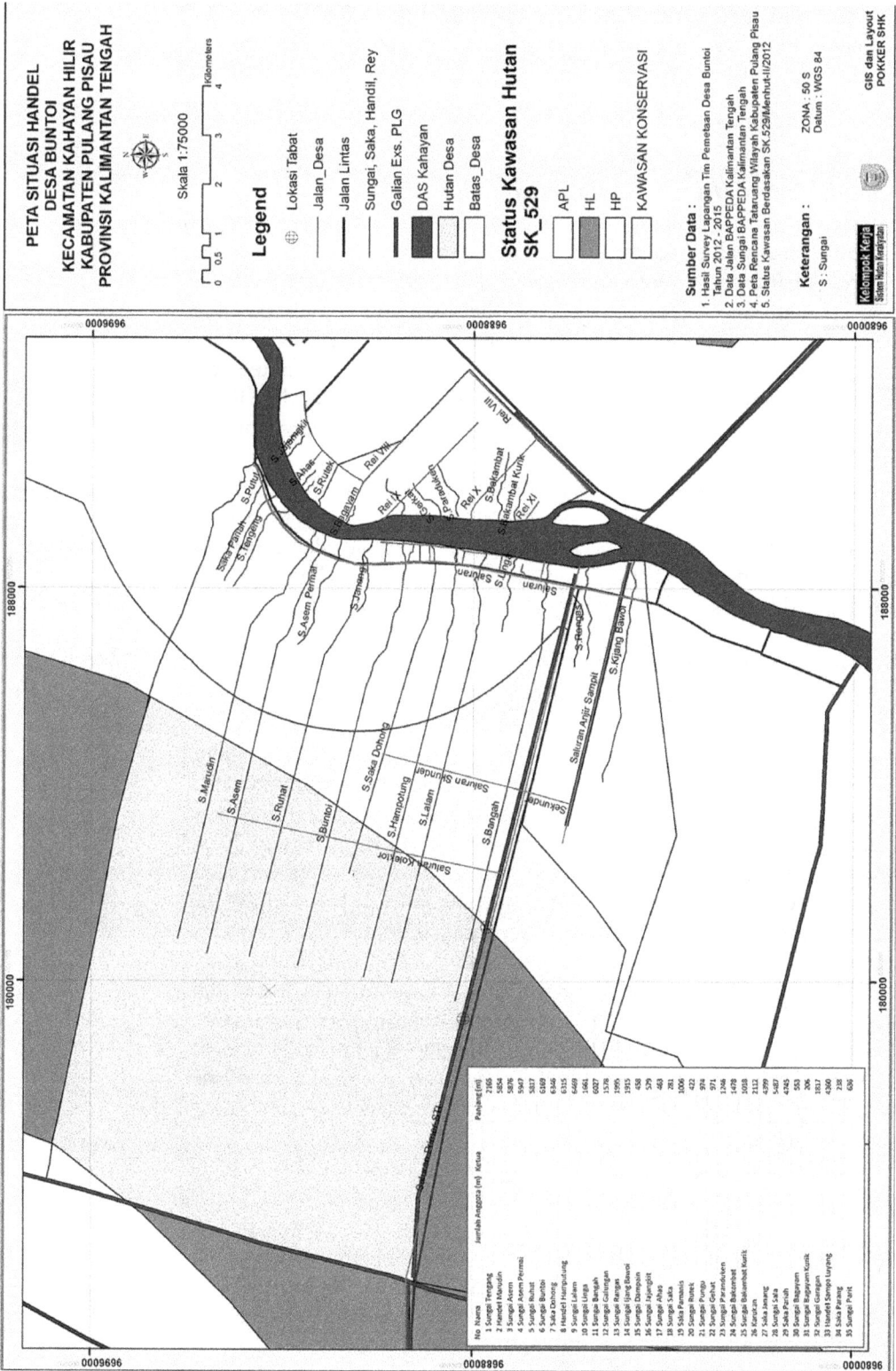

*Figure 1. Map by POKKER SHK.*

*hutan desa* in its legal status). The maps that might be legible but they do not coincide with dwelling experiences. Rather, they enforce and represent a certain viewpoint, one that will contribute to the experience of dwelling in the future.

## Commodifying landscape: New value relations

This specific map was, of course, important because with it villagers could gain access to and conserve approximately 7,000 hectares of land near the village. The map could be used to represent the village and make it possible to see the state forest (categorised as a protected forest) legalised as a village forest area, which was what many, if not all, of the villagers wanted. Yet the map also paved the way for a plan that would commodify the village forest area through carbon trade; it was a tool for imagining a new future of commodified nature.

Since the legalisation of the village forest, it has been managed by the village forest organisation LPHD (*Lembaga Pengelolaan Hutan Desa*), which was headed by an elder, one of the customary experts in the village. He was close to the village head at the time when the village forest was being formed and he worked in close collaboration with the village elite and staff at that time.

The previous village head, my host Pak Nambang, had also been actively pushing for the *hutan desa* permit, but in 2014 was relieved of his duties by substitute staff and later replaced as village head in elections in February 2015. Most of the people I met felt that they did not know about the activities of the head of LPHD; they said he hardly ever communicated with other people or informed them about the organisation's activities. Thus, some of the villagers, including the person elected as village head in 2015, complained that they received no benefit from the village forest area, and feared that the benefits would go to someone else, notably those in LPHD. They also felt that they would not benefit economically either, because it was not then possible to plant oil palm or other harvestable crops on the land. Some villagers, and LPHD, thought that the most important result was that village forest area would prevent oil palm corporations from expanding into the village. For instance, two LPHD heads from the neighbouring villages and Pak Nambang once told me that they had been able to thwart efforts to establish palm oil plantations in their respective villages by establishing a village forest area.

POKKER SHK, which supported the LPHD suggested that carbon trade would solve the problem. Alina, who facilitated POKKER SHK's activities in the village, told me their main concern was to convince villagers that to make money they could sell carbon instead of timber or land to the palm oil corporations. Thus, training sessions were organised to teach people how to measure the size of trees and know how to calculate carbon. Villagers told me that they did not find these techniques difficult, but what was difficult for them to understand, was what carbon is, and how and where people could sell it. This training programme had been launched just as I arrived in the field. The idea was that the carbon generated from the village forest area could be sold through the Plan Vivo Foundation, a registered Scottish charity, which had, and continues to have, its own technical specifications, with technical specifications for calculating carbon sequestered or emissions avoided by allowing trees to grow.[20]

The village forest area is now under the management and control of the villagers through LPHD. They are responsible for devising the forest management plans and implementing them as well as for preventing forest fires and stopping external threats. They also should be the main actors in rehabilitating the forest land, with support from state agencies and the private sector. In an interview with the provincial forestry official, he told me that the village forest area should be profitable because it will operate under a private-sector permit for the next 35 years. However, like many other officials from the district and provincial levels that I interviewed in 2016, he had the view that the village forest organisations were far too small, and that they lacked the financial resources to protect and manage large areas such as this, up to 4000–7000 hectares. There was administrative restructuring going on in central Kalimantan in 2016, but the important issue is that the state ministries at the regional level understood that while they had some responsibility for facilitating management of the village forest area through LPHDs, they did not have the resources to do it. Thus, they hoped the private sector would help.

This brings to mind Tanya Murray Li's discussion on conservation and community-based forest management (2005), where she argues that it tends to transfer responsibility for forest management from the state or corporations to poor communities, something I have also argued in the case of state forest management in Central Java (Lounela, 2009). As it stands, community-based forest management involves demanding work; Ngaju are expected to expend a great deal of energy and time planning their own forest management operations, patrolling the forest, stopping illegal logging and preventing forest fires. Otherwise, they risk losing their permit to manage the forest. It also entails that the villagers should become cheap labour in the production of new valuable types of environment, similarly to what Jason Moore suggests with his concept of "capitalocene" (Moore 2015).

In Central Kalimantan, NGOs and donors have generally taken the view that the carbon trade, eco-tourism and non-timber products could offer economic benefits to the villagers. Furthermore, most REDD+ and climate change mitigation activities involve money: eco-tourism and non-timber products (but not hunting) from the village forest area would bring benefits one could count in financial terms. Indeed, such politics have been enacted in my field sites also, for instance the villagers involved in LPHD had already planted 12 hectares of rubber trees in the village forest area in 2014, but they had burned in the 2015 forest fires. Once again, the disturbed landscape became open for different kinds of assemblages of persons and plans, but also for new fears and dreams for the future.

---

20  Retrieved from http://www.planvivo.org/about-plan-vivo/ (28.9.2015). This plan was probably not actively advanced after the 2015 forest fires.

## Conclusions

In this paper, I have discussed the politics of dwelling, describing various entanglements and encounters between the actors engaged in the production of landscape.

For a long time, people living in Buntoi have engaged in the production of local landscapes through complex environmental practices: swamp forests and gardens around the settlement used to be places of dwelling, practicing hunting, fishing, tapping rubber, collecting forest products and engaging in slash-and-burn rice cultivation. Usually couples, possibly with their children, would be mobile for a relatively long periods before settling in places familiar to them from having used them to gather forest products (*kaleka*). In the past men would typically hunt. However, since the nineteen-sixties, logging corporations, and later, state initiated programs such as large-scale canal digging along with agricultural schemes, have transformed the landscape. Furthermore, especially after the new reform era (1998-), conservation efforts and climate change schemes have contributed to landscape production, including via making maps, that is, detachable representations of the landscape.

Buntoi landscape has become a dwelling place for NGO activists, scholars, donor organisation staff, state forestry officials and others engaged in mapping species, measuring distances and studying the landscape from a detached point of view. It has also become gendered place: what is important today is for men to have physical strength and knowledge about the disturbances and changes. For instance, sometimes villagers engage in conservation through rubber or tree planting or they are patrolling in the forests. These tasks transform accepted social relations: couples no longer walk long distances collecting forest products, hunting is forbidden in the village forest area and (illegal) loggers are considered a problem. In short, changes in the landscape transform social relations. A disturbed landscape is open to new encounters, but these are different kinds of encounters, extending from the locality to global arenas, producing new assemblages.

Such assemblages are also being manifested in the ways people engage in new exchange relations: the Ngaju used to engage in exchange relations with spirits, ancestors, family members and their neighbours, as well as with animals and other materialities that embody their own spirits. But today, as noted by the Kaharingan customary head, only a couple of older people, and those who still know, engage in such exchange relations with spirits and ancestors. Instead, people are increasingly engaging in exchange relations with the state and corporations, not to mention environmental and climate change mitigation schemes, where landscapes appear and are evaluated in terms of money or conservation values.

In general, maps operate as tools to simplify and make legible complicated rights and systems (Scott 1998). Maps also stabilise power relations. The state categories that are reproduced in NGO-made maps, seek to guarantee access rights to some areas, and can also be read as counter-maps (Peluso 1995; Kirsch 2006). This explains why and how maps become popular tools for local people to seek access in places like the village forest area (*hutan desa*). Maps do not just show landscape in the form of zones of state categories and property rights, with a kind of abstract gaze, they redefine use rights: hunting, timber logging and any other 'destructive' activities that are forbidden or frowned upon, but also open limited access to the landscape – here village forest area – that not so long ago was customary forest area

These representations become part of villagers' life: through the work of LPHD, the responsibility for managing and conserving the village forest area is now in the hands of the villagers. The stakes are high: if they fail to manage and conserve the area well enough in state's eyes, or secure additional economic resources for such efforts, they could lose the permit. Thus, some villagers dream of pristine forests in which limited livelihood systems could be developed, new settlements established along the border of the village forest area or forests become valuable in terms of the carbon trade. At the same time, other villagers wish for economic development and, for instance, oil palm plantations, and so they resist the mapping and the politics it brings. In short, I argue that the maps have multiple, sometimes contradictory, effects. They also create new political landscapes.

I have brought together two seemingly contrasting approaches to landscape: the phenomenological and political ecology approaches. However, I have suggested that ethnography is able to combine them into a single frame of analysis: dwelling within disturbed landscape is a socio-natural experience, which involves narratives and representations that give meaning to a landscape at the same time as they constitute its emergence. But landscape is also a representational object: it can be detached from local material practices through mapping and rule making, or what I would call abstraction. The example I have given of experience of dwelling within a disturbed landscape in Central Kalimantan, shows how histories of environmental transformation and related power relations become embedded within a landscape but I have also argued that apparently abstract and detached representations of a landscape become entangled with the experiences of dwelling in such a disturbed landscape. When walking with Karli in the village forest area, he often talked of how he and his brother were alone in trying to stop forest fires and prevent illegal logging; sometimes they succeed, but often they did not. It was a landscape of alienation, death, familiarity and hope – or a landscape of political experiences.

# References

Allerton, Catherine 2013. *Potent Landscapes: Place and Mobility in Eastern Indonesia*. Honolulu: University of Hawai`i.

Angelsen, Arid and Desmond McNeill 2008. The evolution of REDD+. In Arid Angelsen (ed.), 2008. *Moving ahead with REDD: Issues, Options and Implications*. Indonesia: CIFOR.

Árnason, Arnar, Nicolas Ellison, Jo Vergunst and Andrew Whitehouse 2012. *Landscapes beyond land*. Oxford: Berghahn Books.

Béguet, Véronique 2012. Iban petara as transformed ancestors. In Pascal Couderc and Kenneth Sillander (eds), *Ancestors in Borneo Societies: Death, transformation, and social immortality.* Copenhagen: NIAS.

Bird-David, Nurit 1992. Beyond "The Original Affluent Society": A Culturalist Reformulation. *Current Anthropology* 33 (1): 25–47.

Cosgrove, Denis 1983. Towards a radical cultural geography: Problems of theory. *Antipode: A Radical Journal of Geography* 15 (1): 1–11.

Couderc, Pascal and Kenneth Sillander (eds), 2012. *Ancestors in Borneo Societies: Death, transformation, and social immortality.* Copenhagen: NIAS.

Couderc, Pascal 2012. Separated dead and transformed ancestors. In Pascal Couderc and Kenneth Sillander (eds), *Ancestors in Borneo Societies: Death, transformation, and social immortality.* Copenhagen: NIAS.

Dalsgaard, Steffen 2013. The Commensurability of Carbon: Making Value and Money of Climate Change. *HAU: Journal of Ethnographic Theory* 3 (1): 80–98.

Descola, Philippe and Gísli Pálsson (eds) 1996. *Nature and society: Anthropological perspectives.* New York: Routledge.

Descola, Philippe 2013. *Beyond Nature and Culture.* Translated by Janet Lloyd. Chicago: University of Chicago Press.

Descola, Philippe 2016. Landscape as transfiguration. Edward Westermarck Memorial Lecture, October 2015. *Suomen Antropologi: Journal of the Finnish Anthropological Society* 41 (1): 3–14.

Dove, Michael 2012. *The Banana Tree at the Gate: A History of Marginal Peoples and Global Markets in Borneo.* Singapore: NUS Press.

Eilenberg, Michael 2014. Frontier constellations: Agrarian expansion and sovereignty on the Indonesian–Malaysian border. *The Journal of peasant Studies* 41 (2): 157–182.

Emery, Steven B. and Michael B. Carrithers 2016. From Lived Experience to Political Representation: Rhetoric and Landscape in the North York Moors." *Ethnography* 17 (3): 388–410.

Fox, James J. 1997. Place and Landscape in Comparative Austronesian Perspective. In James Fox (ed.), *The poetic power of place: Comparative Perspectives on Austronesian Ideas of Locality.* Canberra: ANU E Press.

Galudra G., U. P. Pradhan, I. Sardi, B. L. Suyanto and M van Noordwijk 2010. Hot spot emission and confusion: Land tenure insecurity, contested policies and competing claims to Central Kalimantan Ex-mega Rice Project area. *Working Paper* no. 98. World Agroforestry Centre.

Gosgrove, Denis 1983. Towards a radical cultural geography: Problems of theory. *Antipode* 15 (1):1–11.

Hastrup, Kirsten (ed.) 2015. *Anthropology and Nature.* London: Routledge.

Hirsch, Eric and Michael O'Hanlon (eds) 1995. *The Anthropology of Landscape: Perspectives on Place and Space.* 1st edition. New York: Clarendon Press.

Howell, Signe 2014. "No rights - no REDD": Some implications of a turn towards co-benefits. *Forum for Development Studies* 41 (2): 253–272.

Ingold, Tim 2011. *Being Alive: Essays on Movement, Knowledge and Description.* London: Routledge.

Ingold, Tim 2000. *The Perception of the Environment: Essays on Livelihood, Dwelling and Skill.* Reissue edition. London: Routledge.

Janowski, Monica and Tim Ingold 2012. *Imagining Landscapes.* Anthropological Studies of Creativity and Perception. Farnham: Ashgate.

Kirsch, Stuart 2006. *Reverse Anthropology: Indigenous Analysis of Social and Environmental Relations in New Guinea.* Stanford, California: Stanford University Press.

Knapen, Han 2001. *Forests of Fortune? The environmental history of Southeast Borneo, 1600-1880.* Leiden: KITLV Press.

Lang, Chris 2015. COP21 Paris: REDD and carbon markets. http://www.redd-monitor. org/2015/12/15/cop21-paris-redd-and-carbon-markets/ <accessed 16 December 2015>.

Li, Tanya Murray 2005. Engaging Simplifications: Community-based Natural Resource Management, Market processes, and State Agendas in Upland Southeast Asia. In Peter J. Brosius, Anna Lowenhaupt Tsing and Charles Zerner (eds), *Communities and Conservation: Histories and Politics of Community-Based Natural resource Management.* Walnut Creek: Altamira Press.

Lounela, Anu 2009. *Contesting Forests and Power: Dispute, Violence and Negotiations in Central Java.* Research Series in Anthropology 17. Helsinki: University of Helsinki.

Lounela, Anu 2015. Climate Change Disputes and Justice in Central Kalimantan, Indonesia. *Asia Pacific Viewpoint* 56 (1): 62–78.

Lounela, Anu 2017. Continuity and Change in Central Kalimantan: Climate Change, Monetization of Nature, and its Bearing on Value Orientations. In Cathrin Arenz, Michaela Haug, Stefan Seitz and Oliver Venz (eds), *Continuity under change in Dayak societies.* Wiesbaden: Springer.

Lounela, Anu forthcoming. Morality, sharing and change among the Ngaju people in Central Kalimantan. *Hunter Gatherer Research.*

McCarthy, John 2013. Tenure and transformation in central Kalimantan: After the "Million hectare" project. In Anton Lucas and Carol Warren (eds), *Ohio RIS Southeast Asia, Volume 126: Land for the People: The State and Agrarian Conflict in Indonesia.* Ohio: Ohio University Press.

Moore, Jason 2015. *Capitalism in the Web of Life: Ecology and the Accumulation of Capital.* New York: Verso.

Peluso, Nancy Lee 1995. Whose Woods Are These? Counter-Mapping Forest Territories in Kalimantan, Indonesia. *Antipode* 27 (4): 383–406.

Peluso, Nancy and Christian Lund 2011. New frontiers of land control: Introduction. *The Journal of Peasant Studies* 38 (4): 667–681.

Robbins, Joel 2003. Properties of nature, properties of culture: Possession, recognition, and the substance of politics in a Papua New Guinea society. *Suomen Antropologi: Journal of the Finnish Anthropological Society* 28 (1): 9–28.

Rumsey, Alan and James F. Weiner 2001. *Emplaced Myth: Space, Narrative, and Knowledge in Aboriginal Australia and Papua New Guinea.* University of Hawaii Press.

Schiller, Anna 1996. An "Old" Religion in "New Order" Indonesia: Notes on Ethnicity and Religious Affiliation. *Sociology of Religion* 57:4 409–417.

Schärer, Hans 1963. *Ngaju Religion.* Dordrecht: Springer Netherlands.

Scott, James 1998. *Seeing Like a State: How certain schemes to improve the human condition have failed.* New Haven: Yale University Press.

Smith, Claire 2005. The roots of violence and prospects for reconciliation: A case study of ethnic conflict in Central Kalimantan, Indonesia. *Social Development Papers.* Paper No. 23/ February. The World Bank.

Suwarno, Hein and Elham Sumarga 2015. Governance, Decentralization and Deforestation: The case of Central Kalimantan Province, Indonesia. *Quarterly Journal of International Agriculture* 54 (1): 77–100.

Tilley, Christopher 1994. *A Phenomenology of Landscape: Places, paths and monuments.* Oxford: Berg Publishers.

Tsing, Anna Lowenhaupt 2005. *Friction: An Ethnography of Global Connection.* Princeton: Princeton University Press.

Tsing, Anna Lowenhaupt 2015. *The Mushroom at the End of the World: On the Possibility of Life in Capitalist Ruins.* Princeton: Princeton University Press.

Joonas Plaan

# Knowing and perceiving the seascape: Local knowledge, human-environment interactions and materiality on Kihnu Island, Estonia

## Introduction

Kihnu Island, a small island off the western coast of Estonia, with only a few hundred permanent inhabitants, neighbouring Manija Island, a further 56 uninhabited islets and the surrounding sea, comprise an area defined by Kihnu residents as the Kihnu cultural space (*Kihnu kultuuriruum*[1] in Estonian). The area has long been a source of inspiration for cultural life beyond, but also a place where knowledge about the natural environment has been and continues to be created. It is also a place where islanders' identity and people's perception of the sea are influenced in interesting ways by the interactions of different actors, including humans and non-humans, the land and the sea.

I argue that the Kihnu cultural space is a fluid and ever-changing space shaped by reciprocal relations with social agents and the environment. The Kihnu seascape, I suggest, is where different knowledge systems and conflicting perceptions meet, putting changing environment, state power and economic forces together to create disputes but also new knowledge, and to alter perceptions of the environment. As I will demonstrate, it is a place where new environmental knowledge and perceptions are created and transformed in continuous human-environment interactions not just in the landscape but, I suggest, in the *seascape*, a relational space of sea and land. It is simultaneously social, material and subjective: a space where islanders' views of nature, their identity and their livelihood practices interact with conservation regulations and state power. On the one hand, Kihnu people claim it is their cultural space: generations of Kihnu people have lived on the island for more than 400 years, during which time they have transformed the land and coastal sea area. On the other hand, conservationists see it as a natural area with great biodiversity: today most of the Kihnu cultural area

---

1   The term 'Kihnu Cultural Space', with capital letters, was first coined in the late 1990s by Kihnu cultural activists preparing an application to give Kihnu a status as UNESCO Intangible Cultural Heritage. Today Kihnu cultural space, without capital letters, is widely used among locals to describe the area where Kihnu people used to historically hunt and gather natural resources. In many cases, they still do so.

is under environmental protection, which, in some cases, restricts human activity. However, knowledge about the seascape is more dynamic than this suggests. It is being constantly recreated and transformed, influenced by the Soviet past, shifting scientific paradigms and practices, dynamics of local-global articulations, and unforeseen transformations in the marine environment.

The chapter builds on three months of ethnographic fieldwork during the fishing season in 2013 on Kihnu Island, and on shorter field trips between 2011 and 2014. The material discussed consists of interviews, archival research, working with fishing crews and marine biologists, and participant observation in meetings. In addition to this work, I have been interviewing officers from the Environmental Board[2] and the Environmental Inspectorate, who work in the regional centre, the city of Pärnu, and in the Estonian capital, Tallinn.

The chapter is structured around three central themes: *seascape*, *human-environment interactions* and *materiality*. Each theme has its own philosophical tradition and they have been brought together only rarely. I draw on them to describe how people know and perceive the Kihnu seascape, beginning with a description of what I call the seascape approach, which I use to describe human-environment interactions on the sea. I continue by describing human-environment relations and the networks they have created in different eras, starting from the beginning of the 20th century, when Kihnu Island was part of the Russian Empire. This will be followed by an ethnographic description of everyday interactions between different actors in the seascape, and how these are changing perceptions and knowledge about the seascape, eventually making the seascape material. Finally, I hope to show how the knowledge and perceptions of the seascape are in constant change, fluid like the water in the sea, yet leaving traces in human-environment interactions and social relations.

## Moving from landscape to seascape

Landscapes in anthropological research tend to represent something holistic and ever-changing, both altered by humans and part of what humans are. In one of the most recent discussions, landscapes "gather topographies, geologies, plants and animals, persons and their biographies, social and political relationships, material things and monuments, dreams and emotions, discourses and representations" (Tilley and Cameron-Daum 2017: 20). Landscapes and the physical processes affecting them, are seen as historically constructed and in continuous relations with resource users and the socio-economic and political sets of relations which shape both

2  The Environmental Board is an organisation whose task is to implement state environmental and nature conservation policies and to contribute to the development and improvement of legal acts and other official documents related to the environment. The Environmental Board falls within the area of governance of the Ministry of the Environment.

landscapes and their inhabitants (Blaikie 1999: 132). Many landscape studies focus on quotidian life, on "everyday experience" (Rose 2002: 457), on "processual daily practices" (Gareth and Metzo 2008: 224), or on "mundane activities and struggles" (Scott 2006: 493).

Sometimes landscape studies, when influenced by political ecology, move beyond such localised and everyday practice. These studies ask what are the aims and desires of the actors who encounter each other in these 'relational spaces,' and what are the social relations of power in their experience of landscape (Neumann 2011: 847). Used to study the relational spaces formed by cross-scalar social, economic and human-environment interactions, this is what is often called the landscape approach. Studies using this approach have shown that the material and discursive relations between landscape and resource users continuously condition both environmental and socioeconomic contexts. The focus is on the ways people are embedded in landscapes through iterative practices (e.g. agriculture or fracking) and on how landscapes are shaped simultaneously by local and extra-local socio-economic and political processes (Zimmerer 1999; Batterbury 2001; Neumann 2011; Huff 2014). Overall, the landscape approach emphasises the ecological and biophysical, and the critical and social dimensions of changing political ecologies (Huff 2014: 87).

This chapter proposes a seascape approach that extends and goes beyond these, inspired by what has been called an amphibious anthropology. The basis of amphibious anthropology is the convergence of land and water and the constitutive relationality of landscape and waterscape (rivers, lakes, glaciers, etc.) (Gagné and Rasmussen 2016). In this case water is seen as part of social production and as a repository of meaning influencing the sense of place and identity, and it is both product and producer of functioning social organisations (Strang 2006; 2009; Stensrud 2014; Rasmussen 2016; Orlove 2016; Willow 2016). By applying this idea of seascape approach, the seascape and people in it are not just in relation to each other; rather the seascape is a relation of material, social and cultural as an organic whole. Nevertheless, I argue that a seascape is marked by a variety of possible relationships between people, ecological environment, materials and geographies. These relationships are based on interactive processes where a seascape is perceived in culturally specific ways (Torrence 2002; Lambert et al. 2006) filled with symbolic meanings (Brown 2015).

As with landscape, the term seascape has commonly been used to refer to a visual representation of the sea, the coast or ships (McNiven 2008), but it need not be considered only as visual representation. Rather, drawing on how Blaikie (1999) and many others have considered landscape, I suggest we can approach it as the reciprocal relations of social agents and the environment. Seascape, like landscape, is "contoured, alive, rich in ecological diversity and in cosmological and religious significance and ambiguity [...]" giving us a new perspective on how people living and working there "[...] actively create their identities, sense of place and histories" (Cooney 2003: 323). Seascape includes the non-human, and it is made up of embodied and lived experiences, representations and perceptions of being in and on the sea, and of the historical and social dimensions that constitute individual and collective understandings of the sea (Brown 2015).

Hence, seascape and landscape have many similar characteristics, but there are two distinctive qualities to note about the seascape. One contrast with landscape, is the fluid and ever-changing nature of seascape. Veronica Strang notes that the "most constant 'quality' of water is that it is not constant" (2004: 49). It is the very notion of the fluid, moving and changing nature of the sea that opens up the space to consider it as a seascape, something that shapes us both through physical processes and social interactions (Steinberg 1999). Moreover, recognising this fluid nature is also to draw attention to the fact that seas cannot be fully controlled, in the way a bounded territory on land can be physically controlled, and so the seascape must be treated as active rather than passive. At the same time, the sea's liquid and fluid nature has often been seen as problematic, and it has led to "categorical difficulty and ontological uncertainty" (Connery 1996). These different perceptions, values and knowledges, often lead to contested debates about what sea is (ontology) and how do we know it (epistemology).

A second contrasting quality, as compared to landscape, come from the fact that little is still known about ecological and biophysical processes in the seascape, and it is often the case that these environmental dimensions reveal themselves only years later, if at all. Perhaps it is because human activity does not leave permanent visual marks on a seascape as happens with a landscape (e.g. agriculture), it has long stayed on the edge of academic inquiry or has been represented as something exterior to research. Consequently, our knowledge about the ecological and biophysical dimensions of seascape is considerably poorer than our understanding of these dimensions of landscapes. Despite the long history of environmental studies of the Baltic Sea, little is known about the fish stocks and biophysical conditions, and there are knowledge gaps relating to the sea floor as well as major threats to the Baltic (Kraufelin et al. 2016). These unknowns of the seascape make way for contestation over knowledge. In these debates, the knowledge there is, is never objective. Rather, it becomes part of "a sociocultural process produced through particular relations of power", in which some natures, knowledges and people are valued above others (Burke and Heynen 2014: 8). What is ethnographically observable, are changing perceptions of something usefully called the seascape.

The seascape is a relational space where new knowledge and perceptions about nature are shaped together with the islanders' identity and their livelihood practices, as these interact with state power and conservation measures. This revealed itself very clearly when I joined high officials and politicians, scientists and managers on a tour of Pärnu County in spring 2013, as they were presenting a new marine management plan for the Gulf of Riga.

It was a sunny afternoon in mid May and we had been sitting in the Kihnu Island Community House for two hours listening to presentations by local politicians, marine biologists and fishery managers about protected species in the marine environment and about new environmental regulations. Robert Aps, the senior marine scientist was giving a presentation about the current health of the fish population, mainly focusing on Baltic Herring and European Perch. Suddenly Mihkel Leas, the representative of the fishers stood up and declared: "We demand that the fishing quotas be reviewed. Today the figures are wrong, which makes us criminals." This surprised the senior marine scientist; after all, a survey is conducted every year and the figures are produced scientifically. This talk of scientific evidence offended the representative of the fishers:

> The scientists come here only in July, when the weather is at its warmest; they put the nets in only a few hundred meters from the shore, and after a week, they declare that there are no fish. Of course there are no fish! The fish are 5 kilometres from the shore, where the deeper and colder waters are. We go out every morning with the scientist from the same harbour and not once do they ask us where we go or where the fish are. (Mihkel Leas 2013)

The marine scientist invited everybody to come and look at the maps, and he asked the fisher to show where the fish are in July. Mihkel Leas agreed to show the location of the traditional fishing grounds but not where they fish today.

Several fishers said in interviews before and after the meeting that actually they also do not know where the fish are; otherwise, they would have fished them out, besides which the environment, including traditional fishing grounds, is changing, and fishing today requires a lot of experimenting because of the rising seafloor and fish behaving in unexpected ways. By the same token, marine biologists and fishery managers admitted later in the afternoon that they too have their doubts about their methods and knowledge. Especially in meetings with locals where fishers argue for their knowledge and perceptions of the sea, they feel unsure about their knowledge of marine environment. This is just one example of how, in the process of trying to understand and manage the seascape as a whole, perceptions of the sea, historical and social dimensions, and a changing political ecology – to which I turn below - meet with the unknown and ever-changing ecological and biophysical dimensions of sea. It is important to remember that this process is always ongoing, with knowledge constantly being transformed and refigured, and perceptions of the sea manifested in divergent ways. The seascape approach becomes useful for understanding these processes. It allows us to understand Kihnu cultural space as a relation of land and sea, humans and environment as an organic whole. It also makes room for analysing the different meanings of seascape that are created when people have differeing relationships with the sea.

## Historical and social dimensions and the changing political ecology of the Kihnu seascape

The Kihnu community has always been more connected to the sea than to the land. Throughout its 400 year-long history, the tiny community has been connected to the rest of the world by marine resources and knowledge about the sea. These have always played a major role in Kihnu's economy and its people's identity (Kalits 2006; Pajula 2009; Rüütel 2012), a story that I now sketch out very briefly.

At the start of the 20th century, Estonian territory, including Kihnu Island, is part of the Russian Empire. This is the heyday of these small island communities: compared to the peasants on the mainland, islanders enjoy political independence from feudal lords, allowing small-island communities to flourish economically and socially (Peil 1999). This was especially clear in Kihnu, where the Kihnu Manor, which had ruled on the island since the 17th century, was liquidated and the land was distributed among the islanders in 1887. The community felt self-reliant and independent (Peil 1999; Kalits 2006), a characteristic that still plays an important role in Kihnu identity. The distance of central power also shaped the relations Kihnu had with the seascape. It connected them more to the sea than to the land.

Marine resources and knowledge about the sea have always connected the community to the rest of the world, saved the islanders from repression, and played a major role in Kihnu's economy (Kalits 2006; Rüütel 2013). Most importantly, the sea connected Kihnu to its overseas neighbours. While the women stayed on the island and worked the land, the men were active seafarers (Rüütel 2013: 32). The resources of the sea were exported to regional centres, and on their return, the men brought back cultural influences. Kihnu seafarers used to be regular visitors as far as London, which had an impact for instance on famous Kihnu women's traditional clothing, which became colourful only once men started to bring dyed cloth from England in the late 19th century. From the mid-19th century until World War I, most of the men on the island were engaged in transporting stones from the coastal waters around Kihnu to nearby cities, or in building cargo ships. The stones were collected manually from coastal shallow waters and transported by sailboat to cities in Latvia, Sweden and Estonia. Most of them ended up reinforcing wharfs and other harbour structures. Since the late 19th century, men from Kihnu started to build their own ships for transporting stone, and by 1914 the Kihnu merchant fleet numbered 67 ships (Kihnu Mereselts 2013). Many Kihnu people like to joke even today that most of the streets of Riga's Old Town are laid with stones from the Kihnu Sea.

Traditionally, in late winters, when the sea was under ice, men hunted seals, mainly grey seals but also smaller ringed seals. For centuries, islanders paid their taxes to the lords of the Kihnu Manor in seal fat and furs. Later fur and fat were sold to Riga, while the meat was consumed as an everyday dish. Fat was, and still is, used to coat houses and boats, seal skins were used for clothes, and meat had, like it still has, an important place in the Kihnu kitchen (Kalits 2006: 81–111). Before the 19th century, the rifle was the main hunting weapon for seal, which limited seal hunting to those men who could afford to buy one. In the mid-19th century, the seal hook technique learned from seal hunters in Finland's Turku Archipelago spread in the region (Pajula 2009). With the new technique, there was no need to invest in rifles and soon all men in Kihnu were engaged in seal hunting in the late winter months. In the process, seal hunting became an even more important aspect of Kihnu socioeconomic life, engaging all men on the island in late winter, while for the young men, their first seal hunt was considered as a step into manhood (ibid.: 2009). The centuries-old practice, a source of food, economic good and social formation, made grey seal Kihnu's 'cultural keystone species' (Plaan 2012), which is to say, "culturally salient species that shape in a major way the cultural identity of a people. Their importance is reflected in the fundamental roles these species play in diet, materials, medicine, and/or spiritual practices" (Garibaldi and Turner 2004).

Overall, the first centuries in Kihnu history were marked with the connection to the sea. It not only connected but also kept islanders protected from oppressors, as sea resources provided economic independence and brought cultural influences from neighbouring trade partners.

As noted, World War I brought great changes to the local political economy. Most importantly the change to a capitalist economic system and privatisation created severe hardships in Kihnu. Between 1920–1921 a fishing licence system is implemented, taxes on fish hooks and sail canvas rise more than 2000% and taxes on fish nets rise 3000% (Kalits 1997: 24). In 1923 the first Fishery Law is created and the state starts to give out loans to buy fishing equipment. In the 1930s, the state imposes tax on seal skins. At the same time, new taxes and state regulations considering seafaring force all working men into fisheries. Women, on the other hand, must find jobs on the mainland to supplement household income in the new economic reality. Overcrowding and economic depression in Kihnu force people to find new places to live. In 1936, the Estonian State allocates land on the nearby uninhabited Manija Island. The same year 20 families (79 people) move to Manija (Leesment 1942). Slowly the state becomes more important in how Kihnu people interact with their seascape.

After the late 1940s, during the Soviet era, fishing becomes even more intense. The former debts of the fishers are forgiven and the entire fleet is motorised, new fishing techniques are introduced and the sale of fish is reorganised (Rüütel 2013: 32). The Russians bring weir nets called *kakuam* from Japan (Jõgisalu 2005: 152), which allows much larger quantities of Baltic herring to be caught. Starting in the 1960s, the local kolkhoz starts buying trawlers, allowing Kihnu fleet to fish the entire Baltic Sea and rendering fishing even more intensified (Kalits 2006: 73). Together the new motorised fleet, cheap fuel and extended state borders comes to support a socioeconomic system that relies on cheap marine resources. Fishing becomes the main activity in the island, and 90% of the income comes from fisheries (Kalits 2006: 78). Most women find jobs at the new fish plant, where they smoke and can herring that their menfolk bring in from the sea. Most importantly, fishing becomes a state-supported activity. Fisheries and fishing people are supported both economically and ideologically, and they are praised as the working class that feeds the nation (Jõgisalu 2006).

All the people in Kihnu were, in one way or the other, involved with fisheries, men with fishing and women in the newly constructed fish plant. Even today, older fishers recall how much better life was during the Soviet era: everybody had a job, fish was plentiful and the state supported the community.

Under the Soviet regime, life in Kihnu did improve gradually, and despite great socioeconomic and political changes in Estonia, the islanders managed to preserve their communal identity (Kalits 1997; Plaan 2012). As the land and the fleet were collectivised and the people were organised into kolkhozes, a systematic economy was introduced, and the men had to catch the amount of fish determined by the state. In many ways, however, the collective fishing and farming system introduced by the new regime was reminiscent of an old way of life, when most work was done communally (Kalits 1997: 26). Despite the collective economic system though, in 1973 the Kihnu kolkhoz was merged into a bigger kolkhoz on the mainland. After that, all decisions about local socioeconomic life were made in the regional capital Pärnu. Several Kihnu women believe that this was a start of a moral downfall of Kihnu men: they got used to not making their own decisions and were spoiled by state support. Nevertheless, both locals and mainlanders remember life in Kihnu as having been much better than elsewhere in Estonia during the Soviet era.

With the collapse of the Soviet Union, the island's economic system also collapsed, which had a devastating effect on social life. The locals had to start rebuilding their life in a new open and more connected capitalist world, which left many islanders unemployed, or forced people to move to the mainland (Kihnu Cultural Space Foundation 2001: 21). This happened throughout the former Soviet Union: the vessels from the Soviet times were too expensive to run, but nobody remembered how to hunt traditionally (Nuttall 2005: 84).

In 2004, Estonia acceded to the European Union, and in 2008, the Kihnu community was included on the UNESCO List of Masterpieces of Oral and Intangible Heritage of Humanity. The process involved making a list of cultural aspects worth protecting on the island, in addition to which the islanders received financial support to promote and protect their culture (Plaan 2012). The area under protection is now identified as the Kihnu Cultural Space:

> An insular place with distinct nature defined by the surrounding seascape, and the livelihood activities of the local community that in the course of history has imminently adjusted to and depended on the natural environment (Kihnu Cultural Space Foundation 2001: 9).

In this process, the Kihnu Cultural Space became a common term among locals. Kihnu cultural space (without capital letters) is used to refer to the area where they have traditionally practiced their livelihood, but more importantly, UNESCO's entitlement marks a point where the islanders' historical living relationship with the seascape became commodified. 'Kihnu culture', a term I would rather not use as an anthropologist, has become part of everyday language among many Kihnu people, as if it were something material, but also distinctive and easy to define. Kihnu weddings, for instance, have become 'staged' shows, where islanders are actually guided by folklorists and anthropologists, and local children perform traditional dances and songs for tourists, not for fun but to earn pocket money. In addition, seal hunting, a once distinctive aspect of traditional Kihnu livelihoods, has become a political tool: through the unique status of being listed in UNESCO's list of intangible culture, it can be used to gain state support, both financial and legal, and to argue against environmental regulations. Not all on Kihnu Island agree with how the UNESCO process is unfolding, but those in leading positions see it as inevitable.

I have tried to show in the above historical overview, how the Kihnu community has evolved through the centuries in constant interaction with the natural environment on the island and with its seascape. Furthermore, the islanders have lived in a certain isolation compared to the mainlanders. The power of the state has not always extended to the island and the Kihnu people were often privileged in that regard. At the same time, the sea that isolates the island has also connected the community to the rest of the world. In the next section I go on to argue that perceptions and uses of the sea and the nearby islets through history, comprise a space were the Kihnu people feel at home, a seascape.

## Interactions in the seascape and transforming the knowledge and perceptions

When I asked people to expand on 'Kihnu culture', one response that I kept hearing, in different forms, was that "we have always fished", and that "it is a cornerstone of our culture. Without fishing there would be no Kihnu culture" (Enn, fisherman 2013). Mare Mätas, a local cultural activist,[3] explained in an interview in 2012: "Fishing, together with seal hunting, are traditional practices. Without support from the state these practices and the knowledge that they carry will be lost." However, not everyone agrees: "I do not understand why they [the Kihnu community] claim that they cannot survive without fishing. If we look at history, traditionally they have transported stones" (Nele Saluver, Head of The Environmental Board, Pärnu Office, 2013).

The local history actually shows that fishing has played a varied role in the life of Kihnu people. Through time, practices have changed as they have adapted not only to environmental changes, but also to political changes and the different restrictions that came with them. In the Soviet era fishing, supported by the state, was indeed the main source of income for the islanders, but today it has lost its importance. The fish population in Baltic Sea keeps declining and the allotted quotas are small, hence, fishing has lost its economic importance. At the same time, the inshore fishery regulated by the European Union's Common Fisheries Policy (CFP), which covers the use and protection of fishery resources, the structure and market organisation policy, decreasing the role of Kihnu people and the control they have over fishing activities.

---

3    Cultural activist refers to person who tries to promote Kihnu and its *unique* culture. Usually they work in Kihnu municipality, museum or school, organise cultural events or write project grants for money to protect and preserve traditions.

After Estonia regained its independence in 1991, fishing regulations were modified and changed frequently as part of the state's programme of internationalisation. With the fish population declining, nets' mesh sizes kept getting bigger and the quotas smaller. Although all the regulations were made with the intent of protecting fish populations, the Environmental Inspectorate found it difficult to police the seas, which meant Kihnu men could conduct their practices in their own way. As Estonia joined the EU in 2004, more new regulations were implemented. In addition, the Inspectorate restructured its work to become more efficient, according to Dora Kukk, Head of the Environmental Inspectorate in Pärnu County, whom I interviewed in 2013. There were several reasons for that. With EU accession, the inspectorate received more funding and acquired new boats. Moreover, many tasks of the Inspectorate were delegated to the Border Guard Board and to the police, who were also patrolling the sea now. And so, even though regulatory efforts go back far into the Soviet era, it was only after 2004 that Kihnu men started to feel increasingly that their activities are being inspected and controlled. What was also happening was that a seascape was being negotiated and produced, as these different social agents and their perceptions, forms of knowledge and practices encounter each other on the sea. What a seascape is, then, is both a product of and producer of everyday practices on the sea, as the following ethnographic narrative will show.

One evening I went with a group of men to put out some nets. Initially it felt like business as usual, but in fact we headed straight for a restricted area under environmental protection. "Today we are going to rob the sea", one of my informants explained in an ironic tone. I had heard from other fishermen how they "rob the sea" as a protest against the regulations, but it surprised me a lot when we came upon three other boats *robbing the sea* in the same area. It was only when we got to the protected area that I understood what they meant by robbery. In earlier interviews I had often heard it expressed that by legally prohibiting traditional Kihnu practices in the name of environmental protection, environmentalists had taken away 'their land'. Kihnu people use often the expression 'their land' when they describe the area that is included in Kihnu cultural space, where they have historically been living or collecting natural resources. Today, simply collecting and catching resources from the area, to which the men felt they were historically entitled, had turned them into criminals. *Robbing the sea,* as many men explained, was a description of their socioeconomic situation.

On earlier trips to the sea, I had noticed the men becoming suspicious on seeing other boats approaching, since you could never know if it might be the inspector's boat. That day the men were as calm as the sea on a quiet day. When I showed my surprise at this behaviour, the men laughed and explained that the inspectors were doing a raid today, but on the other side of the Bay of Riga. One fisherman on the island is related to the head of the Environmental Inspectorate; he had received warning from him earlier. Enn Keeman, who was the head of the inspectorate at that time admitted in a later interview that he is well aware of such illegal activities: "The biggest percentage of violations in my region comes around Kihnu Island [...] I cannot just go and fine all Kihnu people," was how he summed up one story, which involved two Kihnu women in their 80s who were caught illegally ice fishing. In such cases the inspectors usually close their eyes and let Kihnu people *rob the sea.*

Thus as they have shaped practices on the sea, fishing regulations, largely coming outside from Estonia today, have also transformed Kihnu understandings of marine resources. These understandings should not be taken as a product of a dominant ideology, but as a product of less institutionalised, more general forms of power (Foucault 1978) and less organised, more everyday forms of power (Scott 1985). As the ethnographic example above showed, both the fishers and the officials ignore the regulations as long as the audience (made up of higher officials, other fishers, etc.) believes they are fulfilled. This makes local knowledge a fragile product of negotiations between the state officials, scientists and local inhabitants (Mathews 2011: 15) over the seascape. Meanwhile the scientists ignore the local knowledge; the fishers ignore the regulations and go out to *rob the sea*; and the officials ignore what the fishers are doing. The actors and their knowledge about the sea all evolve through these practices, and in the process the meanings of their actions also change (Ortner 1995: 175).

This means that biophysical and social processes produce material transformations in the physical surroundings, which in turn feed back onto transformations in social processes. Even if we were able to draw borders around a distinct seascape, such as the Kihnu cultural space or a marine protected area, both the natural and social processes that produce it, go beyond local; they are intrinsically part of regional and global movements that go back into history. And so, in order to understand the changes in the perceptions of seascape, we must move beyond localised, everyday practice and ask what are the aims and desires of the different actors who encounter each other in these 'relational spaces.' While I both environmentalists and fishermen desire to have more productive marine ecosystem, their aims and practices differ considerably, which also creates a space for the transformation of knowledge and perceptions.

Importantly, today fisheries management observes international regulations that originate outside Estonia. The administration of the fisheries is regulated by the Common Fisheries Policy that applies to all European Union Member States, while its contents are developed based on scientific work. As part of this, every day the fishers have to fill out a fishing diary, which is later presented to officials, and annually fishers have to complete a survey, which should describe their situation, and lastly, ichthyologists make an annual survey of the catch. These three methods combined are the basis of the scientific knowledge about fishing in the Kihnu area. However, as my ethnographic vignette showed, this is problematic. Although it is through scientific practices that scientists become "familiar with things, people and events, which are distant" (Latour 1987: 220), and the fishing diary, the questionnaire and the survey produce data that is deemed scientifically correct, from the fishers' point of view, the resulting knowledge is not always true. While the aim of science is to be familiar with things, which are distant this is not the case for fishing. For fishers, what is important to know about, is the here and now.

In a situation where all conservation officials are trained in the natural sciences, it is not surprising that they admit in personal conversations that they do not know how to assess the impacts of their work on the local communities, or how to incorporate local knowledge into conservation policies. This suggests that conservation officials may speak authoritatively, but they are constantly worried that they lack local knowledge and, conversely, that they do not know how to translate their science-backed knowledge to the locals. This makes official and scientific knowledge vulnerable but not insignificant. As the environmental practices of officials come into contact and conflict with the environmental knowledge of local fishers, this nevertheless transforms local practices, the usage of natural resources and eventually perceptions of the seascape.

## *Material seascape*

I turn now to the meanings that different social groups pour into the seascape, guiding their decisions about how to act there. Various meanings form a deep rationale for using the marine resources. In other words, the scale of resource extraction and the ways seascape is used, are guided by the meanings different social actors have for seascape. Consequently, the seascape becomes a space of struggle over material meanings: an ever-changing historical and cultural realm comes into conflict with ideas of the sea as enclosed and controlled, measurable and marketable. Despite its ever-changing fluidity, it is important not to ignore how certain meanings make the material seascape.

Under the so-called 'derby-style' fishing system (*Olümpiapüük* in Estonian), large number of crews compete with each other to catch their quota in a particular fishing area during a restrictive time window. The quota, the area and the time window are set by the Ministry of Agriculture based on the scientifically produced knowledge that largely ignores fishermen's insights. Instead of the here and now of local knowledge, state power, authorised through scientific knowledge, produces separation and alienation from the nature – symbolically and materially (Moore 2016: 86–87). I will show how the regulations and politics separate 'sea' from 'seascape', since the regulations identify only certain aspects of the situation, specify only particular times and spaces, and select only some people and uses as meaningful or relevant.

In this process, fish become nothing more than a material object, symbolically alienated from social and cultural relations: "Look how we have to work like robots" says Enn, the skipper, "there is no difference between day and night anymore." It was our sixth day catching Baltic herring and there had been barely any time to sleep. The quotas could be reached at any moment. We were out at sea, going to collect weir nets for Baltic herring called *kakuam*. We passed some shoals near an islet marked with a juniper sticking out of the sea, and then arrived at our destination south of Kihnu Island where the men had set their *kakuam* nets. "We have always had our weir nets here", Enn explained when I asked about the location of the nets.

"My father fished here and that's the way it has been throughout history," he said. "The fishing grounds are traditionally divided," ads Kaido, "we set two weir nets, but some crews have as many as four." On the map, they point out and name all the Baltic herring fishing spots in the Kihnu cultural space. I notice that many are not used anymore. These are the historic spots that are 'too far' from the harbour, the men explain, since by going to the more distant spots, fishers risk the quotas getting filled in the meantime by others. The previous year Enn had been out to collecting *kakuam* nets, when he received a phone call saying that the quotas were full. So was the net, but he had to let loose about 2 tons of Baltic herring, most already dead. He decided not to fish at that spot anymore—it was simply too far—much safer repeatedly to visit spots closer to harbour.

These fishing practices reveal two features about changing knowledge and perceptions of the seascape. Firstly, the familiar seascape appears to be shrinking: old fishing grounds become simply dots on the map, separated from Kihnu cultural space, both symbolically and materially. Secondly, by limiting the time and space of fishing activities, the regulations also treat fish simply as material objects that are separate from local sociocultural life. The fisheries management rewards those who tirelessly exploit the same grounds over and over, while dismissing traditional practices that allowed *kakuam* nets to be spread throughout the seascape. Consequently, the fishing grounds near the harbour are under much greater pressure – even overexploited – a point on which both fishermen and fisheries scientists agree, even if fisheries scientists claim that the fish population is declining, whereas fishermen 'know' that there are plenty of fish, just that they are elsewhere.

Drawing from the analytical uses of the landscape concept, we can claim that such interactions take place within a seascape that is similarly the product of specific socioeconomic, spatial and political arrangements, beliefs, knowledge and material culture, as well as ecological constraints and opportunities, that are in continuous change through time (see Hirch and O'Hanlon 1995; Strang 1997; Tilley 2006). Materially and symbolically, the relation of material sea, social action and cultural meanings is tied to the production of place. Yet, from the perspective of the state, the sea is mainly material, as for example, the quantifiable herring, tied to a certain space and time. Excluding the cultural and social meanings, the seascape becomes simply a sea full of marine resources to extract, species to protect and areas to enclose or promote.

At the same time, almost imperceptibly, the seascape itself has become an object to sell. Caught up in a process of objectification but also on a new dependency on nature-based commerce, the Kihnu area is also witnessing a commodification of nature (Castree 2010: 1743–1744). Culture has also been objectified, for instance since the 1990s economic decline, some Kihnu women saw that local, unique, culture was something that would hold the community together. UNESCO was used to get international and national recognition and support for their way of life, while Kihnu cultural activists, specialists of Kihnu traditions and history, anthropologists and folklorists, created a list of what is unique in Kihnu culture and needed protection. This list was made to fit with UNESCO's definition of intangible and oral heritage, and in the process UNESCO's title was used as tool to invoke cultural identity but also to promote the Kihnu seascape to tourists. In this process, the ever-changing Kihnu cultural space is being transformed also into a static Kihnu Cultural Space, a material space to sell and promote.

All this makes perceptions and knowledge about seascapes historically bounded, evolving and changing, uncertain and contested but importantly, these processes are also material. Through interactions with various social actors – marine biologists measuring the state of marine ecosystem, state officials following international fisheries regulations, fisheries inspectors policing the sea, and even an anthropologist, trying to define what is Kihnu culture – Kihnu people find themselves both producers and products of both the material and symbolic seascape. For Kihnu people the seascape has always been a source of income on the one hand, but also a source of social formation and inspiration for cultural life, on the other.

## Conclusion

What I have called the seascape is a place where people's identity and perceptions of the sea are shaped by the interactions of humans and non-humans, the land and the sea. By focusing on Kihnu cultural space I showed how seascape is intertwined with topographies and geologies, plants and animals, persons and their biographies, social and political relationships. Seascape is a source of social formation and inspiration for cultural life, but as I have shown, it is also a place where new material meanings are created and marine ecosystems transformed. In other words, it is a space where material things come together with expectations, discourses and representations.

I have argued that seascape carries two important characteristics. Firstly, perceptions of the seascape emerge as relations of different knowledge systems, that is, conflicting understandings about the seascape as a whole. In their attempts to control and constrain parts of the seascape, for example particular species or specific environmental conditions, different social actors with different types of knowledge become both producers and products of the seascape. Secondly, embedded into social relations and economic networks, the perceptions of the seascape are shaped by the practices of politics and regulations. I have shown how, as the regulations used to control and manage the sea have become formal and bureaucratic, so has local knowledge about the seascape. Overall, seascape is a space where local inhabitant's views of nature, their identity and their livelihood practices interact with distant conservation regulations and state power, making the perceptions and knowledge of seascape dynamic and ever-changing.

The focus on different ways of understanding the Kihnu seascape reveals land and seascapes as contested natures, as struggles over meaning, and simultaneously as struggles over social identity, belonging and exclusion, and marine resource rights and use. The Kihnu seascape is influenced by the Soviet past, by shifting scientific paradigms and practices, by the dynamics of local-global articulations, and unforeseen transformations in the marine environment. It can be known and perceived as series of interactions and encounters of different actors through time and space. This includes humans, such as Kihnu fishers, marine scientists, conservationists, non-humans, such as marine animals and the sea itself, but also intangible ideas, such as 'traditional culture' and state ideology. Based on the empirical case presented above, I suggest that seascape can be usefully thought of as a relational space that draws various perceptions and knowledges together in unstable and ever-changing ways. Different views of the seascape have led to material struggles over meanings of seascape, where commodified nature and uncertain state power meet. Because of all this, Kihnu seascape is not fixed, but in a relational, multiple, fluid, and sometimes conflicted relationships with social actors who know and perceive the seascape differently.

# References

Batterbury, Simon P. J. 2001. Landscapes of Diversity: A local political ecology of livelihood Diversification in South-western Niger. *Cultural Geographies* 8 (4): 437–464.

Blaikie, Piers 1999. A Review of Political Ecology. *Zeitschrift Für Wirtschaftsgeographie* 43 (1): 131–147.

Brown, Mike 2015. Seascapes. In Mike Brown and Barbara Humberstone (eds), *Seascapes Shaped by the Sea*. Farnham: Ashgate Publishing.

Burke, Brian. J. and Nik Heynen 2014. Transforming Participatory Science into Socioecological Praxis: Valuing marginalized environmental knowledge in the face of the neoliberalization of nature and science. *Environment and Society: Advances in Research* 5 (1):7–27.

Castree, Noel 2010. Neoliberalism and the Biophysical Environment 2: Theorising the neoliberalisation of nature. *Geography Compass* 4 (12): 1734–1746.

Connery, Chris 1996. Oceanic Feeling and Regional Imaginary. In Rob Wilson and Wimal Dissanayake (eds), *Global/Local: Cultural Production and the Transnational Imaginary*. London: Duke University Press.

Cooney, Gabriel 2003. Introduction: Seeing land from the sea. *World Archaeology* 35 (3): 323–328.

Foucault, Michel 1978. *The History of Sexuality*. New York: Pantheon.

Gagné, Karine and Mattias Borg Rasmussen 2016. Introduction – An Amphibious Anthropology: The production of place at the confluence of land and water. *Anthropologica* 58: 135–149.

Garibaldi, Ann and Nancy Turner 2004. Cultural keystone species: Implications for ecological conservation and restoration. *Ecology and Society* 9 (3): 1.

Huff, Amber R. 2014. Weathering The 'Long Wounded Year': Livelihoods, nutrition and changing political ecologies in the Mikea forest region, Madagascar. *Journal of Political Ecology* 21: 83–107.

Jõgisalu, Harri 2006. *Meri põlõm'te paljas vesi: Kihnu arhipelaag.* [Sea is not simply water: Kihnu archipelago.] Tallinn: Ilo.

Kalits, Vilve 2006. *Kihnlaste elatusalad: XIX sajandi keskpaigast XX sajandi keskpaigani.* [Subsistence of Kihnu People: From XIX Century till Mid XX Century.] Lina küla: Kihnu Kultuuriruum.

Kihnu Cultural Space Foundation (KCSF). 2001. National Candidature File of Estonia. Kihnu: Kihnu Cultural Space Foundation.

Kihnu Mereselts. 2013. Lühiülevaade Kihnu laevandusajaloost. [Short overview of the history of boat building in Kihnu]. http://www.kihnumereselts.ee/ajalugu/

Kraufelin, Patrik, Zeynep. Pekcnep-Hekim, Ulf Bergström, Ann-Brit Florin, Annuka Lehikoinen, Johanna Mattila and Jens Olsson 2016 Essential Fish Habitats (EFH).

Conclusions from a Workshop on the Importance, Mapping, Monitoring, Threats and Conservation of Coastal EFH in the Baltic Sea. Copenhagen: TemaNord.

Lambert, David, Luciana Martins and Miles Ogborn 2006. Currents, Visions and Voyages: Historical geographies of the sea. *Journal of Historical Geography* 32: 479–493.

Latour, Bruno 1987. *Science in Action*. Cambridge: Harvard University Press.

Leesment, Leo 1942. Kihnu ajalugu: Geschichte der Insel Kühno (Kihnu). [Kihnu history]. Tartu: Tartu University Press.

Mathews, Andrew. S. 2011. *Instituting Nature: Authority, expertise, and power in Mexican forests*. London: The MIT Press.

McNiven, Ian J. 2008. Sentient Sea: Seascapes as spiritscapes. In Bruno David and Julian Thomas (eds), *Handbook of Landscape Archeology*. Walnut, CA: Left Coast Press.

Moore, Jason W. 2016. *Anthropocene or Capitalocene? Nature, History, and the Crisis of Capitalism*. Oakland, CA: PM Press.

Neumann, Roderick. P. 2011. Political Ecology III: Theorizing Landscape. *Progress in Human Geography* 35 (6): 843–850.

Nuttall, Mark 2005. *Protecting the Arctic. Indigenous Peoples and Cultural Survival*. Oxon: Routledge.

Orlove, Ben 2016. Two Days in the Life of a River: Glacier floods in Bhutan. *Anthropologica* 58: 227–242.

Ortner, Sherry. B. 1995. Resistance and the Problem of Ethnographic Refusal. *Comparative Studies in Society and History*. 37 (1): 173–193.

Pajula, Toomas 2009. *Hülgepüük kui kihnlaste traditsiooniline elatusala*. [Seal Hunt – a Traditional Kihnu Subsistence.] Linaküla: Kihnu Cultural Space Foundation.

Peil, Tiina 1999. *Islescapes. Estonian Small Islands and Islanders Through Three Centuries*. Stockholm: Almqvist & Wiksell International.

Plaan, Joonas 2012. *Culture in Nature: Traditional ecological knowledge and environmentalism in Kihnu*. Unpublished Bachelor's Thesis. Tallinn University. Estonian Institute of Humanities.

Rasmussen, Mattias. B. 2016. Water Futures: Contention in the construction of productive infrastructure in the Peruvian highlands. *Anthropologica* 58: 211–226.

Rüütel, Ingrid 2013. *Naised Kihnu kultuuris*. [Women in the Culture of Kihnu] Tartu: EKM Teaduskirjandus.

Scott, James 1985. *Weapons of the Weak: Everyday forms of peasant resistance*. New Haven: Yale University Press.

Steinberg, Philip 1999. Navigating to Multiple Horizons: Toward a geography of ocean-space. *Professional Geographer* 51 (3): 366–375.

Stensrud, Astrid B. 2014. Climate change, water practices and relational worlds in the Andes. *Ethnos* 81 (1): 75–98.

Strang, Veronica 2004. *The Meaning of Water*. Oxford: Berg.

Strang, Veronica 2006. Fluidscapes: Water, identity and the senses. *Worldviews* 10 (2):147–154.

Strang, Veronica 2009. *Gardening the World: Agency, Identity, and the Ownership of Water*. New York: Berghahn.

Tilley, Christopher and Kate Cameron-Daum 2017. *An Anthropology of Landscape. An extraordinary in the ordinary*. London: UCL Press.

Tilley, Christopher 2006. Introduction: Identity, place, landscape and heritage. *Journal of Material Culture*11(1–2): 7–32.

Torrence, Robin 2002. Cultural Landscape on Garua Island, Papua New Guinea. *Antiquity* 76: 766–76.

Willow, Anna J. 2016. Troubling water: Shale energy and waterscape transformation in a North American extraction zone. *Anthropologica* 58:166–178.

Zimmerer, Karl S. 1999. Overlapping Patchworks of Mountain Agriculture in Peru and Bolivia: Toward a regional-global landscape model. *Human Ecology* 27 (1): 135–165.

Jenni Mölkänen

# Making sense of conserved landscapes: From intimate landscapes to new potentialities and differences

The Tsimihety are rice and vanilla cultivators who also hunt, fish and gather forest products, living in the villages of the valleys of the River Lokoho in northeastern Madagascar. In 1998, when the 55 500 hectare Marojejy National Park was set up on the initiative of the World Wildlife Fund (WWF), the establishment of the park was part of the Malagasy state's environmental policies, supported by millions of dollars and euros from development and conservation agencies. The project was based on a scientific inventory conducted by 25 WWF experts from Andapa and Antananarivo, supported by local people working as assistants and porters. The scientific inventory was funded by the Kreditanstalt für Wiederaufbau (KfW), a German investment bank, and the Center for Biodiversity and Conservation of American Museum of Natural History in the Marojejy and the Anjanaharibe-Sud reserve (Goodman 2000: viii–1). It involved large areas of land being demarcated for environmental conservation efforts, with the people living in the vicinity of the park being barred from access to these. Apparently, this was a clear case of pure and pristine nature being harnessed for economic growth promoting development (see KWF 2011; also Walsh 2005; Duffy 2008). Tourists, mainly from Germany, France and the UK were welcomed in the park while some local people were recruited for ecotourism activities as guides, cooks, porters and park rangers. The Tsimihety were puzzled about what all the foreign (*vazaha*) people were doing in the park and what they were looking for there.

In this article, I show that ecotourism has led the Tsimihety to become aware of something new: it turned out that they did not know their landscapes as intimately as they thought they did. Observing tourists and researchers interacting with lemurs, locals could not understand quite what the tourists were looking for in the landscapes they themselves had known over generations. The Tsimihetys' speculations about tourists were based on careful observations as well as cultural understandings and historical experiences. Analytically, the concept of landscape is useful here. It highlights its significance as something that people can walk through, and something that is marked by people's everyday life events, such as marriages and funerals and inherited knowledge.

## Human-made landscapes

The concept of landscape has been used in many ways in scholarship, from highlighting processes of human labour on the environment to focusing on how painters in 16th and 17th century Europe, and later romantic poets and conservation movements, helped generate particular subject-object positions. Overwhelmingly, Euro-American understandings have also imposed a dualist conception of the environment as a physical substratum socialised by human actions (e.g. Sauer 1925; Cosgrove and Jackson 1987). Looking at it anthropologically, this hardly corresponds to the manner in which most people conceptualise the places where they dwell (Descola 2016: 5).

However, landscapes are still imagined in ways that are influenced by Euro-American history. A paradigm case has been the establishment of national parks and other conservation areas in the USA, for example Yosemite National Park, which had its origins in ideas of pristine wilderness promoted by the Sierra Club in 1892 (McCormick 1989: 12–13). One problematic aspect of the wilderness image is to satisfy utopian dreams of Euro-American tourists' visions of primitive people, "ones who somehow belong to wild places such as the wilderness" (Stasch 2014: 203). Nature conservation parks are indeed based on Euro-American understandings of contrasts between wild and domesticated (Tsing 2005: 195). In frontier contexts, tamed and wild came together in creating North American understandings of a new type of citizen, one with the power to tame the wild and one upon whom the wild had conferred strength and individuality (Turner 1894). This also gave rise to ideas of landscapes without people where the nature-human dualism is accentuated (West and Carrier 2009: 3). These understandings of the wild and the tamed, of pristine and managed nature, are still relevant when environmental conservation practices create new types of spaces, ones that are equally constructed, such as those discussed below.

In studies of the Euro-American notion of landscape, vision, sight and looking from a certain perspective, have been major themes (Urry 1992: 3). While scholars have shown that people's sense of place, as well as of nature, can vary hugely and have nothing to do with Euro-American landscape conventions (Feld and Basso 1996), tourist experiences today remain fundamentally visual (Cosgrove 1984: 9; Urry 1992: 172; Feld 1996: 94). Many have argued that nature as visual spectacle is not merely an assemblage of images, but the mediation of relationships between people by images (Debord 1994; Igoe 2010: 376). Following anthropological critiques, this chapter looks at how, in capitalism, images of nature operate to turn environments into commodities eclipsing actual relations between people and environments (Igoe 2010: 275). However, anthropology can also recover ways in which such relationships are being recreated even as commodified nature interferes in the process.

The natural landscapes of the global tourist imagination have to be understood as a historically specific Euro-American social and cultural construction that is essential to the leisure and pleasure –tourism and spectacular entertainment (Green 1990: 6). A crucial notion about space in the Euro-American view, which became globally dominant through modernity, has been that it is empty of contents: space is neutral until it is modified and filled, for instance, with technologies of governance and economising (Li 2007; Mitchell 2011). However, such managerial schemes do not pay enough attention to the dynamism of environments (Pressey et al. 2007) not to mention dynamics of people and nature and historical processes of the landscape formation (Fairhead and Leach 1995; Scott 1998; Tsing 2003: 24; 2015).

Living in villages near rivers running west to east, and cultivating irrigated rice on hillsides and in valleys, the Tsimihety have not conventionally used a concept of landscape. They have referred to the villages, rivers, hills and valleys where they live by their place names, or as a larger continual ancestral territory *tanindrazana*, which gathers all those who have been and will be buried in the same ancestral tomb (Keller 2008). What has most shaped the sense of place is movement between places along paths and transferring bones into the paternal ancestral tomb after secondary burial[1]. In these processes, land, space, movement and different practices have come together to form what, from an anthropological point of view, can usefully be called landscape. To know landscapes by living in them, as Tsimihety do, is very different from how environmental conservationists know them, based on cadastral maps, scientific inventories and GPS information.

This chapter draws attention to the marked but perhaps not obvious differences between the ways that Tsimihety and visitors experience the new park. Foremost, rather than appreciating pristine forests and enjoying nature as tourists do, the Malagasy tend to look admiringly at places they have built or transformed, for example houses and fields (Bloch 1995). I shall further argue that the way of relating to one's surroundings also has a profound effect on efforts to make sense of the processes of environmental conservation and ecotourism. As I discovered during fieldwork in 2012–2013, the Tsimihety have been puzzled by the rise in tourism (see also Walsh 2010). Further, I noted how the resulting rapid rearrangements of space are disruptive, even chaotic, as the emerging literature indicates it is for many people living in environments of interest to tourism (Lowe 2006). In fact, comparative ethnographic cases show how imaginations and material realities based on different political and historical experiences are not merely bringing people together around new shared projects, as in the case of the Masoala National Park, it is actually the case that joint conservation efforts can emphasise differences (Keller 2015).

## Historical landscapes in the Lokoho valleys

The landscape histories of the Lokoho valleys near the present day Marojejy National Park are connected with colonial and state natural resource use,

---

1   *Famadihana* is a secondary burial ritual that is performed five to seven years after the first burial. The bones of the deceased one are dug out from the ground, rewrapped in new clothes, placed in a coffin and reburied in a family tomb.

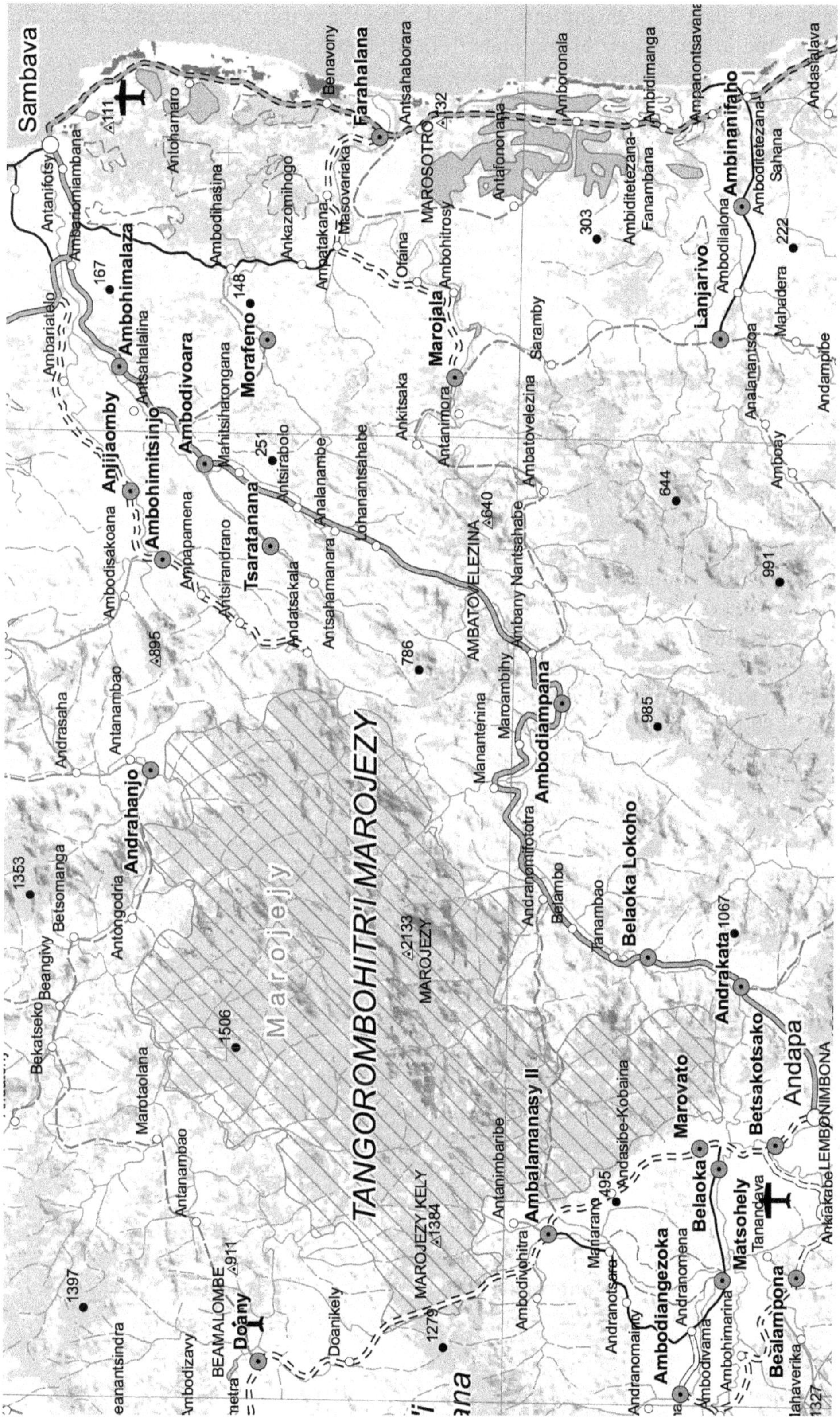

*Figure 1. A map of the Sambava-Andapa and Lokoho valleys' landscapes (Moat and Smith 2007).*

but also with Tsimihety migrations. The Lokoho valleys were intensively settled in the 1920s, mostly by migrants from Madagascar's north-eastern coast who, as it was said, were mainly 'looking for money' (*mitady vola*). The practice of 'looking for money' basically meant young males and, in some cases, whole households, moving to new regions. They either went to work on plantations on the humid eastern coast established by Reunionnaise or, among the Creole population, set up as entrepreneurs encouraged by the Merina and French states, to work the land, either for some relative or for themselves (Cole 2001: 43–45; Brown 2004; Keller 2008). In less than 20 years, the area was transformed into an important corner of the so-called vanilla triangle (Laney 1999: 1) along with Antalaha and Sambava, and it soon provided most of the world's vanilla (Althabe 1968) as smallholders had adopted vanilla into their cultivation systems (Molet 1959).

For European colonialists, the lands and forests of Madagascar were clearly a resource for the development of the imperial economy. The French colonial government (1896–1960) encouraged the creation of plantations of export crops such as vanilla, sisal and coffee (Olson 1984: 180), as well as eucalyptus and ebony (Jarosz 1996). The colonial government gave concessions to European and Creole settlers on the east coast on supposedly empty forest land (Cole 2001: 43–45). The plantations required a work force, and these sometimes became members of the land owner's family (Brown 2004: 626). However, although they also worked for wages, most Tsimihety continued cultivating their own hill-rice fields. New varietals and techniques introduced in the plantations were adopted creating mixed farming systems (Laney 1999: 18; Brown 2004: 626–627).

Implementation of state-led projects has been uneven across Madagascar, but throughout its environmental history, land has always been managed in the interests of the state and foreign people. For instance, the colonial government encouraged the formation of irrigated rice-fields more intensively from 1950s onwards. Government representatives built small irrigation dams and canals and instructed farmers on different techniques for soil conservation and intensive cultivation (Kull 2004: 230). On the other hand, on the north-western hills of the Marojejy mountains, most irrigated fields had already been built by the 1950s before pressure on land had worsened, and they had been contributing a large proportion of villages' subsistence (Laney 2002: 703; see also Jarosz 1993: 370–372).

At the same time, this politically and economically motivated natural resource use was entwined with environmental conservation efforts. One illustration is *tavy* (the Malagasy word for swidden agriculture), which has conventionally been blamed for most of the historical destruction of the eastern rainforest of Madagascar (Jarosz 1993; Kull 2004). Cutting firewood was banned by one of the first rulers of the pre-colonial Merina state, who also encouraged planting trees on the hillsides of the capital, while prohibitions on burning the forest were confirmed shortly before the French occupation by the 1881.[2] In 1909 Governor General Gallieni prohibited the practice

---

2   Code of 305 Articles (Scales 2014, 134).

of shifting cultivation with the aim of protecting Madagascar's forest from further deforestation, and he imposed a system of so-called rational forest management. Gallieni expected that the ban would also force the formerly mobile Malagasy to remain in one place, making it easier for the government to locate and tax them. As the people reacted to the ban by burning the forest, the practice of *tavy* in fact became a symbol of independence and resistance (Jarosz 1993: 374; Kull 2004: 206–207).

Another link between conservation and imperial legacies was made by environmental scientists, biologists and botanists concerned about vanishing biodiversity. The first nature reserves were established at the initiative of the French scientists and naturalists, such as Henri Jean Humbert, who accused French and Creole concession owners as well as swidden cultivators of destroying fragile forests and disrupting biological equilibrium (Humbert 1927: 9; Sodikoff, 2004: 393 fn. 2). The first conservations areas to be established were wholly exclusionary with no local economic benefits. Unsurprisingly, the local populations surrounding these protected areas viewed them as foreign, as additional facets of colonial oppression. Different groups of swidden cultivators have accessed protected areas and resources whenever possible (Kull and Marcus 1999: 1; Kull 2004: 208).

On the other hand, many permanent and enduring markings in the landscape, such as houses, fields and tombs, which have close connections to Tsimihety cosmology and politics, are admired and valued. As elsewhere in Madagascar, establishing tombs on ancestral land, *tanindrazana*, is a way of anchoring kinship and establishing status (Bloch 1971; see also Graeber 2007: 203). Similarly building houses, clearing forests for fields and establishing new tombs, e.g. among the Betsimisaraka of the eastern coast, allows people to become rooted in a place (Keller 2008). Establishing relationships with land is important, and those who have lost their connections with their land are considered slaves, not proper persons. Working in forest areas has enabled people without land to re-establish ancestral land (Brown 2004: 619, 627). In short, the way landscapes are valued for having been modified by people, is in drastic contrast from the way environmental conservation areas have been thought about and planned.

## Abstract knowledge in the making conserved landscapes

The establishment of the Marojejy National Park was part of the Malagasy state's environmental policies upheld by millions of dollars and euros from bi- and multilateral development and environmental conservation agencies (Kull 2013: 146). At the 2003 IUCN[3] World Bank Congress in Durban, Ravalomanana, the president at that time, announced the Durban Vision, an initiative to more than triple the area under protection.[4] In 2013, following

---

3   International Union for Conservation of Nature.
4   From 3% to 10% of Madagascar's area, approximately 17,000 km² to over 60,000 km². The Durban Vision was later entitled the '*Système d'Aires Protégées de Madagascar*' (SAPM) (System of Protected Areas in Madagascar) (Corson 2011).

the guidelines of the United Nations and the IUCN as stated in the 2010 Convention on Biological Diversity, Madagascar met the 10 % requirement of areas under protection (Corson 2014: 193.) In 1998 the WWF, together with Madagascar's Water and Forest Department, authorised a special state agency called The National Association for the Management of Protected Areas in Madagascar (ANGAP)[5], renamed Madagascar National Parks (MNP) in 2007, to manage national parks. Taking over management from the state forest services, ANGAP was supposed to build up local capacity to take over.

In the process of expanding Madagascar's protected areas, non-state actors (e.g. NGOs, INGOs)[6] have used the three key components of what Vandergeest and Peluso (1995) call territorialisation: mapping boundaries, establishing and enforcing new rights and determining acceptable resource uses (Corson 2011: 705). In these processes, certain people are included and others are left out, and usually local people are banned from the park area. This follows the model of the Yellowstone, the world's oldest national park, which was instigated by American elites and designed to remain free of hostile indigenes, if needed, through the use of US Army personnel (Rydell and Culpin 2006), thus setting a precedent "of native dispossession all over the world" (West et al. 2006, 258.)

In Marojejy, intensive conservation efforts were begun in the 1990s. At the time, the WWF negotiated with the villagers (Garreau and Manantsara 2003, 1453–1454). Importantly for the argument in this chapter, top-down processes of imposing a new territorial order require abstract knowledge. In Marojejy, the territory of the park was based on the multidisciplinary research group organised in the 1990s by WWF Madagascar, mentioned above. The group carried out large-scale biological and elevational inventories and used geographical positioning systems, discussions with locals and various mapping techniques at different sites of investigation (Goodman 2000).

As in so many other places, knowledge produced by biologists, animal behaviourists, geographers and other scientists trained in the dominant though contested Euro-American idiom of science, has been crucial in establishing Madagascar as an environmental hot spot. According to biologists and environmental conservationists, to qualify as a hotspot an area must contain at least 0.5% or 1,500 of the world's 300,000 plant species as endemics. In fact, 15 of the 25 hotspots contain at least 2,500 endemic plant species, and 10 of them at least 5,000, where the classification is based on the two criteria: species endemism and degree (Myers et al. 2000). For modern scientists, Madagascar is important because of a proliferation of species that are not found anywhere else in the world. Clearly, to select certain species to represent conservation is simplification. It reduces forests of multiple species to forests of utilitarian rationality. Knowledge of this kind is withdrawn from previous relational contexts, and so translates certain elements into abstract standards (see e.g. Strathern 1992; Scott 1998: 11–12; Tsing 2015),

5    Association Nationale de Gestion des Aires Protégées in French.
6    Conservation International, World Wildlife Fund, and The Nature Conservancy.

and has allowed European science to displace other epistemologies in favor of universal standardisation systems.

Indeed, Marojejy's biodiversity has been recognised globally. Already in the 1950s, Humbert (1954: 45) described Marojejy as a marvel of nature because of its exceptional biological diversity as compared to other protected areas of Madagascar. In 2007, the park was granted UNESCO's world heritage status as a specific ecological region with multiple elevational zones. These zones maintain the ecological processes necessary for the survival of Madagascar's exceptional biodiversity, with high level of endemism (UNESCO 2007). Effectively, designating this as a site of world or global heritage recreates and maintains production of one single global view, while the heritage status is believed to add to the attractiveness and fame of the park, and to support conservation. The global view is not, however, oblivious to local peoples' contribution and management of the environment. These have been explicitly recognised as one reason for UNESCO's nomination of the park as a heritage site (MNP 2007: 8). Since there is a well-known discourse of problems in park creation in Madagascar (Keller 2015) and elsewhere (West et al. 2006), this could be interpreted as an effort to take people living near the national park into consideration. Whatever the answer, the people living near the Marojejy park relate to what westerners call nature in culturally specific ways.

## Intimate and habitual landscapes

When a passer-by asked him, "where are you going?"[7] Willy[8], a local cultivator, park guide and a research assistant for my project in his thirties, answered in the Tsimihety dialect "I am going into the forest".[9] This is a typical greeting between people in the village and on the roads. I followed Willy to his irrigated rice-fields, situated less than half an hour's walk from the village, behind some hills. We climbed a steep, soft, muddy slope, the soil bursting between our toes, and continued on a path between some vanilla fields and vegetables gardens. The pathway led out of the secondary forest (*savoka*) to a cleared hilltop, from where we were able to see rice fields in the valleys, hill-rice, cassava and vanilla fields on the slopes. We could also shout out greetings to the people working on their fields. To reach Willy's fields, we deviated from the main path and followed the side of a hill-rice field full of loose dried soil, an effect of there being little vegetation on the hillside. Thus, the phrase "to go into the forest" could mean ending up working fields, visiting friends or checking gardens or chickens, gathering fruits or firewood, or going hunting. These forests were not empty but full of pathways, houses, fields, channels, people, water, soils and rocks, everything crisscrossing. Nor

---

7   *Mandeha hoeza?*
8   All personal names of the villagers are pseudonyms.
9   *Mandeha any atiala*, a Malagasy expression meaning 'to go into the forest'.

were forests and fields clearly separated[10] into industrialised agriculture and forest land (see also e.g. Scott 1998; Tsing 2005: 165; Descola 2016: 5).

In contrast to conservation landscapes, the Tsimihety landscapes are for dwelling, for people to learn by living, following and observing (Ingold 2000; Bloch 1991). "Whose field is that" I asked Willy, trying to figure out land ownership patterns. "It is Mama ny Karen's field," he answered. "How do you know?" I asked. As was typical, his answer was: "I just know." Since people usually inherit land from their parents, there is no question of seeking new knowledge about it, rather, relations between people and land is how things are, how life is (compare Riles 1998: 419).

In addition, the Tsimihety have intimate knowledge about the places that are suited for vanilla production. Papa ny Georges, one of the biggest producers in the village, explained:

> The land in Antafiro[11] is very smooth. Vanilla produces long fruits that sprout well and weight a lot. Grains are not that good. Weight diminishes after collecting and there are very few grains inside the fruit. Antsahabehasina[12] is cooler than Antafiro. Coffee does not grow well in Antsahabehasina because of the coolness. There is also enough rain for vanilla in Antsahabehasina because it is near the forest and vanilla produces full round grains.

This kind of information is built on a long history of settlement and dwelling. Knowledge about cultivation is created through practical engagement with materials, soils and plants, and is passed from one generation to another. Papa ny Georges explained that his father was known for his knowledge about vanilla and its cultivation. Papa ny Georges has followed in his father's footsteps, and would explain cultivation practices to anyone who was interested.

Whereas knowledge of specific places is detailed, as this example shows, people in the Lokoho valleys do not talk about environment (*tontoliainana*), let alone biodiversity, and they have no word for landscape. Instead, they refer to the elements of their environment with very practical terms, for example animals (*biby*), flowers (*folera*) and trees (*kakazo*) (see also Sodikoff 2012: 87). However, this does not mean that cultivators can not make sense of complex ecological processes and relationships, as is clear from Papa ny Georges's explanation. A similar case among the Baduy in West Java has shown that although they had not adopted many other introduced crops, after several years of careful observing of a Albizia tree, the Baduy wanted to integrate it into their swidden cultivation. This tree was used by the Baduy to fertilise the soil but also to gain some cash income (Iskandar and Ellen

---

10  Tsimihety people have many different words for fields: *tany horaka* (irrigated rice field), *tavy* (swidden cultivation- the concept can refer to the whole process), *tany la vanio* (vanilla field) and people sometimes refer to a specific activity by saying: I cultivate land (*mamboly tany*).

11  A peninsula cultivated rights across the River Lokoho that people cross with their canoes (*lakana*).

12  A place is located about six kilometres away from one of the villages studied.

2000:7). Indeed, people know their environments by observing concrete processes, interpreting them and evaluating potential new crops and plants in the context of existing ethno-ecological knowledge. Agro-ecological knowledge that is based on the generic understanding of the processes is vital for local people just as it is for scientists (Ellen 2006: 165). However, landscapes are not merely objectively observed but are also related to people's cosmologies and ways of being. Next I discuss people's relationships with ancestors and how these exist in the landscape.

## Marked landscapes

The meaning of land and territory for the Tsimihety derives from a cumulative history of occupation and use. Because his father's sister was already living in Manantenina, Willy's father had come there from a village located four day's walk to the west. The sister gave him some land to cultivate and after a while told him that he should clear some forest (atiala) for himself. So he went to Antsahabehasina, a hillside about one hour walk from the village, and cleared some land *(tany)* there.

> Willy: When they [father's sister and father] saw that I was growing up[13] they decided to give my aunt's land to me. That is why I have to send my aunt's bones to where his father is from.
> Jenni: What happens if you don't send the bones back?
> Willy: It is not good. I am afraid of that something will happen.

This was a typical history. Someone in the extended family had gone to look for money (*mitady vola*) in a new place and then (s)he tells the family to come and live there. Indeed, despite historical analysis suggesting that the Tsimihety had fled from the state at the turn of the 20th century, their movements have not been collective, rather individuals and households have moved to look for new opportunities or to avoid misfortune (see also Wilson 1992: 29).

As anthropological literature in Madagascar has shown, by clearing forest, building houses and establishing tombs, shifting cultivators became more and more settled or, to use Eva Keller's (2008) term, rooted in place. Having extra money implies a moral obligation to build a house. For instance, people may work for six months as research assistants in the park, earning a monthly salary. Such people will have built a house, not made of bamboo, which anyone who is capable of carrying it back from the forest can do, but of timber planks, processed by circular saw and paid for with money. Also, several people in the village where I did fieldwork, who had made a big profit

---

13 To grow up refers to understanding of responsibility, how to live as a responsible and respectful person. In this case, it meant taking care of the family, working, respecting customs (*fomba*) and able maintain descendants and many social relationships.

in 2003, when vanilla prices rocketed, had built cement houses with two or three floors.

As a new household is established, usually by a married couple, it generates more wealth: children. Children are a sign of life and good fortune as are rooms to house them. When Willy built an additional room, he had a celebration before anyone used it where he invited the children of his kin and his neighbours to eat very smoothly cooked rice. When I asked why he had invited small children, he answered that "they bring good life and fortune." The ideal is that children help their parents by working in the house and on the fields, and finally by taking care of them when they grew old. Finally, children are responsible of taking care of the *famadihana*, exhumation, "sending the bones [of a dead person] back where the father is from" as Willy put it. Thus, children are very important in maintaining relationships with other people and ancestors.

When people move to a new site they do not lose their ties to previous homes. Rather, after successfully establishing new fields and houses and having children, a site becomes imaginable as a branch of the kin group. For example, Willy could go any time to the village where his father was from and claim his land there. In actuality however, "at the moment, here is good for me" he told me while we walked on the road next to the village he lived. Despite of Willy's notion, father's village further west is also Willy's *tanindrazana*, the place where he will be buried eventually (see also Lambek and Walsh 1997: 317; Keller 2008).

In sum, my research showed that in people's relationships with their environment, it was important to mark the landscape through working, building houses and tombs. Movement expands people's territories in the landscapes where they can claim kinship relations and access to land through these ties. Expansion in space is matched by expansion in time as cultivators return their bones to their family tombs. This world has an axis that is simultaneously temporal as well as spatial (Lambek and Walsh 1997: 320). For the people living in these landscapes, history is thus crucial whereas visitors and tourists have not been so interested in these landscape histories.

## Standardising the nature experience

In the Marojejy National Park, in order to successfully meet sustainability goals introduced by the joint practices of international conservation organisations, investment banks and the Malagasy state, all of which emphasise the economic sustainability of conservation, a new kind of nature experience had to be standardised. The park was built for the needs of the foreign tourists and according to a standardised national park model. Even the visitor information centre in Marojejy was designed in a similar shape to Yellowstone, so that visitors could enter in and look at the photographs of the plants and animals and also read short descriptions of local customs such as swidden agriculture and even taboos. The sign at the entrance welcomes people to the park. The path up to the summit of the Marojejy is built from rocks and sand to facilitate tourists' efforts to reach the primary forest.

Three different camps along the path provide possibilities for cooking and sleeping, in cottages with beds and bedding, kitchen utensils for cooking and even a porcelain pot in the restroom of one of the camps. Between the first and second camps, a terrace is built from which one could admire the primary forest and a waterfall named after the 19th-century botanist Jean-Henri Humbert. As I observed during my fieldwork, tourists had the latest camping equipment, outdoor clothes, hiking boots and durable backpacks. In addition, practically everybody had a camera and they took pictures of plants and animals as their guides pointed to them. In the park, tourists were fascinated by the lemurs that climbed in 10–20 meter trees, ate leaves and jumped from one tree to another. The special moment was when a lemur gazed back at the tourist for the perfect photo (see also Andersson 2013). Tourists called these animals cute, marvellous and exciting, pointed at them and took photographs that they enjoyed looking at.

However, tourism is not just about experiencing and seeing rare things, and importantly, even ecotourism is closely related to capitalist practices. Yellowstone, the model national park, was established in the USA in the 19th century, which was characterised by rapid industrialisation, extractive capitalist expansion and the rise of iconic business tycoons, many of whom became noted philanthropists and nature lovers. Early American conservation strategies involved enrolment of these elites on conservation practices (Tsing 2005: 95–96; Igoe et al. 2010: 490.) Relating economic and environmental conservation practices provides an avenue by which corporations and politicians can become 'green', and through creating new enclosures and conservation-based enterprises, conservation fuels processes of capital accumulation (Brockington 2011: 2). The net result is that "international biodiversity conservation is creating new symbolic and material spaces for global capital expansion" (Corson 2011: 578). The notion of spectacle, introduced by the Situationist Guy Debord (1994 [1967]), is important here because it refers to the mediation of relationships between people and the environment by images (see also Berglund this volume). Following Debord, James Igoe (2010: 376) has insisted that spectacle and material reality are inextricably woven together:

> The spectacle which inverts the real is in fact produced. Lived reality is materially invaded by the contemplation of the spectacle while simultaneously absorbing the spectacular order, giving it positive cohesiveness. Objective reality is present on both sides. Every notion fixed this way has no other basis than its passage into the opposite: reality rises up within the spectacle, and the spectacle is real.

Igoe's conception is important because it points out that by focusing consumers' attention on distant and exotic locales, the spectacular productions conceal the complex and proximate connections of people's daily lives to environmental problems, while suggesting that the solutions to environmental problems lay in the consumption of the kinds of commodities that helped produce them in the first place (Igoe et al. 2010: 504; Brockington and Duffy 2011: 4–5).

Increasingly however, people living in the Lokoho valleys and their intimate knowledge have been put into the service of ecotourism. The Tsimihety have been hired as guides, cooks and porters, since to gain a proper experience of wilderness, tourists require local guides to show them what they have come to find. Guides act as their 'eyes' and as translators of biodiversity, but they are also more general care-takers for the tourists. They explained about local plants and animals, like helmet vanga or medicinal plants such as *aspidium,* or trees that are used for house building, such as *palissandre.* Guides point out animals and plants that tourists are not used to seeing, such as chameleons hiding in the vegetation. In addition, guides observe constantly whether tourists are able to walk on a steep elevating path.

A lot of effort has been made to fulfil tourists' expectations. Some cultivators have worked as so-called simpona[14] guides that tourists can hire to be sure that they definitely find lemurs in the park. A simpona guide will go to the park some days beforehand, depending on tourists' preference, to track down a lemur group. As tourists arrive in the park, their standard guide calls for the simpona guide using a specific call. The simpona guide replies with a double howl and tourists are able to approach lemurs tracked by the simpona guide. This way tourists can catch what they came to see: a spectacle of pristine nature.

Ironically, because tourists and researchers have been following lemurs in the park for so many years, lemurs are no longer afraid of human beings and did not necessarily flee when they saw people. This was not the case when ecotourism and research activities began. A US animal behaviour researcher described how, when he began his work in 2001, he had to walk around the forest just to see a glimpse of lemurs (Pieczenik 2009). This shows how in environmental conservation and ecotourism practices, wild, pure and pristine nature are tamed. While tourists were intrigued by the lemurs, the Tsimihety were not so sure what these foreign people were doing in the park.

## Becoming aware of different potentialities

If guides, cooks and porters were not so interested in following lemurs, they did observe the tourists' behaviour. They were puzzled as to why tourists got so enthusiastic about animals that they and their parents had been hunting and eating for generations. I argue that because of new relationships between tourists and Tsimihety and tourists and lemurs, Tsimihety became aware of different potentialities of lemurs: it is because of these animals that tourists come to visit their landscapes, at the same providing, through ecotourism, a necessary income. In addition, if tourists continue to come to Tsimihety landscapes, it is possible for the Tsimihety to create relationships that, for example, allow selling their vanilla beyond regular middlemen managing vanilla trade.

14  *Simpona* means silky sifaka lemur (*Propithecus candidus*) in Tsimihety dialect.

At the same time, the Tsimihety are puzzled as to how is it possible that *vazaha* (foreigner, stranger) have so much money, can fly around the world and have the latest technology and lots of different things, such as hiking boots, watches, rain jackets. Based on observation, people in ecotourism came to the conclusion that the problem with the Malagasy state was that it was not rich. "Now that the Malagasy state is in charge, there is no money," one guide continued and compared his experiences to those in the 1990s when the WWF worked in the area: "They had nice cars, jackets and watches." Guides had experience in collaborating with tourists: If tourists were satisfied, they could give an extra gift, such as money, shoes, a camera, sleeping bags, old camping cloths, in addition to the regular salary. One guide had acquired four pairs of shoes, at least two hiking coats and one camera that tourists had sent him from France. Tourists had paid his trip to the capital to pick it up so that he would be able to take pictures of species in the park and learn more about them in a local library.

However, my interlocutors appeared uncertain how world economies worked. "How is it possible that you are rich and we here in Madagascar are poor?" a vanilla cultivator and broker asked me after we had been discussing his business on the porch of his house. I started to explain about historical processes of colonialisation, trade agreements, structural adjustment and recent neoliberal policies that I considered relevant because of my Finnish university education. He listened without saying anything. Similar observations have been reported in northwest Madagascar (Walsh 2004; 2005) and in Papua New Guinea (Stasch 2014). In Madagascar, people were aware that someone gained, but they just did not know how (see also Walsh 2010: 236).[15]

In discussing ecotourism practices, a male rice cultivator in his 50s pointed out: "Clever people abroad, they know how to take advantage of Madagascar's forests". Also, an ethnography from the Antankarana national park in Northwest Madagascar shows that some people in Antankarana realised that foreign researchers and tourists have a different way of looking at things than Malagasy people (Walsh 2005). Indeed, tourism is not merely an industry but constitutes as a reflexive inquiry into globalisation itself (Stasch 2014), teasing out the possibilities and methods of different accesses of different people. I would add that this applies also to environmental conservation practices.

Interestingly, unlike in other intensively conserved places (parts of Amazonia, Indonesia), in Madagascar there are not many social movements that create a critical discourse or countermovement against the transnational conservation activities. In Madagascar, there have been a few cases of labour movement (Sodikoff 2005) and there is a transnational NGO (for example Terres Malgasches) that is not based in Madagascar. Researchers have noted that in Madagascar people fear the state (Cole 2001; Graeber

15 If not mentioned otherwise, these cultivators' perspectives came out from the 40 semi-structured interviews that I conducted in the beginning of the fieldwork, in September and October 2012 in four different villages, in order to get general sense of the people and the places.

2007), or that they simply prefer to avoid the state or situations that might possibly put them in the position to take orders. Avoidance has been political. For example, some Malagasy have made clear their opinion of ongoing development practices by burning forests (see e.g. Kull 2004).

Most Malagasy have maintained culturally important relations and practices. Respect and obligations towards the words of ancestors, guide peoples' access to land and their prosperity in general (Keller 2008; see also Jütersoncke et al. 2010). For example, the way of maintaining social coherence and morality has been an ancestral speech, *kabary*, a skilful form speech full of proverbs and metaphors (see e.g. Crossland 2014: 210). When, in the coup d'etat of 2009, the opposition used the concept of ancestral land (*tanindrazana*) in order to halt leasing land to the South Korean company Daewoo, the understanding of ancestral land that had to be kept in Malagasy ownership, mobilised national as well as transnational actors (see e.g. Vinciguerra 2013).[16]

Indeed, when cultivators want success, they ask for blessings (*mijoro*) from their ancestors or in certain sacred places, for example at a big rock in the village near the River Lokoho or at a big tree located in a deep, curved slope along the paved highway. One of the elders living in the village near the tree told me:

> *Tony* [a respectable place] was established before a woman went there. She was hit by a stone on the road and she had to stay at home. She was too tired to stay at home and she went to the place and said: 'If I am healed, I will kill a chicken'. Only a week after her request, she became healthy again. This happened a long time ago.

The elder also mentioned that eight women had made such promises (*voahady*) there, and they all had gone to France. A similar kind of narrative is related to the big rock located by the river in front of the village. For example Willy told me: "Three years ago when the football team from our village was in the finals, we went with *zafintany* [the original settler of the place] to the sacred rock and we asked for a blessing. We won." Being prosperous and successful was thus never solely a matter of individual rational choice. Other powers and relations were also part of allowing success (see also Cole 2001: 138–139).

## Conclusions

In this chapter, I have discussed conserved landscapes in Northeast Madagascar whose creation is strongly informed by transnational environmental or conservation organisations, NGOs, donors and investment banks. As a result of their efforts from the 1990s onwards, wide areas of

---

16  In the national context the question was about national politics while transnational organization, TANY, Terres malgaches was concerned about the food security and inequalities.

land have been occupied for conservation. As elsewhere, these conservation efforts have a longer history tied to state, and later transnational actors' territorialisation processes and modern scientific knowledge production. And, as other scholars have shown in different places (Lowe 2006; Tsing 2005), these types of areas typically exclude people who have long historical relationships with land that have shaped their ways of living, working and building and creating differences between people. However, in Madagascar, globally recognised social movements have not emerged, and the Malagasy have preferred to avoid submitting to foreigners' wishes and commands. On the other hand, their skilful way of speaking and using meaningful metaphors, such as *tanindrazana* (ancestral land), can be made politically significant, as the case of the South Korean Daewoo shows.

The Tsimihety know intimately the landscapes and environments that they live in and practically engage with, and their knowledge is inherited from and distributed through the generations. In contrast, the practices of environmental conservation rely on abstract universal knowledge that has relevance for managerial purposes and capitalist processes. In the recent joint efforts of capitalism and conservation, images have been important in mediating peoples' relations with each other and with different environments. In the processes of ecotourism, different actors and things are not only mediated by the images but come together in the same space.

In the national park, the Tsimihety have followed tourists and scientists that interact differently with the species that the Tsimihety haven been hunting and eating. I have suggested that by observing and comparing, Tsimihety have become aware that there is something in their landscapes that they do not know yet. In addition, they became aware of their economical marginality, puzzled as to how these people, tourists and scientists, can be so rich. Although ecotourism was introduced with the idea of supporting local economic development, it made them aware of economic disparities. I have shown that ecotourism not only affects resource use in a utilitarian sense, but it also affects ways of looking and thus making sense.

I have highlighted that landscape in this case is not created by one group of people, rather its formation is related to different interests, meaning-making processes and ways of seeing. Ethnographic writing and conscious use of metaphors or analytical concepts, such as forest in this article, helps to tease out the nuances that are crucial in understanding the differences between different people and the power relations involved (see also Anderson and Berglund 2003: 10–15). This is also the analytical relevance of the concept of landscape: it allows us to focus on particular actions, practices and materials in actual places that are not seen in just one way but always in relation to other landscapes, histories and intelligible processes of different people. Looked at in this way, it is possible to avoid hegemonic master narratives and point out that stories of landscapes are never one but multiple stories in process (Massey 2005). The anthropologist's task is to think his/her methodology accordingly, and be aware of what and where are the connections and disconnections, things that are seen and not seen, and perhaps hidden.

105

# References

Althabe, Gerard 1968. *Oppression et libération dans l'imaginaire: Les communautés villageoises de la côte Est de Madagascar.* Paris: Maspero.

Anderson, David G., and Eeva Berglund (eds) 2003. *Ethnographies of conservation: Environmentalism and the distribution of privilege.* New York: Berghahn Books.

Andersson, Thomas 2013. Solving Madagascar: Science, Illustrations, and the Normalizing of Fauna of Nineteenth Century Madagascar. In Sandra Evers, Gwyn Campbell and Michael Lambek (eds), *Contest for Land in Madagascar: Environment, Ancestors and Development.* Boston: Brill Academic Publishers.

Bate, Jonathan 2013. *Romantic Ecology: Wordsworth and the Environmental Tradition.* London: Routledge.

Bloch, Maurice 1971. *Placing the Dead: Tombs, Ancestral Villages, and Kinship Organization in Madagascar.* London: Seminar Press.

Bloch, Maurice 1991. Language, anthropology and cognitive science. *Man* (NS) 26 (2): 183–198.

Bloch, Maurice 1995. People into places: Zafimaniry concepts of clarity. In Eric Hirsch and Michael O'Hanlon (eds), *The anthropology of landscape: Perspectives on place and space.* Oxrford: Clanderon.

Brockington, Dan, and Rosaleen Duffy (eds) 2011. *Capitalism and Conservation.* Malden, MA: Wiley-Blackwell.

Brockington, Dan, Rosaleen Duffy and Jim Igoe 2008. *Nature unbound: conservation, capitalism and the future of protected areas.* London: Earthscan.

Brown, Margaret 2004. Reclaiming lost ancestors and acknowledging slave descent: Insights from Madagascar. *Comparative studies in society and history* 46 (3): 616–645.

Cole, Jennifer 2001. *Forget Colonialism?* Chicago: University of Chicago Press.

Corson, Catherine 2011. Territorialization, enclosure and neoliberalism: Non-state influence in struggles over Madagascar's forests. *Journal of Peasant Studies* 38 (4): 703–726.

Corson, Catherine 2014. Conservation politics in Madagascar: The expansion of protected areas. In Ivar R. Scales (ed.), *Conservation and Environmental Management in Madagascar.* New York: Routledge

Cosgrove, Denis 1984. *Social formation and symbolic landscape.* Wisconsin: The University of Wisconsin Press.

Cosgrove, Denis and Peter Jackson 1987. New directions in cultural geography. *Area*: 95–101.

Corson, Catherine 2016. *Corridors of power: The politics of environmental aid to Madagascar.* New Haven: Yale University Press.

Debord, Guy 1994. *The Society of the Spectacle.* New York: Zone Books.

Descola, Philippe 2016. Landscape as Transfiguration. Edward Westermarck Memorial Lecture, October 2015. *Suomen Antropologi: Journal of The Finnish Anthropological Society* 41 (1): 3–14.

Duffy, Rosaleen 2008. Neoliberalising nature: Global networks and ecotourism development in Madagasgar. *Journal of Sustainable Tourism,* 16 (3): 327–344.

Ellen, Roy 2006. *The categorical impulse: Essays in the anthropology of classifying behaviour.* Berghahn books.

Evers, Sandra J. T. M. 2013. Lex loci meets lex fori: Merging customary law and national land legislation in Madagascar. In Sandra Evers, Gwyn Campbell and Michael Lambek (eds), *Contest for Land in Madagascar: Environment, Ancestors and Development.* Boston: Brill Academic Publishers.

Fairhead, James and Melissa Leach 1995. Reading Forest History Backwards: The Interaction of Policy and Local Land Use in Guinea's Forest-Savanna Mosaic, 1893–1993. *Environment and History* 1 (1): 55–91.

Feld, Steven 1996. Waterfalls of Song: An Acoustemology of Place Resounding in Bosavi, Papua New Guinea. In Steven Feld and Keith H. Basso (eds), *Senses of place*. Santa Fe: School of American Research Press.

Feld, Steven and Keith H. Basso (eds) 1996. *Senses of place*. Santa Fe: School of American Research Press.

Garreau, Jean-Marc and A. Manantsara 2003. The protected-area complex of the Parc National de Marojejy and the Réserve Spéciale d'Anjanaharibe-Sud. In Steven Goodman and Jonathan Benstead (eds), *The Natural History of Madagascar*. Chicago: University of Chicago Press.

Goodman, Steven 2000. *A floral and faunal inventory of the Réserve spéciale d'Anjanaharibe-Sud, Madagascar: With reference to elevational variation*. Chicago, IL: Field Museum of Natural History.

Graeber, David 2007. *Lost people: Magic and the legacy of slavery in Madagascar*. Bloomington: Indiana University Press.

Green, Nicholas 1990. *The spectacle of nature: Landscape and bourgeois culture in nineteenth-century France*. Manchester: Manchester University Press.

Hirsch, Eric 1995. Introduction – Landscape: Between Place and Space. In Eric Hirsch and Michael O'Hanlon (eds), *The anthropology of landscape: Perspectives on place and space*. Oxrford: Clanderon.

Humbert Henri 1927. La destruction d'une flore insulaire par le feu. Principaux aspects de la végétation de Madagascar. Documents photographiques et notices. *Mémoires de l'Académie Malgache* 5. Paris: Muséum National d'Histoire Naturelle.

Igoe, Jim 2010. The spectacle of nature in the global economy of appearances: Anthropological engagements with the spectacular mediations of transnational conservation. *Critique of Anthropology* 30 (4): 375–397.

Igoe, Jim, Katja Neves and Dan Brockington 2010. A spectacular eco-tour around the historic bloc: Theorising the convergence of biodiversity conservation and capitalist expansion." *Antipode* 42 (3): 486–512.

Ingold, Tim 2000. *The perception of the environment: Essays on livelihood, dwelling and skill*. London: Routledge.

Iskandar, Johan and Roy F. Ellen 2000. The contribution of Paraserianthes (Albizia) falcataria to sustainable swidden management practices among the Baduy of West Java. *Human Ecology* 28 (1): 1–17.

Jarosz, Lucy. 1993. Defining and Explaining Tropical Deforestation: Shifting Cultivation and Population Growth in Colonial Madagascar (1896–1940). *Economic Geography* 69 (4): 366–379.

Jütersonke, Oliver C., Moncef Kartas, Isabelle Dauner, Julie Mandoyan and Christoph Spurk 2010. *Peace and conflict impact assessment (PCIA): Madagascar*. Geneva: Graduate Institute of International and Development Studies.

Keller, Eva 2008. The banana plant and the moon: Conservation and the Malagasy ethos of life in Masoala, Madagascar. *American Ethnologist* 35 (4): 650–664.

Keller, Eva 2015. *Beyond the lens of conservation: Malagasy and Swiss imaginations of one another*. New York: Berghahn Books.

Kull, Christian 2013. The roots, persistence, and character of Madagascar's conservation boom. In Ivar R. Scales (ed.), *Conservation and Environmental Management in Madagascar*. New York: Routledge

Kull, Christian 2004. *Isle of fire: The political ecology of landscape burning in Madagascar*. Chicago: University of Chicago Press.

Lambek, Michael and Andrew Walsh 1997. The imagined community of the Antankarana: Identity, history, and ritual in Northern Madagascar. *Journal of Religion in Africa* 27 (1–4): 308–333.

Laney, Rheyna 1999. *Agricultural change and landscape transformations in the Andapa region of Madagascar*. PhD Dissertation. Clark University.

Laney, Rheyna 2002. Disaggregating induced intensification for land-change analysis: A case study from Madagascar. *Annals of the Association of American Geographers* 92 (4): 702–726.

Li, Tania Murray 2007. *The will to improve: Governmentality, development, and the practice of politics.* Durham: Duke University Press.

Lowe, Celia 2006. *Wild Profusion: Biodiversity Conservation in an Indonesian Archipelago.* Princeton: Princeton University Press.

Madagascar National Parks 2007. *The Marojejy National Parks. Annual Report.* Madagascar National Parks.

Marcus, Richard R. and Christian Kull 1999. Setting the stage: The politics of Madagascar's environmental efforts. *African Studies Quarterly* 3 (2): 1–8.

Massey, Doreen 2005. *For space.* London: Sage.

McCormick, John 1989. *Reclaiming Paradise: The Global Environmental Movement.* Bloomington: Indiana University Press.

Mitchell, Timothy 2011. *Carbon democracy: Political power in the age of oil.* London: Verso Books

Moat, Justin and Paul Philip Smith 2007. *Atlas of the vegetation of Madagascar.* Royal Botanic Gardens, Kew.

Molet, Louis 1959. *L'expansion Tsimihety: modalités et motivations des migrations intérieures d'un groupe ethnique du nord de Madagascar.* Mémoires de l'Institut Scientifique de Madagascar. Série C: Sciences humaines.

Myers, Norman, Russell A. Mittermeier, Cristina G. Mittermeier, Gustavo A. B. da Fonseca and Jennifer Kent 2000. Biodiversity hotspots for conservation priorities. *Nature* 403: 853–858.

Olson, Sherry 1984. The robe of the ancestors: Forests in the history of Madagascar. *Journal of Forest History* 28.4: 174–186.

Pressey, Robert L., Mar Cabeza, Matthew E. Watts, Richard M.Cowling and Kerrie A.Wilson 2007. Conservation planning in a changing world. *Trends in Ecology & Evolution* 22 (11): 583–592.

Riles, Annelise 1998. Division within the boundaries. *The Journal of the Royal Anthropological Society* 4 (3): 409–424.

Rydell, Kiki Leigh and Mary Shivers Culpin 2006. *Managing the "Matchless Wonders": A History of Administrative Development in Yellowstone National Park, 1872–1965.* National Park Service, Yellowstone Center for Resources.

Sauer, Carl 1925. The Morphology of Landscape. *University of California Publications in Geography* 2 (2): 19–53.

Scales, Ivan R. 2014. A brief history of the state and the politics of natural resource use in Madagascar. Ivar R. Scales (ed.), *Conservation and Environmental Management in Madagascar.* New York: Routledge

Scott, James 1998. *Seeing Like a State: How Certain Conditions to Improve the Human Condition Have Failed.* New Haven: Yale University Press.

Sodikoff, Genese 2004. Land and languor: Ethical imaginations of work and forest in northeast Madagascar. *History and Anthropology* 15 (4): 367–398.

Sodikoff, Genese 2007. An exceptional strike: A micro-history of 'people versus park' in Madagascar. *Journal of Political Ecology* 14 (1): 10–33.

Sodikoff, Genese 2012. *Forest and Labor in Madagascar: From Colonial Concession to Global Biosphere.* Bloomington: Indiana University Press.

Stasch, Rupert 2014. Primitivist tourism and romantic individualism: On the values in exotic stereotypy about cultural others. *Anthropological theory* 14 (2): 191–214.

Strathern, Marilyn 1992. *After nature: English kinship in the late twentieth century.* Cambridge: Cambridge University Press.

Tsing, Anna Lowenhaupt 2003. Cultivating the wild: Honey-hunting and forest management in southeast Kalimantan. In Charles Zerner (ed.), *Culture and the*

*Question of Rights: Forests, Coasts, and Seas in Southeast Asia.* Durham: Duke University Press.

Tsing, Anna Lowenhaupt 2005. *Friction: An ethnography of global connection.* Princeton: Princeton University Press.

Tsing, Anna Lowenhaupt 2015. *The Mushroom at the End of the World: On the possibility of life in capitalist ruins.* Princeton: Princeton University Press.

Turner, Frederick 1894. *The Significance of the Frontier in American History.* https://www.historians.org/about-aha-and-membership/aha-history-and-archives/historical-archives/the-significance-of-the-frontier-in-american-history <accessed 31 October 2017>.

UNESCO 2007: *Rainforests of the Antsinanana, Madagascar* (ID no. 1257). World Heritage Nomination. IUCN Technical Evaluation.

Urry, John 1992. The Tourist Gaze and the Environment. *Theory, Culture & Society* 9 (3): 1–26.

Vandergeest, Peter and Nancy Lee Peluso 1995. Territorialization and state power in Thailand. *Theory and Society* 24 (3): 385–426.

Walsh, Andrew 2004. In the wake of things: Speculating in and about sapphires in northern Madagascar. *American Anthropologist* 106 (2): 225–237.

Walsh, Andrew 2005. The obvious aspects of ecological underprivilege in Ankarana, northern Madagascar. *American Anthropologist* 107 (4): 654–665.

Walsh, Andrew 2010. The commodification of fetishes: Telling the difference between natural and synthetic sapphires. *American Ethnologist* 37 (1): 98–114.

West, Paige and James Carrier 2004. Ecotourism and Authenticity: Getting Away from It All? *Current Anthropology* 45 (4): 483–498.

West, Paige and James Carrier 2009. *Virtualism, Governance and Practice: Vision and Execution in Environmental Conservation.* New York: Berghahn Books.

West, Paige, James Igoe and Dan Brockington 2006. Parks and peoples: The social impact of protected areas. *Annual Review of Anthropology* 35: 251–277.

Wilson, Peter J. 1992. *Freedom by a Hair's Breadth: Tsimihety in Madagascar.* Ann Arbor: University of Michigan Press.

Vinciguerra, Venusia 2013. How the Daewoo attempted land acquisition contributed to Madagascar's political crisis in 2009. In Sandra Evers, Gwyn Campbell and Michael Lambek (eds), *Environment, Ancestors and Development.* Boston: Brill Academic Publishers.

*Online resources*

KFW 2011: http://www.kfw-entwicklungsbank.de/ebank/EN_Home/Countries_and_Programmes/Sub-Saharan_Africa/Madagascar/index.jsp <accessed 10 May 2011>.

*Videos*

Pieczenik, Sharon 2009: Angels of the Forest. Silky Sifaka Lemurs of Madagascar. https://vimeo.com/5894853

FRANCESCO ZANOTELLI
 https://orcid.org/0000-0003-4257-4275

CRISTIANO TALLÈ[1]

# The political side of the landscape: Environmental and cosmological conflicts from the Huave point of view

## *Making room for power in landscape theory*

In recent decades landscape, reconsidered from a phenomenological perspective, has been used as a strategic and powerful ethnographic tool, one that is multifaceted and flexible, and capable of accommodating different forms of agency, materiality and sensorial perception (Feld and Basso 1996; Hirsch and O'Hanlon 1995; Ingold 2000). In this chapter, we would like to push the phenomenology of landscape to engage the issue of power and politics with two purposes in mind: firstly, to explore the theoretical implications of connecting the concept of power with that of landscape; secondly, to better understand processes that originate from the conflicting management of the landscape.

This approach, which is simultaneously empirical and theoretical, emerges directly from our fieldwork with the Huave, fishermen and peasants numbering about 27,000 scattered in four main communities: San Mateo del Mar, San Francisco del Mar, Santa Maria del Mar and San Dionisio del Mar, settled in a lagoon environment facing the Pacific Ocean, on the Isthmus of Tehuantepec (Oaxaca, Mexico).[2] Their rejection of a mega-scale wind

---

1   The whole chapter is the result of comparing and sharing the fieldwork experiences of the authors (Francesco Zanotelli in San Dionisio del Mar since 2009 and Cristiano Tallè in San Mateo del Mar since 1999). Introduction and Conclusions equal contribution; the second and the fourth paragraphs by Cristiano Tallè; the third and the fifth paragraphs by Francesco Zanotelli. This is part of the ongoing research project *Eco-frictions of the Anthropocene* (2017–2020), funded by the Italian Ministry of Education and Research (PRIN 2015–20155TYKCM–SH5). The writing process began with Zanotelli presenting at the session *Landscape ontologies in collision: food, politics and (non)human transformations in the neoliberal era*, convened by Tony Knight and Laura Montesi at Helsinki's Biennial Conference of the Finnish Anthropological Society in 2015, and he would like to thank them their kind invitation to participate.

2   On the 7th of September, and again on the 19th September 2017, the inhabitants of the Isthmus of Tehuantepec were struck by two powerful earthquakes. We hope that they will soon recover their serenity despite the inevitable landscape and social transformation.

farm project designed to exploit the energy of the strong winds blowing over the lagoon, is exemplary of territorial conflicts being not just about land, but also about landscape. We consider that the concept of landscape, together with the classic notion of land, is a powerful analytical instrument for deepening our understanding of Mexican environmental conflicts and the huge processes of land-grabbing, typical of contemporary struggles in Latin America and beyond.

Including landscape in the analysis is particularly urgent in light of prior traditions of Latin American studies into land and territory (Escobar and Alvarez 1992). Early research conducted with indigenous groups was traditionally characterised by the idea of a strong connection between land and the peasant system of production (Redfield 1956; Stavenhagen 1969; R. Bartra 1974; A. Bartra 1979; Warman 1980); a second, politically and economically informed, stage of anthropological inquiry has focussed on the link between territorial autonomy and indigenous citizenship (De la Peña 1995; Bartolomé 1997; Pacheco de Oliveira 1998; Surrálés and García Hierro 2004; Burguete Cal y Mayor 2010; Venturoli and Zanotelli 2013). This political and economic tradition in anthropology has rarely dialogued with the specifically ethnological perspective on cosmovision and indigenous knowledge, or where it has, it has lent itself to naïve interpretations of indigenous environmentalism (Conklin and Graham 1995; Albert 2004; Turner 2000). Only recently has the role of natural entities been investigated in a framework of cosmo-political anthropology (de la Cadena 2010), which brings together three interconnected dimensions of analysis: the neo-liberal specifics of natural resource exploitation; phenomenological and embodied effects on territories and people; moral economy and political resistance (Scott 1976) that includes non-human agents.

Taking a similar anthropological perspective, we propose the concept of landscape to develop a more intimate understanding of contemporary eco-political frictions (Tsing 2005). In other words, the material and sensorial dimension of the landscape is an important characteristic of the local conflicts, which must be considered in conjunction with the economic and political asymmetries concurrently at play at different scales.

The most interesting challenges of this approach include connecting local conceptions and experiences of landscape with complex macro processes (late industrialisation, the management of green energy, land grabbing, national and transnational politics) and the indelible imprints that they leave in "disturbed landscapes" (see Lounela, this book).

Thus, we devote the first section to illustrating the procedures that the Huave have put in place to conceive and describe the landscape in which they live. Through an examination of aspects of the Huave linguistic encoding of landscape forms, we find that the landscape is conceived as a never-ending process of materialisation: it is the precarious result of the constant co-agency between nonhumans (meteorological, geological and liquid elements) and humans, which interact at different timescales.

The significance of this perspective is further revealed in the next section, which considers a second dimension: the representation of the landscape in Huave mythology and rituals, where the landscape is the resulting concretion

*Figure 1. The lagoon region of the Isthmus of Tehuantepec: in red, the main Huave settlements and the ritual place of Cerro Cristo; in blue, the main Zapotec and mestizo cities and settlements (Image elaborated by the authors with Google Earth).*

of political negotiations between humans (especially religious and political authorities) and nonhumans (sea, lagoon, wind, lightning, clouds, animals), a kind of negotiation characterised by conflict and its resolution.

In the third section we stress how the relationship of Huave people with the water-scape and aero-scape is intimately connected with forms of their ethnic identification, for example in a contrasting opposition with the neighbouring Zapotecs, who are identified with inner-land and farms. In this framework, we will discuss the hypothesis that the local agrarian conflicts that historically characterise inter-ethnic relations here, can be explained on the basis of a historical process of 'ethno-naturalisation'.

Finally, we take the present strenuous opposition to the huge eolian industry spreading wind farms all over the region, as a struggle for indigenous sovereignty that cannot be reduced to an exclusive right over a plot of land, but embraces the whole web of aquatic and air agents shaping the landscape.

As we stress in the conclusions, the radical and abrupt transformation of the landscape caused by the high density of turbines, together with the massive occupation of land that they entail, assumes an immediate political significance for indigenous people living on the edge of the lagoons. This process of 'landscape grabbing' seems to endanger indigenous self-determination in a more radical way than ever before. Moving from ethnography towards a more theoretical perspective, we consider that attending to the 'political side' of the landscape helps us to better understand the intimate reasons for opposition to the so-called sustainable energy industry: these go beyond the concerns of twentieth-century political economics, such as struggles founded on a quantitative conception of land.

## The landscape from the Huave point of view: Co-agency and metamorphosis

The landscape that the Huave inhabit is a hydro-geographic *continuum* where forms of land and water interpenetrate in a fluctuating way (Zizumbo and Colunga 1982). The alternation of heavy rains (typically from June to September) with a dry period of strong winds (about November to February) creates a patchy lagoon landscape that can change dramatically within a year or a cycle of several years, depending on intensity of rainfall, the strength of ocean currents and waves, and the force of the northern winds that dry the stretches of water and move sand dunes. Historically lagoon fishing has been the main way of appropriating this metamorphic landscape, coexisting, wherever possible, with livestock farming (cattle and sheep) and agriculture.[3] Although fishing is practiced today in a market regime it still retains some of the territorial characteristics of a foraging economy. The lagoon fishing is traditionally practiced with dragnet and trammel, and requires an extensive mobility (coextensive to the resources). It involves walking along the banks and through the fords, or moving with canoes into the lagoons. We could define this type of fishing as a 'walking fishing', in and out of the water, which is at the same time a technique of the body and an expert use of places: one learns to fish while learning to move in the lagoons, one learns to move in the lagoons while learning to fish.

In this economy, the agency of meteorological elements in shaping the landscape is therefore very tangible, not only on a geological timescale, but also on a human one of months, years or decades. The morphogenesis of landscape is indeed a recurrent topic of cosmological memory as constructed in mythological tales, as well of biographical memory and everyday conversations. In this context, the local way of speaking of the landscape seems to constantly reflect a kind of "interanimation" (Basso 1996: 107–108) between human and the meteorological agency.[4] This interanimation is detectable at every level of local discourse, from the linguistic coding in single words to the construction of stories.

The Huave lexicon does not have a unitary concept that corresponds to the English landscape. Rather, there is a lexical mechanism that, by connecting body part terms to topographical terms (aquatic and terrestrial)

---

3    This ethnographic description of the conception of landscape refers specifically to San Mateo del Mar (notably the linguistic documents studied as part of Cristiano Tallè's fieldwork). Its territory is very exposed to the hydro-morphology of the ocean and the lagoon, and fishing rather than agriculture predominates. By contrast, the fertile lands of the Eastern territories of San Dionisio del Mar and San Francisco del Mar give a major role to agriculture, together with fishing.

4    Basso's notion of interanimation refers to the experience of sensing places: "As places animate the ideas and feelings of persons who attend to them, these same ideas and feelings animate the places on which attention has been bestowed" (1996: 107).

*Figure 2. A lagoon close to the shore in the surroundings of San Mateo del Mar (picture by Cristiano Tallè).*

(Tallè 2017), defines the metamorphic forms of the local environment and their affordance for human actions (Gibson 1979; Ingold 2000; 2007).[5]

For example, in the *ombeayiüts* ('our mouth') of San Mateo del Mar,[6] the landform of ford is encoded by the compound term *o-mal iüt* (his-head of land/the land's head) to indicate the land summit that is submerged where a sand dune, crossing a lagoon in its seasonal movement driven by the northern winds, forms an elevation on the lagoon bottom. Focusing on the vertical discontinuity underwater, the term echoes a very relevant sensory-

5   The term *püjchiün* indicates the specific topographic morphology of an open and level ground (from the verb *apüüch* /to extend/). Only recently has this term acquired the visualist and general connotation of landscape, understood as an extensive view of land scenery in front of the eyes of the viewer (Flavia Cuturi, personal communication, 2016).

6   The Huave language is an isolated language that is extremely endangered in three of its four variants: the *ombeayiüts* (literally: our mouth) of San Mateo del Mar is spoken by more than 95% of the inhabitants, the *ombeayiüjts* of San Dionisio del Mar by around 50% of the population, the *umbeayajts* of San Francisco del Mar by around 15%, the *umbeayüts* of Santa Maria del Mar by less than 10% of people (INEGI census 2010). The pronunciation of the phonemes in *ombeayiüts* of San Mateo del Mar is the following (according to the International Phonetic Association): *ch* = [tʃ] (as in Spanish), *ü* = [œ] (an intermediate sound between *u* and *e*), *x* = [ʃ] (like English *sh*), *j* is aspirated (as in Spanish) and *w* is a semi-consonant (as in English *water*), *g* = [ɣ] (hard *g* as in Spanish *ga, go, gu, gue, gui*). When it is useful for a better understanding of their meaning, the words are segmented into their morphological components, followed in brackets by literal and free translations, such as: *o-mbeay ndek* (his-mouth lagoon / the bank of the lagoon).

motor experience in local fishing practice, which involves wading through a stretch of water, where one can perceive (first by foot, then by eye) *niüng ajlüy awaag* (where it is dry). The lagoon bank is encoded by the compound term *o-mbeay ndek* (his-mouth of lagoon/the lagoon's mouth) or *o-mbeay yow* (his-mouth of water/the water's mouth) to indicate the perimeter of the bodies of water, such as a mouth top view. This term, marking the variable perimeter of the lagoon, resonates with a different experience of walking, one that is very common in the daily movements of every lagoon fisherman, namely walking along the coastline (*ajüy mbeaymbeay* /walking coast-to-coast/). Differentiated again from the bank of a lagoon, the ocean beach is encoded by the body-part term *o-mal* (his-head), namely *o-mal wiiüd* (his-head of the sand (dune)/the crest of the sand): the term indicates the emerging profiles of the shore as it is moulded by the perpetual undertow of ocean waves, forming a crest. Marking this prominent profile of the sand, the term records a specific experience of walking, which is to say 'walking up' (on the top) and 'out of the waves', going to fish or looking for turtle's eggs (Tallè 2016: 97–129).

This linguistic encoding of a water-land-scape *continuum* does not label topographic forms as a series of discrete objects existing 'out there' (on a geological scale) well separated from human experiences 'within' (on a historic scale). Instead, it seems to reflect a fleeting morphology of the landscape (the shifting sand dune forming fords, the rhythmic 'to and fro' of the undertow moulding the shore, the intermittent filling and emptying of the lagoon basins) resounding with the sensory-motor experiences of humans moving within it.

On the other hand, walking seems to be a prototype of the agency that encompasses many processes, human and nonhuman. In the *ombeayiüts* of San Mateo del Mar, the verb *ajüy* (walk) defines processes and 'paths' in many different domains of experience: the motion of human bodies moving on foot but also the gliding of canoes within the lagoons (*ajüy müx* /walks the canoe/), women's weaving (*ajüy mandel* /walks the napkin/) and men's weaving of fishing nets (*ajüy ndok* /walks the fishing net/), as well the movement of lightning during summer storms (*ajüy teat monteok* /walks father lightning/), the sun's movement across the sky (*ajüy teat nüt* /walks father Sun/), the movement of the sand dunes driven by north winds (*ajüy wiiüd* /walks the sand dune/) and more. Thus, at a timescale relevant to human and nonhuman lives, path (*tiiüd*) and footprint (*akwüüch oleaj* /tread the foot/) are better concepts for expressing the emic sense of temporality of this morphogenetic landscape.

A prototype of how this kind of meteorological and human co-agency shapes the landscape exists in local mythology. Meteorological phenomena are represented in myths as persons, with specific social, moral and emotional characteristics (Lupo 1997), but their morphogenetic agency over the landscape is not described as 'demiurgic'. That's to say, it is not described as an intentional (ego-centred) act of creation, moulding or production, but rather as the solidified imprint of the motion of meteorological bodies in resonance with parallel co-actions of one (or more) human and animal bodies.[7] What follows is an excerpt from a larger narrative, focused on the specific morphology of the landscape that is such a consequence of the inter-action between humans and nonhuman agents. It concerns a ravine, called *nots weak* (one horn), like the gigantic one-horned snake that dug it:

[...] *kiaj ajmbaj a tiük aaga ndiük, nadaam ajmbaj a tiük* [...] *nadam aaga xeech tiük, nadaaaam; tamb at nej yow, nej maw chük ngana a ndiük, ndoj teat Dios ngomüüch lugar, kiaj chük mandooig onik, mandooig onik ngana, tilüy iün chük matüch miyow nej, tawün nej andüy kawak.*

[...] there the snake breaks the mountain, makes a large breach in the mountains [...] it is huge that mountain, really huge; [the snake] went like water, the snake went out – it is said – but Father God (an old man-lightning) didn't allow it, he cuts off his neck there – it is said – now he cuts off the neck, he came at once – it is said – to reject his water, he pushed him southwards.

[...] *Aaga kiaj mejaw nganüy kiaj ngitow aaga jarraw kiaj, asoik nots weak, awün aood andüy tiüt ndiük, nadam ata tiük niüng ajmbaj, nadam yow ajoy, nadam, aag naw tiül tiük kiaj, hasta tamb ngana nej, teat Dios nepal andüy kawak* [...] *Tandüüb andüy kawak, aag tamb ngineay awün nendondonrojpüy, jarraw netejngieyay ajntsop mal wiiüd, ijaw ngineay* [...]. *Tajntsop, tajntsop mal wiiüd, apmatüch kiaj... mbi kos nangaj nadam ndek, ngoj ajponch ngwa? tatüch mal wiiüd, aag lamapal ombeay niüng awün zanja.*

[...] Now you can see there how big this ravine is, it is called "One Horn", the snake digs down a ravine as big as the breach of the mount, he carries a large flow of water, big, he comes out there from the inside of the mountain, until the moment He went, until the moment when Father God (an old man-lighting) went to block [his path] southwards [...]. He continued southwards, and dug a channel stream, a curved ravine, led to the head of the sand (the ocean bank), you can see how it is [...]. Led to the head of the sand (the ocean bank)... but because of the great sacred sea (ocean) and its waves, the mouth where comes out the channel was closed.[8]

## The landscape from the Huave point of view: Cosmology and power

As mentioned, the mythology of the Huave makes numerous references to the weather and to atmospheric elements. Furthermore, in the mythology, these elements are usually engaged in conflictive situations.

It means that through the language of myth, the narrator is talking about the locally shared ideology of power. This aspect is fully reported in the analysis elaborated by Lupo (2015) of the myth of *the son of the silly*

---

7   In San Mateo del Mar the same term *ombas* (which means 'body' but also 'form', 'color' among other things) indicates the human anatomical body as well its non-human *alter ego* (animal or atmospheric), which are semantically assimilated because they are existentially and agentively coupled (compare with *nagual* in Mesoamerican ethnographic literature, e.g. Tranfo 1979).

8   Extract from a myth narrated in 2006 by the elder *teat* (Father/Mr.) Juan Zaragoza (Tallè 2016: 258–259).

*town-crier* (*el hijo del pregonero tonto*), collected in San Mateo del Mar. Like many other local stories, it narrates the fight between cosmic forces: on one side lightening (*monteok*) and his ally the southern maternal wind (*müm ncharrek*) that bring rain and prosperity; on the other side the horned snake (*ndiük*) that is able to transform itself into a hurricane, endangering the territory. The possibility of reproducing the lagoons, the fish, the shrimps, the harvest – in one word life – depends on the balancing of these forces.[9] In the myth, the fight ends with the recovery of unity and harmony: control over the hurricane is gained, but only temporarily. Transferred to the social realm, the same myth talks about the power of one special child, who is able to get in touch with the snake and to obtain knowledge about the flood and the stormy wind, surpassing even the village authorities in wisdom. Then he dies, his death caused by his audacity. When he dies, sacrificed to the snake, he then transforms himself into a red cloud full of rain. In Lupo's interpretation, taking a perspective intimately related to the social life of the community, the myth represents the conflict between the young and old generations over power (Lupo 2015: 111).

The same conflictual dynamic that involves power and meteorology is at the heart of another myth (Warkentin and Olivares 1947: 230–231), but on the scale of the huge territory encompassing the four Huave municipalities and some neighbouring Zapotec communities. It tells of the robbery of some bells from Juchitán (the Zapotec municipal centre) by two Huave who were also able to make clouds on which they could carry the holy bells to San Mateo, where the bells are guarded carefully to this day. Cuturi (2003a: 41–45) reports a different version of the same myth focusing on the origin of the Huave villages. It was because of the risk of a big flood announced by San Vicente (the eponym of the municipality of Juchitan) that the Huave population left the original site of Huazantlán del Río (today a hamlet near San Mateo del Mar) and went to found the villages of San Dionisio del Mar and San Francisco del Mar. Because of the contrast between the saints, San Mateo went to ask for the help of southern lightning, which cut off the head of San Dionisio, though not completely.

We conclude this discussion with an analysis of a myth that is widespread in the region (Ramírez Castañeda 1987: 50–51; Millán 2003: 62), which, like those discussed above, is about a confrontation over knowledge, wealth, power and landscape imprints. But it refers to an even higher territorial level where colonial and postcolonial relations between the Huave and the central government are played out (Zanotelli 2016: 174–188). This narrative tells the story of a child prodigy born to a virgin. The version we report, collected in San Dionisio del Mar, refers to the child as *ñutyok* (the one who does exceptional things).[10] His special nature is underlined by his capacity to multiply fish and

---

9   See Signorini (2008: 381–388) for a general explanation of the conflictual relationship between *teat monteok* (father lightening) and its enemy *ndiük* (water snake) in the Huave mythology.

10  This has been collected by Francesco Zanotelli in San Dionisio del Mar in 2009 from the voice of *teat* Otilio Castellanos, an 87 year old man of authority. In San Mateo del Mar, the same myth is well-known as *ndeaj*, the orphan.

crops, to build a church in just one night, to invent all the machinery that corresponds to the idea of modernity among the Huave: helicopters, ships, trains and so on. However, the child prodigy's fame reaches the *gobierno*'s ear,[11] a military force from outside of the Huave territory that wants to catch, imprison and take him out of the Huave lands, towards Mexico City.[12] The Huave ancestors are unable and unwilling to protect the *ñutyok* against those who want to take him away, so the child decides to escape and to bring his exceptional abilities and wealth to other people all over the world. Before leaving the region, he leaves to his people unmistakable signs of his passage, such as the unfinished church of San Dionisio Pueblo Viejo and the imprints of his little hands on the inside of a cave in Cerro Cristo, a desert island located in the northern part of the Laguna Superior. In a similar version collected in San Mateo del Mar (Millán 2007: 207) the child prodigy, with his imprints, creates the coastal lagoons, the mountains and salt marshes of the coast, and he also leaves his moustache from which shrimps are created.

This brief journey into Huave mythology allows us to add something to the character of the landscape as perceived from the Huave point of view: not only is it shaped in the continuous co-agency between humans and nonhuman elements, it also results from the effects of confronting forces, which can have potentially disruptive impacts. The implication is that it is worth being careful about behaving correctly.

The spillover between moral and political behaviour is evident in the realm of ritual work, as can be seen by examining the administration of public life. Like elsewhere in the region, in San Mateo del Mar this involves two hierarchical systems of authority: civil (linked to national institutions) and religious (linked to the Catholic Church).[13] These authorities have common ritual obligations aimed at the reproduction of life in connection with aquatic manifestations (sea, rain, lagoons). The high point of this system falls before and after Holy Week, when, following special ritual techniques (Millán 2007: 139; Signorini 2008), the mayor and other civil authorities bring their offerings to the sea and the lagoons. The mayor's conduct and moral reputation in this context impact the fishing economy since he is seen here as more or less fit to rule the meteorological and ecological cycles of water exchange between the Ocean and the lagoons, and so to propitiate an abundant or poor rainy season (Tallè 2016: 235–236).

By contrast, in San Dionisio del Mar, the political and religious authorities are neatly separated. The religious field is in flux, with a high level of conversions from syncretic Catholicism to several variants of Protestantism (Montesi 2016: 125). However, among the rituals of the annual Catholic calendar, there is one that seems to be respected by everyone, and supported

---

11 The Spanish word was used while the narrator was speaking in *ombeayiüjts*.
12 In the version collected by Ramírez Castañeda (1987) in San Mateo del Mar, the orphan (*ndeaj*) was initially brought to Mexico City to be educated in Spanish schools.
13 This dual political system takes varied forms but is well-known in Americanist ethnology as the *cargo* system. See Pellotier, Dehouve, Hémond (2011) for a comparative review.

*Figure 3. The island of Cerro Cristo (Christ Mountain), a ritual place in the northern part of the Laguna Superior (picture by Caterina Morbiato).*

by the political authorities (whether they are Catholics or not): every Holy Week, the "Catholic Society"[14] organizes a sailing trip through the lagoons with the aim of reaching *Cerro Cristo* (Christ Mountain) in order to celebrate one day and one night of rainmaking rituals. The island of *Cerro Cristo* is the setting for the myth sketched above.[15]

Thus, as well as in the realm of mythology, it also seems that the co-agency between humans and nonhuman entities is at work in the rituals performed by political and/or religious authorities. Echoing the ethnographers cited above, we conclude that these specific rites performed in known places, and cosmologically located in the landscape, aim to maintain a delicate balance between excessive rain, abundant rain and scarce rain, a condition that is inherently unstable, ecologically, morally and politically.

## Disputing ethnic frontiers: Landscape or land?

On the basis of the ethnographic outline above, it could be said that for the Huave the political control of their 'dwelling space' has happened more

14  It is an unofficial association of people from the community who play ritual roles in the ceremonies and liturgies of the Catholic Church.
15  Francesco Zanotelli's fieldwork notes, August 2010, San Dionisio del Mar.

through the careful monitoring of the landscape and its morphogenetic cycles than through the control of land. In other words, although they have always had a 'landscape politics' played out in certain places through ritually caring for the cosmo-political (de la Cadena 2010) control of its metamorphosis, they have been much less effective in territorial politics, that is, the control of a portion of land within boundaries (Tallè 2016: 77–85). Such landscape politics is principally based on a way of appropriating the environment through the careful control of circumscribed places and waypoints, which is essential for the effectiveness of the walking practice of lagoon fishing.

Ingold has shown how this way of appropriation of the environment contrasts the great family of foraging economies with those practicing the exclusive ownership of a plot of land (such as a ranch), and shows how it has been the historic reason for countless disputes between hunting and gathering societies on the one hand and agricultural societies on the other (Ingold 1987: 130–164; 2000: 40–60). Such a dispute was the reason for the progressive taking of the Huave lands by the neighbouring Zapotecs and *mestizos* farmers, and for the long-standing agrarian conflicts that have plagued the region from the time of the Colony until today.[16] As the historical anthropologist Zárate Toledo has shown, it was precisely through the settlement mode of the *ranchos* operating in the pre- and post-revolutionary era, that agricultural penetration into Huave territory was made by some Zapotec villagers, and consolidated through land tenure rights (Zárate Toledo 2010: 262–269).

Within the colonial economic-political order and later with the formation of the Mexican Nation state, the conflictual land-tenure process went together with a process of naturalisation and ethnicisation that pitted the Huave people – 'underdeveloped' lagoon fishermen – on the one hand, against the Zapotec people – 'evolved' ranchers from inland – on the other. The *de facto* identification of the Huave with waterscapes – fluid, empty, open and fordable – and with lagoon fishing techniques requiring a high level of mobility through water, has gone together with a structural weakness of the Huave municipal boundaries. These have always been vulnerable to infiltration by Zapotec settlers (Castaneira 2008; Zárate Toledo 2010). It is important to stress how far the negative identification of the Huave with the waterscape has moulded their image in regional and national contexts. In fact, the term Huave seems to have been imposed by neighboring Zapotecs with the eloquent but derogatory meaning of 'people rotted by the water' (León 1904; Signorini 1979: 17–18). The exo-ethnonym is a reflection of what was perceived ethnocentrically as a misguided fishing practice, one

---

16  In the early Colony, the entire Isthmus of Tehuantepec was the private property of Hernán Cortés, who was gifted the *Hacienda del Marqués del Valle* by the Crown (Cuturi 2009, Machuca Gallegos 2001). Throughout Mexico, landlordism continued after independence (1821) and it was only with the Revolutionary process (1910–1917) that economic restructuring became thinkable. Agrarian reform from the 1930s onwards has served as a powerful means of national identity construction.

that did not require the art of navigation in open water, but that of walking in shallow waters like fords, shores and estuaries.[17]

Since the Huave municipalities' boundaries were defined after national independence at the end of the 19th century, this process of 'ethno-naturalisation' has continued and been accompanied by chronic agrarian conflicts. In the western part of the lagoon system, the municipal territory of San Mateo del Mar has suffered a steady erosion of its borders, a process legalised through various official decisions.[18] The beneficiary was the nearby pueblo of Santa Maria del Mar (*agencia municipal* of the Zapotec town of Juchitán de Zaragoza) to the east,[19] and to the west, the Zapotec municipality of San Pedro Huilotepec and the *ejído* of Boca del Río. In the eastern part of the lagoon area, the municipalities of San Dionisio del Mar and San Francisco del Mar also have a long history of conflict with the neighbouring Zapotec *rancherias* that caused an almost forced relocation of both villages. Between the 19th and 20th centuries they were relocated inland from their original isolated locations on the lagoon in order to maintain better control over disputed lands and are today known as San Dionisio Pueblo Nuevo and San Francisco Pueblo Nuevo (Zárate Toledo 2010).

By making a distinction between a landscape-based appropriation and a land-based one, between a 'landscape politics' and a land politics, we can better analyse this history of agrarian conflicts. Here, the degrees of trust and familiarity with the technologies of representing the earth (maps, cartography, etc.) as well as with each national bureaucratic regulation designed to objectify a customary law (Cuturi 1996), have played a fundamental role, from the Colonial period to well after national independence. In the case of San Francisco del Mar (the Huave municipality most known for its fertile lands), the rediscovery of the *título primordial* (primordial title) in the nineteen-seventies meant the legal recognition of their homelands, which halted the land dispossession they had suffered 50 years earlier, caused by the neighbouring Zapotec municipality of San Francisco Ixhuatán. In the case of San Mateo del Mar (the Huave municipality where lagoon fishing is by far the most dominant economic activity), the occupation of lands unfolded in a process of complete disregard for maps and documents: these were lost, counterfeited or never even submitted to the agrarian courts.

---

17 The terms *Ikoots* (in San Mateo del Mar and Santa Maria del Mar), *Ikojts* (in San Dioniso del Mar), *Konajts* (in San Francisco del Mar) (which means 'us', as inclusive form) are used as endo-ethnonyms starting from the nineties of the last century, as the result of a self-representation tending to free itself from a negative image (Tallè 2015: 393–403).

18 San Mateo del Mar was recognised as municipality by a decree of 1825. Due to recurrent agrarian disputes the Agrarian Court issued during the 20th century different *Resoluciones Precideciales* (in 1904, in 1945 and in 1984), that is official acts of recognition and titling of communal property, that changed the land endowment of the community of San Mateo del Mar.

19 The settlement of Santa Maria del Mar has an agrarian history that binds it jurisdictionally to the town of Juchitán since the end of 19th century (Zárate Toledo 2010).

Today, in San Mateo del Mar it is commonly held that the incapacity to defend ancestral lands in the past went hand in hand with the widespread ignorance of Spanish and illiteracy among the authorities of that time. Added to this, there is a perceived decline in the public morals of present-day authorities, viewed as ever ready to transform their turn at community service into robbery. All this is felt as a heavy historical loss that weighs more and more on the community, eroding conditions for continuing with their own form of life. In fact, land disputes with neighbouring communities are shrinking the fishing area more and more, resulting in a severe scarcity of land and undermining mobility through the lagoons. It is becoming increasingly clear to the new generation of agrarian authorities that defending and claiming rights to ancestral land is the inescapable condition for safeguarding the free movement of fishermen across the lagoons that is the very footing of 'landscape tenure'.

For this reason, indigenous place names turn out to be an unexpected political tool in territorial claims. In 2010 Cristiano Tallè was involved in writing an anthropological expert's report, based on a glossary of native place names, to be submitted to the local agrarian courts in order to resolve a dispute relating to a portion of border territory. Mexican legislation requires that native right to land be proven by exhibiting judicial evidence (artefacts, maps or traditional knowledge supported by anthropological expertise), and so the place names in *ombeayiüts* were recognised as the best evidence of the ancestral ties of the community with the disputed land. They were in the indigenous language and still in everyday use. Reflecting in such a transparent way the forms of landscape and waterscape and the movement of humans within them, they reveal in an immediate way that the appropriation of the environment is founded on the control of landscape. In fact, the place names mark crossing lines and waypoints, anchoring the right to mobility in the local landscape, however unstable. In the courts, however, where national and international laws oriented towards a productivist conception of land and work align indigenous land tenure with the legal and policy standards of Western law (Povinelli 1995), these waypoints can easily turn into border-points.

## A new frontier of dispute: Eolian energy and the aero-scape

In the following, we try to demonstrate that a similar reduction of the idea of landscape to one of land and territory is also at work in current disputes over the aero-scape. This perspective will serve to better understand the strong local resistance to the installation of wind farms. In the Isthmus of Tehuantepec, opposition to wind power projects has grown in the last decade. Those in favour have been a network of transnational and national actors like the Inter-American Fund for Development (a regional commission of the World Bank), the Mexican government, the Oaxaca state governor and, at the local level, a variable number of administrative authorities and inhabitants affiliated to them, attracted by the potential for financial compensation – or, to go with local gossip, by bribes.[20] On the other side, against the proposals are many different actors united by discontent with how the sustainable energy industry has been brought to the region: individual farmers who want to annul the rental contracts previously signed by intermediaries for the power companies; whole communities opposed to the exploratory surveys carried out by technicians (the municipalities of Álvaro Obregón and San Mateo del Mar), or who have cancelled previously granted permits (San Dionisio del Mar); organised movements with anti-capitalist and neo-zapatista leanings such as the *Asamblea de los pueblos indígenas del Istmo en defensa de la tierra y el territorio* (APIIDTT), based in Juchitán.

There are two related explanations for the intense development of wind parks here, amongst the highest in the world as reported by the NREL.[21] The first is technical: the wind on the Pacific side of the Isthmus is constant all year round, and from November to February has a power rating equivalent to the force of off-shore wind. The second is linked to the shift in Mexico towards the use of renewable energy. On a legal level, we are also seeing public energy production being transformed into a system contracted out by the state to private multinational companies (Boyer 2014; Howe et al. 2015: 99). Both public and private institutional actors view the wind, and the territories that it passes through, as a quantifiable resource that can be converted into money. This point of view reveals the intimately neoliberal matrix they embody, which according to Pellizzoni (2015: 19), is based on the ability to stimulate competition and to create new goods for new markets. The peculiarity of new goods in a neoliberal economy is that they concurrently take on the function of new exchange values. This also applies in this case: the wind is a material good which, thanks to the industrial process, is converted into a kind of commodity (energy) to buy and sell, but it is also a medium of financial exchange through an emerging international system of free carbon market emissions. The final effect is the 'financialisation of landscape'.

Importantly, this neoliberal system can transform the landscape, the shared experience of living beings as we have defined it, into a commodity to be exploited by the few. Furthermore, the renewability of these kinds of meteorological resources is compromised by the fact that the industry needs to preserve some of the land and some parts of the landscape by occupying them. In the Isthmus, the wind resource is abundant and technically cheap to extract. This makes the level of occupation so aggressive that instead of

20  The case is reported extensively in national press, especially during 2012, when the conflict arose explicitly. See for instance *La Jornada*, 8/9/2012, *Denuncian comuneros ikoots amenazas del gobernador de Oaxaca, Gabino Cue*; *La Jornada*, 12/15/2012, *Empresas eólicas y derechos de los pueblos en el Istmo de Tehuantepec*; *La Jornada*, 1/9/2014, *Muerto proyecto eólico en San Dionisio, Oaxaca*.

21  This report, authored by the National Renewable Energy Laboratory, was originally promoted by the United States Agency for International Development (USAID) on the request of the Mexican government, and distributed by the U.S. Department of Energy, Office of Scientific and Technical Information. See National Renewable Energy Laboratory (NREL), 2003, *Wind energy resource atlas of Oaxaca*, report accessed on-line the 28 of May 2017 from: www.nrel.gov/docs/fy04-osti/35575.pdf

Figure 4. Map of the location of wind farms and mining concessions in the Isthmus of Tehuantepec (picture by www.geocomunes.org).

land grabbing it is possible to talk of massive scale 'landscape grabbing'. This is visible in how wind power companies on the Mexican isthmus have divided the space not only into plots of land but also into areas of air space corresponding to groups of turbines owned by multiple transnationals. In this context, the concept of ethnography of the atmosphere is useful or, to use Cymene Howe's (2015) language, we can talk about an anthropology of life above earth:

> Life Above Earth cannot simply suggest air, sky, and space as new ethnographic opportunities; it must instead indicate how lives and materialities in these suspensions represent specific forms of human and non-human being. It is to see these spaces [...] as constitutive, not simply as contextual (ibid.: 206).

This helps understand why opposition has grown in the last two decades as wind farms have been installed, especially in the inland territories inhabited by the Zapotecs. Stated reasons for the protests have included, firstly, fear of damage by the wind turbines to animals (cattle who no longer produce milk, interference in the migratory routes of birds) and to the land (pollution caused by the leakage of lubricants from the turbine motors, contamination of mangroves); secondly, farmers' difficulties in accessing their land, and an increasing sense of encirclement by wind-turbines in close proximity to settlements (Dunlap 2017); thirdly, lack of adequate information about, and dissatisfaction with, the agreed economic terms, which give land owners only paltry compensation for the sale of their land (Manzo 2011, Nahmad et al. 2014). Last but not least, some inhabitants have criticised the loud and persistent noise pollution produced by the turbines, and the visual obstruction, perceptible dozens of miles away, in the flat land-sea-scape.

One project in particular, the *San Dionisio* Wind farm, prompted great opposition. We will look at this briefly here as it highlights the struggle over the political dimension of the landscape.

The project was initially put forward by another company with mostly Spanish capital, but subsequently passed to a multinational company with Australian and Dutch capital, thanks to Mexican intermediaries. The project was supposed to become operative in 2011, with 102 wind turbines situated along the *barra de Santa Teresa*, a narrow sandy peninsula located in the centre of *Laguna Superior*, in the municipal territory of San Dionisio del Mar; another 30 wind turbines were to be located along the *Barra Tileme*, in a territory disputed by the communal land owners of Santa Maria del Mar and by their neighbours of San Mateo del Mar.

We believe that the key to understanding the opposition has to do with territorial sovereignty, or rather the legitimacy of those who should be responsible for the decisions regarding it. However, from the local point of view that anthropology is interested in, the concept of sovereignty cannot be reduced to an exclusive right over land. In fact, as we have argued above, lagoons and borders between communities are constantly disputed, and when we consider the tenuous link between sovereignty and atmosphere, the case is even stronger.

Until 2012, the people of San Dionisio del Mar were quite unaware and rather unconcerned about the wind farm project (Zanotelli 2016: 168–169). They were doubtful about the intention of the multinational to create it, and some of them considered wind energy to be a resource 'high up' enough not to disturb their ordinary life.[22] In that sense, it could be shared, but only under some conditions.

By the beginning of 2012, the situation had completely changed and tension was very high. In January the mayor, a member of the PRI (*Partido de la Revolución Institucional*), signed a new contract with the wind power company, giving them a thirty year permit to use the land for the installation of wind turbines. This agreement was communicated to locals at a meeting, where people expressed strong dissatisfaction with the decision, considered an affront to the community. There was fear about the possible consequences for the delicate lagoon ecosystem because, in the period from 2010 to 2012, local inhabitants had been informed about it at meetings organised by the neo-zapatista APIIDTT. Here people learned that, in addition to the wind turbines, there was a plan to build several pier moorings in proximity to some shrimp farms, as well as to install a large underwater cable. The construction work would certainly disturb the lagoon currents, and the lighting on the wind turbines could potentially frighten away the fish. The heavy cement foundations on which the wind turbines were to stand could impede the interflow of waters between the lagoons separated by the peninsula. Following an announcement by the civil authority, a resistance group occupied the town hall and the mayor was forced to flee, making him unable to continue with the agreement made with the company. In the months that followed, the members of the Assembly and the APIIDTT activists had to face the organised violence of groups ready to destroy any resistance to the project.

The events that followed were favorable to the Assembly resistance group. In 2013, a legal action filed by some dwellers was upheld by the judge in Salina Cruz who called for the immediate suspension of any activities related to the wind farm project until wider investigations had taken place.[23] Those who brought the case had appealed to treaty 169 of the International Labour Organization (ILO) regarding the rights of indigenous peoples to give their prior and informed consent to any actions implemented in their territory. In the ruling, the judge recommended that a popular consultation should take place at the end of this process. In the face of legal opposition, the company decided to abandon the project and move its investments to the nearby municipality of Juchitán de Zaragoza.

To understand the level of opposition, it is necessary to raise the socio-political analysis from the level of specific complaints to a much wider concern, namely that the wind farm might completely compromise the ecosystem and the local economy, based as it is on the commercial sale of fish and on subsistence fishing (Castaneira 2008: 67–86): "[...] la laguna nos da de comer" (the lagoon feeds us), claimed a woman from San Dionisio.

22  Francesco Zanotelli's fieldnotes collected in San Dionisio del Mar in 2009, 2010.
23  Source: http://www.noticiasaliadas.org/articles.asp?art=6907, accessed on the internet the 11/16/2013.

In conclusion, there are at least two aspects which define the sovereignty of the Huave and the Zapotecs who live in the lagoon context: on the political side, these peoples do not agree to give up the rights to their land and their territory to others who want to take possession of it (Howe et al. 2015: 108). On the economic side, sovereignty includes the whole lagoon system, which for them represents an environmental continuum and guarantees the existence and survival of future generations.

A further and deeper implication is the cosmo-political dimension of the conflict which cannot be ignored. As we have shown, meteorology and the productivity of fishing and crops are materially connected, but locally they are further related to a moral dimension. The common sense of the locals is full of moral judgements that connect human behaviour with the non-human agency of lightning, southern and northern winds, and clouds. It is precisely in this elaborate moral economy that an external element, the turbines, is a threat that could affect the most intimate elements lives of the indigenous people: the aero-scape and the water-scape. The concept of sacred places sometimes used by the companies in order to show respect for the indigenous culture (for example avoiding to install the turbines in *Cerro Cristo*),[24] is very revealing in this sense: it shows that they have misconceived the local sense of place, which is the idea that places are not unrelated, stable and unique locations, but the variable materialisation of the co-animation between humans and not-humans. If some specific places are in some sense 'sacred', or rather, are part of local ritual practices and mythological narratives, it is because they are inserted into a wider conception of relatedness among meteorological, aquatic and terrestrial activity, as we have shown.

## Concluding remarks

We started by considering how, given the rapid and radical metamorphosis of local landscapes caused by inclusion in the technological framework of late neoliberal industrialization, the almost apolitical phenomenological concept of landscape, as outlined by Ingold, needs to be more politically oriented. From our point of view, the phenomenological approach needs to be integrated with a multilevel analysis covering both native cosmologies and a historical analysis of territorial conflicts, within a political-economic frame in which the various participants (local communities, movements, institutions, transnational corporations) move along different scales. Expanded so far, the phenomenological approach can be a powerful heuristic device to explore the political, economic and existential dimensions that landscape embodies.

---

24 It is one of the responses that the multinational used to contrast the accusation of being disrespectful of the local knowledge carried by the social movement against the wind farms. The other was to contract an anthropologist to recollect huave legends published in an instant book that was circulating in the locality at the time of our investigation. Zanotelli's fieldnotes, San Dionisio del Mar, 2010.

Starting from the analysis of the Huave conception of the landscape combined with the forms of resistance taking place around the area, we make some concluding remarks. The political dimension of the Huave landscape is deeply rooted in body techniques and practices, as well as in linguistic code, in mythology and ritual, as well as in the historic memory of interethnic territorial conflicts. This dimension remains largely implicit in the public sphere of the eolian conflict, perhaps a plane of "cultural intimacy" (Herzfeld 1997). Nevertheless, in order to understand the resistance of the indigenous population towards the reduction of the landscape to a space of massive extraction, it is a core dimension. The conflict around the wind farms cannot be reduced to a process of negotiation or appropriation of resources, rather, it involves an entire form of life.

Our analysis reveals the appearance of two new frontiers of neoliberal exploitation in the long history of agrarian conflicts in the region. The first is sustainable energy, which reduces the wind to an energy resource that can be extracted and marketed for private purposes (Boyer 2014); the second is the massive technological occupation of the landscape by particularly invasive alien objects. In this framework, the grand-scale exploitation of renewable energy resources takes on the characteristic of 'landscape grabbing', which proves to be unsustainable in an unexpected way. Within the indigenous cosmology, the radical and irreversible transformation of the local landscape that the installation of more than one-hundred wind turbines could provoke, seems to make concrete all their unsustainability.

According to many testimonies collected in San Mateo del Mar, the wind turbines are described as *nendalalüy* (twirling objects), which is the same word that defines the domestic fan, from which it differs only by its giant size. Another word that is used to describe them is *najal tarrap owix manchiük nendalalüy* (high and wide twirling iron arms/high iron fan). Another fairly common term defines them as *nepal iünd* (that which stops the north wind), and other similar variations on the theme (e.g. *najal oleaj manchiük nepal iünd* /very high iron wind barrier/). All these terms attempt to describe technological objects that are quite mysterious from the local point of view. They are emphasising the turbines' agency over the wind and not vice versa: they are colossal objects that move the wind, like a fan does, or they block its flow. Interfering with the biggest metamorphic agents of local landscape – the blowing of *teat iünd* (father northern wind) or the currents of the *nadam nangaj ndek* (great sacred sea-lagoon/ocean) – these machines seem to be able to subvert the 'hierarchy of agency' between elements, cosmologically rooted at the core of indigenous political practice and ideology.[25]

On the other hand, their gigantic presence, while transfiguring the local landscape, goes with a massive occupation of land, and could impede the free mobility, so constitutive of the Huave experience of the environment.[26]

---

25 Cristiano Tallè's fieldwork notes, San Mateo del Mar, 2013, 2016. This analysis was presented for the first time by Tallè at the *Living Environments and Imagined Environments. New Challenges for Anthropology* IV Biennial Conference of ANUAC (November 5–8, 2015, Free University of Bolzano, Italy).

26 The research of Dunlap (2017), conducted in the Zapotec municipality of La Ventosa where a huge windpark have been already installed, shows some outcomes

*Figure 5. Wind turbines on the horizon from the Laguna Inferior (Picture by Cristiano Tallè).*

A further upshot of our analysis is the redefinition of the concept of sovereignty and self-determination. The case examined here suggests that these concepts, usually restricted to land and territory, should be applied at an enlarged scale, including the landscape and the web of relations among humans and nonhumans that it implies. Without doubt, paying attention to the atmospheric level, as well as to the terrestrial and aquatic levels, allows us to highlight this dimension of sovereignty that has been so little explored up to now.

Considering that the waterscape is where fish and shrimps breed, and where humans earn a livelihood, and considering that reproducing the waterscape depends fundamentally on the aero-agents, from the Huave point of view, reproducing this entanglement between waterscape, aeroscape and fishing practice, corresponds to what more abstractly is thought of as sustainability.[27]

that are predictive for the Huave case, even if in the lagoon environment the consequences could be even more disruptive.

27 The *ombeayiüts* of San Mateo del Mar can well capture the concept of 'sustainability' through the concept of *monapaküy*, which can be translated as 'life and health' or 'healthy life'. *Monapaküy* is the condition of a delicate balance between meteorological and water agents that must be preserved at all costs, and it can refer to any living being, human and non-human. In fact, during the procession held on the shore after Holy Week, the mayor begs the meteorological agents for *monapaküy*.

We can say, therefore, that the landscape continues to be at the core of the political concerns of the Huave people. In fact, increasingly landscape is a major reason for conflict in the region, since even its most immaterial dimension (as wind) it enters into the sphere of interest of a neoliberal political economy. In our view, it is precisely on this latter point that the sustainability of the industrial conversion to 'green energy' implemented in the region reveals a clear limit (Zanotelli 2014).

In fact, the case-study that we have summarised here shows the unsustainability of such a grand-scale exploitation of wind energy, since it reduces the landscape to a space of massive extraction, treating wind (an indivisible and intangible subject) as a quantitative and divisible resource. For those people for whom the wind, like other landscape agents, is a social actor in the continuation of their way of life, all this is a threat to their sovereignty and even more to their existence.

# References

Albert, Bruce 2004. Territorialidad, etnopolítica y desarrollo: A propósito del movimiento indígena en la amazonía brasileña. In Alexandre Surralés and Pedro García Hierro (eds), *Tierra adentro: Territorio indígena y percepción del entorno.* Copenhagen: IWGIA.

Bartra, Armando 1979. *La explotación del trabajo campesino por el capital.* Mexico City: Macehual.

Bartra, Roger 1974. *Estructura agraria y clases sociales en México.* Mexico City: Editorial Era.

Bartolomé, Miguel Ángel 1997. *Gente de costumbre y gente de razón: Las identidades étnicas en México.* Mexico City: INI–Siglo XXI editores.

Basso, Keith H. 1996. *Wisdom sits in places: Landscape and language among the Western Apache.* Albuquerque: University of New Mexico Press.

Boyer, Dominic 2014. Energopower: An introduction. *Anthropological Quarterly* 86 (1): 1–37.

Burguete Cal y Mayor, Araceli 2010. Autonomía: la emergencia de un nuevo paradigma en las luchas por la descolonización en América Latina. In Miguel González, Araceli Burguete Cal y Mayor and Pablo Ortiz-T. (eds), *La autonomía a debate: Autogobierno indígena y estado plurinacional en América Latina.* Quito: Flacso Ecuador.

Castaneira, Alejandro 2008. *La ruta mareña: Los huaves en la costa del Istmo Sur de Tehuantepec, Oaxaca (siglo XIII–XXI). Territorios fluidos, adaptación ecológica, división del trabajo, jerarquizaciones interétnicas y geopolítica huave-zapoteca.* Tesis de doctorado en Ciencias Antropológicas, Mexico City: UAM Iztapalapa.

Conklin, Beth A. and Laura R. Graham 1995. The shifting middle ground: Amazonian indians and eco-politics. *American Anthropologist* 97 (4): 695–710.

Cuturi, Flavia 1996. Messico: dall'immaginario dello stato all'ecumenismo indigeno. In Pietro Scarduelli (ed.), *Stati, Etnie, Culture.* Milano: Edizioni Guerini e Associati.

Cuturi, Flavia 2003a. *Juan Olivares: Un pescatore scrittore del Messico indigeno.* Roma: Meltemi.

Cuturi, Flavia 2003b. El aparecer del paisaje en la textualidad del tejido huave. In Davide Domenici, Carolina Orsini and Sofia Venturoli (eds), *Il sacro e il paesaggio nell'America indigena.* Bologna: CLUEB.

Cuturi, Flavia 2009. *Africanos e indígenas en el Istmo de Tehuantepec colonial ¿Un mestizaje olvidado o no reconocido?*, unpublished paper, 53° Congreso Internacional de Americanistas, Mexico City, 19-24 July.

de la Cadena, Marisol 2010. Indigenous cosmopolitics in the Andes: Conceptual reflections beyond 'politics'. *Cultural Anthropology* 25 (2): 334-370.

de la Peña, Guillermo 1995. La ciudadanía étnica y la construcción de los indios en el México contemporáneo. *Revista Internacional de Filosofía Política* 6: 116-140.

Dunlap, Alexander 2017. 'The town is surrounded': From climate concerns to life under wind turbines in La Ventosa, Mexico. *Human Geography* 10 (2): 16-36.

Escobar, Arturo and Alvarez, Sonia A. (eds) 1992. *The making of social movements in Latin America: Identity, strategy, and democracy.* Boulder: Westview Press.

Feld, Steven and Keith H. Basso (eds) 1996. *Senses of place.* Santa Fe, New Mexico: School of American Research Press.

Gibson, James J. 1979. *The ecological approach to visual perception.* Boston: Houghton Mifflin.

Herzfeld, Michael 1997. *Cultural Intimacy: Social poetics in the nation-state.* London: Routledge.

Hirsch, Eric and Michael O'Hanlon (eds) 1995. *The anthropology of landscape: Perspectives on place and space.* Oxford: Oxford University Press.

Howe, Cymene 2015. Life above earth: An introduction. *Cultural Anthropology*, 30 (2): 203-209.

Howe, Cymene, Dominic Boyer and Edith Barrera 2015. *Wind at the margins of the state: Autonomy and renewable energy development in Southern Mexico.* In John-Andrew McNeish, Axel Borchgrevink and Owen Logan (eds), *Contested powers: The politics of energy and development in Latin America.* London: Zed Books.

Ingold, Tim 1987. *The appropriation of nature: Essays on human ecology and social relations.* Iowa City: University of Iowa Press.

Ingold, Tim 2000. *The perception of environment: Essays on livelihood, dwelling and skill.* New York: Routledge.

Ingold, Tim 2007. Earth, sky, wind, and weather. *Journal of the Royal Anthropological Institute*, 13(s1): 19-38.

León, Nicolas 1904. *Catálogo de la colección de antigüedades huavis del Estado de Oaxaca, existente en el Museo Nacional de México.* Mexico City: Imprenta del Museo Nacional.

Lupo, Alessandro 1997. El monte de vientre blando. La concepción de la montaña en un pueblo de pescadores: los huaves del Istmo de Tehuantepec. *Cuadernos del Sur* 11: 67-77.

Lupo, Alessandro 2015. La serpiente sobre la mesa: Autoridad y control de la lluvia en una narración oral huave (México). *ANUAC* 4 (1): 88-123.

Machuca Gallegos, Laura 2001. *El Marquesado del Valle en Tehuantepec, México (1522-1563).* Lima: Pontificia Universidad Católica del Perú.

Manzo Carlos 2011. *Comunalidad, resistencia indígena y neocolonialismo en el Istmo de Tehuantepec, siglos XVI-XXI*, México City: Ce-Acatl.

Millán, Saul 2003. *La comunidad sin límites: Estructura social y organización comunitaria en las regiones indígenas de México.* Mexico City: INI.

Millán, Saul 2007. *El cuerpo de la nube: Jerarquía y simbolismo ritual en la cosmovisión de un pueblo huave.* Mexico City: INAH.

Montesi, Laura 2016. Vivir en (dis)continuidad: Reconfiguración de subjetividades religiosas en una comunidad ikojts de Oaxaca. *Desacatos* 50: 122-137. http://www.redalyc.org/articulo.oa?id=13943562009.

Nahmad, Salomon, Abraham Nahon and Ruben Langlé (eds) 2014. *La visión de los actores sociales frente a los proyectos eólicos del Istmo de Tehuantepec.* Mexico City: Consejo Nacional de Ciencia y Tecnología.

Pacheco de Oliveira, Joao 1998. Uma etnologia dos "índios misturados"? Situação colonial, territorialização e fluxos culturais. *Mana* 4 (1): 47–77.

Pellizzoni, Luigi 2015. *Ontological politics in a disposable world: The new mastery of nature.* Farnham: Ashgate.

Pellotier, Victor Franco, Daniele Dehouve and Aline Hémond (eds) 2011. *Formas de voto, prácticas de las asambleas y toma de decisiones: Un acercamiento comparativo.* Mexico City: Ediciones de la Casa Chata.

Povinelli, Elizabeth A. 1995. Do rocks listen? The cultural politics of apprehending Australian aboriginal labor. *American Anthropologist* 97 (3): 505–518.

Ramírez Castañeda, Elisa 1987. *El fin de los montiocs: Tradición oral de los Huaves de San Mateo del Mar, Oaxaca.* Mexico City: INAH.

Redfield, Robert 1956. *The Little Community and Peasant Society and Culture.* Chicago: University Chicago Press.

Signorini, Italo (ed.) 1979. *Gente di laguna: Ideologia e istituzioni sociali dei Huave di San Mateo del Mar.* Milano: Franco Angeli editore.

Signorini, Italo 2008. Rito y mito como instrumentos de previsión y manipulación del clima entre los huaves de San Mateo del Mar (Oaxaca, México). In AnnaMaria Lammel, Marina Goloubinoff and Esther Katz (eds), *Aire y Lluvias: Antropología del clima en México.* Mexico City: Centro de Estudios Mexicanos y Centroamericanos.

Scott, James 1976. *The Moral Economy of the Peasant: Rebellion and Subsistence in Southeast Asia.* New Haven: Yale University Press.

Stavenhagen, Rodolfo 1969. *Las clases sociales en las sociedades agrarias.* Mexico City: Siglo XXI.

Surralés, Alexandre and García Hierro, Pedro (eds) 2004. *Tierra adentro: Territorio indígena y percepción del entorno.* Copenhagen: IWGIA.

Tallè, Cristiano 2015. La gramática de la identidad: La escuela bilingüe, los maestros y el "rescate" de la identidad en San Mateo del Mar (Oaxaca, México). *ANUAC* 4 (2): 157–188.

Tallè, Cristiano 2016. *Sentieri di parole: Lingua, paesaggio e senso del luogo in una comunità indigena di pescatori nel Messico del sud.* Firenze: SEID.

Tallè, Cristiano 2017. L'anatomia del paesaggio fuor di metafora: L'uso dei termini anatomici negli enunciati locativi in ombeayiüts (Oaxaca, Messico). *Lares* 2: 235–268.

Tranfo, Luigi 1979. Tono e nagual. In Italo Signorini (ed.), *Gente di laguna: Ideologia e istituzioni sociali dei Huave di San Mateo del Mar.* Milano: Franco Angeli editore.

Tsing, Anna L. 2005. *Friction: An ethnography of global connection.* Princeton: Princeton University Press.

Turner, Terence 2000. Indigenous rights, indigenous cultures and environmental conservation: convergence or divergence? The case of Brazilian Kayapó. In Jill Conway, Kenneth Kenniston and Leo Marx (eds), *Earth, air, fire and water.* Cambridge: University of Massachusetts Press.

Venturoli, Sofia and Francesco Zanotelli 2013. Inacabadas: Etnicidad y ciudadanías sustantivas en México y Perú. In Lobato Mirta and Venturoli Sofia (eds), *Formas de Ciudadania en America Latina.* AHILA. Madrid: Iberoamericana/Vervuert.

Warkentin, Milton and Juan Olivares 1947. The holy bells and other Huave legends. *Tlalocan* 2 (3): 223–234.

Warman, Arturo 1980. *Ensayo sobre el campesinado en México.* Mexico City: Nueva Imagen.

Zanotelli, Francesco 2014. Green Economy. *AM. Rivista di Antropologia Museale* 34/36: 86–88.

Zanotelli, Francesco 2016. Il vento (in)sostenibile: Energie rinnovabili, politica e ontologia nell'Istmo di Tehuantepec, Messico. *ANUAC* 5 (2): 159–194.

Zárate Toledo, Ezequiel 2010. La territorialización entre mareños y zapotecos en el sistema lagunario del sur del istmo de Tehuantepec. In Salomon Nahmad Sittón, Margarita Dalton and Abraham Nahón (eds), *Aproximaciones a la región del Istmo. Diversidad multiétnica y socioeconómica en una región estratégica para el país.* Oaxaca: CIESAS, Secretaría de las Culturas y las Artes de Oaxaca del Gobierno del Estado de Oaxaca, CONACULTA.

Zizumbo Villareal, Daniel and Patricia Colunga García 1982. *Los Huaves: La apropiación de los recursos naturales.* Mexico City: Universidad Autónoma de Chapingo.

Tiina Järvi
https://orcid.org/0000-0002-3508-9389

# Marking landscape, claiming belonging: The building of a Jewish homeland in Israel/Palestine

In northern Israel, near the coastal city of Haifa, lies the Mount Carmel National Park. Within its territories one can find forests, historical sites, hiking routes and picnic areas. There is also a pine forest known as Little Switzerland because the landscape it forms resembles those of the mountainous Alpine country. When we drove the serpentine roads to reach the beginning of the hiking trail in summer 2016, the signs of a forest fire that had destroyed large parts of the said pine forests in 2010 were still very much present in the landscape, notwithstanding that the burned areas have been undergoing reforestation by the Jewish National Fund (JNF), an organization that manages many of the Israeli natural reserves. Forest fires are a common, almost a yearly occurrence in the pine forests of Israel/Palestine, as pines are not well-adjusted to the hot and dry summers of the region. The tree was imported from Europe in the early twentieth century by Zionist settlers, and planted across wide areas, nowadays known as the 'green lungs' of Israel. The fast-growing pine trees in Mount Carmel were planted by the JNF in 1948 on top of the ruins of the Palestinian villages Ijzim, Umm al-Zinat and Khubbaza, which had been destroyed earlier the same year.

The case of Mount Carmel National Park illustrates how Israel has altered the landscapes here, obscuring the history of the Palestinian presence on the landscape. In 1947 and 1948, almost 800,000 Palestinians were forced to flee from their homes and turned into refugees or internally displaced people, after over 500 Palestinian villages and eleven urban neighbourhoods were emptied, and as their Palestinian inhabitants fled the violence of Zionist paramilitary forces (Masalha 2012: 3; Pappé 2006). Later, the depopulated Palestinian villages were either bulldozed to prevent Palestinians from returning or, in a few cases, renamed and repopulated with Jewish immigrants. Some of the ruined villages were covered with forests, as in Mount Carmel, and thus any traces of them hidden from view. Palestinians know the events of 1948 as *al-Nakba*, a catastrophe.

In this chapter, I scrutinise how Israel has worked with the landscapes of Israel/Palestine in order to hide its Palestinian history – and to enable the rooting of an Israeli settler nation. I do this by theorising the processes with Mitch Rose's (2012) idea of marking and claiming. In an article titled 'Dwelling as marking and claiming', published in the journal *Environment and Planning D: Society and Space*, Rose introduces a way to approach world-building by reinterpreting Heidegger's notion of dwelling and being-in-the-world. For Rose, marking constitutes a claim of ownership, not necessarily in a concrete sense, but as a way of building a world in a manner that makes it possible to belong, and landscape is one of the mediums through with such claims are made. Rose concentrates on the philosophical demonstration of what marking and claiming are, and explains it as Dasein's way of building its own world (Rose 2012: 763–766). Here, however, my aim is to adapt his idea to analyse the concrete dimension of Israel's practices to build belonging in the context of settler colonialist nation building. I hope to highlight that transformation of landscapes through marking is not practised only by individuals who hope to belong, but also by states and other institutional actors, which makes it a highly political practice penetrated by power hierarchies.

I ground Rose's notion of dwelling by contemplating it together with Tim Ingold's (2000) idea of landscape as the carrier of the dwelling of former generations. The layers of dwelling present in the landscape make it clear that marking and claiming are not only spatial but also temporal, as the pre-existing world carries markings to which new claims of belonging need to be related. This approach allows me to consider the destruction of Palestinian dwellings as a ground on which Israeli Jewish claims for belonging are built. In the first part of the chapter, I describe how the signs of past dwelling have been eradicated from the landscapes of Israel/Palestine, after which I proceed to address how marking and claiming have taken place by giving examples from afforestation and archaeology. I concentrate on these two cases because they have reordered the landscapes in a manner that has materialised the narratives embedded in Zionist imagery. They function on two different levels that are both crucially involved in materially marking the landscapes as solely Israeli Jewish. On the one hand, planting forests on the ruins of destroyed Palestinian villages is obscuring markings left by Palestinian dwelling, while on the other, it is realising the Zionists' modernist vision of making the desert bloom. Archaeology, in turn, has created sites that legitimise Israeli-Jewish belonging by marking landscapes with ancient histories of Jewishness. It has been utilised in building evidence of Jewish rootedness and indigenousness. Simultaneously, findings that indicate the historical presence of other people are disregarded and even erased, which highlights how archaeology in Israel has been highly politicised to serve the settlers' nationalist aims.

The paper is largely based on several short visits to Israel/Palestine from 2008 to the present and on two-month long fieldwork conducted in 2016. During these visits, my own perceptions on the landscapes of Israel/Palestine, both inside the 1948 borders[1] and in occupied West Bank, changed as my knowledge of the history and political conditions increased. When I travelled to Israel/Palestine the first time in 2008, the history of Palestinian

---

1    1948 borders refer to the borders that were enforced after the war between Israel and coalition of Arab states in 1948 and which currently form the internationally recognised borders of Israel.

dwelling was not part of the landscapes I witnessed within the 1948 borders, as I was not familiar then with the dispossession of Palestinians that had taken place in 1948. Only after learning more about the history of the settler colonialism and ethnic cleansing that define the founding of Israel did, I start to see the traces of absence on the landscapes. These observations form the basis of this chapter. Yet, the aim is not to expose new forms of landscape practices that the state of Israel has utilised to create belonging. Rather, I contemplate the specific means that have been used in marking the landscapes by the state of Israel and other actors, and how these uphold Israeli Jewish belonging.

## Marking and claiming in a context of a settler nation

The creation of and belonging to the Jewish homeland are processes that have been studied from numerous perspectives, such as nation-building, Zionist ideology, history, identity politics and territoriality (e.g. Sternhell 1998; Yiftachel 2006; Piterberg 2008; Fields 2012; Sand 2012). This extensive literature includes many insightful and sophisticated pieces on the landscapes of Israel/Palestine (see e.g. Falah 1996; Benvenisti 2000; Azaryahu and Golan 2004; Braverman 2009; Long 2009; Grunebaum 2014), many of which are written by geographers. Among anthropologists, Susan Slyomovics (1998) has discussed the national importance of landscapes of Israel/Palestine and the changes that have taken place in them, though she does not concentrate on landscape per se. Emily McKee (2014), meanwhile, has written about the present-day Nagab/Negev desert and how landscape has become a site of struggle between the local Bedouin and the Israeli state, and how visibility in a landscape is one of the strategies used by the Bedouin. Also, the metaphorical importance of landscapes for building the identity of the Israeli nation has been contemplated by Tom Selwyn (1995), but what is absent in his account is the recognition that the Israeli Jewish landscapes are built on destroyed Palestinian ones. His emphasis on the multiplicity of Zionist discourses fails to acknowledge the material reality that was, in fact, created after the establishment of the state. My aim is to concentrate precisely on that by scrutinising the material landscapes as an important dimension of settler colonial nation-building. Settler colonial framing has gained prominence in research on Israel/Palestine, and here I bring landscape into those discussions by focusing on the ways the landscapes have been altered, or even manufactured, with the aim to legitimate the settlers' arrival and sense of belonging.

In theorising the role landscape practices have played in settler colonial nation-building, I found useful Rose's (2012) article discussing marking and claiming. In 'Dwelling as marking and claiming', Rose introduces an argument that dwelling, which takes material form through building, can be considered a way of marking the world as one's own. I apply this idea in demonstrating how material sites in the case of Israel/Palestine function as markings, as described by Rose, and are used by the Israeli state in claiming the land. Rose's idea of dwelling as marking and claiming has been cited to some extent (e.g. Pyyry 2016; Whyte 2015), but it has been hardly used in empirical analysis (see however Schelly 2014), even less in research focused on institutional actors and power-saturated contexts such as Israel/Palestine. Rose has even been criticised for a lack of political perspective (van Dyke 2013), but I believe that when adapted to other than individual actions, it is possible to overcome such shortcomings. Interestingly, Israel/Palestine seems to present an example par excellence of how ownership is declared through markings in a state context.

In fact, in Israel/Palestine, struggle over land is part of everyday reality, both within the 1948 borders and in the occupied territories. In the occupied West Bank, land confiscation for settlements and 'military purposes' is commonplace especially in Area C.[2] Within the internationally recognised borders of Israel, on the other hand, Bedouin in Naqab/Negev desert face the constant threat of dispossession as their villages are repeatedly demolished and sometimes transformed into Jewish settlements or recreational areas. In this reality, claiming ownership gains prominence: when the settler nation needs to both justify conquest and make it visible, and help its people to connect with the acquired lands, marking in Rose's sense is practised on a daily basis, for instance by setting up flags, signs and buildings and by embedding the materiality with narratives that manifest belonging. These material signs make control over the land(scape) visible, as through building, landscapes are 'marked out' by mortals (i.e. human beings) who seek to claim ownership of a pre-existing world they are thrown into (Rose 2012: 759). Building is always initiated in a world that precedes us and that is constantly in motion, and it is thus inevitably not only historical and temporal but also finite practice. Highlighting both the temporal and spatial nature of marking and claiming, Rose (ibid.) summarises:

> To dwell is not only to build the world we are always already within but also to build it in a manner that makes it visible to ourselves and other beings from a distance. Dwelling, as building, is (in short) to mark and claim. While it is the world that delivers mortals to a particular situation, it is mortals who mark and claim it as their own.

In this it becomes clear that for Rose marking is not a form of intentional world building, but rather, it is part of every mortal's being-in-the-world. In his conceptualisation, building is thus something that is part of being itself, rather than something that one chooses to do or not to do. By engaging in marking, one is trying to make a place for oneself as a being, someone who is thrown into a world made up of already established connections and understandings. Marking and claiming is thus a way of confronting one's 'out-of-placeness' through trying to appropriate the world one dwells in.

---

2   In the Oslo II Accord (1995) occupied areas were divided to three zones: A, B, and C. According to the agreement, Area A is under full Palestinian control, Area B under Palestinian civil administration but Israeli military control, and Area C under full Israeli control. Roughly speaking, major cities in West Bank form Area A whereas villages and agricultural lands fall under Areas B and C.

Though Rose looks at marking and claiming through Dasein's[3] way of existing in the world through building, I consider it important to note that world-building can never be a solely individual practice as the existing ordering of the world and the power relations in it direct the forms that any individual marking and claiming can take. Especially when one considers the markings present in a landscape, it is apparent that in building them, states, companies, municipalities, NGOs, settler organisations and similar institutional actors are central. Correspondingly, national narratives – and nation-states in themselves – can be materially involved in individual beings' efforts to build their world as belonging to themselves. For example, official, state-approved geography school books in Israel teach Jewish citizens of the state to see themselves as masters of the land, "to control its population, its landscape and its space" (Peled-Elhanan 2012: 136). This type of collective narrative, which exists in the work to which the mortals are thrown into, affects the ways human beings dwell and are able to claim spaces for themselves. It is not thus only the finitude of being and the vulnerability it creates, as described by Rose, that define marking and claiming, but also the historical situatedness in a pre-existing world with specific political structures. Also for Heidegger, on whose work Rose builds, it is not only the spatiality of being but also its temporality that is a central part of a mortal's existence. Both of these are framed not only by mortals as individuals but also by the formations that have the power to arrange the world in which mortals live.

For marking to function as a claim of belonging, it should be noted that it must be recognisable to ourselves and to others. If we consider that marking is a way of declaring the world as one's own, and we approach it as a practice involved in nation-building, then not all building can be interpreted as constituting a marking. Marking should be recognisable so that it is possible to tell from a distance that it belongs to one sovereignty rather than to another. If one perceives the landscapes of Israel/Palestine, this recognisability is created with flags and specific forms of building, which make it clear who is claiming the landscape as their own. The importance of recognisability is further increased when marking happens as part of settler colonial conquest, because in such a context it becomes crucial to distinguish the constructions of the settler nation from those of the groups who dwelt there before. That the majority of the Palestinian Arab villages were demolished after they were emptied in 1948, rather than used to house the Israeli Jewish population, can also be interpreted from this perspective. When Palestinian villages were used for housing the newcomers, those placed in them were usually Arab Jews from countries such as Iraq and Yemen, whose Arab

---

3   Rose defines this central term of Heideggerian philosophy as "the type of being that best characterizes a human being" (Rose 2012: 760). However, geographer Mikko Joronen (2008: 599) notes that "interpreting Dasein in a purely anthropocentric sense misses the essential point". He continues that "[a]s the German word Da refers to place in a sense of 'there' and 'here' and the word sein refers to being, to the open itself, Dasein means literally a place of openness in the midst of beings, wherein being renders itself as a possibility for something to be as something".

identity itself became a problem for the new state because it challenged the clear-cut dichotomy between the Jews and the Arab other (see e.g. Shohat 1999). Besides being a reminder of the former dwellers, a record of their dwelling in the landscape as Ingold would describe it, Arab villages were associated with a backwardness not deemed to fit the modernist (European) landscapes of the Jewish state. A similar temporal framing of indigenousness exists also in other settler colonial contexts. In Australia, the dispossession of the Aboriginal populations was justified on the grounds of their being a hindrance to progress (Banivanua Mar 2010), while in the United States, the Native Americans were routinely described as a remnant of the past (Spence 1999). Similarly, the change of a landscape can be detected in many other settler colonial settings than Israel/Palestine, and Tracey Banivanua Mar and Penelope Edmonds (2010) write:

> the impact of settler colonialism is starkly visible in the landscapes it produces: the symmetrically surveyed divisions of land; fences, roads, power lines, dams and mines; the vast mono-cultural expanses of single-cropped fields; carved and preserved national forest, and marine and wilderness parks; the expansive and gridded cities; and the socially coded areas of human habitation and trespass that are bordered, policed and defended. Land and the organised spaces on it, in other words, narrate the stories of colonisation.

It is this material narration of colonial rule, I suggest, which can be theorised as marking. Now I proceed to elaborate how it has taken place in Israel/ Palestine.

## From the landscape of Palestine to the landscape of the Jewish homeland

In most nation-states, existing material landscapes are invested with meanings that contribute to nationalist ideology. In settler states, however, the processes of signification are not always as straightforward because settled land does not yet carry the marks of their dwelling. Though there were Jewish people living in Mandatory Palestine among the Palestinian Arab population before Israel was established, and though the land does carry histories of Jewish dwelling also materialised in the landscapes, establishing Israel as a Jewish state required reorganisation and resignification of existing landscapes. It became imperative to bring forth those layers of history that enforced the belonging of the Jewish people and rooted this settler nation into the land, while concurrently obscuring and ignoring other layers that might be reminders of the fact that in recent history other people have also belonged to the land. The reasoning for such action can be found in the words of Fred Inglis (1977: 489) for whom "a landscape is the most solid appearance in which a history can declare itself". This also makes perceiving a landscape in itself an act of remembrance. As Tim Ingold (2000) has famously written: landscapes are always pregnant with the past. In Ingold's words, "the landscape is constituted as an enduring record of – and testimony to – the lives and works of past generations who have dwelt within it, and

in so doing, have left there something of themselves" (Ingold 2000: 189).
Thus, when the aim is to enforce the belonging of one group over others
in a landscape, which, for centuries has been inhabited by diverse peoples,
the problem faced by the settler state is how to treat the material marks of
dwelling left by previous inhabitants. In the case of Israel/Palestine, the most
pressing challenge to the legitimacy of the settler populations' belonging, are
the marks of dwelling left by those Palestinians dispossessed in the process
of creating the new state.

Israel was established in May 1948. By the end of the same year, close to
800 000 Palestinians who had previously lived in the area were turned into
refugees or were internally displaced (history of Palestinian dispossession,
see e.g. Morris 2004; Pappé 2006; Masalha 2012). The expulsions were
implemented by Zionist militias with methods such as intimidation,
bombing of villages and population centres, arson attacks, demolitions and
planting mines to prevent Palestinians from returning to their homes and
agricultural lands (Pappé 2006: xii). These expulsions created a reality that
resembled the notion of an empty land, an ideal common to many settler
colonial projects (see e.g. Banivanua Mar and Edmonds 2010 [eds], part 1),
that in the case of Israel, was brought forth in slogans such as "a land without
people for a people without land". Actual encounters with the realities of
mandate-era Palestine had, however, challenged this idea of empty land
(Leshem 2013), and the Zionist thinkers were not ignorant of – nor did they
ignore – the presence of Palestinians. Yet, the land was considered empty in
a deeper sense: emptiness was perceived at a spiritual level, and early Zionists
in particular saw that as long as there was no Jewish sovereignty over it, the
land itself was as if forced into exile – much like Jews themselves (Piterberg
2008: 94–95). Zionist leaders, from Theodor Herzl to Israel's first prime
minister David Ben-Gurion, had been consistent in their wish to create
a Jewish state with as small an Arab population as possible (Pappé 2006: 47),
and the events of 1948 were central in actualising this wish. Yet, even after
the expulsions, the landscapes still bore witness to the previous inhabitants.
To create 'the empty land' also at a material level, landscapes needed to be
cleared of the dwellings of the population that had *de facto* lived there for
generations.

When Palestinians were driven from their homes, the practical challenge
faced by the Zionist forces was to prevent people from returning. It quickly
became apparent that many Palestinians aimed to do precisely that: they
crossed the newly created state border back to their villages to live in their
houses and to care and harvest their crops. These people were treated as
infiltrators, and they were repeatedly expelled, or even killed, as they tried
to return to their homes (Korn 2003). To ensure that the dispossessed
Palestinians would have no place to return to, the military forces of the
newly established state started to demolish the emptied villages, and by the
mid-1949, most of them were either completely or partly in ruins (Morris
2004:342). Following the destruction of the Palestinian villages, between
1948 and 1952, around 300 Jewish settlements were erected on the border
area, either in the exact location of a destroyed village or on village lands
(Korn 2003: 5). As Alina Korn (2003) has noted, this formed  a Jewish

presence that in practice restrained the return of expelled Palestinians. As well as creating a buffer-zone that effectively blocked the possibility of return, the newly-established Jewish settlements created facts on the ground that brought Israeli Jewish presence to places where the new sovereignty needed to be enforced and shown to those across the border. In this manner, the new Israeli Jewish villages functioned as markings that made ownership over land material and visible, especially for those in the neighbouring countries.

The material destruction of villages and other dwelling places was implemented also on the level of representation of space, as maps were redrawn with new locales and new names. The Arab history of the land was obscured by replacing Arabic names with new Hebrew ones, a systematic process that has been documented for example by Meron Benvenisti (2000). Many names were direct translations from Arabic to Hebrew, in other cases the new Hebrew name had a similar pronunciation as the original Arabic one. There was also an effort to derive names from the Bible, as biblical-sounding names would have an ancient ring to them (Benvenisti 2000: 20). Palestinian dwelling places were removed from maps as demolished villages were first marked as destroyed and later left out altogether (Grunebaum 2014: 214). Naming also had its material manifestations, with sign-boards that introduced the new names into the landscapes. Now these are the names one encounters when travelling through them.

The destruction of Palestinian neighbourhoods and villages radically transformed the material reality of Israel/Palestine, but it also obscured the history of Palestinians in the most concrete way, on the landscape. The landscapes went through *an erasure of memory* (Bender 2001: 2), a destruction of the material signs of former dwellers. Though such destruction is never absolute, and though there are always material markers that can trigger a memory for those who want to remember, by demolishing the villages, Israel removed an important dimension of Palestinian history. Importantly, this erasure transformed how the landscapes are perceived. When travelling from Jerusalem/al-Quds to Tel Aviv/Yafo, I have many times tried to locate the destroyed villages by using a mobile application iNakba created by the civil society organization *Zochrot*, which marks all the destroyed villages on a map. Yet in most cases, the villages just are not there to be seen; not as material sites nor as names on signposts. Thus, destroying the villages not only removed the material marks left by Palestinian dwelling, it also produced a transformation in perception as well as in the kind of gathering now possible in these landscapes. To paraphrase Ingold, by erasing the history of the Palestinian people's presence from the landscapes, Israel removed the signs of dwelling left by generations of Palestinians who built, worked and lived in those very settings. These transformations have altered what kind of remembrance is possible in the act of perceiving the landscapes, and they show that signs of dwelling that are present in a landscape can be an outcome of a highly political practices. For Palestinians, the very absence of their material history on the landscape is part of the dispossession and unjust treatment caused to them by the rupturing events of *al-Nakba* and that still continues today in different forms.

Villages here used to gather landscapes in a particular way, as places of human presence and work, and they gave meaning to things surrounding them. Heidegger's description of the role of a bridge in gathering its surroundings in *Building dwelling thinking* (1993, German language original 1951) is helpful here: in the same manner as the bridge, the villages allow a certain type of unfolding of the world to happen. Villages form an *Ortschaft*, meaning in fact village, town or another sort of settled locality, which in Heideggerian philosophy manifests how it is not only one structure but a coming-together of structures that gather and form a place that is both a gathering and itself gathered (Heidegger 1973; see also Malpas 2006: 262–263). Thus, making it impossible to perceive the villages transformed how places in Israel/Palestine are gathered. It formed a step in the process of settler-colonial world-building. The obliteration of old markings is often intentional during the conquest of space and, I would argue that for settler colonialism to reach its aims, not only the elimination of the natives is required, as Patrick Wolfe (1999; 2006) suggests, but also the removal of their markings from the landscape. Without this transformation, it would be easy for the indigenous population to make claims that would convincingly challenge the legitimacy of the settler society's right to the land. Removing marks of former dwelling and building markings that foster the belonging of the settler nation, allows the new state to claim the landscapes as its own. In Israel/Palestine, by destroying the old and building anew, landscapes were, and still are, redefined as a Zionist homeland. Still, this process is not unique to the context of Israel/Palestine; it can be identified in other settler colonial histories, as was noted in the previous section. As W. J. T. Mitchell (2000: 218) puts it, "it is not enough to drive out the inhabitants; the very landscape must be purged of their traces, their claims, their history, their idols".

Though marking and claiming rests on the material unfolding of changeable landscapes, it also involves narratives that attaches meaning to different aspects of that materiality. Hence, in Israel/Palestine the erasure of memory is implemented not only in the material world-building but is evident also, for example, in schoolbooks that downplay the two millennia of Jewish exile and barely mention the life of Palestinians on the land (Peled-Elhanan 2012: 91). When landscapes are produced specifically as what we can call *homelandscapes*, they are a combination of material and narration, which according to Azaryahu and Golan form together "an ideate: an actual existence that corresponds with an idea" (Azaryahu and Golan 2004: 497). In Israel/Palestine, like arguably in countless places around the world, national and historic narratives give depth to the material settings highlighting that the markings belonging to *our* world rather than to *theirs*. I believe anthropologist Joost Fontein (2011: 707–708) summarises this process eloquently in writing about how

> the remains of different pasts present in the landscape, as ghosts and ancestors, graves and ruins, are 'active' in the varying ways that they materialize, constrain, enable, and structure different, entangled discourses and practices of autochthony and belonging at play in the reconfiguration of authority over land.

This 'authority over land' is made visible through materiality that direct both perceptions of landscapes and how people can corporeally engage with them. It is further strengthened by narrating the material settings in a manner that upholds the dominant authority.

As a consequence of this destruction, at many sites in Israel/Palestine one shares the landscape with 'ghosts and memories' (Wylie 2009: 277). Shadows of absent or past landscapes are still present in many places, for instance in the form of ruins, feral fields and orchards. Thus, a record of dwelling, in the sense Ingold describes it, manifests itself also from amid destruction and can be further enforced by social imagining of landscapes through remembering and narration (see Khalidi 1992; Khalili 2004; Davis 2011; Ramadan 2013). These places can be seen as markings of absence, and for Palestinians, in turn, they form a part of their national world-building. Furthermore, these markings of absence can be negated by revealing and naming, an approach John Wylie (2009) calls *bringing-to-presence*. The actions of civil society organisations such as *Baladna* and *Zochrot*[4] aim to do precisely this when they put up signs and name plates at places where Palestinian villages and habitations used to exist, and organise tours to destroyed villages, thus marking them by their corporeal presence. By their actions but also merely by their presence, Palestinians who still live in Israel, especially the internally displaced, ensure that total forgetting of their history on the land is not possible. Nevertheless, for those who now live in exile, landscapes transformed from experienced locales of everyday life to abstract spaces of the past that can be narrated and commemorated, but which are not accessible for them as their presence continues to be denied by Israel.

## Marking landscapes as Israeli-Jewish

As Ingold has noted (2000: 199), transformation in and of landscapes is always inevitable, indeed the anthropological conception of landscape popularised by him is that they are never still and complete, but constantly under construction through the process of dwelling. Yet, as I have shown, that transformation can also be manipulated through deliberate destruction of the signs left by earlier dwellers. This was the case in the first years after the establishment of Israel. I will now turn to consider how the concepts of marking and claiming can be further utilised in analysing settler nationalist world-building, as I proceed to examples of how landscapes were claimed for the Israeli-Jewish homeland. I consider how afforestation and archaeology function as markings through which landscapes were, and still are,

---

4   Baladna, literally meaning our land or our country, is a youth organization for Palestinians within Israel. One of its projects is to facilitate activities for internally displaced youth to engage with their villages of origin. Zochrot, on the other hand, aims to educate the Jewish population of Israel on al-Nakba and the Palestinian history of the land. They organize visits to destroyed villages and neighborhoods and make the Palestinian history of the places visible by installing signs with the Arabic names of the destroyed locales.

transformed to support the belonging and sense of rootedness of the Jewish population of Israel.

## Afforestation: Planting roots in the landscape

Forests are highly visible parts of landscapes, yet they are not intuitively perceived as markings. Forests carry an aura of naturalness and originality; they are part of wilderness and thus are seen as the opposite of the kind of dwelling materialised in building. It may be questionable whether forests can be considered to engage in the kind of building that constitutes marking and claiming. Yet, returning to Heidegger, we can see that what we understand as nature gathers things that are built much in the same way as more obviously human-made things do (Malpas 2006: 234–235). Ingold stresses the same when he recognizes that a tree gathers the landscape around it in a similar manner to how buildings do (Ingold 2000: 204–205). Furthermore, the forests under scrutiny here can even be considered as having been built in a literal sense, as they are clearly a result of human action: Jewish National Fund, the main player in afforestation in Israel/Palestine, boasts on the 250 million trees they have planted since the organisation was founded in 1901, on how their actions have transformed the "desert-nation into a "garden oasis".[5] But even when the afforestation is explicit and even underlined, it is easy to think that a forest belongs to a landscape in a different manner than a built environment. Forests carry an atmosphere of timelessness, or, as Theodor Adorno (Adorno 2002: 105) writes, "the beautiful in nature is history standing still and refusing to unfold". Given this association, when trees are used as markings, their power relies on narratives that are tied to them. That forests can be seen as markings in the context of Israel/Palestine rests upon their narrated form that creates connection between people and specific type of tree, but as mentioned, forests function also on another level, by obscuring Palestinian dwelling in the landscape.

The Jewish National Fund (JNF) is an important actor when it comes to afforestation in Israel/Palestine, as it has engaged extensively in tree planting ever since its foundation in 1901. Since the establishment of the state of Israel, it has set up around seventy forests and national parks in different parts of the country. According to the organisation *Zochrot*, more than two-thirds of JNF's forests and sites are located where there are destroyed Palestinian villages (Bronstein Aparicio 2014). This means forty-six forests and parks planted and established after 1948 and 1967 on the ruins of eighty-nine Palestinian villages. The practical function of this planting was to prevent the Palestinian refugees from returning, and the forests were thus machinated into the landscapes to hinder the possibilities of human habitation in the form of village life and an agricultural livelihood. In Heidegger's terms, the forests made it impossible for the landscapes to form a *clearing-away*, that "brings forth the free, the openness to man's settling and dwelling" (Heidegger 1973: 9). Planted on the sites of destroyed villages, the forest redefined the landscapes of Israel/Palestine: instead of witnessing

---

5   https://www.jnf.org/menu-2/our-work/forestry-green-innovations

a destroyed site of dwelling, one now sees a tall pine forest: this obscures the ruins making them invisible from a distance.

Nowadays it is possible to participate in afforestation via the JNF website by giving donations and 'planting' trees for loved ones. This continues a long history of fund-raising for tree-planting by the organisation: JNF has planted over 250 million trees in Israel/Palestine, most of them pine. This choice of species has an important symbolic function as it connects the Jewish exile with the material landscapes of Israel/Palestine. Many Jews in exile have memories of the JNF's blue box in which donations for tree planting were collected (Long 2009). Historian Simon Schama (1995), for instance, remembers how as a child in a Jewish school in London, he participated in collecting funds for JNF. His recollections exemplify the symbolic value of the forests, as for him they represented the opposite of diaspora: Israel was to be fixed and tall as a forest, and this would negate the landscape of rocks and sand associated with exile (Schama 1995: 5–6).

JNF's tree planting is the one of the most significant actions to have transformed perceptions of the landscapes of Israel/Palestine. Covering over 250 000 acres, the JNF forests have in many places determined that landscapes are no longer construed as Palestinian villages but open to visitors as forests and parks. However, in addition to transforming material reality, afforestation has also invested the landscape with narratives of Zionism and thus symbolically rooted the Jewish people in the land. Elsewhere too, as for example Richard J. Martin and David Trigger (2015) highlight, the human-plant relationship has been relevant in the settler colonial setting. Plantings have had clear impacts on how indigeneity and nativeness are perceived and produced, as it brings forth the question on what is indigenous and what is introduced. As Martin and Trigger (2015: 278) phrase it, "what does it actually mean for plants and persons to belong in a place". Interestingly, in Israel it has been the relation to an introduced species of plant that has been central in fostering belonging and producing the specific sort of national identity. The mainly single species pine forests that were planted after the establishment of Israel were involved in 'modernising' and 'Europeanising' the landscape. Furthermore, the pine tree has had a special national importance here, and Irus Braverman (2009) even states that there is a totemic identification between the pine tree and the Jewish people. This has allowed an otherwise politically neutral plant to function as marking, especially as it constitutes 'counter' flora to olive trees and cacti, which in turn are closely associated with Palestinian presence on the land (Abufarha 2008). The pine tree also links modern landscapes to ancient Jewish history. Joanna C Long reviews the belief that biblical landscapes were covered with forests of pine trees, rather than appearing as rugged and thorny hills with bushes and olive trees. Pine forests thus contributed to building 'originality' and 'ancientness' (Long 2009: 66–67), and as such they form markings that recreate the landscapes associated with early Jewish presence.

In Zionist imagery, historic Palestine was described as desolate, rocky and uncultivated, covered with bushes and thorny plants, and the mission of the Jewish settlers was to tame this harsh landscape and, as noted above, to 'make the desert bloom'. This also highlights the relevance of labour. If simply

145

roaming the landscape was seen to create a bond between Jewish immigrants and the lands they now deemed to be their own, physical engagement with the land was viewed as important when it was also a way of investing in the land. Working the land was also linked with modernisation narratives and in JNF documents, it is described how the organisation managed to perform 'an agricultural and botanic miracle' in overcoming two millennia of neglect (Long 2009: 65). Again, these accounts contributed to the erasure of Palestinian dwelling as they ignored the fact that the land was already cultivated and looked after.

Even though forests have effectively made places of Palestinian dwelling invisible from a distance, once inside forests, it is still possible to see the ruins of villages. Nevertheless, a video from Canada Park, located by the highway between Tel Aviv and Jerusalem, produced by Israeli magazine +972 (2013), exemplifies how the ruins remain unacknowledged and un-narrated, and thus left without meaning. While being closely connected to Israeli transportation networks and named as an Israeli national park, the majority of Canada Park's lands are in fact on the West Bank side of the Green Line, and thus in occupied areas. Its areas exhibit multiple layers of history from Roman and Second Temple eras to Crusaders' times. Yet, before the Six Day War, it was also the location of three Palestinian villages: Imwas, Yalo and Beyt Nouba. Though the Roman sites and other archaeological remains from earlier eras are described on information boards, the Palestinian villages that were destroyed after the Six Day War are not mentioned, even though their remains too can be seen. This is the case in many other forests and parks in Israel, and in publications about them; even when villages are named, they are never referred to as Palestinian and their history and former dwellers are narrated only vaguely, and thus "expressing forgetfulness and neglect", as Noga Kadman (2015: 115) puts it. This practice renders the ruins nameless, something that can be easily disregarded by visitors to the nature reserves.

Even when one is aware of the presence of Palestinian ruins, it is not always easy to recognise them. I specifically went looking for marks of the destroyed villages in Mount Carmel, but when I came across the ruins of houses and walls, it was hard for me to tell for sure which were of Palestinian origin, as there were no signs that would have indicated their history. This highlights the importance of other forms of remembering besides material landscape, in producing memories of place (see e.g. Hoelscher and Alderman 2004). Palestinians themselves have challenged these types of deliberate forgetting by different means. One is by corporeal presence on the destroyed landscapes which they do through return visits to villages (see e.g. Ben-Ze'ev and Aburaiya 2004). There are also political activities, such as an annual March of Return organised by internally displaced Palestinians, that commemorate their history on the land and call for an end to the dispossession. These attempts to claim Palestinian dwelling in the landscape challenge official Zionist narratives and contest the conscious forgetting of the Palestinian past that is practised so widely in Israeli society (e.g. Ram 2009).

ARCHAEOLOGY: BUILDING A JEWISH PAST INTO THE LANDSCAPE

Proving historical belonging and indigenousness have been central processes in the building of Israeli national identity. If, as I have argued alongside others (Mandelman 2014), landscape is a key medium for its tangible manifestation, then archaeology is one way of bringing historicity back into actual landscapes. It helps to materially redefine their meanings as "any excavation inevitably changes and often destroys the given situation" (Lemaire 1997: 15). Archaeology thus plays a central part in building material cultures, in the sense that excavation transforms landscapes as it makes particular histories concrete by marking them in space. It is, however, rather unique to Israel that as a settler colonial nation it can claim rootedness and belonging through archaeological evidence. In other settler colonial contexts, such as Australia or the United States, it has not been possible to root the nation by relying on an ancient past, though archaeology does have a nationalist dimension in these countries as well (Silberman 1995). In Israel, archaeology has been valued highly as a national hobby and even as a substitute for religion during the early years of the state (Feige 2001: 91), and thus it has been highly important in nation-building and in marking Jewish belonging in the landscape. The ancient history of Jewish people in the areas that now comprise Israel and the occupied territories, and its articulation as the Promised Land of the Jewish people, is one of the elements on which belonging is built, and this sacred connection is cemented with archaeological markings that confirm the historic existence of the Jewish population here.

Archaeological excavations have played an important role in this process, as they are material and visible signs of rootedness in a place. Within Bruce G. Trigger's (1984) classical typology examining the nature of archaeological research and its relation to the social milieu of the nation state in which it is practiced, archaeology in Israel can be described as nationalist, though in its approach to the material history of the Palestinians, it also has some characteristics of colonialist archaeology. In excavations, layers of former dwelling are revealed, which in many occasions happens at the expense of the current dwellers. It has been widely reported by academics (e.g. Abu El-Haj 1998, 2001; Feige 2001; Silberman 2001; Pirinoli 2005; Piterberg 2008) and civil society organisations (e.g. Emek Shaveh; Centre for Jerusalem Studies) that archaeological sites and excavations are used for settler colonial purposes and for building national narratives, that is, for opening them up as not simply "*a* world but as *our* world" (Rose 2012: 769; italics in original).

After the establishment of the state of Israel, archaeological interest mainly focused on what Nadia Abu E-Haj (1998: 168) has called "mythological digs", which formed the core of the Israeli national-colonial imagination. Even before the state, the aim of archaeological excavations was to proof the continuity of Jewish presence in the land (Abu El-Haj 2001: 73–74). By creating connection to the past, archaeology too has helped the immigrant society to set 'instant roots' (Feige 2001: 91). And it had a great symbolic value as it was centrally involved in forging national identity by constructing a narrative of ancient Israel's greatness (Feige 2001: 91). This exploitation

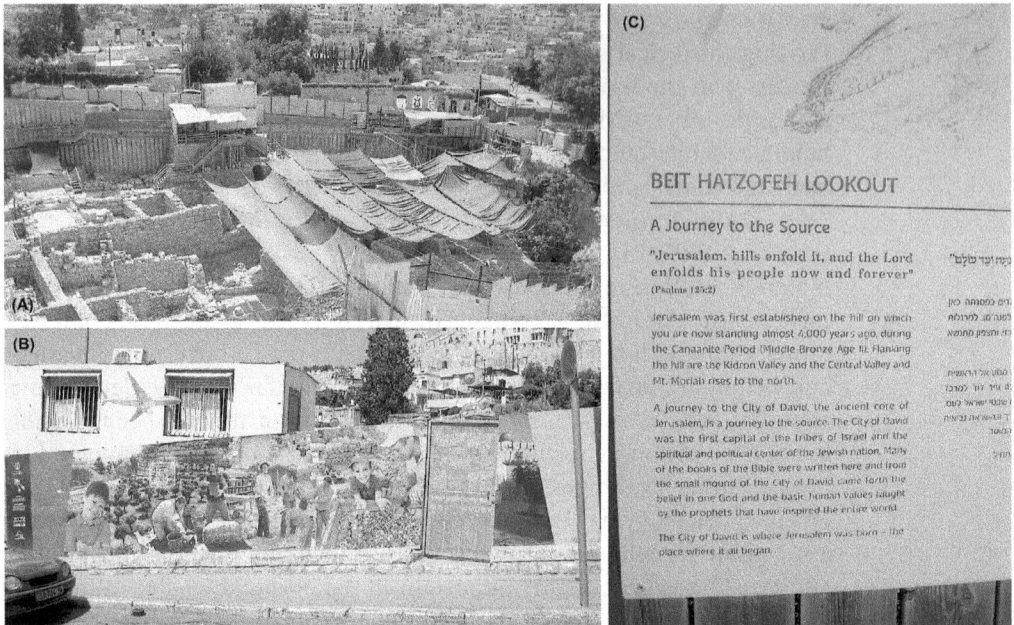

*Figure 1. The City of David and its surroundings. On the top-left, the entrance of City of David can be seen behind the Givati Parking Lot excavation site. On bottom-left is the barrier surrounding the said excavation site, seen from the entrance of City of David. The photo on the righ introduces an information board, one amongst many similar found within the tourist site of the City of David.*

of archaeological findings for nationalist ends is further reinforced by the fact that monuments and findings from the Arab and Ottoman eras are not considered to have great value. An extreme example of disregarding findings from these eras that do not manifest the Jewish history of the land, is the use of bulldozers in excavation sites. Nadia Abu El-Haj recounts how in an excavation she participated to, bulldozers were used to reach the older strata as quickly as possible. In the process of accessing layers "saturated with national significance" (Abu El-Haj 2001: 148), the markings left by non-Jewish others were removed and, in practice, destroyed without any closer inspection. This highlights how the bearing given to different layers of history in the practice of excavation defines the historicities that landscapes are able to disclose, and which dwelling is animated for those perceiving the landscapes.

A specific example of how archaeology is appropriated for colonial practices of materialising biblical narratives of landscape can be found in the City of David, a tourist site that lies right next to the southern walls of Jerusalem's Old City. The site is believed to be the place where the palace of King David was situated (for the history of the place, see e.g. Greenberg 2009), but now it is on lands belonging to the Palestinian village of Silwan. I visited the site in 2015, and before I had even entered, its Israeli-Jewish nature became evident as the abundance of Israeli symbols and Hebrew writing effectively concealed the fact that the site is located in a Palestinian neighbourhood of occupied East Jerusalem. This impression was only strengthened as I approached the City of David from the Old City of Jerusalem, crossing the Plaza of the Western Wall to reach the outer walls of the Old City from where the road leads to the historical site. Both the Old City and the village of Silwan are in East Jerusalem, yet there is no evidence that one is in an occupied area as the trash cans and lampposts with the West Jerusalem municipal emblem on them continue to line the roads. At the entrance of the City of David, there are Israeli flags and a sign in Hebrew and English. Opposite the entrance, where there is a parking lot turned to the excavation site of Givati (Figure 1a), there is a protection barrier. This shows pictures of findings from the Second Temple era, children and adults working on the excavations, and information written again in Hebrew and English (Figure 1b). On the site itself, all the information boards start with a direct quotation from the Bible and most of them use the Bible as a reference (Figure 1c). Tellingly, the boards refer solely to the Jewish history of the place, mainly to the First and Second Temple eras, and the more recent history is left un-narrated. Even the Palestinian houses within the tourist site, which are still there and inhabited, are not mentioned on any information boards. The site is managed by the militant settler organisation El'ad, which is also involved in Judaising the village of Silwan, and especially its neighbourhood Wadi Hilwah, where the excavation sites of the City of David are located.

## Conclusion: Continuous marking and claiming

In this chapter, I have demonstrated how landscapes have been transformed and appropriated through the process of marking in the context of Israel/Palestine. I have highlighted that the destruction and disregard of the material sites of Palestinian dwelling have formed the basis for Israel's settler colonial nation building and I have further shown how, accompanied by efforts to root the Israeli Jews in the land through afforestation and archaeology, this destruction has produced belonging for Jewish Israelis while denying it from the Palestinians. These processes have radically changed the way the landscapes of Israel/Palestine can be perceived, and thus they also define *whose* belonging can be witnessed via the presence of material markings. Concentrating on this dimension of landscape practices has enabled me to acknowledge that landscapes are not always an 'innocent' record of dwelling, rather they can be an outcome of violence, dispossession and destruction. Power structures, hierarchies, and dominant narratives affect what there is to perceive, and what meanings are animated for the perceiver. Though this in undoubtedly the case in all landscapes, its relevance is amplified at contested sites where landscapes are used in claiming belonging.

Though the focus of the chapter has been on the first years of the Israeli state, both archaeology and afforestation are still used in appropriating land. Importantly, the practices described in the article have enabled and continue to enable the creation of a certain type of Israeli identity, which highlights how landscapes do not only represent identity but in fact make it possible (Rose 2006: 548). By creating landscapes with markings that foster national belonging of the Jewish population of Israel, the state of Israel has forced the landscapes through violent transformations that have changed how things are gathered. Landscapes changed in a process of creating sites that enabled the settler nation to belong as natives[6]. A corollary has been that the history of Palestinian dwelling was obscured.

Bearing in mind that no national identity is homogeneous, and the narratives that construct it are always open to challenge, my aim has been to show how landscape materialises and thus enforces certain narratives in ways that are easily channelled into the national consciousness in the process of nation-building. I have concentrated on reviewing actions of state and state-related entities and put forward the idea that marking and claiming are not only individual actions but also institutional practices. As the condemnable destruction of Palestinian cultural heritage that I have described demonstrates, markings made by institutional actors can be both symbolically and materially violent, as they support a certain type of identity, belonging and dwelling, and in doing so deny belonging and dwelling from others. There is no doubt that all people hope to dwell in a manner that they can feel they belong and have an ownership of the world they are living in, yet in Israel/Palestine the possibility to do so is not equally accessible to all.

Unequal possibilities to engage in world-building can be detected in most projects of nation-building, so in this sense the situation in Israel/Palestine is not exceptional. Yet, settler colonial contexts have their own specificities, and Israel's settler colonialism has some unique manifestations. As highlighting these specificities has been the emphasis of the chapter, the claim-like nature of markings has not been discussed in an equal manner. It should, however, be remembered that marking is by nature vulnerable to the constant unfolding of the world. It is finite and open to destruction and can thus be challenged through building differently. This has also been done, as I have mentioned, by Palestinians and others who have reminded us about landscapes that were destroyed to build a state based on Jewish exclusiveness. Though the markings that tell the history of Palestinian dwelling can no longer be retrieved in their material form, the lost landscapes are nevertheless still enacted in different ways, bringing forth the diversity of dwelling that defines the historical landscape of today's Israel/Palestine.

6   Native is a problematic concept for many reasons, mainly as it assumes that certain people are more deeply connected to specific geographies than others, and further as it freezes a random point from history to be the beginning when measuring indigenousness. Here my use of the word is intentional as it highlights the political processes that have, in fact, tried to claim Jewish belonging as deeper and stronger than that of others who have dwelt in the area. An example of this is a video published by Israel Ministry of Foreign Affairs on their Facebook page on 6 October 2016. It is introduced with a statement "[n]o matter who came knocking at the door, the Jews stayed put in their home-sweet-home, the Land of Israel, for 3,000 years" and presents all other people as visitors and sidesteps Palestinian presence all together by presenting them as someone who only after the establishment of Israel come to claim the land for themselves. https://www.facebook.com/IsraelMFA/videos/vb.101995411316/10154038006641317/?type=2&theater

## Acknowledgements

I wish to thank Dr. Mikko Joronen and prof. Laura Huttunen, and people who took part in the panel Landscape and Memory in the Biennial Conference of the Finnish Anthropological Society for their comments and support. Further thanks go to Finnish Institute in the Middle East for the travel grant and position in its visiting researcher programme that enabled me to do fieldwork in Israel/Palestine in the summer 2015 and in the spring of 2016, respectively.

# References

Abu El-Haj, Nadia 1998. Translating Truths: Nationalism, the Practice of Archaeology and the Making of Past in Contemporary Jerusalem. *American Ethnologist* 25 (2): 166–188.

Abu El-Haj, Nadia 2001. *Facts on the Ground: Archaeological Practice and Territorial Self-Fashioning in Israeli Society.* Chicago: University of Chicago Press.

Abufarha, Nasser 2008. Land of Symbols: Cactus, Poppies, Orange and Olive Trees in Palestine. *Identities* 15 (3): 343–68.

Adorno, Theodor 1984. *Aesthetic Theory.* London: Routledge & Kegan Paul.

Azaryahu, Maoz and Arnon Golan 2004. Zionist homelandscapes (and their constitution) in Israeli Geography. *Social & Cultural Geography* 5 (3): 497–513.

Banivanua Mar, Tracey 2010. Carving Wilderness: Queensland's National Parks and the Unsettling of Emptied Lands, 1890–1910. In Tracey Banivanua Mar and Penelope Edmonds (eds), *Making Settler Colonial Space: Perspectives on Race, Place and Identity.* Basingstoke: Palgrave Macmillan.

Banivanua Mar, Tracey and Penelope Edmonds 2010. Introduction: Making Space in Settler Colonies. In Tracey Banivanua Mar and Penelope Edmonds (eds), *Making Settler Colonial Space: Perspectives on Race, Place and Identity.* Basingstoke: Palgrave Macmillan.

Ben-Ze'ev, Efrat and Issam Aburaiya, 2004. 'Middle-Ground' Politics and the Re-Palestinization of Places in Israel. *International Journal of Middle East Studies* 36 (4): 639–655.

Bender, Barbara 2001. Introduction. In Barbara Bender and Margot Winer (eds), *Contested Landscapes: Movement, Exile and Place.* Oxford: Berg.

Benvenisti, Meron 2000. *Sacred Landscape: The Buried History of the Holy Land Since 1948.* Berkeley: University of California Press.

Braverman, Irus 2009. Planting the Promised Landscape: Zionism, Nature, and Resistance in Israel/Palestine. *Natural Resources Journal* 49 (2): 317–361.

Bronstein Aparicio, Eitan 2014. Most JNF – KKL forests and sites are located on the ruins of Palestinian villages. *Zochrot.* https://zochrot.org/en/article/55963

Davis, Rochelle A. 2011. *Palestinian Village Histories: Geographies of the Displaced.* Stanford: University Press.

Emek Shaveh (2013) *Nabi Samwil – A Village Trapped in a National Park.* http://alt-arch.org/en/nabi-samuel-national-park/

Falah, Ghazi 1996. The 1948 Israeli-Palestinian War and Its Aftermath: The Transformation and De-Signification of Palestine's Cultural Landscape. *Annals of the Association of American Geographers* 86 (2): 256–285.

Feige, Michael 2001. Identity, Ritual and Pilgrimage: The Meetings of the Israel Exploration Society. In Deborah Dash Moore and S. Ilan Troen (eds), *Divergent Jewish Cultures: Israel and America.* New Haven: Yale University Press.

Fields, Gary 2012. "This is *our* land": Collective violence, property law, and imagining the geography of Palestine. *Journal of Cultural Geography* 29 (3): 267–291.

Fontein, Joost 2011. Graves, ruins, and belonging: Towards an anthropology of proximity. *Journal of the Royal Anthropological Institute* (N.S.) 17 (4): 706–727.

Greenberg, Raphael 2009. Toward an Inclusive Archaeology in Jerusalem: The Case of Silwan/City of David. *Public Archaeology* 8 (1): 35–50.

Grunebaum, Heidi 2014. Landscape, complicity and partitioned zones at South Africa Forest and Lubya in Israel-Palestine. *Anthropology Southern Africa* 37 (3-4): 213–221.

Heidegger, Martin 1973. Art and Space. *Man and World* 6 (1): 3–8.

Heidegger, Martin 1993. *Basic Writings*. San Francisco: HarperCollins.

Hoelscher, Steven and Derek H. Alderman 2004. Memory and place: Geographies of a critical relationship. *Social & Cultural Geography* 5 (3): 347–355.

Inglis, Fred 1977. Nation and Community: A Landscape and its Morality. *The Sociological Review* 25(3): 489–514.

Ingold, Tim 2000. *The Perception of the Environment: Essays on Livelihood, Dwelling and Skill*. London: Routledge.

Joronen, Mikko 2008. The technological metaphysics of planetary space: Being in the age of globalization. *Environment and Planning D: Society and Space* 26 (4): 596–610.

Kadman, Noga 2015. *Erased from Space and Consciousness: Israel and Depopulated Palestinian Villages of 1948*. Bloomington: Indiana University Press.

Khalidi, Walid (ed.) 1992. *All That Remains: The Palestinian Villages Occupied and Depopulated by Israel in 1948*. Washington D.C.: Institute for Palestine Studies.

Khalili, Laleh 2004. Grass-roots commemoration: Remembering the land in the camps of Lebanon. *Journal of Palestine Studies* 34 (1): 6–22.

Korn, Alina 2003. From refugees to infiltrators: Constructing political crime in Israel in 1950s. *International Journal of the Sociology of Law* 31 (1): 1–22.

Lemaire, Ton 1997. Archaeology between the Invention and the Destruction of the Landscape. *Archaeological Dialogues* 4 (1): 5–21.

Leshem, Noam 2013. Repopulating the emptiness: A spatial critique of ruination in Israel/Palestine. *Environment and Planning D: Society and Space* 31 (3): 522–537.

Long, Joanna C. 2009. Rooting diaspora, reviving nation: Zionist landscapes of Israel-Palestine. *Transactions of the Institute of British Geographers* 34 (1): 61–77.

Malpas, Jeff 2006. *Heidegger's Topology: Being, Place, World*. Cambridge, Mass: MIT Press.

Mandelman, Adam 2014. Unstrategic essentialism: Material culture and Hawaiian articulation of indigeneity. *Social & Cultural Geography* 15 (2): 172–200.

Martin, Richard J. and David Trigger 2015. Negotiating Belonging: Plants, people, and indigeneity in northern Australia. *Journal of the Royal Anthropological Institute* (N.S.) 21 (2): 276–295.

McKee, Emily 2014. Performing Rootedness in the Negev/Naqab: Possibilities and Perils of Competitive Planting. *Antipode* 46 (5): 1172–1189.

Mitchell, W. J. T. 2000. Holy Landscape: Israel, Palestine, and the American Wilderness. *Critical Inquiry* 26 (2): 193–223.

Morris, Benny 2004. *The Birth of Palestinian Refugee Problem Revisited*. Cambridge: University Press.

Pappé, Illan 2006. *The Ethnic Cleansing of Palestine*. Oxford: One World.

Peled-Elhanan, Nurit 2012. *Palestine in Israeli School Books: Ideology and Propaganda in Education*. London: I.B. Tauris.

Pirinoli, Christine 2005. Erasing Palestine to Build Israel: Landscape Transformation and the Rooting of National Identities. *Etudes Rurales* 173–174: 67–85.

Piterberg, Gabriel 2008. *The Returns of Zionism: Myths, Politics and Scholarship in Israel*. London: Verso.

Pyyry, Noora 2016. Learning with the city via enchantment: Photo-walks as creative encounters. *Discourse: Studies in the Cultural Politics of Education* 37 (1): 102–115.

Ram, Uri 2009. Ways of Forgetting: Israel and the Obliterated Memory of the Palestinian Nakba. *Journal of Historical Sociology* 22 (3): 366–395.

Ramadan, Adam 2013. Spatialising the refugee camp. *Transactions of the Institute of British Geographers* 38 (1): 65–77.

Rose, Mitch 2006. Gathering 'dreams of presence': a project for the cultural landscape. *Environment and Planning D: Society and Space* 24 (4): 537–554.

Rose, Mitch 2012. Dwelling as marking and claiming. *Environment and Planning D: Society and Space* 30 (5): 757–771.

Sand, Shlomo 2012. *The Invention of the Land of Israel: From Holy Land to Homeland.* London: Verso.

Selwyn, Tom 1995. Landscapes of Liberation and Imprisonment: Towards an Anthropology of the Israeli Landscape. In Eric Hirsch and Michael E. O'Hanlon (eds), *The Anthropology of Landscape: Perspectives on Place and Space.* Oxford: Clarendon Press.

Schama, Simon 1995. *Landscape and Memory.* London: Harper Perennial.

Schelly, Chelsea 2014. Are residential dwellers marking and claiming? Applying the concepts to humans who dwell differently. *Environment and Planning D: Society and Space* 32 (4): 672–688.

Shohat, Ella 1999. The Invention of the Mizrahim. *Journal of Palestine Studies* 29 (1): 5–20.

Silberman, Neil Asher 1995. Promised lands and chosen peoples: The politics and poetics of archaeological narrative. In Philip L. Kohl and Clare Fawcett (eds), *Nationalism, politics, and the practice of archaeology.* Cambridge: University Press.

Silberman, Neil Asher 2001. If I Forget Thee, O Jerusalem: Archaeology, religious commemoration and nationalism in disputed city, 1801–2001. *Nations and Nationalism* 7 (4): 487–504.

Slyomovics, Susan 1998. *The Object of Memory: Arab and Jew Narrate the Palestinian Village.* Philadelphia: University of Pennsylvania Press.

Spence, Mark David 1999. *Dispossessing the Wilderness: Indian Removal and the Making of the National Parks.* Oxford: University Press.

Sternhell, Zeev 1998. *The Founding Myth of Israel: Nationalism, Socialism and the Making of the Jewish State.* Princeton: University Press.

Trigger, Bruce G. 1984. Alternative Archaeologies: Nationalist, Colonialist, Imperialist. *Man* (N.S.) 19 (3): 355–370.

WATCH: 'Canada Park' built on destroyed Palestinian villages. (2013, December 17). *+972.* http://972mag.com/watch-canada-park-built-on-destroyed-palestinian-villages/83861/

Van Dyke, Chris 2013. Plastic Eternities and the Mosaic of Landscape. *Environment and Planning D: Society and Space* 31 (3): 400–415.

Whyte, Nicola 2015. Senses of Place, Senses of Time: Landscape History from a British Perspective. *Landscape Research* 40 (8): 925–938.

Wolfe, Patrick 1999. *Settler Colonialism and the Transformation of Anthropology: The Politics and Poetics of an Ethnographic Event.* London: Cassel.

Wolfe, Patrick 2006. Settler colonialism and the elimination of the native. *Journal of Genocide Research* 8 (4): 387–409.

Wylie, John 2009. Landscape, absence and the geographies of love. *Transactions of the Institute of British Geographers* 34 (3): 275–289.

Yiftachel, Oren 2006. *Ethnocracy. Land and Identity Politics in Israel/Palestine.* Philadelphia: University of Pennsylvania Press.

MORGAN MOFFITT[1]

# The enduring imaginary of the 'northern frontier': Attending to stories about entangled landscapes

The circumpolar world is experiencing accelerated changes to ecosystems and climate, one result of which has been the melting of year-round sea ice and an increase in international interest in northern resources that were previously considered inaccessible. At the same time, many Northern regions are also experiencing a resurgence of local political and social activism. Indigenous northerners' right to self-determination is increasingly supported by international governmental and non-governmental organisations, and colonially rooted power relations are questioned and challenged. In this context, contested ideas about land are colliding in an ever more fraught and public sphere. The necessity and struggle to adapt to a quickly changing environment and to confront the realities and consequences of a century of unequal power relations, makes the relationships between local peoples and extractive industries in northern regions an important, timely and deeply political issue.

Industry and the Northern Nations often envision and frame arctic and subarctic landscapes as frontiers for development.[2] Often, these powerful actors are located far from the northern regions they envision and represent as frontier spaces. Their frontier discourse has significant social, political and material implications for northern indigenous peoples, specifically their relationships with their home territories and their right to self-determination. This is particularly the case in the Canadian North. This chapter examines how indigenous peoples living in Tulít'a (the Dene and Métis) conceptualise

1   This chapter would not be possible without the wisdom and support of the people in Tulít'a who have shared this knowledge with me. In particular, thank you to the families who took me out to Willow Lake and patiently taught me to harvest and process moose and fish, and to the mountain people who took me under their wing to teach me the stories of their Elders. Thank you as well to: Jean Polfus, Joe Hanlon, Dr. Deb Simmons, the Sahtu Renewable Resources Board, Dr. Mark Nuttall and Dr. Thomas D. Andrews.

2   There is an emerging body of literature on arctic geopolitics that brings together academics from anthropology, geography and political science. See Dodds and Nuttall (2016) for an excellent survey of the contemporary interests of northern nations and the globe in the arctic and how these are linked to longer histories of resource extraction, exploration and colonialism.

land and hydrocarbons in the context of local ontologies, past and present development, and in a national discourse that is politically and historically rooted in the social imaginary of the northern resource frontier. I historicise the image of the northern resource frontier as it is discursively figured by industry and government, and use the stories about land and hydrocarbons told by Dene and Métis people in Tulít'a, to explore the plurality of landscape, thereby complicating and challenging the enduring image of the frontier. Questioning the northern frontier through 'the stories people tell' unveils how stories impact development in the Canadian subarctic, demonstrates that both past and present experiences of extraction clash with the idea of the resource frontier, and highlights the need for new narratives rooted in northern lifeworlds.

The Sahtu region of the Northwest Territories (NWT), Canada, has been publicly imagined and portrayed as a frontier for hydrocarbon exploration and extraction since the 1920s and particularly ardently since the 1970s. The most well-known iteration of the northern hydrocarbon frontier emerged in the mid-1970s, when an international conglomerate of oil and gas companies proposed to build a pipeline from the Arctic Ocean through the NWT to reach southern markets. In response to this proposal, the Canadian government put together the Mackenzie Valley Pipeline Inquiry. The inquiry was led by Justice Thomas R. Berger who was tasked with evaluating whether or not a pipeline should be constructed. Justice Berger framed the essential question of the inquiry – whether or not a pipeline should be built through the region – as two competing visions of northern landscapes: the "northern frontier" versus the "northern homeland" (Berger 1977). This image resonated deeply with the local population and it remains popular today, often mobilised in debates about resource development. It has set up a powerful dichotomy that has unintentionally simplified the wide networks of relations and forces that contribute to the way in which landscapes are shaped, and the social, political, and temporal forces that influence indigenous peoples' relationships with landscape and development. This temporal amnesia silences the complexity of indigenous peoples' relationships with land, as well as the past relationships that government, indigenous peoples, and industry have with the land and the oil within it. By silencing the 'northern frontiers' of the past, both oil and gas companies and government strategically frame northern lands as sites of economic potential yet to be tapped. This occurs despite an important and locally well-known history of oil and gas exploration and development.

In the Sahtu, local perspectives of the land are intertwined with family histories as well as development histories, challenging the ideas that non-local Euro-Canadians have about northern landscapes and how they are perceived and depicted. The research informing this chapter involved direct engagement and participation in daily life in the community, trips on the land with research participants, work in NWT and Glenbow archives and a review of northern and national media coverage. Using an assemblage of qualitative research methods to capture the richness of local knowledge and histories, including participant observation, oral history, and semi-structured interviews, I listened and learned from the stories and experiences of Dene and Métis, who kindly shared stories with me and patiently taught me about local cosmology and storytelling practices. This approach captures the various ways in which hydrocarbons have become a part of the community. The stories that are discussed in this chapter were shared by indigenous elders and community members, and are employed to demonstrate how stories are shared and worked into individual and community approaches to hydrocarbons and environmental decision making. Oral traditions and stories are a part of daily life in Tulít'a, and these narratives are considered an integral part of Dene culture and communication. Stories are used to understand, negotiate and interact with local histories, places and non-human beings, as well as reflect and orient local cosmology within the changing modern world (Ridington 1988; Cruikshank 1998; 2005). Recent work with other Dene groups in the territory has focussed on the centrality of stories and the ways in which they are employed to teach, share knowledge and navigate cosmological differences between Dene and non-Dene ways of life (Legat 2012; Scott 2012). Incorporating stories as a research method and a key source of data supports a more holistic understanding of Dene and Metis experiences of landscape and development, and it also encourages non-indigenous researchers and readers to listen more closely to the stories they hear and are taught.

## The Sahtu and the Tulít'a Dene and Métis

The Sahtu region was officially created by the settlement of the Sahtu Dene and Métis Land Claim agreement (SDMLCA)[3] in the Northwest Territories in subarctic Canada. It encompasses an area of 41,437 km² and borders the Yukon Territory to the west, the Inuvik Region to the north (which includes the Gwich'in and Inuvialuit settlement areas), the Territory of Nunavut to the east, and the North Slave and Dehcho regions to the south. There are five communities in the Sahtu: Tulít'a, Délįnę, Norman Wells, Fort Good Hope, and Colville Lake. The region is cut through by the Mackenzie River, known as the 'Deh Cho' or big river. The Deh Cho is the largest river in Canada and the second largest river in North America. It is an important watershed and a vital part of the landscape. The hamlet of Tulít'a is located at the confluence of the Deh Cho and the Sahtu Deh (Great Bear River).

3   'Sahtú' is the name of the Great Bear Lake in North Slavey, the traditional language spoken by Dene and Métis in this region (though there is variation in local dialects). The SDMLCA was initiated in the 1970s by territory-wide political activism by Dene and Métis peoples who were pressuring the federal government to address their issues with Treaties 8 and 11. This political organisation and legal action was in part spurred by the first Mackenzie Valley pipeline proposal. The Dene and Métis did not want a pipeline to be built on their land until their claims for rights and title be addressed, and it was for this reason that, following a commission on the possibly pipeline project, it was recommended that no pipeline be built until land claim agreements were settled (see Berger 1977). In 1993 the SDMLCA was signed between the Dene and Métis of the Sahtu and the Government of Canada (see Irlbacher-Fox 2009, 13–18).

There were 516 people living in Tulít'a in 2015, 456 of whom identify as indigenous (Dene or Métis).[4] For eight months of the year, the community is only accessible by air and water. For the other three months of the year, the territorial government opens a winter road that connects the region to the rest of the territory and Canada. Because of the seasonal changes, there is also a period of several weeks between the freeze up and break-up of the Deh Cho during which travel to communities on ice or water is not possible.

Dene (and some Métis) living in the Sahtu speak North Slavey, an Athapaskan language. Historically, Dene identified and organised themselves on the basis of socio-territorial groups sometimes referred to by anthropologists as "bands" (Helm 1965). They further define themselves on the basis of the traditional territories where they and their ancestors lived and travelled and are known as the people of that particular territory.[5] For example, a Dene Elder living in Tulít'a may broadly identify as Dene and then further specify this as being either Shúhtaot'ıne (Mountain people), Kàálogot'ıne (Willow Lake people), Dǝogaot'ıne (River people), or Sahtúgot'ınę (Bear Lake people). The largest groups in Tulít'a are the Shúhtaot'ine and Kàálogot'ine, with fewer people identifying as Sahtúgot'ınę and Dǝogaot'ıne. Anthropologists believe that the ancestors of the Dene and Métis who live in Tulít'a today to have inhabited the region for thousands of years (Andrews et al., 2012; Hanks and Winter, 1986), a belief that is supported by a rich oral history. In the 1950s through to the 1970s, the Canadian government drastically increased its direct intervention into the lives of the Dene. Dene and Métis children were sent to residential schools and families were forced to settle more permanently in Tulít'a. Though many families continued and continue to hunt, trap, and fish in their traditional territories, their ability to do so was limited by these changes. The Métis in Tulít'a are the descendants of European traders and, Dene peoples throughout the Sahtu region, primarily Dene maternal ancestry and northern European paternal ancestry. They are indigenous peoples who maintain a distinct identity from the Métis in other regions of the territory and country. Collective political identification emerged first during the early twentieth century during the treaty process and again more fervently during the 1970s (Slobodin 1981: 362). In Tulít'a, most Métis families claim Dene and Scottish heritage[6] and, like the Dene, have specific areas where their families historically travelled, trapped, hunted and fished. Many of the Métis families were also pressured by government policies and an increased reliance on wage labour to settle more permanently in Tulít'a.

The most recent phase of oil and gas activities in the Sahtu region began in 2010–2011 when Industry interest in the Canol shale resulted

---

4   From the Government of the Northwest Territories (GNWT), Bureau of Statistics (accessed 11/10/2016): http://www.statsnwt.ca/community-data/infrastructure/Tulita.html.

5   For example, as Helm (1965: 363) points out "got'ine" means "the people of". Thus, groups of people identify and historically organized in a particular area (often a meaningful place or feature of the landscape in that area).

6   Based on personal communications.

in exploration licenses being granted by the National Energy Board. This interest was spurred by the stable oil market in southern parts of Canada (primarily Alberta) and the horizontal hydraulic fracturing[7] boom in the United States which made "frontier" exploration a popular and exciting investment for companies once again. The exploration followed closely behind the second failed attempt to build a pipeline through the Mackenzie Valley. This pipeline project is referred to as the Mackenzie Valley Pipeline. Like the project proposed and assessed in the 1970s, the idea was that it would effectively create a new energy corridor through the NWT, making oil and gas deposits in the Beaufort Sea and other regions of the NWT more accessible for exploitation, and thus a less risky and expensive investment for industry. Together with government, industry has promoted the pipeline as a practical guarantee for local economic prosperity in the Sahtu and the territory.

Similarly, industry and government signal another possible economic boom as a result of exploration and development in the Canol and Bluefish shale formations.[8] Oil companies began canvassing communities almost immediately, both to fulfil consultation[9] requirements and to seek support from community organisations and businesses. Oil and gas companies in particular promise employment and financial opportunities for local peoples and businesses, as well as community development through the provision of funds for community programmes, along with large donations to support important projects or events. The fracking activities in the Sahtu lasted for roughly two and a half years and have since halted as a result of the recent global drop in oil and gas prices and by December 2015, industry activities were limited to well-capping. For the people living in the Sahtu community of Tulít'a, fracking is the newest development in a long continuum of oil and gas activities in their traditional territories. This is partly because of the permanent material changes to the landscape and partly because of the socio-political impacts that the oil and gas activities have had on the region; however, it is also because of the nature of a boom-and-bust industry like oil and gas. The result is that oil and gas activities hold a significant place in local histories and are often figured prominently in people's discussions of past, present and future well-being. Fracking, and the controversy that surrounds it, has been met with much debate and has once again enlivened local, regional and territorial discussions about Dene and Métis relationships with the land, water, animals and each other.

---

7   Horizontal hydraulic fracturing is a controversial extraction method for accessing unconventional oil deposits. It is commonly referred to as 'fracking'.

8   The Canol and Bluefish Shale formations rock reservoirs located in the Sahtu region of the NWT made up of Shale, a fine-grained sedimentary rock that is formed from clay minerals in Devonian rocks.

9   Industry and government are legally required to consult with indigenous communities about development projects on their traditional territories. The requirement for consultation on the exploration and development of subsurface resources in the Sahtu is also outlined in chapter 22 of the Sahtu Dene and Métis Land Claim Agreement (1993). See Newman (2009) for more details on the duty to consult.

## Dene and Métis conceptualisations of land

Tulít'a Dene and Métis conceptualise land (*né*) through local cosmologies and historically situate land within personal practical experiences and collectively held and shared oral traditions. Dene scholars and academics have written about how Dene in the Northwest Territories conceptualise land as a living entity (Blondin 1996; 2005; Andrews et al. 1998; Andrews and Buggey 2008; Legat 2012). Legat (2012: 79) explains that, "*Dè* includes everything because all entities are in the state of existing and have spirit." This includes land, water, rocks, mountains, animals and non-human entities. In her work with the Tłįchǫ Dene, Legat (2012: 67–69) builds on the concept of dwelling as developed by Ingold (2000) to describe Tłįchǫ ways of dwelling in *dè*.[10] The Tłįchǫ emphasise the importance of respectful behaviour as a means of maintaining harmonious and predictable relations with land and the other beings who dwell in it. Dene and Métis living in Tulít'a have expressed similar beliefs about the relationships between *né*, humans and non-humans. These beliefs are fundamental to their perception of the landscape, which is considered to have material and immaterial properties. Oral traditions and narratives are a crucial mechanism through which knowledge about land and being a good Dene are communicated.[11] Of particular importance are the creation stories, which tell of a time when the world was new and animals could talk (Blondin 1990), and similarly, the Yamoria[12] narratives, which provide order to the landscape, naming geographic features and spirits and emphasising the importance of following Dene law.

*Né* and relations with *né* must be regulated and tended to in order to maintain respectful relations between all beings and ensure survival. Research participants in Tulít'a explained to me that healthy and respectful relationships with the land are maintained through ceremony (such as feeding the fire) and respectful behaviour (such as cleaning up and tending to important places, observing blood taboos, and paying the land and the non-human entities who inhabit particular places with offerings of tea, tobacco or shells). *Né* and the observance of healthy relations with *né* are seen as integral to Dene and Métis identity. Maintaining healthy relations with *né* includes pursuing traditional activities, like hunting, fishing and trapping. These activities are understood as important to subsistence as well as vital practices that maintain cultural and historical connections to *dé* and maintain balance and harmonious relations between all entities. As a

10  In the Tłįchǫ dialect land translates as "*dè*" with a low tone whereas in the Sahtu, land is known as *né*. These two concepts are treated as synonymous in this paper as the Tlicho are closely related to the Sahtu Dene and Métis and are their southern neighbours in the NWT.

11  The work of Cruikshank (1998; 2005) clearly describes this practice among indigenous peoples in the Yukon Territory.

12  Yamoria is a cultural hero who moved throughout Denendeh (land of the Dene) creating order and setting down Dene law. He is known by several different names, depending on the Dene group.

result, skills and participation in these activities are highly valued, as is local knowledge of the landscape (which is required to travel safely).[13]

In his work with the Western Apache, Basso (1996a; 1996b) examines both the individual and collective understandings and relationships that the residents of Cibecue have with the landscape, as well as the processes through which this cultural landscape is produced. Basso (1996b: 55) argues that landscapes are "inevitably a product and expression of the self whose experience it is, and therefore, unavoidably, the nature of that experience (its intentional thrust, its substantive content, its affective tones and colorings) is shaped at every turn by the personal and social biography of the one who sustains it." Places are reciprocally and dynamically sensed through what Basso (1996b: 55–56) refers to as 'interanimation':

> This process of interanimation relates directly to the fact that familiar places are experienced and inherently meaningful, their significance and value being found to reside in (and, it may seem, to emanate from) the form and arrangement of their observable characteristics. Animated by thoughts and feelings of persons who attend to them, places express only what their animators enable them to say.

This process becomes a shared and dynamic artefact in communities, a "universal tool of historical imagination," that is communicated through oral histories and storytelling as "what is remembered about a particular place – including, prominently, verbal and visual accounts of what has transpired there – guides and constrains how it will be imagined by delimiting a field of workable possibilities," (Basso 1996a: 5). The concept of interanimation aptly describes the way that landscapes, as conceptualised by Dene and Métis in Tulít'a, include more than land. This chapter demonstrates how imagined pasts and future possibilities for landscapes are created and challenged through individual and collective relationships with land and water, traditional conceptualisations of land, traditional beliefs and practices (such as dreaming or prophecy), and how these are linked to family histories as well as resource histories. These histories are often embodied in and communicated through stories and exercised politically through processes such as land claim and self-government agreements, local government organisations, and the resource management organisations that were created as a result of the land claim.

## *Complicating the 'frontier': Hydrocarbon histories in the Sahtu*

Dene and Métis people in the Sahtú have known about geophysical materials (today referred to as resources), including oil and gas, since time immemorial. These materials and their attributes are part of local knowledge

---

13  Tulít'a Dene and Métis travel throughout their traditional territories, often by boat or snowmobile, visiting friends in other communities, attending spiritual or cultural gatherings (such as handgames tournaments), or for the subsistence activities mentioned above.

and are often conceptualised as active features of the world, meaning that depending on their properties, they can move, transform or effect change on land and other beings. This is because, as Cruikshank (2005: 4) argues, "local knowledge is never crudely encapsulated in closed traditions, but is produced during human encounters, rather than 'discovered'. It is dynamic and complex, and it often links biophysical and social processes." Some examples of this include Tłı Dehdele Dıdlo (Red Dog Mountain) where oral tradition holds that the mountain once opened up to swallow the river and the people travelling on it, until the day a powerful Dene medicine man paid the water for safe passage; similarly, *dekʼone* (the smokes), a coal seam just upriver from Tulít'a, is the site where the culture hero Yamoria is said to have cooked the two giant beavers he killed after chasing them down the Sahtú Deh (Great Bear River). Several open seams are still burning today, and they represent for many the continued significance of indigenous cosmology. As these examples show, not only do Dene and Métis recognise oil and gas and related geophysical materials and processes as active and important features of landscapes, but they connect these features to the past, present and future, thereby linking temporality, locality and sociality.

It is important to note that in figuring hydrocarbons and in local histories, almost all of the Dene and Métis I worked with distinguished between knowing about oil as a material and knowing about oil as a *commodity*. Oil as a commodity cannot be separated from the industry it is associated with, particularly the extensive exploration, development and extraction activities that the material represents.[14] Dene and Métis often distinguished the two when asked for clarification. When used in daily conversation 'oil' is not distinguished from the industry and activities that it symbolically and ideologically represents. This was not always the case. Prior to the twentieth century, Dene used oil for practical purposes, like applying it to the tracks of sleighs. The black, sticky substance that seeped to the surface was known as 'tłeh'. A self-government negotiator and Métis man from Tulít'a, recalls: "It was just people who used to travel in that area [Norman Wells] and every time they passed by that area they used to see this black stuff on the ground and they used to share with each other that if you put this black stuff under your sleighs it goes really fast, you know." A Shúhtaot'ine Elder, explains that Dene were aware of both oil and gas because of their extensive local knowledge: "And people are hunting here and there, you know, and they stop [on the] land to make fire and then they can detect some of those natural fumes, and the air takes up on them. So, they, in those senses, they start to get some idea that maybe there is some things here and there." The Elder explained to me that people would learn about oil, as well as how to think

---

14 When asked if Dene and Métis people knew about oil, almost all research participants understood me to be asking about whether they knew about oil as a substance of value or as a material representation of the industry itself. This denotes the hybrid character of oil as well as how the material, social, and conceptual worlds intertwine in this area. It is similar to what Rogers (2012) talks about when he discusses the "materiality of the corporation" in Russia. This is explored more thoroughly in my dissertation.

about oil, from creation stories and that knowledge of minerals is also passed down in this manner.

Although Dene and Métis families were clearly aware of and using certain hydrocarbon materials in the Sahtu prior to and throughout early contact with Europeans, it was not until the beginning of the twentieth century that hydrocarbon exploration and later development by Euro-Canadians began in the Sahtu. Up until World War II, the Canadian government had limited interest in its northern territories and residents. Most of the northern lands that were acquired by Canada in the 1868 transfer of Rupert's Land and the North-west Territory (which then encompassed Alberta, Saskatchewan and present-day Yukon, NWT and Nunavut), were considered less important because these regions lacked agricultural potential. Consequently they were less appealing for Euro-Canadian settlement. Except where there was interest in developing land or extracting resource wealth from these newly acquired territories, Canada did not feel the need to establish treaties with indigenous peoples in the North. Because of this, the history of federal involvement and intervention in the North is more recent than other parts of the country. There was little thought or concern for the interests or well-being of northern peoples and places.

The whaling operations in the Beaufort Sea and the discovery of gold in the Yukon, encouraged Canada to create the Yukon Territory and begin negotiating northern treaties. During the negotiations of Treaty 8, which reached into the southern portion of the Northwest Territories, Dene and Métis people living further north of the Treaty 8 boundaries indicated that they were not interested in meeting with the government and forming a treaty. At the time, the government was satisfied with this response. Later, when Imperial Oil indicated interest in developing the hydrocarbon resources in the Sahtu, Canada formed a treaty party to negotiate Treaty 11 (Fumoleau 1973; Coates and Morrison 1986). Dene and Métis connect Treaty 11 with the emergence of extractive industry activity in the Sahtu, and they identify the late 1910s and early 1920s as the beginning of local hydrocarbon development. They explicitly tie the development of Norman Wells oilfield by Imperial Oil with the treaty they signed with the government, a controversial agreement that the Dene understood as a promise to share the land, but which the government recorded as a cession of territory and title[15] (Fumoleau 1973). A Métis participant explains:

> Treaty was signed in this area 1921. But they found, they knew about the oil before, probably 1920. And, ah, as I understand anyways, is that they wanted to get the treaty signed because there was potential for *oil* and they wanted to get the resources and – but, ah – so that's how it all started off in those days.

---

15 These divergent understandings of the Treaty resulted in decades of conflict as Canada failed to fulfill treaty promises and ignored indigenous rights and title. The issues with Treaty 8 and 11 came to a head in the 1970s, once again due to the potential of oil and gas activities, this time in the form of a pipeline. For a more thorough study of the issues with Treaty 8 and Treaty 11 see Fumoleau (1973).

Dene and Métis in Tulita describe Imperial's exploration in the 1910s as their first important experience with the industry. Local oral tradition holds that oil was first "discovered" or brought to the attention of Euro-Canadians by Dene. Many Dene and Métis from Tulít'a recalled that it was an indigenous resident from the Blondin family who provided a sample to a missionary, trader or geologist – depending on the version of the story – who was passing through the region. Written records from this period hold that the first serious investigation of petroleum potential in the area was conducted by J.K. Cornwall of the Northern Trading company in 1911 (Bone and Mahnic 1984: 53). Cornwall sent samples of crude oil to Pittsburgh, where analysis revealed it was good quality, similar to that found in Pennsylvania (Page 1981: 16; Bone and Mahnic 1984: 53). In 1914, mineral claims in the area around Tulít'a, near present day Norman Wells, were obtained by P.O. Bosworth and later purchased by Imperial Oil through its subsidiary, the Northwest Company. There is no mention of Dene involvement in the Euro-Canadian written record of this early exploration, yet the similarity to Dene oral accounts, according to which a sample of oil was sent down south in this period, is noteworthy and it provides important detail on indigenous involvement and the key role of local knowledge.

The Imperial Oil exploration during the late 1910s and early 1920s was the most northern oil and gas activity in North America. On August 24, 1920, oil was struck on a well known as 'Discovery' (Bone and Manic 1984: 54). Activity in the area was limited and eventually shut down because of the small local market and limited viability of transporting northern oil to southern markets. Yet despite the small scale of this first exploration, it had lasting political and social consequences for the indigenous peoples.

Imperial's activity encouraged the government to settle a treaty in the area, and it marked the first significant resource extraction other than fur in the Sahtu. It is telling that prior to the activity Dene and Métis peoples were largely not consulted, and that they were then left out of official accounts. A very different perspective on this early activity emerges from local accounts, wherein the Dene and Métis play a pivotal role and the injustice of their experiences in treaty making, failure of the government and industry to respect their rights, and their exclusion from the Euro-Canadian records, is underscored. Substantiation of the role of Dene and Métis in early exploration, and their experiences with the industry at this time, can be found in both written and oral records. For example, in the diaries and notes kept by Ted Link, geologist for Imperial Oil, we can see that he hired both indigenous and non-indigenous labourers to work for the company staking claims and supporting exploration. Although Link's journals from this period are not detailed, he did author articles on his experience in the *Imperial Oil Review* as well as write a geological report, which only mentions indigenous peoples in passing. Yet, in his journal from 1921, Link records the names of at least two indigenous men (and one non-indigenous man who married a local indigenous woman) who worked with him: Hib Hodgson, Ted Trindell and Jean Blondin. On both June 28th and June 29th, 1921, Trindell and Blondin are recorded as labourers in Link's planner and on August 11th, 1921, Link records that Blondin is "taking a skiff to another of his labourers" (Link 1921). In notes accompanying the journal, Link records that Hodgson was hired and worked for three days before quitting; Trindell was hired on June 18th and off on June 25th; and Blondin was hired from June 20th to June 25th. Such evidence makes it clear that Dene and Métis were involved in the early Imperial Oil activity, and this involvement is communicated today as a critical example of the silencing and erasure of local people from Euro-Canadian histories. This became evident in my fieldwork in the ways children, relatives and community members have incorporated this involvement into their own history of hydrocarbons.

The initial oil strike at the Discovery well led to the construction of a small refinery that provided petroleum products to the communities along the river. The refinery was closed in 1925 because the cost of producing in such a remote location with a limited market was not economically viable for the company (Bone and Mahnic 1984: 54). Drilling recommenced in the 1930s with new demand from mineral development in the area, which led to increased demand from new mines. A new refinery was built to supply diesel fuel to the mines being developed in the territory, specifically Port Radium, Con and Negus (Bone and Mahnic 1984: 56). The sale of oil continued to slowly increase until the outbreak of World War II, when Norman Wells would become embroiled in a key wartime project, known as the Canol[16] Pipeline. The Canol project, which I discuss below, involved an aggressive expansion of the Norman Wells oilfields and the construction of a 960 kilometre pipeline to the Yukon (Bone and Mahnic 1984: 54). The Canol played a large role in the industrialisation of the NWT. Once again, indigenous peoples were not consulted about the expansion of the oil fields, and many Elders remember well the shock and surprise of the intense changes associated with this period. It was not until the late 1960s and early 1970s, when indigenous activism was taking root throughout the country and Canadian indigenous policy was increasingly critiqued, that indigenous northerners would have their opinions on hydrocarbons heard.

The Mackenzie Valley Pipeline Inquiry, also known as the Berger Inquiry after the Judge who led it, was created to assess the social, economic and environmental impacts of constructing a gas pipeline across northern Yukon, down the Mackenzie River Valley and into Alberta (Berger 1977). Building it would effectively create an energy corridor through which other pipelines were expected to follow.

The Berger Inquiry played a key role in laying the foundation for contemporary social and environmental assessment processes in Canada. It was also a widely-publicised process that brought indigenous grievances with the state to the national stage and recognised the importance of settling indigenous rights and land claims issues in the country.[17] Berger's report in

16  Canol (or CANOL) is an acronym for 'Canadian Oil'.
17  Prior to the Inquiry, Francois Paulette and fifteen Dene chiefs in the NWT filed a caveat stating that the indigenous peoples of the NWT had never seized title of the land in Treaty 8 and 11, and that the terms of Treaty's 8 and 11 had never been honoured by Canada (Abel 2005: 251). Justice William Morrow heard the case and found that the Dene and Métis concerns needed to be addressed.

1977 highlighted the importance of Canada addressing these issues. Berger determined that no pipeline should ever be built across northern Yukon, and furthermore that there should be a moratorium on oil and gas development and the construction of pipelines for at least ten years, during which time Canada could address the unresolved issues of aboriginal rights and title (Berger 1977: xxvi). Berger titled his report *Northern Frontier, Northern Homeland*. Doing so effectively highlighted that the popular image of the northern territories as resource frontiers benefitted the state and the southern populace. He powerfully contrasted this depiction with the perception of local peoples for whom the north is a homeland. Berger wrote:

> We look upon the North as our last frontier. It is natural for us to think of developing it, of subduing the land and extracting its resources to fuel Canada's industry and heat our homes. Our whole inclination is to think of expanding our industrial machine to the limit of our country's frontiers. In this view, the construction of a gas pipeline is seen as the next advance in a series of frontier advances that have been intimately bound up with Canadian history. But the native people say the North is their homeland. They have lived there for thousands of years. They claim it is their land, and they believe they have a right to say what its future ought to be. (Berger 1977: 1)

This duality – the north as a frontier on the one hand, and a homeland on the other – has been maintained over the last fifty years in public and political consciousness, and the failure to adequately attend to it continues to feed conflict and questions surrounding northern resource development.

Anthropologists have demonstrated in their work on landscape and place, that the past plays an important role in place-making practices and in creating an individual's and/or a community's sense of place.[18] Julie Cruikshank examines stories about glaciers and how these narratives reveal the values and beliefs that both indigenous peoples and Euro-Canadian explorers and scientists possess. Cruikshank (2005: 9) argues that "Because narratives energize both exploration practices and local meanings, it is worth paying attention to what such stories accomplish, how they move, and why they persist." Similarly, narratives about past oil and gas activities reveal the diverging values and practices that characterised early interactions and exploration in the Sahtu.

Local knowledge about hydrocarbons is shared through oral traditions, stories and personal narratives. These relate individual and shared knowledge and experiences. For this reason, some Dene and Métis living in Tulít'a emphasize certain moments in history over others, just as other stories related to hydrocarbons are more highly valued among different individuals and groups. For example, Kààlogot'ine and some Métis tend to emphasise the story of the Blondin family discovering oil and being forced out of Norman Wells by Imperial Oil. This may be because of their kinship connections to the Blondin family or because they appear to have

---

18 I am thinking in particular of Basso (1996a; 1996b), Cruikshank (2005) and Thornton (2008).

historically spent more time in and around Norman Wells and Tulít'a during this period of early oil and gas development. Shúhtao'tine peoples – who tended to spend less time around Norman Wells and Tulít'a during this period – emphasise the Shúhtao'tine involvement in the building of the Canol pipeline and the passage of this pipeline through the mountains. Taken together, however, these narratives work to form a shared community story of hydrocarbon development in the Tulít'a district of the Sahtu region. These stories are deployed strategically and are used as tools to conceptualise and understand, as well as to "act on" listeners. Dene and Métis are quick to point out that the oil and gas industry (and by association the government of Canada, which issues licences and supports exploration and development) is considered responsible for negatively transforming the landscape in the Sahtu, albeit many are equally quick to note that the changes are not "all bad." Flying over the region easily supports these observations, criss-crossed as it is with seismic lines and abandoned well sites.

Recent ethnographies provide examples of how to begin addressing historical fissures and periods of transformation in landscape, place and space studies (Gordillo 2004; Stewart 1996). Gastón Gordillo's work in the Chaco with the Toba explores how the spatialisation of memory is embodied, turning past memories into new values and resulting in contradictions and social tensions. This also speaks to the situation in the Sahtu. Places and their attending memories can conjure up and connect particular people and events. Spatialised memories figure significantly during periods of transition, such as the period that has occurred with the advent of exploration using horizontal hydraulic fracturing.

Some places, people and events have been officially commemorated by the Historical Society in the regional centre of Norman Wells, and by the territorial government. Memories of other events, as well as important stories, prophecies or legends, are evoked when traversing the land or visiting a particular site, as well as when talking about oil and gas. One example is the story of the Dene men who worked as guides for the Canol pipeline. A second is how Dene and Métis today reference prophecy and prophets in their narratives of development, to communicate how they are temporally and materially connected to hydrocarbons and their development through ancestors and local knowledge. This practice demonstrates how recent hydraulic fracturing activities have verified Dene metaphysics and beliefs about development, whilst simultaneously representing a future of known uncertainty. Both of these examples are 'stories people tell' when asked about past and present oil and gas development.

## Fred Andrew Sr., George Blondin Sr., and the Canol pipeline project

During the Second World War the government of the United States found its oil tankers on the Pacific front under threat from Japanese forces. In an effort to guarantee the safety of oil – necessary to fuel the war – the Canadian Oil (Canol) pipeline project was created (Barry 1982: 1985). The pipeline moved crude oil from the Imperial oil field in Norman Wells, NWT, across the Mackenzie Mountains to a refinery in Whitehorse, Yukon. From there, oil was transported by air on the Northwest Staging Route and used as fuel for the Alaska Highway project (Barry 1985). Large numbers of American military men, as well as a Canadian civilian labour force, arrived in the Sahtu to expand the Imperial oil field and build the pipeline, the first in the Canadian subarctic.[19]

The terrain in the Mackenzie Mountains can be rough and dangerous, particularly for those who do not know its geography. Prior to the 1940s, very few non-indigenous peoples were familiar with the geography and the region. Since the military needed to scout a possible route through the mountains, they sought to employ local Dene, who had travelled through these mountain passes and valleys quite frequently, to assist with their project. The Tulít'a Band Chief explains:

> What they were telling people at that time was that, you know because the war, war was happening, so they had to build the Canol pipeline to bring some gas over to Alaska. So that's, that's when they start working. And some of the, some of the – my uncle Fred [Andrew] was one of them that guided the people over that way, because the people they walk back and forth [from the mountains to the town].

Two of these men were Frederick Andrew Sr. and George Blondin Sr. Fred Andrew Sr. was a Shúhtaot'ine from the Tulít'a area and George Blondin Sr. was a Sahtúogot'ine from the Délįnę area who later moved to Yellowknife for work and then moved his family to Behchokǫ̀ (personal communication). George Blondin has two accounts of his work on the Canol in print (Barry 1985; Blondin 1990). Fred Andrew Sr. shared his stories with his children, extended family and friends, who in turn shared some with me. Andrew's experiences are often referenced or recounted in conversations and interviews I've had with community members about oil and gas development. George Blondin's story 'Working on the Canol Pipeline' is included in one of his books of Dene stories and teachings published in the NWT (Blondin 1990: 227–228). In it, he recounts how he and his father, as well as other Dene men, scouted to the pipeline route to the Yukon.

Different fragments of this story, and the role that these Dene men played in the construction of the Canol, have been shared with me several times throughout my fieldwork, by people living in Tulít'a, particularly when I ask about what it was like for the Dene and Métis during the Canol project. It has also been conveyed when I inquire as to how Dene and Métis may have been included or not in early hydrocarbon development. The stories of the Dene who led the pipeline survey team in the mountains have been performed in different settings and for different audiences, each serving different purposes, and have become a part of both local and family histories. For

---

19 It is worth noting that in addition to the construction of an oil pipeline, this period also saw a drastic increase in the production and extraction of oil. This was made possible by the advent of aerial surveying and the construction of new roads and infrastructure.

example, sometimes they are told in a classroom by an Elder who has been invited to talk to the students about his or her history. I have also heard them shared in community meetings with industry and government.

Local Dene and Métis involvement in the Canol project is commemorated at the museum in Norman Wells (referred to as Ɫe Gǫhlįnį, 'the place of oil', in the above narrative by George Blondin) on a large sign outside of the museum. The stories are brought up sitting around kitchen tables over tea and dry meat, as well as in official community meetings with different companies interested in extracting minerals or oil and gas in the region. There are also specific aspects of these stories that are left out for particular audiences, because they involve spiritual beliefs and practices deemed inappropriate to share with outsiders. On December 6, 2013, the Government of the Northwest Territories (GNWT) announced that a mountain in the Mackenzie Mountain range would thereafter be named "Mount Fred Andrew" in honour of Fred Andrew Sr.'s leadership in Tulít'a and the Sahtú, as well as his involvement in the Canol project. These commemorations and retellings invigorate connections to the land and pride in the skills and accomplishments of local people. They also establish a connection between local indigenous peoples and officially recognised hydrocarbon histories.

Stories of Dene and Métis involvement in the Canol project link to ruins of the pipeline itself, which was abandoned in 1946 after operating for just one year (Bones and Mahnic 1984). Today the pipeline route (now known as the Canol heritage trail) is considered one of the most challenging hiking trails in Canada and an important part of the Sahtu peoples' heritage. Sites along the route included abandoned buildings and vehicles, worn-down bridges and related materials left behind by the military and the oil company, although government funded remediation and clean-up work has recently removed much of this material from the route. Clean-up and remediation from the project is ongoing. Tourists can, however, still buy paintings and photographs of the abandoned oil barrels and military vehicles, which are sold at the museum in Norman Wells. Outside, plaques and signs recognise and honour local involvement in the oil and gas industry, along with trucks, tugboats and other vehicles once used by the industry.

The Canol project involved two years of extensive exploration, construction and extraction in the Sahtu, and was a period of intense change for people and land. It came following decades of intermittent oil and gas activities during which time hydrocarbons and their associated infrastructure gradually became a part of the local landscape. As a result, oil and gas development is sometimes assumed to be inevitable. What is more, following Canol, the Berger Inquiry and the land claims process, oil and gas have become for many a potential source of future economic prosperity. Thus, particularly in Norman Wells, where the exploration in the Sahtu region is based and where oil and gas company geologists, engineers and business men are often present, pro-development discourse runs rampant and alongside speculation about the 'future'. For example, Mason (2006) examines the resource extractive industry to describe how oil and gas companies create futures through the practice of "inserting the future into the present." He notes that oil and gas companies have "an aesthetic fascination for images of the energy future" (Mason 2006:4). This fascination with the future is combined with the material remains of past developments in the region, such as the equipment left behind by the Canol. Thus, like the decaying metal from workers' shelters, oil barrels and the military trucks that once peppered along the Canol trail, or the landscapes scarred with seismic lines, narratives are carried into communities as past, present and future. The stories told about past relationships and involvement in industry, combined with present-day government policies and practices that favour and at times outlandishly cater to hydrocarbon development, serve to create a region where development is possible and most importantly, perceived as necessary and inevitable.

## Prophecy and hydraulic fracturing

Throughout my fieldwork in Tulit'a, people referred to how certain Dene prophets foretold current hydrocarbon development and related resource extraction through dreams or visions.[20] Sometimes this was offhand, at other times, surreptitious. The example most often provided by my research participants has to do with the current site of Husky Energy Ltd.'s exploration across the river, north-west of the community. The general outline of this prophecy and its retellings goes like this: Elders (or a specific prophet, depending on the telling) told community members about how, in the future, there would be a lot of oil and gas exploration and drilling in the Sahtu. So much development would occur that there would be numerous lights shining from an area across the river from Tulít'a. In some versions of this story, this marks the beginning of a period of great environmental decline and hardship, but this has not been a theme in all of its tellings.

The prophecy has significance in terms of landscape, though this may not be immediately evident to an outsider not familiar with the sheer size of the Sahtu, or with the likelihood that a gas well would be drilled exactly where Elders said it would be. Yet this prophecy has resonated with many Dene and Métis living in Tulít'a, because of the specificity of the area prophesised for development, and because they can see the area being explored and developed today for themselves. This legitimises prophecy and the importance of traditional knowledge and beliefs. Dene and Métis remind listeners and researchers such as myself that Elders knew where oil was. For example, one good friend of mine explained to me: "My Dad used to always talk about oil and gas. They knew where oil and gas was; not only my Dad,

20  It is important to note that many Dene and Métis take discussions about prophecy very seriously and some are hesitant to share or discuss them, in line with cultural beliefs about knowledge and authority (see Ridington 1992). In some cases individuals chose not to share this knowledge with me, either explicitly denying its existence and their knowledge of it, or explicitly stating they knew it existed but did not possess the ability or knowledge to share it with me. In other instances Elders requested that I document and note its importance. Respecting my interlocutors, I treat references to prophecy or prophets selectively and carefully.

there's other Elders. Like, there's [lists names of local Elders]... All of them, they *all* talk about oil and gas; they knew where it was on our land."

Community members have identified important connections between prophecies and the area where Husky Oil Ltd. was drilling and working between 2012–2015. They have also pointed out that prophecy can be used to foretell Husky's return (or that of another company) to the area in the future. First, they note that the site of Husky's hydraulic fracturing exploration project is currently located where their Elders foretold it. They also point out that this is significant because the hydraulic fracturing activities differ from previous exploration projects because of the controversial drilling that is being used, and because Husky built a permanent road to their site, something that had not occurred in recent times. The road was new, and the horizontal hydraulic fracturing drilling method had not been used in this area before. A second feature people commented upon was how the prophecy is being fulfilled at a time when the community is feeling particularly vulnerable to socio-political changes linked to the global economic climate, and are being given conflicting information by industry, government and anti-fracking activists about the environmental impacts of hydraulic fracturing. Finally, they were able to reflect on this prophecy and its potential fulfilment in the future, after the hydraulic fracturing exploration was abandoned due to the downturn in oil and gas prices. People interpret the meaning of prophecy differently. For some who see oil development as critical for improving the local economy, increasing jobs and improving living conditions, the likelihood of industry once again returning is framed hopefully and discussed with promise. For others, those who are critical of the environmental and social impacts that may occur alongside development, or cognisant of the negative impacts that may deteriorate access to important places and traditional practices, the return of industry is a sinister possibility.

## Discussion and conclusion

Stories about hydrocarbons in the Sahtú act across and within locality and temporality to connect peoples' understandings of the past, as well as determine how histories and futures are produced, defined and contended with in the present. Individual and collective narratives are part of working out the incommensurability or commensurability of hydrocarbon development with past practices and beliefs, and they support individual and group efforts to imagine possible futures. Recent hydrocarbon exploration using horizontal hydraulic fracturing has become particularly controversial because of the relative unknowns associated with the unconventional extraction method. The differences between past oil and gas extraction and horizontal hydraulic fracturing appears to have taken the communities of the Sahtu by surprise.

Willow and Wylie (2014: 225) argue that "fracking is an outgrowth of established energy production patterns, as well as a novel socio-technical phenomenon." Because of the relative remoteness of the Sahtu (in comparison to other areas of Canada and the United States) and the extremely limited infrastructure in the region, hydrocarbon production takes place on a smaller scale than it does in the south, but it has an equal or larger impact. In addition, fracking activities and their negotiation have followed the patterns of earlier oil and gas development: promises of significant economic benefit and job creation; assurances of vast wealth from hydrocarbon resources that could create sustainable economies and communities.

Dene and Métis initially handled hydraulic fracturing exploration as a continuation of previous oil and gas activities in the region rather than as a novel technical phenomenon. As this new socio-technological phenomenon came under increased scrutiny in the global media, some local people began to question the safety and impacts on the environment and people. Nuttall (2010) highlights how the dreams of extracting resources in the circumpolar world have been fuelled by and created through the notion of the arctic as a frontier for oil and gas development. This imagined potential for development has similarly shaped the political and discursive imaginary of the northern territories in Canada. He notes that many indigenous peoples feel helpless in the face of what appears to be inevitable development, while many others perceive oil and gas as an economic opportunity, particularly important where there are few opportunities for jobs and where communities are extremely vulnerable to global market fluctuations and environmental changes, most notably climate change.

As the Canol and Blufish cases indicate, many indigenous peoples in the territory view oil and gas development as an important economic opportunity, but are wary of the environmental risks associated with development and the impacts this will have on livelihoods and health (Kakfwi 2004; Nuttall 2010). A part of this move towards supporting oil and gas development can be explained by the land claim settlement and the expectation that any development now will be decided by indigenous peoples themselves and cannot proceed without their consent. It can also be explained, as this chapter has argued, by the longer and increasingly active acknowledgement of Dene and Métis involvement in past development and the increasing reliance on short-term industry for seasonal wage employment. This is not just happening in the Canadian North. Anthropological work on oil and gas corporations in Siberia provides a possible comparison to the situation in the Sahtu due to the similarities of the region and the colonial histories of development, as well as industry practices (Tuisku 2002; Rogers 2012).

Rogers (2012) argues that oil and gas companies in the Perm region of Russia have developed new patterns of sociability by strategically implementing material and semiotic depictions of their projects alongside local histories and beliefs. These have formed part of an effort to sustain public support and evade critiques of their projects. In the Sahtu Oil and gas companies provide large donations to community programs, and in recent years they have also begun entering into Impact Benefit Agreements (IBAs) prior to exploration and development (see Dokis 2015). Furthermore, old equipment from industry activities, as well as the Canol trail itself, are materially and symbolically meaningful and highly regarded throughout the region for their historical significance. The case of the Perm region of Russia is similar, as companies deploy the material qualities of hydrocarbons strategically, such as likening the geological depth of resources to the cultural and historical 'depth' of local communities. Thereby they evoke a material connections between the natural gas pipeline and the local communities (Rogers 2012: 285). These depictions can result in local people identifying culture and tradition with oil. There are clear similarities between the Perm region and the situation in the Sahtu region of the NWT where, during public meetings, industry representatives make notable efforts to depict their projects as favourable to potential workers, and to establish continuity between past and present projects in the area. They speak to local relationships to land and place if possible. In these contexts, 'traditional knowledge' is used as a buzzword rather than engaged with as a concept. And as I indicated, the material connectivity of land and oil and gas is perceptible in the scarred remnants of seismic lines, the abandoned American vehicles along the Canol pipeline trail, and most recently, the road built by Husky Ltd to access their exploratory wells.

The NWT has been and continues to be imagined as a 'northern frontier' by industry and government. This chapter has demonstrated that there is in fact a long history of resource extraction in the region. In contemporary discussions of 'developing' the material wealth of the Canadian North, however, this history is disregarded by industry and the state. Perhaps Abel was right when he said that "Because the region is marginal in southern consciousness, Canadians often assume that its history is marginal as well" (2005 [1993]: 265). The industrial history of the NWT has been marginalised in contemporary discussions about oil and gas. On the other hand, the image of the northern homeland – the place that Berger came to know through the stories and testimonies shared with him by Dene and Métis people living throughout the NWT – has been equally strong and limiting for many, because it fails to acknowledge how hydrocarbons are a part of contemporary Dene and Métis landscapes, family and individual life stories. It also disregards the role Dene and Métis played in creating political and governance structures in the area. Berger made a very clear distinction between the Dene homeland, which he understood as distinct and set apart from hydrocarbons, and the northern frontier which has been, throughout Canadian history, intertwined with hydrocarbon exploration, development and extraction. His definitive separation resulted in a very powerful imaginary of the Dene and Métis traditional territories, but it did not accurately represent their own conceptualisation of hydrocarbons as they relate to and are a part of land, nor did it represent their historical and practical connections to hydrocarbons and their development. Today, it can be recognised that the Dene and Métis homeland is a landscape of which hydrocarbons are an active part. They are inescapably a part of the landscape and history, but they are also apart from it. As Tsing argues, "frontiers have their own technologies of space and time: Their emptiness is expansive, spreading across the land; they draw the quick, erratic temporality of rumour, speculation, and cycles of boom and bust, encouraging ever intensifying forms of resourcefulness" (2005: 27). In this light, one of the most illusory impacts of the frontier concept in the Sahtú is how it has co-opted the past as part of a pro-development narrative, and has managed to both stall and omit new discussions as the debate continues to be framed as one of 'frontier versus homeland' and 'nature versus culture'.

# References

Abel, Kerry 2005 [1993]. Drum Songs: Glimpses of Dene History. Montreal & Kingston: McGill-Queen's University Press.

Andrews, Thomas D. 2004. "The Land is Like a Book": Cultural Landscape Management in the Northwest Territories, Canada. In Igor J. Krupnik and Tonia W. Horton (eds), *Northern Ethnographic Landscapes: Perspectives from circumpolar nations.* Washington: Smithsonian Institute.

Andrews, Thomas D. and Susan Buggey 2008. Authenticity in aboriginal cultural landscapes. *APT bulletin* 39 (2–3):63–71.

Andrews, Thomas D., Glen MacKay, Leon Andrew, Wendy Stephenson, Amy Barker, Claire Alix, and the Shúhtagot'ine Elders of Tulita 2012. Alpine Ice Patches and Shúhtagot'ine Land Use in the Mackenzie and Selwyn Mountains, Northwest Territories, Canada. *Arctic* 65 (Supp.1): 22–42.

Andrews, Thomas, John Zoe and Andrew Herter 1998. On Yamòzhah's Trail: Dogrib Sacred Sites and the Anthropology of Travel. In Jill Oakes, Rick Rieve, Kathi Kinew, and Elaine Maloney (eds), *Sacred Lands: Aboriginal World Views, Claims, and Conflicts.* Edmonton: Canadian Circumpolar Institute.

Barry, Patricia S. 1985. *The Canol Project: An adventure of the U.S. War Department in Canada's northwest.* Edmonton: Patricia Barry.

Basso, Keith H. 1996a. *Wisdom sits in places: Landscape and Language among the Western Apache.* Albuquerque: University of New Mexico Press.

Basso, Keith H. 1996b. Wisdom Sits in Places: Notes on a Western Apache Landscape. In Steven Feld and Keith H. Basso (eds), *Sense of Place.* Sante Fe: School for Advanced Research Press.

Berger, Thomas R. 1977. *Northern Frontier, Northern Homeland.* The Report of the Mackenzie Valley Pipeline Inquiry: Vol. 1. Ottawa: Minister of Supply and Services Canada.

Blondin, George. 1990. *When the World was New: Stories of the Sahtu Dene.* Yellowknife: Outcrop.

Blondin, George 2005. *Trail of the Spirit: The Mysteries of Medicine Power Revealed.* Edmonton: NeWest Press.

Bone, Robert M. and Robert J. Mahnic 1984. Norman Wells: The Oil Centre of the Northwest Territories. *Arctic* 37 (1): 53–60.

Canada 1993. *Sahtu Dene and Métis Land Claim Agreement.* Indian and Northern Affairs Canada. Ottawa: Government of Canada.

Cruikshank, Julie 1998. *The Social Life of Stories: Narrative and Knowledge in the Yukon Territory.* Vancouver: UBC Press.

Cruikshank, Julie 2005. *Do Glaciers Listen? Local Knowledge, Colonial Encounters, and Social Imagination.* Vancouver: UBC Press.

Dokis, Carly A. 2015. *Where the Rivers Meet: Pipelines, Participatory Resource Management, and Aboriginal State Relations.* Vancouver: UBC Press.

Fumoleau, Rene 1973. *As Long as This Land Shall Last: A History of Treaty 8 and Treaty 11, 1870–1939.* Toronto: McClelland and Stewart Limited.

Gordillo, Gastón R. 2004. *Landscapes of Devils: Tensions of Place and Memory in Argentinean Chaco.* Durham: Duke University Press.

Goulet, Jean-Guy A. 1998. *Ways of Knowing: Experience, Knowledge, and Power Among the Dene Tha.* Vancouver: UBC Press.

Hanks, Christopher C. and Barbara J. Winter 1986. Local Knowledge and Ethnoar-chaeology: An approach to Dene settlement systems. *Current Anthropology* 27 (3): 272–275.

Helm, June 1994. *Prophecy and Power among the Dogrib Indians.* Lincoln: University of Nebraska Press.

Ingold, Tim 2000. *The Perception of the Environment: Essays on Livelihood, Dwelling, and Skill.* London: Routledge.

Irlbacher-Fox, Stephanie 2009. *Finding Dahshaa: Self-government, Social Suffering, and Aboriginal Policy in Canada.* Vancouver: UBC Press.

Janes, Robert R. 1993. Ethnoarchaeological Observations among the Willow Lake Dene, Northwest Territories, Canada. *Musk-ox* 33: 56–67.

Kakfwi, Stephen 2004. *A Review & Assessment of the NWT Protected Areas Strategy.* Toronto: World Wildlife Fund.

Link, Theodore A. 1921. Ted Link's diaries and journals relating to trips to Norman Wells, Northwest Territories, 1919–1946. Daily Journal, M-9449-1. Ted Link Fonds, The Glenbow Archives, Calgary, Alberta.

Legat, Allice 2012. *Walking the Land, Feeding the Fire: Knowledge and Stewardship Among the Tlicho Dene.* Tucson: The University of Arizona Press.

Mason, Arthur 2006. Images of the energy future. *Environmental Research Letters* 1: 12–17.

Nadasdy, Paul 2003. *Hunters and Bureaucrats: Power, Knowledge, and Aboriginal-State Relations in Southwest Yukon.* Vancouver: UBC Press.

Nadasdy, Paul 2007. The Gift of the Animal. *American Ethnologist* 34 (1): 25–43.

Newman, Dwight G. 2009. *The duty to consult: New relationships with Aboriginal peoples.* Saskatoon: Purich Publishing.

Nuttall, Mark 2010. *Pipeline Dreams: People, Environment, and the Arctic Energy Frontier.* Copenhagen: IWGIA.

Page, R.D.J. 1981. Norman Wells: The Past and Future Boom. *Journal of Canadian Studies* 16 (2): 16–33.

Ridington, Robin 1988. *Trail to Heaven: Knowledge and Narrative in a Northern Native Community.* Iowa City: University of Iowa Press.

Ridington, Robin.1990. *Little Bit Know Something: Stories in a Language of Anthropology.* Iowa City: University of Iowa Press.

Rogers, Douglas 2012. The materiality of the corporation: Oil, gas, and corporate social technologies in the remaking of a Russian region. *American Ethnologist* 39 (2): 284–296.

Scott, Patrick 2012. *Talking Tools: Faces of Aboriginal Oral Tradition in Contemporary Society.* Edmonton, AB: CCI Press.

Slobodin, Richard 1981. Subarctic Métis. In June Helm (ed.), *Handbook of the North American Indians, Vol 6: Subarctic.* Washington: Smithsonian Institution.

Stewart, Kathleen 1996. *A Space on the Side of the Road: Cultural Practices in an "Other" America.* Princeton: Princeton University Press.

Thornton, Thomas F. 2008. *Being and Place Among the Tlingit.* Seattle: University of Washington Press.

Tsing, Anna Lowenhaupt 2005. *Friction: An ethnography of global connection.* Princeton: Princeton University Press.

Tuisku, Tuula 2002. Nenets Reindeer Herding and Industrial Exploitation in Northwest Russia. *Human Organization* 61 (2): 147–153.

Willow, Anna J. and Sara Wylie 2014. Politics, ecology, and the new anthropology of energy: Exploring the emerging frontiers of hydraulic fracking. *Journal of Political Ecology* 21: 222–236.

Jasmin Immonen

# Ephemeral landscapes: Contrasting moralities in a city of sand

## *Introduction*

In February 2015, Kenny, then sixteen years old, posed the interesting question about how globalisation is materialised in a landscape through objects of speed. We were in Pachacutec, north of Lima, Peru, where I had taught him at Our Lady of Sorrows school as part of my fieldwork between October 2012 and September 2013. Pachacutec, named after a famous Inca Emperor, consists of around two hundred settlements[1] known in the Peruvian official lexicon, as well as in common speech, as *asentamientos humanos* (human settlements). As it was the summer holidays, Kenny and I did not meet at the school, but at a nearby crossing where buses left the teachers to climb the last stretch of the steep, sandy hill up to the school. During fieldwork, I had often seen students here in their uniforms, roaming around and greeting teachers. After my fieldwork, Kenny and I had stayed in contact through Facebook, our correspondence enabled by our smartphones. We both had Nokia 520s. As my home country was often a focus of conversation, I had been quick to point out that Nokia was a Finnish brand.

Kenny had grown since I had last seen him, and he looked down somewhat shyly as he descended from the school. He soon got over his shyness and enquired about Europe in his typically curious way. Reflecting back on Pachacutec, Kenny said in a casual, perhaps even cynical, manner: "You see? Nothing has changed here". Kenny was using a vocabulary I had grown accustomed to during fieldwork, for in daily conversation in Pachacutec the subject of 'change', and whether it had been accomplished or not, was very common. We sat down to drink our Inca Kola (a local soft drink now acquired by Coca-Cola), in a restaurant that catered to travellers. A new, yellow bus passed by, taking people to Lima. I had not seen these buses during my fieldwork, and I pointed out to Kenny that they were new. Kenny agreed, but with some hesitation: "Yes, change happens, but too slowly". This comment went to the heart of a major concern among the youth of Pachacutec: the evident lack of the speedy progress that had been

---

1   In 2013 there were reportedly 136 settlements making up Pachacutec, but online sources suggest the number had vastly increased by 2015.

175

promised through the connectivity brought by objects such as smartphones. Inspired by our discussion on 'change' and smartphones, Kenny then turned to a question that I sensed had been in the minds of many: "If Finland gained its independence nearly a hundred years after Peru, why it is so much more advanced than Peru?"[2]

I take Kenny's question as a good point of departure for examining discourses that I heard in Pachacutec on a daily basis. I will suggest that the ways materiality emerged in certain narratives and practices on the city peripheries, point to tensions between their lives on the one hand and official narratives of advancement through economic growth on the other. There has been a long tradition of ethnographic studies of the spontaneous formation of new settlements by people 'invading' areas in the margins of Peru's capital city (e.g. De Soto 1989; Imparato and Ruster 2003; Stefano Caria 2008) focussed on community organisation and infrastructural provision. They mostly view such settlements as primarily fulfilling aspirations for housing and gaining a foothold in the urban economy. This chapter seeks to go beyond this by adding a socio-material dimension to the study of urban anthropology. Indeed, Ian Hodder (2012) has pointed out the peculiar absence of attention given to materials in social anthropology until recently in contrast to the high importance placed on the material quality of 'things' in archaeology.[3] For example, the material quality of excavated pottery reveals a whole range of issues regarding the society under question. In a similar vein, the material qualities of the landscape in Pachacutec reveal a lot about the conflicts around 'advancement' today, and about the more complex entanglement of humans, things, history and ideology.

More specifically, this chapter aims to link the moral values associated with linear time and advancement with the settings within which people live, in particular their everyday encounters with materiality. For instance, that 'advancement' carries with it expectations that do not always deliver as expected, or that there are ambiguities in an ideology that separates humans from their material surroundings. A terminology of 'less' or 'non-advanced' has long been applied to people living in these areas and, as illustrated by what Kenny said, there is a degree of entrapment experienced in constantly waiting for 'change'. This has a lot to do with the material quality of the landscape surrounding him, but also with the struggles the people of Pachacutec have gone through in their desire to obtain 'things' as well as

2   The most typical answer to Kenny's question builds on work by Peruvian scholar Mariategui (1971), who argued already in the early 20th century that the Independence of Peru (or of Latin America more broadly) was 'fictive', for it only served an elite willing to be mediators for foreign powers such as the USA and Britain, and seeking to guarantee the export of minerals. At the turn of 21st century, the discourse of 'participating in globalisation' only increased this export and today Peru's wealth comes mostly from the export of minerals such as copper and gold (Murakami 2014).

3   Hodder is one of many theorists highlighting the importance of things. He notes the continuous interplay between our relationship with things and generalised systems of discourse and value.

to transform the landscape. Indeed, I want to pick up on Hodder's (2012) insight that there is a darker side to the entanglement of humans and things. The sources of transformation and constraint in human society are not in the material facts of existence, but in the mutual dependencies between humans and things. As things have a limited ability to produce themselves, in our dependence on them we also become entrapped in their dependence on us. In order to illustrate this point, this chapter will pay special attention to houses in Pachacutec and how their appearance has been entangled with notions of ownership and permanence, as well as with notions of linear time. The people of Pachacutec need houses and land-plots for living, but the houses also need to be built of stronger materials. Issues around legal ownership and lack of resources have inhibited this, and one result has been talk of the need for 'change', as illustrated by Kenny.

As anthropological work on the landscape concept shows, materials mediate sentiments and ideas with other dimensions of experience. To explore the implications of finance capitalism for everyday experiences and landscapes, it is also useful to attend to discrete 'things' like mobile (or cell) phones and houses, with their material and social qualities. Through looking at the ways by which the people of Pachacutec interact with these objects, we can infer that they have not been passive in the process of landscape change, but they have actively participated in its transformation and, by their own standards too, have made gains by doing this. New cities anyway are dynamic places, where people modify legal frameworks, for instance through practice, by claiming inclusion. And although they are often 'not included' in the legal sense of the term, they are participating in consumption, exchange and distribution in ways that challenge the victimising position implied in the idea that they are 'less advanced'. Furthermore, recent years in Latin America have seen the emergence of new forms of abundance in terms of consumption, work, entrepreneurship, territorial organisation and money (Gago 2017). This abundance is particularly visible in the circulation of objects such as smartphones, which have opened up new forms of communication that enable territorial distance to be bridged. As Arjun Appadurai (1990) argues, 'mediascapes' or the distribution of the electronic capabilities to produce and disseminate information, and the images created by these media, "provide large and complex repertoires of images, narratives and 'ethnoscapes' to viewers throughout the world, in which the world of commodities and the world of 'news' and politics are profoundly mixed" (1990: 299).[4] There are globally shared sentiments that often disrupt alleged views of national differences, in a way that could even be called post-national. The use of social media, frequently accessed via the mobile phone, has also given youth

---

4   Appadurai's theory of five main 'scapes' pertaining to globalisation is famous (see also the introduction to this volume). In proposing these deeply perspectival constructs, Appadurai is extending Benedict Anderson's idea of nation-states as imagined communities, to "perspectival sets of landscapes", which are the building blocks of "imagined worlds" in a world where international capital and international clothing are given local meaning by contextual conventions (1990: 296–297).

*Figure 1. A fairly new 'invasion' by the beach of Pachacutec.*

a degree of freedom to rework norms. These re-workings have, however, often been fragile and fleeting, making the term ephemeral landscapes a suitable metaphor to capture the situation.

I also suggest that while Kenny asked the question about advancement, he may not have believed the premise of the question himself. A few years after that meeting in 2015, as part of a funding application he wrote an essay, which he shared with me, about the boredom of everyday life. In it, he questioned calls for progress and modernisation, as well as the linear time that makes life so dull. He ended his essay with a call for freedom for Peru, indicating how nationalist sentiments are deeply entwined with the multiple contradictions generated by global capitalism. Considering this, my intention in this chapter is thus not to say that national identifications are waning, or that they will necessarily wane, but to show that paying attention to 'things' allows us to better recognise how narratives of 'advancement' produce ephemerality. This should be reiterated even after many years of sustained critiques of teleological meta-narratives of modernity (Ferguson and Li 2018). The chapter thus puts forward the view that at a conceptual level, to foreground entanglement over advancement, is not to deny the existence of cores and peripheries. Rather, it aligns with a political shift from narratives of national growth that place responsibility on the individual, to recognising a shared material world that is not separate from human interaction, and to highlighting the significance of distribution (see Li 2014). Such shifts may well be more suited to addressing the multiple paradoxes experienced in empirical reality.

## *The promise of "getting ahead" and its contradictions*

The importance of the city as the space where "imagined worlds", to borrow Appadurai's (1990) term, are sought, has been emphasised in the last century. The last decades have seen the birth of megacities with populations larger than that of some nation-states. Today Lima's population is more than 10 million, but what is relevant is not the figure, but the speed at which the city has grown. In the book, *Lima y sus arenas* (Lima and its sand) (2015), Danilo Martucelli records the following seemingly unbelievable figures: Lima's population has multiplied roughly 90 times within the past 115 years. What accounts for this vast growth has been the mass migration to the city from the 1940s onwards. In the Peruvian social science literature this has been named the 'rise of the masses', *ascenso de masas* (Matos Mar 2004). People migrating from other areas of Peru, most prominently the Andes, were first lured by the possibilities generated in the 20th century by small industrialisation processes on the coast. The initial settlers ran out of space in the city centre, and built their houses in the peripheries, starting with simple straw mats and rugs for building materials. The migrants are known as *pobladores* (settlers), and to each other as *vecinos* (neighbours). A large proportion of those living in settlement towns are born there, which means the nomination *poblador* does not apply to them anymore; they are children of the city. Moving to settlements from the older residential area of Lima is also increasingly common.

This process of settlement formation, by more or less organised invasions, has changed the landscape of the city of Lima entirely. Lima is built on flat land, in a type of oasis in the middle of the desert, and after Cairo it is the world's largest desert city. The Rimac River runs through its old colonial centre. In geographical terms, the areas surrounding Lima with their many settlements, spread north, east and south, are known accordingly as *cono norte* (North Cone), *cono este* (East Cone) and *cono sur* (South Cone). On the northern and southern edges, the settlements cover a vast expanse of sandy mountains known to Peruvians as *arenales* (from *arena*, sand) that form the last stretches of the Andean *cordillera* reaching the coast. In the east, the settlements are formed in rockier hills, closer to where the Andes begin. These three areas have shopping malls, highways and microenterprises. They began to grow at a fast pace in the 1960s and continued to absorb migrants from other regions.[5] At the turn of the millennium, the population in the cones grew at a more accelerated pace than in residential Lima (Calderon 2005; Joseph 1999; Matos Mar 2004) so that in 2010, only 2 million people lived in the old parts of Lima, whereas 6.5 million lived in the cones (Martucelli 2015).

The self-built townships in Lima and its peripheries all have distinct histories that shape the everyday experience of their inhabitants. Pachacutec

---

5   In Peru, areas outside of Lima, including Callao where Pachacutec lays, are termed as regions. These regions are subdivided into provinces and districts, and they have an elected government. Lima instead maintains the status of a province.

built on top of the *arenales* north from Lima, was officially established in 1989, but records state that it has been settled at least from 1968 (Calderon 2005; 2009). It is built next to Ventanilla, a municipality and a district that also started as a settlement town, and it lies next to a beautiful coastline also visited by *Limeños*, the inhabitants of Lima. At the time of writing, Pachacutec is home to approximately 200 000 people. The settlements that make up Pachacutec have been formed through a combination of people settling on previously uninhabited land in the desert, resettlement programmes, and buying of land-plots on the legal and 'illegal' land-markets.[6] In 2015, Pachacutec was listed by the Map of poverty of Peru[7] as an area where 38,9–46,2 % of the population is poor. The majority of its inhabitants do not possess legal title to their land-plots, also known as lots. Despite these ambivalences, Pachacutec continues to grow at a fast pace. This indicates that settlement towns in city peripheries continue to hold hope and potential for their inhabitants.

In Peru, the 20th century marked a stage when settlement towns came to encapsulate a promise of citizenship still visible today in places like Pachacutec. The migrations to Lima, and aspirations of mobility that transformed the desert landscape surrounding it, were motivated by a goal epitomised in the phrase heard all over Peru: *salir adelante*, 'getting ahead' or 'moving forward'. *Salir adelante* in common speech often refers to a present state that is characterised by a struggle (*lucha*). It was geographically expressed in a downward movement, as the altitude of the highland Andes often denotes poverty. In the name of 'getting ahead' (*salir adelante*), the *pobladores* were defined as those who could claim access to money circulating in the city of Lima by working in commercial activities, construction, cleaning and domestic work. Their story did not, however, end with gaining access to the capital. That was merely the beginning. The telos of modernity (e.g. Ferguson 1999) posits education as a symbol of 'progress', and so every settlement has a large land-plot reserved for building a school. The sacrifices that sometimes accompanied migration, such as losing lands in the home village, were compensated by the promise of 'upward social mobility'. This idea held that the children of the *pobladores* would eventually be rewarded by the work of their parents, and over the course of time become 'better than their parents'. This entailed such things as a professional career, 'a happy family' and a 'better way of speaking', or *mejor habla*. A mother of a student said to me: "Maybe we cannot give them proper housing, they'll have to do it when they are grown up. But we can give them education". 'Getting ahead' was thus accompanied by a new vision and division where ascendance through the social strata was defined by education and respectability, both racialised characteristics according to old colonial classifications (e.g. De la Cadena 2000; Wade 2009).

6  The biggest difference between 'legal' and 'illegal' inhabitant is that the latter only holds a 'proof of possession' but not legal ownership (Calderon 2005).
7  The Map of Poverty of Peru drafted by the INEI (National Statistical and Informational Institute) is backed up by various national and international agencies.

We could thus argue that while 'getting ahead' was an expression of a desire to break free from asymmetrical social relations implanted through colonialism, it implied moving up through a hierarchical scale that paradoxically was also implanted by colonialism. Geopolitical alignments have been decisive in perpetuating this linear movement, and historically the linear hierarchical scale has served the purpose of classifying people according to colonial reductionist logics in order to legitimise resource extraction. If, since colonial times, the Peruvian economy has been understood to be part of a world economy where the rhythm is set by export (Golte and Adams 1990), the situation continues today in the multiple loans that Peruvians have been forced take out in order to meet the needs of 'getting ahead'. These loans in turn have had an influential role in how citizenship has been forged through the formation of settlement towns. In 1960s global development discourse, the urban debate carried out by the architect John Turner and anthropologist William Mangin, posited that settlements were not so much the problem as the solution. Auto-construction turned into a space of 'alternative futures', and many planners and donor agencies became convinced that shantytowns are as much 'slums of hope' as they are 'slums of despair' (Corbridge 1995: 258; Davis 2007: 71–72; Turner 2009). Foreign aid money was directed to projects that supported settlement formation throughout the latter half of 20th century (Calderon 2005).

Yet policy as such is less important here than the ways people's actions get entangled with it, along with local material and social histories, in short, with the landscapes they inhabit but also construct. For one way by which some measure of equality inside the nation has been achieved in Peru, have been the discursive frames of foreign loan companies and donor agencies, which, when combined with national efforts, shaped the city but also got rid of the oligarchic relations of past regimes. Land-reforms by the leftist government of Juan Alvarado Velasco in 1968–1975 expropriated land from wealthy landowners and were a symbol of this type of democratisation. At the same time, land reform contributed to the disorganised growth of Lima, as large landowners became frightened of losing their lands to the state, and began selling on their land illegally, thus also reducing its value (De Soto 1989; Calderon 2005; Davis 2007). The land reform was also a period when Peru became more dependent on the rest of the world and was forced to rely more on foreign debt (Teivainen 2002; Klaren 2004). This scenario remains structurally unchanged, and strengthening citizenship via land distribution is a practice continued up to this day, serving as a mechanism for securing votes (by right- and left-wing governments alike). Continuing the theme of the emancipatory potential of settlement towns, as promoted by Turner and Mangin, the influential economist Hernando De Soto posited at the end of the 1980s that the legalisation of ownership would have a positive effect on the residents' tendency to invest, e.g., by starting restaurants or by subletting their property, and hence over the course of time, owners of lots would become the middle-class of the nation (1989). In the 1990s, the right-wing political leader Alberto Fujimori, to whom De Soto served as main economic adviser, initiated neoliberal structural reforms that liberalised the market in favour of foreign investment, while at the same time retaining

*Figure 2. Parts of the settlements of Pachacutec.*

multilateral agencies' approval via loans in public investment[8] (Teivainen 2002; Oliart 2011).

The result of the alignments taken during the 20th century was that a house in the periphery of the city, no matter how fragile and in what condition, became a marker of citizenship. At the same time, providing the settlements with adequate infrastructure got ignored. Nonetheless, through their visibility, these fragile houses disturbed the status quo.

The entanglement of people's efforts with national and foreign policy thus also yielded concrete results that redefined the meanings of citizenship. Several authors have argued that in the newly emerging cities of the global South, citizenship and its entitlements are not defined through labour, as had been the case in 19th century Europe, but rather through residence (Davis 2007; Holston 2008). This process has been accompanied by a new social praxis. Martucelli (2015) argues that the city of Lima has become a theatre for the creation of a new form of sociability stemming from changes in interpersonal dynamics that have been accompanied by a new type of individualism, something that has progressively taken over all social classes. People's worldview has begun to centre around the market, rather than the subservient and patronising relationships of old. In the political and economic realms, this can be seen in the expansion of certain ways of doing business and forming alliances. In Pachacutec, this new sociability as well as the linear movement of 'getting ahead' is seen in how the material of houses is used and how the land is divided.

---

8   For example, in 1996 the Urban Property Rights Programme was established with the support of the World Bank (Stefano Caria 2008) to legalise property. For educational reforms supported by the World Bank, see Oliart (2011).

*Figure 3. Middle-class aesthetics.*

Once the boundaries of lots are drawn, owners take charge of house construction, each lot being associated with a family nucleus that owns it. The houses most often have a backyard reserved for a possible extension. Cement is a valuable construction material that denotes more permanency and affluence than either straw mats or wood sheeting. Over time, as settlements have grown and become more established, houses made of straw matting have been replaced by wood and tin. Today, almost all the houses in Pachacutec are made of wood, and straw mats figure mostly in people's conversations and references to the neighbourhood's past. When straw mats are mentioned, they are used to describe a prior state, from which people have managed to 'move forward' or 'get ahead'. Houses are often painted with bright colours that signal successes in citizenship and individual ownership, since rarely do two neighbours have the same colour house. Graduating to a wooden house, however, signals but another state of impermanence, as ideally the wooden boards should eventually be replaced by cement. A reminder of the impermanence of wooden houses, some of the windows do not have glass. This allows people to jut their face out a window opening to greet a visitor with a kiss on the cheek. Alternatively, some houses do not have window openings at all.

I suggest that this construction process is a way of claiming or performing citizenship by residence. For citizenship is most visible in the layout of the houses. The orderly shape of the settlements, more than individual people, is what underpins understandings of citizenship. The lots and their owners are the first things to be registered in the municipality after an invasion, while the number of people actually living in a lot remains vague. Sometimes a census is carried out, but generally with poor results. Furthermore, the way settlements are designed by engineers before an invasion takes place, as well as the satisfaction people get from their lots being registered and mapped, suggest that there is a desire for a particular spatial order. The houses are aligned in firm blocks, with the *asentamientos humanos* referred to in official papers with the letters A.A.H.H. or A. H., regularly laid out in official maps and preliminary designs. This differs from the public perception that settlements are founded in disorder and occupied by lawless, invading people. In these designs, the areas reserved for parks and commercial activities are marked in colours, showing how they are planned with forethought, and how different forms of inclusion are expected to transpire over time, reaching social and political goals in almost tangible ways. Green is a highly valued colour in the desert landscape as it symbolises a state of permanence as opposed to the ephemerality of the sand and for this reason houses were often also decorated with green plants. The Peruvian flags were popular decoration too, an assertion of the pride of citizenship and of participation in the national society. Here, the temporality of linear progress had generated considerable hope among *pobladores,* hope that at times over-rode the everyday struggles of living in a settlement, like lacking proper access to infrastructure. In part then, the landscape is being transformed to meet the needs of 'inclusion', the rules of which are set by the land market. Indeed, in James Ferguson's (2015) work on the renewed need of a politics of distribution, he describes how people do not aspire simply to democracy or political equality, but also to ownership. This is particularly easy to see in land-politics, and as we have seen in the case of Peru, it has important consequences for the ways landscape is transformed, what people expect and how they experience and live through this transformation.

The state, with its own, shifting conceptions of citizenship, obviously also plays a significant role. As elsewhere, analysing official representations like maps gives insight into this. New maps do not just erase histories (see e.g. Järvi and Uusihakala, this volume), they also reproduce historical divisions as they seek to create new orders. Benjamin Orlove (1993) has showed that whereas the colonial orderings emphasised racial differences, the newer Republican maps with their postcolonial ordering stressed natural regional differences. It was also in Republican Peru that the state essentially began to measure elevations, with the effect that the Andes and its people were depicted as an obstacle to national integration. The Highlands became represented as a uniform elevation dividing the nation, and Peru gained the tripartite characteristics of today: the Andes, the Amazon and the Coast. As Orlove's descriptions indicate, through maps new means of controlling were put in place as previous mechanisms of imposing order evaporated. Today, the ambiguous non-presence of *Pachacuteños* in the national census has made them appear an 'obstacle' to progress and an object to be developed through national integration via orderly settlement planning. To some degree, the people living in settlements are also de-racialised and this might indeed be a desired attribute for the migrating people, and a reason to move to Lima. But while they are de-racialised, they are also increasingly classified on a more or less non-governmental scale as the 'urban poor'. There is thus an ever-present ambiguity in the process of citizenship via residence, and the existence of classificatory categories like 'the global/urban poor' as well as the problems in census making, exhibit this. The next section will indicate how the material quality of the landscape, often ignored in policy, contributed to this ambivalence.

## Sand and the moral conflicts of 'advancement'

Foregrounding the entanglements of material and ideology means attending to how power travels through discursive frames and local efforts. One of the seductions of the narrative of advancement, which in this setting became encapsulated in performing citizenship through residence, is the potential rewards it promises. As it has been recorded in other settings also, the linear narrative of growth presumes everyone will receive a fair reward for their work (e.g. Li 2014). Reverberations of a similar trend can be seen in Pachacutec. Besides material markers such as flags and houses, the moral discourses present in Pachacutec are significant in making citizenship claims. Specific groups of people who lacked a common history but were for one reason or another – through the forces of global capitalism – joined together in this area, had to forge a common identity to counter the dispossessing mechanisms of capitalism.

During my fieldwork this happened through a narrative of humbleness. Indeed, in the discourse in Pachacutec, humility was an attribute through which claims to citizenship and its entitlements were made. When I arrived there for the first time, an informant called it a *ciudad fantasma,* a ghost town: people left it to work in the early hours of the morning and returned at night time. He described the people as 'supportive' and 'humble'. They worked hard to 'get ahead' and did not steal and trick as much as a *Limeño*. And yet, 'getting ahead' was not an entitlement that was given just with the act of moving, one had to demonstrate one deserves it by labouring to transform the sandy landscape into a habitable place. This required coordinated effort, and indeed, a settlement requires an organisational unit to be formed, known as *directivo* that takes charge of matters pertaining to the settlement. The *directivo* is comprised by a leader, a secretary and a treasurer, elected by vote, who are charged with the responsibility of obtaining legal access to land that has already de facto been settled  as well as infrastructures such as a water sewerage system (see De Soto 1989). The residents or *pobladores* are required to attend settlement meetings and take part in communal work duties, known as *faenas,* to make roads and build schools, all activities that are decided upon in settlement meetings run by the *directivo*.

*Faena* is a public exchange of labour that involves the community as a whole and some institutions. Clearing out the hard sand in order to build houses is the first duty carried out in *faenas* as soon as a settlement is formed. The systems of exchange, reciprocity and redistribution present in the *faena* have historical roots. The Incas used *mit'as*[9] in order to extract large amounts

---

9   Michael Malpass (2016) describes that while *faena* is a work that the community does in a common project, *mit'a* is rotating work that members of a community do in turns for another institution, such as the church or state government.

of labour, but also provided for labourers in a way that was typical to their communities' exchange systems (e.g Klaren 2004). *Faena* was also a form of labour exploitation by large estate owners (*hacendados*). Later the state took to using *faenas* in order to meet its needs for labour, providing materials and technical knowledge in exchange for the labour of commoners gathered by district officials. Peasant communities have also adopted this form of labour mobilisation, and *faenas* are an important part of the community identity and politics (Gose 1994; Borg Rasmussen 2015; Malpass 2016). An important component of these labour exchanges was providing the labourers with food, drink and coca leaves, a practice that is still carried out in some regional areas (Malpass 2016), but not really anymore in settlement towns like Pachacutec. These forms of labour practices have become an important symbol of citizenship and its entitlements in settlement towns.

In Pachacutec, performing collaboratively through *faenas* was a sign of humility, and thus also a way of making a citizenship claim, I shall argue. Humility highlighted the distinctiveness and autonomy of these spaces. While 'humble' would also be a word used to describe poverty, the meanings associated with it in Pachacutec implied resistance and ability to overcome obstacles. 'Humble people' didn't 'need great things', but 'valued themselves for what they had'. A 'humble person' thus had sensitivity towards other people and did not allow his/her own personal successes to disturb social relations with others. Sometimes, 'being humble' was extended to describe Peruvians in general. When Yosimar, a quiet boy in the 9th grade, commented on Peruvians, he rejected the traditional view set out by the development discourse that Peruvians 'need help': "We are good. We are caring. We don't need help. If there is need, we help each other", he said. 'Humble people' essentially helped each other, extending their solidarity via collective work and raising funds with *polladas* – selling dishes of chicken with potatoes – in order to raise funds for some cause, such as care of a person suffering ill health. At times such cooperation was undoubtedly idealised, and at others it was hoped that it would eventually extend to the whole world, perhaps reverberating with past socialist movements. Explaining to me the principles of cooperation, whisking her hand backwards as a sign of past times, 7th grader Barbara said the practice of collective work went 'back to the time of the Incas':

> It's like in the community they make a collection for a woman. Right now, there is a woman who has cancer. And so, everybody gets together to make a *pollada*, to get the money together, and all the [ones who have] collected go to see the woman [...]

> It's mutual help, help for the woman, like sometimes when we need help, that same person is going to help the people who helped her. And also you can count on help [...] when you have problems in the family. You can trust in other people or in works...between the women they help to clean the community because sometimes...there is so much rubbish [laughs]... And so, everyone gets together and starts to clean everything that is dirty, and from there they agree they have to help each other, so that one day, they will help between everyone.

And this chain will keep ascending from our comrades (*compañeros*) to the rest of the world.

Indeed, solidarity is pragmatic, and authors writing of similar settings have written about the importance of social relations over money, the ephemerality of the latter confusing the very meaning of 'economy' (de L'Estoile 2014). Interpersonal and social commitments like solidarity often create more tangible and lasting relationships than mere money, and this might be more the case in such instances where resources and revenues are irregular. The Peruvian economy has certainly shifted towards irregularity in income generation, and today, 60% to 70% of the population make their earning through the informal sector.[10] Much of the development narrative places emphasis on people as income generators and responsible for their own economic growth and the presence of the discourse of humility indicated the tensions of this model. The development narrative obviously had in some respects failed the residents of Pachacutec, who have had to forge a collective in order to combat the most dispossessing effects of capitalism. As Ferguson and Li (2018) point out, in the South, wage labour has anyway often attained a kind of aspirational universality that it nowhere achieved in reality.[11] Barbara's quote suggests that the principle of mutual aid in Peru's settlement towns has an element that defies ideas of deservingness and meritocracy: it functioned as a distribution mechanism for those in need.  But it also contained an element of negotiation. As in this case, it was the women more than men who participated in communal labour duties. Further, it has been argued that the informal sector's cooperative practices function on a 'compensating logic' (Quijano 1998), performing roles 'for the time being' until more security of income is established. Thus, here we see a peculiar combination of a desire for autonomy on the one hand, and dependence on the other. The autonomy of the community is celebrated via notions of humility, yet its ultimate aim is to establish another type of dependence altogether: citizenship with all its promises of mobility and equality, to which infrastructural markers are crucial. Here I would go back again to the desire to be inserted into the national map, and the importance of ownership to achieve that goal. In anticipation of that, different labour forms have been mobilised validated through the narrative of 'humbleness'. This can also be something to exploit in order to become visible to the state. In this process, the natural quality of the landscape became secondary.

As it has been suggested thus far, gaining citizenship through the ownership of land-plots, and the consequent transformation of the landscape through *faenas,* are not processes free from frictions. Just like the narrative of humility, the way by which people interacted with materials spoke to me about the fragility and tensions of formal citizenship. Undoubtedly the

---

10 In 2014 19% of the Peruvian GDP was produced by the informal sector and it employs 61.5% of the population (Martucelli 2015: 198).

11 The authors argue this requires going beyond narratives of the 'proper job' as the cornerstone of 'advancement' (Ferguson and Li 2018)

most overwhelming material in the narratives was sand, reminding that the material quality of the landscape so easily ignored in policy could not really be ignored in reality. Indeed, while the linear logic of progress had a considerable potential to instil hope, present for example in the ways houses were painted and decorated, perhaps the greatest contradiction in 'getting ahead' via land ownership is the way capitalism operates in the market: it always gives preference to those with more capital. This had profound consequences for the way landscape could – or could not – be transformed in Pachacutec. In 2013, around 80% of the land-titles were not legalised, despite the emancipatory legalisation attempts hailed by De Soto in the 1990s. An official working for a state organisation in charge of land-titling gave me the official reason for this lack of legalisation: the land was reserved for military use. The unofficial rumour circulating in Lima was that people were not given titles for fear of 'landowner mafias'. These have been gaining influence and consolidating their power since 2000 (Martucelli 2015) when, due to the rapid increase in land prices, owning land in peripheral areas of the city became recognised as a viable business. It was also known that people from Lima and other places, recognising rapid increases in the price of land as infrastructure arrived, were buying plots in settlement towns in order to re-sell them when the prices went up, leaving the houses unoccupied or renting them out in the meantime.

There is thus a startling and suggesting ephemerality in the landscape itself. Land speculation has generated disciplining discourses among government officials and bitter rumours among the *pobladores* about 'selfish people' hoarding plots while not living in them. Meanwhile the people who do live in the settlements have to carry out the labour of sweeping sand away through *faenas*, constructing streets and negotiating for infrastructure. These tensions are also expressed through housing materials. Anthropological work in Peruvian settlement towns has demonstrated that while the straw mat used by the incoming migrants displayed precariousness simultaneously with a promise of 'a modern identity' (Nugent 2006), it also symbolised a prior state of social relations, when people were more cooperative. Writing of Lima's district of San Martin de Porres, which grew out of settlements like those of Pachacutec, Ivan Degregori et al. (1986) record how the *pobladores* recounted that the material of the straw mat had allowed them to have conversations with each other through their walls. In the narratives of the *pobladores*, there was a sense of growing 'selfishness' that accompanied individualism and the change of straw mats to brick walls, and the subsequent decline of shared activity. The *pobladores* recounted that people 'don't care anymore', *ya no se preocupan*. Similarly, in Pachacutec, rumours circulated about settlement leaders who took the best pieces of land for themselves, or took the money gathered for the construction of parks and ran away. These activities contributed to the sense of impermanence characteristic of Pachacutec and they were perceived to contribute to the ephemerality of the landscape.

Lack of legal title caused by fears of land hoarders, or because the land indeed was meant to be for military use (which is a peculiar claim given that part of the settlements were born as government projects), has also meant

*Figure 4. "The people of Pachacutec united will never be defeated."*

that water companies and other agents in charge of infrastructure have not been willing to invest, fearing that they might lose their profits if the people are evicted. In some houses, blue water tins are a reminder that water is not available on tap. The people themselves sometimes are not inclined to invest in their houses for the same reason. The 'selfishness' accompanying the desire for accumulation was met with some resistance, however. During my fieldwork, I saw empty houses left to accumulate in value being vandalised by the *pobladores* with graffiti's stating *no vive* 'does not live'. In some cases they were vandalised with explicitly political statements, such as the leftist statement: "The people (of Pachacutec) united will never be defeated".

The principle of growth through land ownership has stumbled on its own principle: accumulation. Furthermore, the policies entangled in a web of global relations have ignored the fundamental material quality of the landscape, which is its sandiness. While ignored in policy, in people's narratives, sand is a significant part of everyday politics and the continuous efforts to keep the sand at bay through sweeping, contribute to a sense of impermanence, just as the empty houses do. People laugh about the presence of sand, or lament how there is too much of it. Sand is also used to discipline. The *pobladores* can evaluate whether their land speculating neighbours really are living in their houses by peering over the fence. If the sand in a backyard had been made hard by daily watering, it is a sign of someone living there. But sand that appears unkempt indicates that no one really lives in the house. These features were often given as proof to the municipality inspectors in charge of land legalisation, who came to verify whether the settlers actually lived on their plots or not. Sand was thus a constant reminder of the elusiveness of 'getting ahead'.

*Figure 5. Peruvian flags were often placed in the lots as a sign of citizenship.*

The narrative of advancement also ignores many matters of family and community relations, such as who gets to benefit from the end result of the arduous process of clearing away the sand, and who is treated as the owner of the land. These questions generate conflicts, and in so doing, also call 'advancement' into question. The sand and empty, fragile houses show that while 'humility' is the attribute through which citizenship had been forged, providing the *pobladores* with autonomous spaces, it is constantly taken advantage of by larger capitalist forces. It also shows that the successes of citizenship via land-ownership are limited in their neglect of the natural material surrounding.

## The 'street' and the ephemeral landscapes of social media

Thinking of the way material and conceptual become entangled in these ephemeral landscapes, also allows us to grasp the heterogeneity of experience that disrupts the linear timeline in these new cities. Recalling my introduction above, I would reiterate how young people in recent years almost anywhere have been similar in their access to a mobile phone and/ or a Facebook account. And there are sentiments expressed via social media that cross borders. This too, has implications for how citizenship is embedded in the landscape, particularly for the young. For instance Saskia Sassen has persuasively argued that globalisation and electronic networks, both as material processes and as imaginaries, bring about changes in the formal and informal relationships between the state and the citizen. Among them are a range of emergent political practices often involving hitherto silent or silenced populations. Through their destabilising effects, globalisation and electronic networks produce operational and rhetorical openings for the emergence of new types of political subjects and spatialities (Sassen 2006: 292).[12] This has been accompanied by a certain flexibilisation of citizenship, where borders become more porous (Ong 1999). Indeed, mediascapes may create severe problems for the ideoscapes with which they are presented (Appadurai 1990: 301), and it is reasonable to assume that today social media, often accessed via mobile phones, has the potential to challenge ideoscapes – such as 'advancement'. Although Daniel Miller (2010) has pointed out that the first and most important impacts of new media tend not to be radically disruptive, but the tendency is to seize upon it to finally realise some previously existing but hitherto frustrated desire.

Digital media has the effect of bridging territorial differences. It joins people in different places through common types of posts, about everyday wisdom or environmental destruction. At the same time, social media offers the potential for self-creation. Miller (2011) sees social media very much as a public arena, where a 'self' is created to be exhibited to an imagined audience. The self being portrayed is often a mobile subject that knows how to 'have fun' and 'enjoy the moment'. Consumerism can bring a lot of destabilising social capital. The youth in Pachacutec use social media to create a 'self' that is street smart and pragmatic, and not necessarily buying into standard tropes of progress.  In the Peruvian youth culture I witnessed, the 'road to development' was accompanied by the 'street', and the youth gained social capital through embracing traits of a street culture that borrowed influences from American Hip Hop and Rap, elements made more popular throughout Latin America by Reggaeton artists. The youth would post pictures of Converse shoes, skateboards and other items that accrue social capital on 'the street', using tropes that defied notions of progress and ascending through a meritocratic paradise. 'Love' also entered the discourse as a sign of 'liberation' accompanying consumerism (see also Abu-Lughod 1990; Lukose 2009).

Other frequent wall posts by girls displayed romantic disillusionment, and cynical tropes of amorous love, reflecting their pragmatic response to dominant gender hierarchies, where girls were still given the role of 'falling in love', while boys sought 'conquest'. Morality was thus implicit in the way in which youth chose to create themselves, and these posts had the potential to rework some of the more constraining norms. By showing how well they knew how to manoeuvre multiple constraints experienced in the everyday, and not be categorised by their circumstances, the youth gained respect (Miller 2010).

The temporal dimension of these new forms of communication is an important aspect of their popularity. While waiting (for infrastructure, cement houses and so on) is felt to be characteristic of Pachacutec, social media promises immediacy and speed. But social media also reconfigures

---

12 Sassen (2006) asserts however that the weakening of the imagery of the nation state as to where solidarity belongs to does not necessitate a move to postnational citizenship, while it does reconstitute the national.

notions of space and time, paradoxically making its transformative potential rather fleeting. Instead of trusting grand narratives that 'getting ahead' present to them, life comes to be 'enjoyed in small moments'. This also reflected a lack of predictability in the future. The relationships formed on social media can be ephemeral and easily sidelined, practicing a new ethics in relationships where less time is given to other people, while time becomes consumed in perfecting the image of the 'self' (Turkle 2011). Indeed, the relationship of digitalisation with youth's increased precarity has been a widely noted process. Guy Standing sees it as a direct reflection of how young people know less and less what to do with their time (that is certainly spent less in employment). In Standing's (2016) formulation, the spread of social media as a means of communication that has accompanied the retrieval of the state and dominance of liberal policies worldwide has gone with the emergence of a new class of people who can no longer be adequately described as either working class or middle-class: the 'precariat'. Precarity however is not to be associated with a shared set of substantive economic conditions, instead, the concept surfaces a set of issues that go far beyond purely economic ones, such as identity, gender, family and national membership (in Ferguson and Li 2018). Precarity thus is not to be viewed as the opposite of an ideal, but it does reflect a change brought by global finance capitalism, a change that requires reconfiguring what we even mean by class, mobility and labour, and to some extent even national citizenship.

We have also seen that while digitalisation may bring precarity, at the same time it has given young people some agency to challenge previous norms. When, in social media, they display robust landscapes, this suggests that they are well equipped to deal with transnational connections and local conditions, and that there is something non-victimising in their position. In these re-workings of power, however, it is important to pay attention again to how power travels through them, for example in preferred images. Young people's shaky, irregular and fleeting ideals shaped by global currents, can allow norms to be disrupted and they form potential spaces of re-articulation, but as Kenny's desires for 'freedom' in his essay and his ambivalent stance on 'advancement' showed, these re-workings do not change the systems of inequality that generate ephemeral spaces.

## Conclusion

The ethnographic examples above show how people's engagement with the material things of the landscape, such as houses and smartphones, can illuminate challenges to the parameters of 'advancement'. If mass migrations to the city were driven in the 20th century by the command to 'get ahead' or 'move forward' into a class-based society, the materiality of colourful houses and national flags later has attested to people having achieved at least some of this, as well as some degree of freedom to rework earlier relations of inequality. The people of Pachacutec further validate their claim to citizenship and 'getting ahead' through the moral discourse of 'humility', which, at the same time, has helped counter some of the most dispossessing effects of capitalism. The ephemerality of the landscape however, generates contrasting moral discourses. The other side of 'advancement' are the empty houses left to accumulate in value while being devalued by graffiti, lack of infrastructure and the ever-present sand. There is also moral condemnation of such selfish people buying lots with houses but not living in them. The losers are those who do not have sufficient capital to live somewhere else. They are the ones subjected to the cruelties of living in sand. These conflicting oppositions reveal the messy entanglement between policy, people and things that also urges scholars as well as others to go well beyond political master-narratives of growth and advancement, and to take materiality more seriously.

At another level of analysis, the global and consumerist tropes that the youth of Pachacutec displayed on social media and gave them meaningful agency, can also be seen as a type of politics on their own. That is, there are sentiments and experiences that shape youth subjectivity in a way that question the use of national categories such as 'advanced' and 'non-advanced'. These currents brought by global capitalism also show the seductive potential that lay in a notion of a unified cosmopolitan world where those with social capital too 'get ahead'. What this chapter has suggested, is that new conceptualisations and approaches are needed that acknowledge better the ephemeral landscapes accompanying narratives of growth and policies advancing accumulation as a sign of citizenship. Ephemerality or precarity, unites wider geographical spaces, but also reconfigures power relations. This requires of us to constantly look back critically to the pernicious concept of advancement. It also highlights the value of an activist-academic stance that would seek to unravel the entanglement of humans, things, history and ideology in favour of a distinctive narrative. Such a stance recognises how meanings and feelings materialise in the surroundings. In doing so, it could also challenge victimhood by taking the people on the ground and their empirical experiences more seriously.

# References

Abu-Lughod, Lila 1990. The romance of resistance: Tracing transformations of power through Bedouin women. *American Ethnologist* 17 (1): 41–53.
Appadurai, Arjun 1990. Disjuncture and difference in the global cultural economy. *Theory, Culture, Society* 7 (2–3): 295–310.
Borg Rasmussen, Mattias 2015. *Andean waterways: Resource politics in Highland Peru.* Seattle: University of Washington Press.
Calderón, Julio 2005. *La ciudad ilegal: Lima en el siglo XX.* Lima: Universidad Nacional Mayor de San Marcos.
Calderón, Julio 2009. La producción de la ciudad formal e informal. In Julio Calderón (ed.), *Foro Urbano: Los nuevos rostros de la ciudad de Lima.* Lima: Colegio de sociólogos del Perú.
Corbridge, Stuart 1995. *Development studies, a reader.* New York: Arnold.
Davis, Mike 2007. *Planet of slums.* London, New York: Verso.
Degregori, Carlos Iván, Cecilia Blondet and Nicolas Lynch 1986. *Conquistadores de un nuevo mundo: De invasores a ciudadanos en San Martin de Porres.* Lima: IEP.
De la Cadena, Marisol 2000. *Indigenous mestizos.* Durham: Duke University Press.

De L'Estoile, Benoit 2014. "Money is good, but a friend is better": Uncertainty, orientation to the future and the 'economy'. *Current Anthropology* 55 (9): 62–73.

De Soto, Hernando 1989. *The other path: The economic answer to terrorism*. New York: Basic Books.

Ferguson, James 1999. *Expectations of modernity: Myths and meanings of urban life on the Zambian copperbelt*. Berkeley: University of California Press.

Ferguson, James 2015. *Give a man a fish: Reflections on the new politics of distribution*. Durham: Duke University Press.

Ferguson, James and Tania Murray Li 2018. Beyond the "proper job": Political-economic analysis after the century of labouring man. Working paper 51. PLAAS, UWC: Cape Town.

Gago, Veronica 2017. *Neoliberalism from below: Popular pragmatics and baroque economies*. Durham: Duke University Press.

Golte, Jurgen and Nora Adams 1990. *Los caballeros de Troya de los invasores: Estrategias campesinas en la conquista de la gran Lima*. Lima: IEP.

Gose, Peter 1994. *Deathly Waters and hungry mountains: Agrarian ritual and class formation in an Andean town*. Toronto: University of Toronto Press.

Hodder, Ian 2012. *Entangled: An archaeology of the relationships between humans and things*. Oxford: Wiley-Blackwell.

Holston, James 2008. *Insurgent citizenship: Disjunctions of democracy and modernity in Brazil*. Princeton: Princeton University Press.

Imparato, Ivo and Jeff Ruster 2003. *Slum upgrading and participation: Lessons from South America* Washington D.C.: The World Bank.

Joseph, Jaime A. 1999. *Lima, megaciudad: Democracia, desarrollo y descentralización en sectores populares*. Lima: Alternativa, UNRISD.

Klaren, Peter F. 2004. *Peru: Society and nationhood in the Andes*. New York: Oxford University Press.

Lukose, Ritty 2009. *Liberalization's India: Gender, youth and consumer citizenship in globalizing India*. Durham: Duke University Press.

Li, Tania M. 2014. *Land's end: Capitalist relations on an indigenous frontier*. Durham: Duke University Press.

Malpass, Michael 2016. *Ancient people of the Andes*. Ithaca: Cornell University.

Mariategui, Jose Carlos 1971. *Seven interpretive essays on Peruvian reality*. Austin: The University of Texas Press.

Martucelli, Danilo 2015. *Lima y sus arenas: Poderes sociales y jerarquías culturales*. Lima: Cauces Editores.

Matos Mar, Jose 2004. *Desborde popular y crisis del estado: Veinte años después*. Lima: Fondo Editorial del Congreso del Perú.

Miller, Daniel 2010. *Stuff*. London: Polity.

Miller, Daniel 2011. *Tales from Facebook*. London: Polity.

Murakami, Yusuke (ed.) 2014. *La actualidad política de los países andinos centrales en el gobierno de izquierda*. Lima: IEP, CIAS.

Nugent, Guillermo 2006. Elencos ingeniosos: Que todo parezca igual para que todo cambie. In Eduardo Toche Medrano (ed.), 2006. *Perú hoy: Nuevos rostros en la escena nacional*. Lima: DESCO.

Oliart, Patricia 2011. *Políticas educativas y la cultura del sistema escolar en el Perú*. Lima: IEP, Tarea.

Ong, Aihwa 1999. *Flexible citizenship: The cultural logics of transnationality*. Durham: Duke University Press.

Orlove, Benjamin 1993. Putting race in its place: Order in colonial and postcolonial Peruvian geography. *Social Research* 60 (2): 300–336.

Quijano, Anibal 1998. *La economía popular: Sus caminos en América Latina*. Lima: Mozca Azul Editores.

Sassen, Saskia 2006. *Territory, authority, rights: From medieval to global assemblages.* Princeton: Princeton University Press.

Standing, Guy 2016. *The Precariat: The new dangerous class.* London: Bloomsbury Academic.

Stefano Caria, Antonio 2008. *Estudios urbanos: Títulos sin desarrollo.* Lima: DESCO.

Teivainen, Teivo 2002. *Enter economism, exit politics: Experts, economic policy and damage to democracy.* London, New York: Zed Books Ltd.

Turkle, Sherry 2011. *Alone together: Why we expect more from technology and less from each other.* New York: Basic Books.

Turner, John 2009. *Housing by people: Towards autonomy in building environments.* New York: Marion Boyars.

Wade, Peter 2009. *Race and sex in Latin America.* New York: Pluto Press.

Eeva Berglund

 https://orcid.org/0000-0003-0269-562X

# Troubled landscapes of change: Limits and natures in grassroots urbanism

## Introduction: The city as a landscape of alternative politics

Seeking above all to make sense of the fraught politics of contemporary urban change, this chapter is informed by grassroots urban activism and, looking towards anthropology, by the socialised concept of landscape developed in this volume. Anthropology's interest in phenomenological research approaches and 'lived experience' could be put to good use in analysing the kinds of technologised, right-angled (or almost) surroundings in which most of us (have to) dwell: cities and towns.

Granted, there is something counter-intuitive about approaching the city, long associated with modern machines, through phenomenological lenses. Urban life is not obviously akin to the embodied, organically embedded and slowly meandering experiences highlighted in the anthropological landscape literature, which builds on Tim Ingold's extensive and influential work. Besides, as the physical footprints of (some) cities today grow with unprecedented ferocity, attention is grabbed rather by physical constructions and the struggles over open space, housing, ecosystems and infrastructures that follow. Nature's zigzags, as Ingold has shown (2013: 137) do offer theoretical insight, but life for most of us has long unfolded amidst the more engineered geometries of the city (Berglund 2011). In a discussion of landscape, it is important to recall that people are at home also in towns and cities, often also enjoying the quintessential pleasures of urban life. This is not just in famously dynamic cities like New York City, Rio de Janeiro, Berlin or London, whose trajectories have informed urban policy the world over. Alas, having tried to emulate their apparent success, many cities are now troubled by the ways everyday life and entertainments, not to mention homes, fetch increasingly eye-watering prices, while the scale and appearance of new construction defy convention, taste and often public legitimacy.

Projections of urban growth suggest that also environments beyond them will continue to be made over to the intensifying requirements of economically dynamic, cities: mega-dams, artificial islands, mountain-top removal, fracking and so forth. This frenzied remaking of landscapes follows on from European fossil-fuel-driven harnessing of 'hinterlands' for industry, and earlier waves of innovation that so dramatically altered solar-based landscapes around the world (Mitchell 2011). The unending economic growth associated with these processes is no longer so clearly on the horizon though. Rather, hydrocarbons, climate and economics mix in historically new ways that defy political imaginations. And so, other futures are being anticipated and built, as cities around the world witness a growing phenomenon of low-budget but intellectually and technically ambitious alternative Do-It-Yourself (DIY) practices.

As a sympathetic observer, I see these practices as opening up spaces for radically different technological and environmental futures. As well as expressing preferences about them, anthropologists can and must critically analyse these processes. Fortunately, the anthropological concept of landscape[1] is helpful as it highlights the social character of the environment, both where it seems stubbornly resistant to human action (as nature) and where it is artificial (technologically complicated or capital intensive). The concept of landscape is surprisingly useful for approaching urban change and its troubles today.

Landscape is an ordinary yet complex word that resonates across many different conversations. In work centred on mostly remote and even quiet places, anthropology has understood landscape to be "beyond land" (Árnason et al. 2012), experienced in movement and perception and generating togetherness as well as separation. Urban landscapes too display similar dynamics, being textured by social practices that persist over time, and harbouring sensuousness, open-ended creativity and contingency. Like non-urban landscapes, cities too set the conditions of life and establish constraints on action and on choice itself (Kirkman 2009; Easterling 2016), while structuring groupings of people and their things, and inviting their inhabitants' heightened attention. Cities are layered with symbols and technical apparatuses of different kinds and periods, they may be alienating in various ways, yet for all that, they can still be home.

This chapter seeks to make a theoretical point about the pertinence of anthropological approaches to landscape in cities, but this needs to be approached through specifics. My example is the Finnish capital Helsinki where I was born and where I have again been living, researching and engaging in a range of urban initiatives, with different levels of intensity, for almost ten years now. Helsinki is now a little over a decade into what the city has itself branded the biggest construction boom in a century, a process presented as the only right response to the incontestable pressures of our times. But many see this trajectory as disastrous, particularly in environmental terms, as well as in producing new social inequalities. Building on this opposition, I posit two contrasting ways of imagining and practicing, but also planning, landscapes. Both arise out of urban experience and both involve the relative privilege of planning for a future. At one extreme is an intensification of

---

1   See introduction: an experience of movement, a shared category, a target of political projects and a memory bank. Also, following geographer Kenneth Olwig, a body politic substantively enfolded within a geography. Our understanding of landscape "cannot focus on the country or the city, but must incorporate the mutual definition and relations of both" (Olwig 1996: 45).

a detached landscape building that originated in the generic, fast-growing, city of industrial capitalism with its organisation based on "seeing like a state" (Scott 1998). At the other extreme is a more or less self-conscious working against this legacy, namely grassroots urbanism and particularly urban gardening. Specific sociotechnical and political histories are always key to shaping landscapes, but painting with a broad brush, Helsinki appears rather typical in the dominance of internationalism in architecture and commerce, standardised infrastructures and global metrics of success. At the other pole, countering this, are forms of grassroots urbanism, also familiar from around the world that build on social media and ideals of global environmental sustainability. Both the mainstream and the alternative are part of global circuits of many kinds, including somewhat abstract technical knowledge. I argue that like scientific authority, this participation informs how city dwellers perceive, produce and inhabit their surroundings, that is, their landscapes.

Like previous social movements, today's grassroots or DIY urbanism is an emergent and often influential force on the urban stage, and as before, it creates spaces for exploring and not simply rejecting technoscience (e.g. Berglund and Kohtala, forthcoming). This notwithstanding, it is also a way of bringing nature into the city. Whether as food production, anarchist inspired nocturnal (usually) acts of city beautification or gatherings of people experimenting across a range of alternative practices and values, these often informal and collective initiatives for urban change are both cause and effect of socio-technical as well as politico-epistemic change, as anthropologists (Estalella and Corsin-Jimenez 2016) and others (e.g. the sustainable design pioneer Ezio Manzini [2015]) have noted. This is not quite protest or resistance, rather, it is an effort to construct or prefigure a different world, as the snappy Zapatista slogan long ago aptly put it.[2] As a type of activism, it has shifted the focus of environmentalist critique toward cities, which though full of artifice and modern hubris, are no longer inimical to environmental agendas, quite the opposite.[3]

The myriad practices of remaking urban environments to better suit uncertain futures are endlessly fluid and self-consciously creative (Rosa and Weiland 2013; Bialski et al. 2015),[4] but tend to seek a reattachment or re-enchantment with practical activity and the human scale. This sensibility is usually guided by respect for limits somewhere. Whereas incumbent ideologies and dominant economic sectors like finance and construction and even mainstream environmentalism elide questions of limits (Meadowcroft 2013), activism questions the mainstream's desire for economic growth and its assumed benefits, even where activists are not anti-capitalist as such.

---

2   At the turn of the millennium, the slogan was often heard: "Another world is possible!" It was attributed to Mexico's Zapatistas, now recognised as a key inspiration for alter-globalisation and anti-capitalist actions around the world.

3   This is not the place to labour a clear definition or typology. The phenomenon is dynamic and the literature is fast growing, some listed below.

4   They can also have perverse effects, and examples of green agendas unwittingly or intentionally supporting standard neoliberalisation abound (e.g. Checker 2011).

Whether bolstered by scientific authority or not, in the older language of 'limits to growth' or recent calls to respect planetary boundaries (Jackson and Webster 2016), a notion of nature as limits somewhere fuels their commitment. Not waiting for government, business or other agencies to do it for them, urban initiatives are prefiguring tomorrow's world today, combining social and ecological critiques into new repertoires of action. This is so even where activism involves beneficiaries of contemporary capitalism, 'creatives' and professionals (or not-quite-professionals) of many kinds. In fact today's urban activism connects the (still) comfortable city life with troubles elsewhere (whether close by or distant) that enable it. They are acutely aware of – and often distraught by – proliferating global assemblages spawning endless wicked problems whose adverse effects are getting closer to 'us' in time and space. Whereas decision makers and academics appear oblivious to limits and limitations, for activists these realities loom large though vague.

An anecdote illustrates the point. One day in spring 2016, I found myself in a dispiriting but not surprising conversation with a young (then under 30) activist I know, who was setting up a new urban garden for Helsinki residents to learn about local edible plants. We had both attended a one-day symposium on environmental policy for researchers and practitioners. The event had been premised on the increased urgency of an all-encompassing shift away from a resource intensive economy. She was scathing about the speakers, several of whom I count as friends and colleagues, and then did an imitation of the day's "blah, blah, blah" -level of discourse that made me cringe as well as laugh. Having recently graduated from university, she had attended the event in the hope of finding inspiration for an educational project. After we parted I felt deeply saddened. Since my first meeting with her six years earlier, she had been doing urban gardening and promoting sustainable energy, either as a volunteer or poorly paid project worker. Compared to all that, however, the environmentalism of those of us at the symposium, those with power – she guessed – was hyped up but constrained and lacking in intellectual merit let alone anywhere near the political force required. Ouch! She is not averse to a little gentle civil disobedience, like many activists of her age in Helsinki, but she is not a protester and hardly militant. Rather, she is a do-er, a team player impatient for massive social change. With another summer season of urban gardening over, she was once again looking for work.

As they turn their backs on – or are denied – conventional capitalist aspirations, activists are not, though, heading in droves to the backwoods (or deserts) to establish eco-villages or other back-to-the-land initiatives as was the case 50 years ago. They are making space in the city, from their own starting points but enmeshed in others' projects, not least large-scale construction. If not protestors, they are social critics. Indeed, starting from mundane experiences of cities designed for some activities more than others, activist researchers have been scathing critics of fast-growing industrial cities since at least the 19th century, and even more so, of the sprawling and car-based cities since. In this frame, my friend at the symposium is an activist-researcher of the city, not unlike Lewis Mumford (e.g. 1938) and

Jane Jacobs (e.g. 1961) in the mid-twentieth century and Richard Sennett (e.g. 1996) and others since. These writers' complaint that the experts (planners particularly) are not up to the task allocated to them is as old as the professions themselves, as is their observation that greed for money and power corrupts city politics. They have specifically drawn attention to the way that conventional, politically powerful, thought has allowed – or erected – a chasm between the city and the wider socio-ecological world beyond. Not unlike phenomenologically inspired landscape research, their work has highlighted everyday feelings and doings, as well as standardised technologies, as what makes up the city.

## Spectacle as disembedded landscape

The dominant urban imaginaries of the last two-plus hundred years, have been rather different. In *The Country and the City* Raymond Williams (1973) brilliantly traced the rise of bourgeois images and understandings of the city and how they captured the imagination and obedience of modern or would-be modern audiences. In an analysis based on London but relevant beyond it, he showed that while the mutual dependencies between what became known as centres and peripheries actually became more intense, their supposedly essential differences became exaggerated and reified in ideologically informed representations. Metropolitan self-delusion, extending to belief in the superiority of city life and people, was made possible in part by disembedded, detached conceptions of rural landscapes contrasted with the city. The modern period's re-arrangement of socio-natural life prioritised the image – the picturesque, the scenic, the deftly composed and pleasing prospect – over the material and intensely experienced struggles that actually produced this epoch-making change. If Williams concentrated on poetry and literature, other authors have drawn our attention to the image as, literally, pictures (Cosgrove 1983).

As the twentieth century saw the expansion and acceleration of consumer-led capitalism, such detached images increasingly took the form of spectacle. This, at least, was a key argument among the Situationist International, whose anti-establishment and militantly convivial protests in mid-twentieth-century Paris still inspire urban activists.[5] At issue was not just the penetration of capitalism into our innermost experience. The Parisian critics posited an image-saturated social system where alienation is total, but they were also critical of the destruction of our physical world too: post-war Paris experienced mass expulsions, distressing demolitions and vast rebuilding projects (Pinder 2005: 137).

Such a literal yet extreme polarisation of landscapes into centre and periphery has only intensified in recent decades. Iconic leisure or ecology-oriented landscapes (see the chapters by Mölkänen and Järvi in this book) have become entrenched and enclosed, often emptied of the people whose activities substantially shaped the attractions that now draw in tourists

---

5   As elaborated upon in Guy Debord's *The Society of the Spectacle*, published in 1967.

and settlers. With just that perversion in mind, William Cronon (1995) dubbed these "the wrong nature". At the other end of this notionally centre-periphery spectrum, are mono-functional central business districts (CBDs). The absolute extreme may be the decidedly fictional skyscraper cities of advertising, for instance the island of thrusting architecture that promoted the (not unreasonable) idea that "we live in *Financial Times*" in an advertising campaign in 2007.[6] Like the modern city of capitalism, the city of the twenty-first century also thrusts upwards from privately owned land and enjoys a reputation as the seat of progress and novelty. However, now city governments also operate as if exempt from temporal, spatial and social limits, and even from accountability to their residents (Easterling 2016).

The fantasy of a global evolutionary trajectory to wealth remains astonishingly tenacious. This is so even though it is now possible (in some quarters) to ponder on the end of global economic growth (Frase 2016). Dogged commitments to growth are arguably driven by urban experiences: paradigmatically consumerist and aspirational, capital-intensive and mediated through such imagery. We now have the alienating spectacle of 19th and 20th century modernity in super-turbo-over-drive, an aesthetic for the epoch-making intensification of both the extractive industries and waste-processing that deal with the excrement or 'externalities' of this mode of economy on the other. The city is disconnected in thought from its hinterlands even as landscapes are produced as conservation areas, traditional villages, mining concessions, industrial-scale agriculture and aquaculture, topologies that only deepen existing complex forms of interdependence and vulnerability. All that there is, is ever more clearly and consciously the result of human design if not shared human benefit. Meanwhile, though knowledge of spatial interdependencies grows, a further polarisation unfolds: gargantuan corporate entities and hyper-wealthy families tear away from most people's lives and certainly from the grassroots capillary actions of those squeezed out of central locations or, like many activists, just outraged by this.

Mega-projects and DIY-projects jostle for space in cities almost everywhere. Helsinki, long presented as human scale and nature loving, offers a not untypical illustration of how such troubling change prompts contrasting responses[7]. The urban gardening hub I discuss below, is one of several initiatives that have offered a low-threshold entry for people to try their hand at self-organised activism. Since 2012 it has been engaging with the future of the city from a greenhouse built into a former railway turntable,

---

6   As explained on an online forum for the creative industries, (http://theinspirationroom.com/daily/ accessed December 2018): "World business in one place is depicted with an island containing recognizable business buildings from all over the world, including the Jim Mao Building and Oriental Pearl Tower in Shanghai, Arche De La Defence in Paris, Petronas Towers in Kuala Lumpur, IFC 2 in Hong Kong, Shurfit-Stone Building in Chicago, Commerzbank Tower in Frankfurt, New York Stock Exchange, Taipei 101, The Gherkin in London, TransAmerica Pyramid in San Francisco, Landmark Tower in Yokohama".

7   It is possible for these contrasting modes to co-exist, e.g. when mega-projects include DIY-elements.

raised beds surrounding it, and former office and service buildings to house small-scale operators in typical post-industrial occupations (like social entrepreneurs, architects, designers) to use as performance spaces and indoor leisure. All this exists here cheek by jowl with an enormous regeneration scheme (www.uusipasila.fi/) projected to construct approximately 183 000 square metres of new floorspace in a cluster of high-rises for shopping, office uses, transport and residential development on a scale never before seen in Helsinki.

Agreeing with activists (and many others), I see this as an overproduction of spaces – or landscapes as I am suggesting – that serve commerce and narrow down the space of other operations. They are defined by infrastructures that are convenient to pass through rather than dwell in, that extract rather than reproduce and whose maintenance and replacement is out of local hands. Meanwhile little is achieved to alleviate chronic shortages of other things (time, green, air, attention). As activists' journey in their altered landscapes – around ever larger building sites – they face concrete obstacles that, ironically, are presented as serving the common good. Paradigmatically, familiar pedestrian and cycle routes become blocked and lengthened as new roads, buildings and other hard infrastructures appear. Other obstacles faced by city dwellers seeking alternatives are more abstract – a less resource intensive urban fabric and less exhausting life choices that do not compromise biotic processes crucial to sustaining human society – but equally out of reach. Paraphrasing activists,[8] what the mainstream is really offering is not about growth for the future, it is about diminishing it.

## Urban activism and its attachments

Activists increasingly talk about how even to try to escape the infrastructures of the contemporary 'successful' city and its daily routines, is to confront irresolvable contradictions of modernity (Brennan 2000; Fortun 2014). Working through these conundrums is an intellectual journey I too find myself taking, often with anthropologists who are also activists (e.g. Juris 2008; Krøijer 2015). Since 2009 I have been an observant participant in various projects of urban change in Helsinki, getting my hands dirty each summer as an occasional gardener and kitchen help, as well as sitting in meetings, including, for one year, as board-member of Dodo, an environmental organisation strongly identified with Helsinki's urban gardening. Besides a handful of interviews and many conversations with people in other initiatives in Helsinki, my analysis also builds on the rapidly expanding literature – activist, academic and hybrid – ranging from how-to manuals to critical analysis (see also Berglund 2017). Restricting my focus here to loose groupings with practical aims, I discern important similarities among them that are also found in this literature: activists share an often unspoken yet strongly felt imperative to act (Williams 2008; Krøijer 2015) and are self-conscious about futures being matters of choice, as plural. In

8    https://kaantopoyta.fi/manifesti/#intro (in Finnish), accessed November 2018.

what follows, I argue that those I know best reattach with the city, contrasting their sensibilities with the global reach of the mainstream that I modelled above. I argue further, that they nurture a feeling for limits – vague but consequential – again, something that those attaching to global circuits of finance and spectacle evade.

'They' are a mixed bunch, of course (see e.g. Bialski et al. 2015), variously influenced by mainstream politics and middle-class morals, but also by 'environmentalism of the poor' (Martinez-Allier 2002), 'environmental justice' (Checker 2011) and anti-austerity mobilisations (Estalella and Corsín Jímenez 2016) and even radical left politics (Krøijer 2015). Traces of environmentalist concern are ubiquitous though in contemporary cities North and South, offering an abundance of examples from what S. Ravi Rajan and Colin A. M. Duncan (2013) refer to as small "mutinies" (2013, 70) and "ecologies of hope". Hazier on detail, William Connolly (2013) writes of more or less hesitant "role experiments" impelled by experiences of neoliberalism, micro-level responses to the fragility of the ecologies that all humans now inhabit. Whatever their political positioning, such people value nature through practical action.

Three typical features of grassroots urbanism will help show how it works towards (re)attachment and perhaps even re-enchantment with a landscape understood in the anthropological sense outlined in the introduction to this book. The three characteristics discussed, though emergent and diffuse, are given further shape by a respect for limits – a nature – elsewhere. The increasing confidence to signal limits is significant as well as novel, although it does continue long-standing critiques of the way modern society despoils the environment. The first characteristic I want to discuss is valuing and protecting what exists; the second, a desire for learning; the third is sharing, particularly food.

Valuing what exists, grassroots urbanism typically operates along the grain of older layers of a city, seeking not to replace, but to reclaim and care for, what is already there. Although commentators, whether activist, academic or other, tend to emphasise how grassroots-initiated new public spaces, gardens for food or pleasure, educational and health projects enliven social and community networks (e.g. Hickey 2012; Rosa and Weiland 2013), each initiative is usually also a re-use, a repurposing of an artefact. The social centres and info shops of radical and autonomist politics in cities around Europe are also examples of physical spaces created cheaply and sustainably, often squatted. Putting value on what exists can also be practiced in relation to actual buildings. These change almost imperceptibly slowly but also need to be maintained and cared for. Thus enfolded into human attentions and actions, buildings then also become part of people's sense themselves. When it comes to thinking about shared heritage, grassroots urbanism can thus align in interesting ways with broadly speaking conservative politics.

An example of how re-use and heritage combine in activism with building anew is beautifully written up by Cindy Kohtala and Andrew Paterson (2015), two design activists (although at the time they would not have used the title themselves) who were involved in the so-called *Oxygen Room* in Helsinki in the early 2000s. This was a pavilion and greenhouse that became the centre of alternative design art and urban culture. Though technically rather centrally located, the initiative was set up in the margins – derelict land awaiting development – by relatively privileged city residents (primarily a women's network and a group, o2 Finland, promoting sustainable design and architecture). It was built from windows that the city had discarded from its own winter gardens. Although the structure was only supposed to be temporary, it hosted exhibitions, practical workshops and other events exploring different way of creating futures for seven years until development projects caught up with the plot. The construction was dismantled in 2007 and the site now houses office, residential and cultural buildings. In their essay, the authors compare the feel of the *Oxygen Room* to another greenhouse pavilion, mentioned above, the *Turntable* that was built in a disused railway turntable with funds from Helsinki's World Design Capital project in 2012. "Like [the *Oxygen Room*], it is located by the railway tracks, it too has plants, vegetables and herbs, inside and out. It too bridges art, design and urban agriculture with ideals of living with greater ecological consciousness" (Kohtala and Paterson 2015: 70). Contemplating its aesthetic and ethic makes the authors nostalgic for the now vanished *Oxygen Room*. Their nostalgia is tempered, however, with a tenacious drive to learn.

This brings me to the second feature of grassroots action I wanted to highlight, learning and strengthening expertise, also picked up on in anthropologists' analyses of activism (Estalella and Corsín Jiménez 2016). Initiatives like the *Turntable* literally seek to build different tomorrows through building differently or nurturing new or new-old skills like climate-friendly food preparation and preservation. Whether they are cooking, gardening, rigging up sustainable energy supply or working on any of the climate-friendly and small-scale initiatives that have spun out of the Turntable, participants are generally aware of using their intellectual resources.

One concrete practice that typifies urban initiatives is workshops where people learn by doing. Building and furniture-making workshops are a common practice that punctuates the lives of many grassroots urban initiatives, drawing attention to skills but also directly addressing the destructive material flows on which modern cities depend. The workshop is a place and time that brings both the past and future into the present through collective, possibly experimental activities. Learning events including workshops are a staple of Helsinki's *Turntable*. This is a product of a longer-term initiative, *Dodo* (www.dodo.org), which was set up in the mid-1990s as Finland's first explicitly urban environmental organisation. Its founders wanted practical change but it was definitely born of learning and talk. It is similar to many social movements throughout modern history, in that its origins lie in small meetings of friends reading together. Indeed, despite the public image of grassroots urbanism being all about creating practical change, most initiatives I know, in Helsinki and elsewhere, have strong roots in some kind of self-education, an urge to replace or complement what mainstream schooling has offered with alternative pedagogies. Alongside learning about sustainability and efforts to behave sustainably, activist networks seek to enhance their knowledge about policy, planning and political processes.

These arenas are matters of design and artifice rather than the organic unfoldings of nature, but as activists engage with and attach themselves to their surroundings, they engage with these more technocratic domains quite fluently. And abstract practices like communicating online, informing oneself about climate science or alternative technologies, combine rather easily with more hands-on practices, like re-using materials or repurposing open urban space. I argue this is analogous to or at least continuous with landscape anthropology's myriad examples of activities that enfold social life within land, materials and meanings and vice versa, in temporal rhythms.

Skills and expertise thus bump along together, and it is fair to say that participants often say they value doing and making over talking. The challenge is to ensure that skills not be 'enclosed' along with other resources and monopolised. Not everyone is considered an expert, but the prefigurative politics of grassroots activism is a way of developing everybody's potential and capacities. Within a wider neoliberal context where skills and learning have become 'resources' that individuals 'invest' in, a shift to something different that is experimental, DIY, accessible and remunerated poorly if at all, is bound to be ambivalent. Still, with other elements of activist practice, these explorations feed alternative ways of being a person and cultivating an accepted identity. This can also give an uncomfortable sense to learning: it is not understood as schooling but as an aspect of being human that is losing its social value.

A third feature of activism to highlight is sharing, particularly of food. No matter what the material or political goals of a grouping, grassroots urbanists everywhere eat together and so create community. Even when an initiative is not primarily concerned with the politics of food – as most urban gardening initiatives are – they often have some kind of kitchen. The rhythmic anarchy of the grassroots urbanists' kitchen can be encountered From Helsinki to Berlin, Budapest and Rio de Janeiro and beyond. Besides repurposed parts of buildings, the pizza oven and the dry toilet – designed for capturing a key resource rather than flushing it out of sight as useless and troublesome waste – are elements of an international repertoire of grassroots urbanism that shows little sign of disappearing. Sanitised versions have been co-opted for commercial purposes.

Sharing is morally valued and has significant economic implications and it shapes the quality of social interaction in these groups with their strong orientation away from the acquisitive individualism considered the norm in contemporary, economy-driven society. Sometimes this sharing mentality dovetails with critical political reactions to capitalism after the economic chaos of 2008, but sharing can be apolitical in tone (Berglund 2017). Whether projects are driven by more or less utopian hopes for a better future or by the need to compensate for the loss of state or other social support systems (most initiatives address multiple issues simultaneously anyway), they foster an alternative sense of ownership – both literal and psychological – closer to the idea of the 'commons'. This is a concept as well as a practice that activists are developing intellectually, alongside 'sharing', 'simplicity', 'conviviality' and 'care'. The extent to which participants seek to spell out or elaborate these underlying motivations varies hugely. However, there is a broad mutual understanding of a need for social and material life to be organised without the enclosures of commercial or state institutions. Using the word 'commons' as a verb, 'commoning' or 'making the commons' thus captures much of the ethos and underlying motivation of these new urban initiatives.

Marginal though it is, this diffused activist work presents itself as more hopeful, less pointless, than a politics of talk – recall my activist friend's views on the vacuous talk of environmental policy. But it is hard and contradictory. As Helfrich and Bollier (2015: 75) put it, initiatives "generally are not based on money, legal contracts, or bureaucratic fiat, but on self-management and shared responsibility". At least these are ideals to which they aspire even if in practice it is often difficult to reach them. Often they find themselves seeking leases on buildings and collaborating with big NGOs or local governments. Of course, even when they succeed in their aims, however small, by establishing something new, making their presence felt or even achieving temporary notoriety, the political impact of any individual urban initiative usually remains weak. Indeed, many activists (and not just in Finland) deny having ambitions to make a political difference, even though they highlight the urgency of total social change. Overt explanations aside, compared to protest events involving large numbers of people that create new and often strong forms of agency (Juris 2008; Krøijer 2015), the longer term sustained work involved in urban initiatives draws its power from more diffuse sources. It has to be sustained against not very good odds in a complex context of many different and competing claims on people's energies and allegiances. Treating developers, municipal offices or the police as adversaries, does not really help, so flexibility and compromises are in frequent demand.

Activists are often eloquent about how resources can be managed without bureaucratic and centralised power, partly thanks to Elinor Ostrom's (e.g. 2009) Nobel prize-winning work on common resource management. This can give them leverage, particularly where their project involves designing alternatives to dominant economic practices, for instance in co-operatives or time-banks. But it is self-organising and horizontality that hold particular attraction among activists. This is underscored by recent anthropological literature (Juris 2008; Graeber 2009; Krøijer 2015) that demonstrates how productive self-organising can be and, through activist research, perhaps strengthens its cultural if not (yet) institutional traction in wider society. Decision making may be less speedy and efficient through 'horizontal' or self-organising processes, but it appears to be superior to 'vertical', voting-based practices in holding people's allegiances and commitments. Rules exist and are learned, through trial and error, but also by explicit coaching. Here the role of workshops is key, putting skills and materials together with people and their aspirations. Of course, it takes far more than sharing food or workshops to sustain voluntary commitment, and the tensions of governing initiatives are a perennial topic in activist groups as in the literature (Berglund and Kohtala, forthcoming). Suffice to mention a well-known urban intervention, Campo de Cebada, in Madrid, which has been a platform for a variety of alternative practices, from political meetings and artistic performances to urban gardening and architectural experiments.

Documented by anthropologists like Alberto Corsín Jiménez (2014) here too, as the initiative grew, both politically and materially, the strictly horizontal principles of decision making associated with protest came increasingly into tension with the need for stability. Indeed, "self-organisation beyond a certain scale is painfully difficult" (McGuirk 2014).

This view is easy to endorse. However, though sometimes painful and often peripheral, the work of activists produces and reproduces not just social groups but landscapes. My argument is that activism gathers things and people together to care for and reflect on them in all their interdependencies, vague as these may be. Self-organised or DIY urbanism can certainly not guarantee change or sustainability, all it can do is continue its work in progress, inhabiting the landscapes it is working on.

## *The idea of limits*

My argument is premised on the idea that urban life too is 'lived experience'. I have also suggested that decisions about urban change are largely pursued through a spectacular imaginary that detaches everything: the investor from the fabric and frictions of his investment, abstract profit from places to live, and so on, and ignores or disavows limits to human endeavour. My illustration was how the city of Helsinki has promoted capital-intensive, commercially driven development oriented to global concerns, while activism has sought to re-attach or re-embed life in material circuits and social processes closer to hand.

I think this is captured in the anthropological landscape concept. It points to the activities but also of actors that constitute our dwelling places. Landscape in this sense is definitely not cultural image or symbol alone, but nor is it natural substrate for life let alone scientific, impersonal, fact. As something that people care about, it is folded into decisions taken by groups, that is, politics, even as it is animated by non-human forces, making it not so much spatial as spatiotemporal. Landscape gathers into itself sociability that remains hidden – ties and the agents they bind – and points to material processes and political decisions unfolding together. Such processes, furthermore, involve not just phenomena close by or available to sensuous experience (as emphasised in phenomenological research traditions), they include circuits of things and ideas that, like 'the market', travel the world in both abstract and concrete forms with both global and local impacts. That is why I have emphasised that learning and abstract information are important in activism just as they are in the construction sector, and further that they too become enfolded in the landscape.

Thus, understanding projects of future building as something that both generates and is generated by landscape need not and should not be limited to the small-scale, technologically and administratively simple or marginal. Building on Ingold's academic insights about landscapes I have suggested that the political and the material, the present and the future, become foci of concern and negotiation in the process of constructing the spectacular cityscapes of our financial times as well. The landscape concept helps even if it remains, perhaps of necessity, somewhat imprecise. Attaching to what already exists in urban initiatives combines very low-tech with very sophisticated and highly mediated knowledge, as activists also find themselves negotiating surrounding technological infrastructures: (more) hazardous waste deposits, (more) motorways and (more) centralised energy production. Other detailed empirical studies, my own early work for instance (Berglund 1998) or Kim Fortun's ethnography of the Bhopal disaster (Fortun 2001), also show that for urbanites too, experiences of learning are embodied but are often far from the sensuous engagements that anthropology typically foregrounds. Thus attention to institutional politics and technoscientific expertise is a key ingredient of critical engagements with changing landscapes. For if activists care about the things they seek to influence, in part this is due to their scientific literacy and other skills they share with the denizens of urban modernity.

The idea that artifice and human intentions are entangled need not, of course, depend on a concept of landscape. Assemblages and actor networks also foreground the entanglements of the material and the meaningful (McFarlane 2011). In urban studies this has led to developing a vocabulary to draw attention to "small, lateral and almost peripheral changes" (Farías and Bender 2010: 1) and helped to think about the nonhumans and the unfamiliar assemblages that can and do scupper human designs, sometimes in quite dramatic and unwanted ways. Jane Bennett (2005) has inspired this work, for instance the much-cited and evocative example of the black-out that struck North America in August 2003. The difference made by "quirky electron flows to cocky economists' assumptions" (2005: 451) was massive and destructive, the lesson being that political and philosophical attention needs urgently to be paid to places and processes not usually imagined or spoken of as political.

Kim Fortun (2014) writes of late industrialism, with its "natural, technical, political-economic, social, and discursive systems, all of which are aging, often over-wrought, ossified, and politicized" (2014: 310) that are easily rendered banal through a postmodern academic discourse. We may never have been modern, she writes referring to Bruno Latour, but we do have what she calls "a modernist mess on our hands" (Fortun 2014: 312). Dirty industries fuelled by disempowered people service overconsumption even as the concreteness of this human and environmental devastation goes unacknowledged by those who benefit from it. Approached with the vocabularies of assemblages and networks, all urban building projects also appear multiple and inherently unstable even as they shape familiar and meaningful surroundings. Even the most gargantuan projects are assembled from resources and affordances that (despite universal pretentions) fall prey to local resistance and obstruction. In pitting one utopia (endless growth) against another (better futures), grassroots urban initiatives in fact foster an acute sense of these instabilities and they sometimes resist politics as an imperative to grow wealth, money or the so-called economy. They experiment with what can and cannot be done in this place with these resources: soils, seeds and other material inputs, available bodies and forms of expertise, and of course time, energy and the political space and cultural acceptance to sustain such endeavour. While landscapes of spectacle are landscapes of hubris and speculation that test limits and disavow mutual dependencies, grassroots landscape making is usually the opposite: it works with limits and interdependency very much in mind.

This vague respect for the limits of what is, is taken for granted rather than spelled out. Most of those involved routinely refer to nature or orient themselves towards it. Activists in Helsinki may or may not talk of 'nature' but they do recognise a bundle of forces *not* amenable to human design. This largely implicit reference to limits somewhere on the horizon – and getting closer all the time – needs to be highlighted, since the action is about producing intentional change, which might be misconstrued as a disavowal of limits.[9] It is not necessarily a strong or even explicated notion of what nature might be. In fact, rather than seeking to protect 'nature' or even the 'environment', the challenge activists make concerns potentially everything: as Kim Fortun writes, at issue is the "tight coupling between natural, technical, political-economic, social and discursive systems" (2014: 310). In studying or doing intentional change, the complex relationship between limits and creativity of course never goes away. Nature remains salient, but invoking it signals not so much the inevitable or the normal as much as resistance to human desire and action. If nature constrains, it also makes possible, and it is something to be worked with, learned from and enjoyed.

The anthropogenic dimensions of the systems that people find themselves in also explain why the academic discipline of geography, which was once about rivers, mountains and continents, now appears to be more about Marxism (Lanchester 2016). Anthropology has a similar record of analysing the human and environmental costs of this (neoliberalising) process, training its lens on everywhere that neoliberal logics operate, in short, pretty much anywhere (Ortner 2016). Anthropology therefore deals in landscapes anyway, despite strong traces of an older language of nature and culture.

The contrast between the country and the city has not gone away, but it has changed its meaning. Limits, like boundaries, are very much present everywhere, including the city, and sensed in material and embodied engagement as well as in intellectual debate. Both matter. As urban initiatives test out ways of arranging material, particularly food and waste, their concern is that practices in Helsinki do not rebound in toxic ways on already vulnerable people and places. Put differently, activists attach to their immediate surroundings with planetary limits – however vague – in mind. The landscape of speculation attaches to quite different things.[10]

Casting landscape as a gathering of people and things that is at once social, experiential and, of course, material and not as a representation separate from the thing it refers to, can refocus critiques of urban development on what matters to city folk of many stripes – the world around them, to the side and

---

9   In contrast, thinking glossed as eco-modernist shares the belief in needing to redesign, confident that technology will come to fix problems, known and as-yet unknown, before it is too late.

10  These attachments are hugely consequential, but have been hard to study as 'lived experience', a situation that I hope is changing.

up, in their dreams and their everyday journeys: in short, in the landscapes they care about. Though my illustration has been Helsinki, there is a general tendency for urban transformation today to be dominated by the rather placeless values and future visions of finance capital. I have drawn attention though to the contestation, which is a also transnational phenomenon. And I have shown, using landscape as empirical as well as theoretical coordinate, the multiple commitments and capacities needed to shape and sustain urban life. Further developing anthropology's landscape concept in urban settings, I believe, would raise more forceful critiques of the city-focussed and image-based hubris, which devastates landscapes anywhere.

# References

Árnason, Arnar, Nicolas Elison, Jo Vergunst and Andrew Whitehouse (eds) 2012. *Lansdcapes Beyond Land: Routes, Aesthetics, Narratives.* Oxford: Berghahn Books.

Bennett, Jane 2005. The Agency of Assemblages and the North American Blackout. *Public Culture* 17 (3): 445–465.

Berglund, Eeva 1998. *Knowing Nature, Knowing Science: An ethnography of local environmental activism.* Cambridge: White Horse Press.

Berglund, Eeva 2011. Tangled and Tangible, Straight and Abstract: Anthropology and Helsinki Architecture. *Suomen Antropologi: Journal of the Finnish Anthropological Society* 36 (3): 5–22.

Berglund, Eeva 2017. Steering clear of politics: Local virtues in Helsinki's design activism. *Journal of Political Ecology* 24 (1): 566–580.

Berglund, Eeva and Cindy Kohtala forthcoming, 2019. Collaborative Confusion among DIY Makers: Ethnography and expertise in creating knowledge for environmental sustainability. *Science & Technology Studies.*

Bialski, Paula, Heike Derwanz, Birke Otto and Hans Vollmer 2015. '*Saving' the City: Collective low-budget organizing and urban practice.* Special issue. *Ephemera: Theory & Politics of Organization* 15 (1).

Checker, Melissa 2011. Wiped Out by the "Greenwave": Environmental Gentrification and the Paradoxical Politics of Urban Sustainability. *City & Society* 23 (2): 210–229.

Connolly, William 2013 *The Fragility of Things: Self-organizing processes, neoliberal fantasies, and democratic activism.* Durham: Duke University Press.

Corsín Jiménez, Alberto 2014. The right to infrastructure: A prototype for open source urbanism. *Environment and Planning D: Society and Space* 32 (2): 342–362.

Cosgrove, Denis 1985. Prospect, Perspective and the Evolution of the Landscape Idea. *Transactions of the Institute of British Geographers* 10 (1): 45–62.

Cronon, William 1995. The trouble with wilderness; Or, Getting back to the wrong nature. In William Cronon (ed.), *Uncommon Ground: Rethinking the Human Place in Nature.* New York: Norton.

Easterling, Keller 2016. *Extrastatecraft: The power of infrastructure space.* New York: Verso.

Estalella, Adolfo and Alberto Corsín Jiménez 2016. Matters of sense: Preoccupation in Madrid's popular assemblies movement. In Anders Blok and Ignacio Farías (eds), *Urban cosmopolitics: Agencements, assemblies, atmospheres.* London: Routledge.

Farías, Ignacio and Thomas Bender (eds) 2010. *Urban Assemblages: How Actor-Network Theory Changes Urban Studies.* London: Routledge.

Fortun, Kim 2001. *Advocacy After Bhopal: Environmentalism, Disaster, New Global Orders.* Chicago: University of Chicago Press.

Fortun, Kim 2014. From Latour to late industrialism. *HAU: Journal of Ethnographic Theory* 4 (1): 309–329.

Frase, Peter 2015. *Four futures: Visions of the world after capitalism*. London: Verso.

Graeber, David 2009. *Direct Action: An Ethnography*. Oakland: AK Press.

Helfrich, Silke and David Bollier 2015. Commons. In Giacomo D'Alisa, Federico Demaria and Giorgos Kallis (eds), *Degrowth: A vocabulary for a new era*. New York: Routledge.

Hickey, Amber (ed.) 2012. *A Guidebook of Alternative Nows*. The Journal of Aesthetics and Protest Press.

Ingold, Tim 2000. *The Perception of the Environment: Essays in livelihood, dwelling and skill*. London: Routledge.

Jackson, Tim and Robin Webster 2016. *Limits Revisited: A review of the limits to growth debate*, Report to the UK's All-Party Parliamentary Group, online: limits2growth. org.uk/revisited. Accessed December 2018.

Jacobs, Jane 1965. *The Death and Life of Great American Cities*. Harmondsworth: Penguin Books in association with Jonathan Cape.

Juris, Jeffrey 2008. *Networking Futures: The movements against corporate globalization*. Durham: Duke University Press.

Kirkman, Robert 2010. *The ethics of metropolitan growth: The future of our built environment*. London: Continuum.

Kohtala, Cindy and Andrew Paterson 2015. Oxygen for Töölönlahti. In Eeva Berglund and Cindy Kohtala (eds), *Changing Helsinki? 11 Views on a City Unfolding*. Helsinki: Nemo.

Krøijer, Stine 2015. *Figurations of the Future: Forms and temporalities of left radical politics in northern Europe*. New York: Berghahn Books.

Lanchester, John 2016. Brexit Blues. *London Review of Books* 38 (1): 3–6.

McFarlane, Colin 2011. The city as assemblage: Dwelling and urban space. *Environment and Planning D: Society and Space* 29 (4): 649–671.

McGuirk, Justin 2014. DIY cities: On citizen agency and government accountability. *Uncube Magazine*. http://www.uncubemagazine.com/magazine-28-14819803. html#!/page5 Accessed December 2018.

Manzini, Ezio 2015. *Design, When Everybody Designs: An introduction to design for social innovation*. Cambridge, Mass: The MIT Press.

Martinez-Alier, Juan 2002. *The Environmentalism of the Poor: A study of ecological conflicts and valuation*. Northampton, MA: Edward Elgar publishing.

McKay, George 2011. *Radical Gardening: Politics, idealism & rebellion in the garden*. London: Frances Lincoln Ltd.

Meadowcroft, James 2013. Reaching the limits? Developed country engagement with sustainable development in a challenging conjuncture. *Environment and Planning C: Government and Policy* 31 (6): 988–1002.

Mitchell, Timothy 2011. *Carbon democracy: Political power in the age of oil*. New York: Verso.

Mumford, Lewis 1938. *The Culture of Cities*. New York: Harcourt Brace.

Olwig, Kenneth 1996. Recovering the substantive nature of landscape. *Annals of the Association of American Geographers* 86 (4): 630–653.

Ortner, Sherry B. 2016. Dark anthropology and its others: Theory since the Eighties. *HAU: Journal of Ethnographic Theory* 6 (1): 47–73.

Ostrom, Elinor 2009. A General Framework for Analyzing Sustainability of Socio-Ecological Systems. *Science* 325: 419–422.

Pinder, David 2005. *Visions of the city: Utopianism, power and politics in Twentieth-Century urbanism*. New York: Routledge.

Rajan, S. Ravi and Colin A.M. Duncan 2013. Ecologies of Hope: environment, technology and habitation – case studies from the intervenient middle. *Journal of Political Ecology* 20 (1): 70–79.

Rosa, Marcois L. and Ute E. Weiland 2013. *Handmade Urbanism: From Community Initiatives to Participatory Models*. Berlin: Jovis.

Scott, James 1998. *Seeing Like a State*. New Haven: Yale University Press.

Sennett, Richard 1996. *Flesh and stone: The body and the city in Western civilization*. New York: WW Norton & Company.

Williams, Gavin 2008. Cultivating Autonomy: Power, Resistance and the French Alterglobalization Movement. *Critique of Anthropology* 28 (1): 63–86.

Williams, Raymond 1973. *The Country and the City*. London: Chatto and Windus.

Katja Uusihakala

https://orcid.org/0000-0001-6432-6323

# "God's own country": Temporalities of landscape in postcolonial nostalgia

## Introduction

This article examines how white former 'Rhodesians', who have emigrated to South Africa since Zimbabwe's independence in 1980, remember and recount the landscapes of colonial Rhodesia, thereby making affective claims of belonging to the land they have left behind but which they hold onto as 'homeland'. In the ex-Rhodesian vernacular, the landscape in which the memory narratives are embedded, and which they in turn shape, is referred to as bush, *bundu*[1], country, or wide open space. The article will explore the central place that 'bush' occupies in the former Rhodesian memory work. I argue that it is at the heart of their moral and spiritual well-being. The article will also examine the ways that the idea of 'empty land' is intertwined with that of the bush, and suggest that the emptiness – embedded in nostalgic reconstructions of the homeland and at the core of the commonplace version of white settler landscape narrative – is far from simple. It is an idea and an image of landscape, which consists of complex and contradictory temporalities and moral connotations. Further, the article examines the kinds of interrelationships that are formed with landscapes through recollecting them. It shows how shared stories about homeland constitute a pivotal element of diasporic nostalgia and are, as such, emblematic to the production of the community.

Zimbabwe's independence was followed by a large wave of white migration during the early 1980s. Of the approximately 100 000 whites who left Zimbabwe, about a half settled in South Africa, a third moved to Britain and the rest mostly to Australia, New Zealand, the US and Canada (Eaton 1996). The more or less voluntary postcolonial migrants, whose lives I researched in South Africa between 1999 and 2002 as part of my doctoral work (2008), had mostly represented the urban middle class of British background in colonial Rhodesia. They chose South Africa as their new home for several reasons. First, migrating to the neighbouring country required far less economic

---

1   *Bundu* (used in South African and Zimbabwean English) signifies an uninhabited wilderness region, remote from towns. The word derives from a Shona word *bundo,* meaning grasslands.

resources than moving to Britain or Australia. Second, restrictions regarding age, occupation, education and assets foreclosed other potential destinations from many. Third, and most important, as a society the apartheid South Africa of the 1980s was a country which resembled most closely the colonial 'homeland' the whites were leaving behind, and which resonated strongly with their worldview. Many reckoned they could continue a familiar, privileged lifestyle in South Africa more easily than elsewhere.

Like many other diaspora communities, the ex-Rhodesians in South Africa are in part united by a shared memory of an idealised homeland, with which they maintain an enduring relationship. Thus, despite the fact that colonial Rhodesia no longer exists, in the lives of post-migrant Rhodesians it continues to have intrinsic weight as the preeminent place of belonging. Although very few of my interlocutors imagined they would re-migrate to Zimbabwe in any foreseeable future, a sense of rootedness with the homeland was actively maintained by sharing stories about Rhodesia.[2] A white postcolonial narrative fixated on emotional affinity with a territory the whites had formerly colonised, is obviously politically highly ambiguous. While ownership, occupation and rights to land are always at the heart of settler colonial politics, the question has been particularly volatile in Zimbabwean politics. It was a fundamental issue in the country's struggle for independence and a problem, which has remained unresolved for decades. When I was doing fieldwork in 2000, the land question re-emerged with force, and the political turmoil concerning redistribution of commercial, mainly white-owned farmland in Zimbabwe turned violent. At that stage, approximately 4 500 commercial farming families owned roughly about a third of the land area in a country of 12 million mainly black inhabitants. The forced, and at times violent, acquisition of about 95 % of the commercial farmland was justified as a final resolution of the land question (Hammar 2010: 396). Removals and relocations of commercial farmers, farmworkers, and their families, as well as the political violence and economic crisis in Zimbabwe, have since been widely documented and analysed (e.g. Alexander 2006; Moyo 2011; Rutherford 2017).

The land crisis in Zimbabwe therefore forms a vital part of the historical and political context in which my fieldwork took place and in which the nostalgic narratives of homeland were recounted. Although the postcolonial struggle over land is not the analytical focus of this article, it is significant to recognise this background, and particularly to observe how very little the political context penetrated the homeland stories I was told. Such silence, disregard and oblivion, however, are never total. In subtle ways they hover and echo at the back of these stories. I will return to the silence and dismissal

---

2    Although 'return' may have been pivotal in the original concept of diaspora – applied to classic and paradigmatic cases of Jewish, Armenian and Greek diasporas (Cohen 1999) – it is apparent that not all committed relationships with homelands materialise in concrete desires to return. Diasporas, rather, are considered to manifest themselves as stances which may be used to make claims, mobilise energies or to appeal to loyalties (Brubaker 2005: 12) or as personal relationships and moral gestures within the diaspora itself (Werbner 2000).

at the end of this paper and suggest that they form an integral part of the postcolonial nostalgic stance this article attempts to sketch.

In the familiar colonial imagery of 'empty land', the landscape is represented as an unmapped, virgin land devoid of (other) human involvement and engagement (Hughes 2010; Pilossof 2012). The emptiness, of course, is a result of cultural imagination and requires particular dismissals and blind spots. In her analysis of white Kenyans, Janet McIntosh (2016: 10–11) adopts a term *structural oblivion* to capture such a mode of moral consciousness. It necessitates erasure, ignorance and denial, and is grounded on a refusal to recognise ideologies that uphold one's elite position as well the experience of others (Uusihakala 2008: 214–215).[3] Understanding the varied meanings, ambivalent sentiments and distinct moral valuations connected with the 'emptiness' or 'wildness' of the remembered landscape, is thus a central question this article addresses.

There are two main ways of representing the landscape in white colonial and postcolonial discourse. In the first version, the land is presented as a resource to be utilised; in the second, as an environment to be conserved and cared for. In the first form, the allegedly empty land is viewed as an unbounded resource and a potential possession; a terrain lacking ownership and yearning for development. The value of land lies in its potential to produce something of material worth. Such a representation has tended to dominate studies – as well as self-analysis – of settler colonials. It was also very much evident in my earlier research on postcolonial whites in Kenya, in which I suggested that the Kenyan whites' commitment to the country and their self-legitimation of belonging are prominently demonstrated in investments in land. The investments relate both to the engineering of landscape – arguments that farmers should ceaselessly labour to build and improve their land – as well as to embodied knowledge and conservational care of the terrain, flora and fauna (Uusihakala 1999; Fox 2012).

The idea that investments in land do not necessarily imply transformation but focus rather on preservation, brings us to the second, antithetical interpretation of the whites' relationship to land. Not only developers and builders, settler colonials have also been described as anti-modern and strongly resistant to social change. This anti-modernity is connected both to a desire to conserve what is considered as the pure and primeval essence of the landscape and to coat it with "rural moral values" (Godwin and Hancock 1999; Dominy 2001). In such a view, the landscape is represented either as a timeless, eternal wilderness or as a pastoral idyll (Chennels 1996; Pilossof 2010). In contrast with a developers' and builders' version, the preserver imagines the landscape as a pristine space unharmed by human touch and values it for its true essence, which is considered to emit its emotional force. This perception has become preeminent in much of the more recent research on postcolonial whites in contemporary African societies (McIntosh 2016;

---

3   Melissa Steyn's (2012) phrase *ignorance contract* also refers to such a form of moral consciousness and structural position. Drawing from critical philosophy of race, she argues that ignorance contract – a tacit agreement to entertain ignorance – is at the heart of society structured in racial hierarchy, such as South Africa.

Gressier 2015; Hughes 2010). For example, in her study on whites in contemporary Botswana, Catie Gressier describes the centrality of the bush in white Batswana cultural values. She argues that the construction of the Okavango environment is central to the white identities, spirituality, social relationships and national belonging. These constructions, however, must be understood in terms of a white minority subject position, which renders "nature a considerably less fraught means than the social environment through which to develop identities and senses of belonging" (2015: 40).[4]

The places people most strongly identify with are not necessarily the ones they inhabit. This is the case for many individuals and groups of people voluntarily or forcibly removed from their homelands. Longing for a place where one feels one most comprehensively belongs, is essentially what the concept of *nostalgia* signifies. Stemming from the Greek words *nóstos* (homecoming) and *algos* (pain, grief, distress) (e.g., Boym 2001), the term nostalgia was coined by a Swiss scholar Johannes Hofer in the late 17th century to refer to a severe homesickness, an illness-like longing for home and for homeland landscapes from which mercenaries suffered. Svetlana Boym (2001) defines nostalgia as a sense of loss and displacement, a longing for a home, which no longer exists or might never have been. Nostalgia, she suggests, may manifest itself in restorative forms, which stress *nóstos*, the return. As such it often signifies nationalistic or revivalist attempts to transhistorically reconstruct a lost home. Alternative nostalgic projects and sentiments might not centralise either the return or a particular place, but fixate on *algos* – the grief and pain – and on the ambivalence between longing and belonging.

In contemporary anthropological studies on memory, nostalgia has become one of the key concepts used for analysing the interlinking of place and memory, and for understanding temporal positions and processes where the past and the future are tied to sociospatial changes (Bissell 2015: 219). Imaginaries, hopes and yearnings related to the past are projected via the present – often characterised by discontinuity and disappointment – towards a future, which, it is hoped, will resemble and remind one of the past (Angé and Berliner 2015). Often such political temporalities gain strength in situations where the past is, in one way or another, irrevocably gone and structurally disrupted. Diasporas, forced migrations and removals, as well as breakdowns of social systems such as colonial order or state socialism, are examples of such fundamental breaks.[5] Nostalgia, in such contexts of epochal change, appears to be projected to a time or a place which is situated before or beyond traumatic events. The ex-Rhodesian diasporic

4 David Hughes considers the relationship white Zimbabweans have with the landscape to be defined by alienation and disconnection. He describes it as a form of "nature-obsessed escape". The postcolonial whites, Hughes argues, have preferred to invest themselves emotionally and artistically in the environment and negotiate their identity with land forms rather than with other humans or social forms (2010: xii).

5 On colonial nostalgia, see Bissel 2005; Smith 2003. On post-socialist nostalgia, see Berdahl 2010; Boyer 2006.

recollections – the sentimental imaginings and evocations of homeland landscapes characterised by their remoteness, emptiness and removal from social upheavals – are a paradigm case of postcolonial nostalgia, which is what this article explores.

In what follows, I first present two memory narratives to illustrate the cultural construction of white postcolonial relationships to the 'homeland' and the complex temporalities they convey. In both narratives the protagonist is a young boy for whom 'the bush' was the world. These young boys, David and Norman,[6] are now middle-aged and keep returning to their childhood places in memory. Both claim a passionate longing for the place intertwined with a sense that the place is calling them and longing for their return as well. I analyse the narratives from two perspectives. I first situate them as part of a genre of white colonial landscape narrative, tracing the temporalities of landscape embedded in the different meanings given to 'bush', 'wilderness' or 'wide open space'. I propose that despite the fact that Norman and David frame their recollections in the familiar narrative of empty space, the landscape they present in their stories, is much more complex. The flickering emptiness appears as a moral commentary more than a lived reality. Secondly, I examine how the moral landscape commentary becomes an integral part of postcolonial nostalgia and the shaping of diasporic stances and subjectivities.

## A place in the bush

### "The mountains had lost none of their presence"

In the 1950s when David was a small boy, his family left behind their urban life in the country's capital and established a farm near Inyanga[7] on Zimbabwe's eastern border. In the discussions I had with my interlocutors, the eastern borderland area, together with the Matopos Hills, were presented as the two epitomes of the natural, majestic beauty of the Rhodesian landscape. Unlike the Matopos with its sturdy, arid terrain and topography dominated by spectacular boulders balancing on each other's shoulders, Inyanga was described as beautiful in a pleasant, European-kind-of-a-way. In these descriptions, Inyanga exemplifies the picturesque in contrast to the sublime beauty of the Matopos.[8]

According to David, farming in the borderland area wasn't very successful.

6   I use first name pseudonyms for the ex-Rhodesian people who have been involved in my research in order to protect their anonymity.

7   The use of place names is a deeply political issue. The colonial placename *Inyanga* was changed to *Nyanga* after Zimbabwe's independence. Here the colonial name is used to cohere with my informants' recollections. Their use of names may be conceived of both as a nostalgic revival and a nostalgic forgetting.

8   According to J. M. Coetzee (1988: 52) the beautiful, the sublime and the picturesque were, in the 18th and 19th centuries, the three categories of European landscape classification. They are so fundamental that they have since organised how landscape is seen and, as Coetzee shows, affected the perception and understanding of colonial terrain.

The soil was poor, rainfall unreliable, droughts recurrent, and hyenas once killed all their cattle. During the liberation war years of the 1970s, the area became a virtual war zone and eventually the family had to abandon the farm.[9] David had recently been back to his childhood home for the first time in more than twenty years, during which time the family farm had become a resettlement area. In our discussion, David contemplated on the mixed feelings he had about his return and on his intense longing for the place.

> The farm was very isolated. And it was quite a distance from Inyanga, which is the nearest settlement. It was bad roads. There were no proper bridges; you just drift though the water, through the rivers. I spent all my time exploring, 'cause it was a very interesting area. And I used to spend all the time in the mountains [...]. We always used to call it the Raingod Mountain. And there was a legend that whenever there was a cloud in the sky, there would always be one over this. 'Cause they used to have these important rainmaking ceremonies there. It was also this belief that whenever a chief was crowned [---] they used to sort of leave him up this hill or something. And there's a guy and he used to have to go up there and make various offerings and if the gods were impressed they used to give rain. There was all these signs of this sort of ancient civilization. There was all these terraces and built structures, and it covers an incredible area. [...] My father picked up a lot just from talking with the locals. And then I read books on it as well. [...] There were some very imposing mountains, quite a stupendous view. And our house was a bit further along.

> ['What was it like to go back after twenty years?' I asked.] It was a sort of mixture of feelings. You know, there was sadness for what it was, what had gone, and yet it was very nice to be back. It hadn't really changed. [...] You know, it was now a resettlement area. It was no longer a farm. But the mountains had lost none of their presence. ['But people had moved in,' I commented.] Yeah, it was now very settled. In that point of view it had changed a great deal [...]. In a way I sort of felt that it was right that this land, which had great religious significance to the locals, should actually have been given back to them. The sad thing was that all the actual blacks they brought in were actually not from the local tribes. They were from outside areas. And the local belief systems meant very little to them. [...] When we gave it over, I liked to think it was to be handed over to the rightful occupants and to the people to whom this mountain was so important. Wish they had got back their land.

> The landscape [...] just has a very powerful spiritual feel about it. I just have this emotional connection with it. I don't really feel down here [in South Africa] with the land. I seem to be drawn back. Inyanga, it's a very mystical area. It's very powerful. [...] As I'm getting older, I'm harking back more and more for, I don't know, for Zimbabwe. I seem to be going back more and more often. I think it's the pull of the land, I suppose. I've never quite got over that part of it. You know I really love the country. The country itself. I never much cared for the society. I made do with the society but I really loved the actual country itself. My sisters

9    Zimbabwe's independence was preceded by nearly 15 years of civil war in which the white-minority government fought against Zimbabwean nationalist movements ZAPU and ZANU and their guerrilla armies.

go back with me too. We always go back; we will make this pilgrimage back to the farm. They also feel the very strong pull. [...] But as I said, in more recent years I find myself harking back more and more for that. Like my life's gone a circle in a way, and I'm sort of going back to beginning.

"The farm was very isolated," David begins, immediately setting the tone of the narrative. In it one faintly hears the opening of many other stories of white farms in Africa, which so intensely stress solitude and seclusion, as well and the vastness of the surrounding space.[10] While it is evident that David knows the landscape through his explorations and wanderings on the mountains, what he accentuates instead, is his interpretation of meanings that landscape has in indigenous belief systems. He elucidates his sense of belonging in a way that suggests a conscious reflection on the experience of others – the indigenous inhabitants of the area. According to Paul Mupira (2003), Mt Muozi (the area that David refers to) is the most sacred place for the VaNyama people inhabiting the area. The mountain was named after Muozi, a powerful diviner and rainmaker among the VaNyama. According to a legend, Mupira writes, the Sawunyama chiefs used to be installed on the mountain and anybody who wanted to become chief had to climb the mountain and be ceremoniously accepted or rejected by the spirits. Eventually the diviner Muozi became so popular and powerful that paramount chief Sawunyama felt threatened and had his army kill him, which subsequently brought a curse on the land and the Sawunyama chieftainship. Numerous droughts followed until Sawunyama managed to appease the avenging spirit. Since then ceremonies have been held on Mt Muozi to prevent misfortune befalling the VaNyama people.

Despite the melancholy tone evoked by ruins of his home, "sadness for what it was, what had gone," David reiterates the solidity and eternity of the mountains. He takes comfort in their firm, physical presence. When I note that new people had moved in since their departure, David consents and explains how the landscape had changed: the isolation of colonial times had given way to a densely populated resettlement area. At the end of that paragraph, David makes a political statement, which at the time of the interview – the farm invasions in Zimbabwe had then intensified markedly

---

10 Examples of white farming novels set in Africa are numerous. One immediately thinks of Doris Lessing in Rhodesia and Elspeth Huxley in Kenya, who both grew up on farms in Africa, and whose novels are often written from a lonely child's perspective. This is where the similarities end, however. Huxley and Lessing read very different meanings into the experienced isolation of farming life. For Huxley, the wide open spaces were about opportunity, they called for initiative and development. (See Huxley's trilogy 1981; 1982; 1987.) For Lessing on the other hand, the isolation of farming life is profoundly ambiguous and cannot be considered outside her general frame of social insulation, which is seclusion both for the individual who cannot belong to the community and for the nation cocooned in itself. (See *Martha Quest* (1973 [1952]), and the short story *The Old Chief Mshlanga* in *Collected African Stories* 1979.) For a discussion of the farm novel in South Africa, see Coetzee (1988: chapters 3–6 in particular). For post-2000 pastoral white writing, see Pilossof (2012).

– was quite unique: he felt that the land, *because of its spiritual significance*, should have been given over to its *rightful occupants*.

At the end of his narrative, David connects his longing to the spiritual feel of the landscape. He feels that the land is pulling him to return; to "make a pilgrimage". Although David's pilgrimage was not exactly of a religious kind, his return to the ruins of his childhood home does resonate with Victor and Edith Turner's classic notion of the concept. Turners consider pilgrimages as movements away from the mundane centres and everyday social structures to a sacred periphery "to a far place intimately associated with the deepest, most cherished, axiomatic values of the traveler" (1978: 241). Thus, leaving behind his secular ordinary life in South Africa where he does not "feel with the land", David travels to the random remains of his childhood home. He then returns to his ordinary life with a sense of some transformation; he feels that his life has "gone a circle" and he's "back in the beginning".

## "THE LAND IS CALLING"
The protagonist of the second narrative, Norman, was introduced to me as a man I absolutely must talk to "because he grew up in the bush", a phrase designed to convey to me, I presume, that within the diaspora community he was considered "the archetypal Rhodesian". And indeed, Norman did capture the image of a Rhodesian 'bush type' heart and soul. Approaching sixty, he was big, bearded and bear-like, invariably clad in khaki shorts, bush shoes and long striped socks. Norman grew up in a very large family in a small town in central Rhodesia. After finishing school, he had worked at a post office, tried farming and then worked around Rhodesia at various power stations. Subsequently he had driven a loading truck at Durban harbour in South Africa, picked fruit in Australia, worked on a salmon fishing boat in Canada and caught tropical fish in Malawi. "But," Norman said, "I always used to get homesick." From all of his journeys he always returned home, "to this small town in the middle of the bush." "Having travelled the world, I wouldn't give you anything for Europe. Or America. Or Canada. I'm an African!" he declared. During our discussion, Norman kept returning to the particularity of his home place, which he felt was constantly calling him. When he recalled the place, his rather rough appearance seemed to melt. His spoke softly and tentatively, tenderly and persuasively.

And you spent your life just shooting at birds. I think I killed one. And just pure running around. You knew all the wild fruit, and there was lots there. Lots and lots of wild fruit. So you knew the seasons, you knew where to look. And there, there's a big river, fishing. 99% of your time was spent at the river [...]. The only restriction: suppertime. The power station used to blow the hooter to tell everybody it's four o'clock. They used to blow this big siren hooter. And then you know everybody's going home. And this could be five, six, eight miles away. As soon as that was heard, we used to run home [...] through the bush.

So this place is always calling me. [...] There's a river, a hill, normal hills, and you get the power station, the power line. And then the hill and all the houses are on the hill with the club on the top. The club you could see for miles. But as far as you could see, it was bush. Just pure God's bush. Not this stupid plantation. Just God's bush. We're gonna go back. I wanna go back now. It's calling me very much. Saying: 'Come, come, come, come back!'

I don't know if you're ever gonna go there, but if you drive from Messina to Beitbridge, when you cross the bridge, you enter God's own country. [...] And when you start climbing on the hills, you will see the baobabs and the green hills and then you'll know what I'm talking about. It's God's own country. God made Africa and just to make it so everybody's happy, he made the top and the bottom the worst places to be. Whereas the middle he kept for himself. [...] The middle of Africa God reserved for himself. And whenever I've had a garden, I've always left a space for God in the middle of the garden. With that piece of land God could do whatever He wished. Whatever He wished to grow in it, would grow.

Norman sets up the scene by describing the bush as an active playground of a child. Through his illustration, one can imagine a bush busy with bare feet treading the ground, the brush swarming and twigs twisting and snapping. He reflects on himself as a child who knows the bush from within – through running, shooting, fishing and picking fruit. But the narrative not only sets the scene in the physical environment; it also forms a setting of a small-town community of colonial Rhodesia. The sounds of kids flocking and rushing through the vegetation are interrupted by a blow of the power station siren. Every day at the same hour, it would tell everyone now is the time to run home. Thus, Norman's bush is not exactly a pristine, untouched piece of nature. Instead, the bush he portrays is constructed by activity and play, as well as by social engagements, which are scheduled and ordered by a modern, repetitive timetable of a colonial industrial small town.

Norman then attempts to capture the sense and spirit of the place by depicting a painting-like landscape image. He portrays a colonial small town set-up dominated economically, socially and visually by the power station and furnished with the communal centre, the club. Having verbally painted the scene and placed the club on the top, Norman then looks at the scene he has re-created from that very top. What he sees now retrospectively is a bush on a different level to that of his previous description of his childhood engagement with it. This is a landscape morally evaluated: it is *pure God's bush*. It is bush delineated as an untouched wilderness set in opposition and understood in comparison to "this stupid plantation", which he encounters in South Africa. Norman's stepping in and out of the picture – his recollections of both moving through the bush as well as his morally evaluative gaze of the scene – reflects the difference between what Tim Ingold (1993; 2011) refers to as a dwelling perspective on landscape on the one hand and the cartographer's or the surveyor's sense of space on the other. However, Norman's dichotomous portrayal also reflects temporal and analytical shifts in the memory narrative. The recollection of how one used to move about captures continuous engagement with landscape as expressive of a way of life in the past, while the evaluative gaze offers a moral retrospection of that engaged landscape from a spatiotemporal, diasporic distance.

Norman senses intensely that the place is animate and calls him; it actually speaks with a voice of its own. It is saying: "Come, come, come, come back!" Norman's voice changes as he enunciates these words. He whispers in a tempting, begging voice attempting to make me understand the power of the call. He then appears to give me driving directions to the sacred land and explains what crossing the bridge over the Limpopo River, a physical landmark demarcating the boundary between the two countries, signifies.[11] The border post and the bridge create a transition – concrete and metaphorical – between two realms of being, two irreconcilable ways of life. Although the terrain and the topography do not change dramatically, in many of the diasporic "homecoming narratives" (Basu 2004; see also Gressier 2015: 54–55), the natural scenery does seem to change. On the South African side, it is as if the landscape barely exists; it is just mileage, something to get through as fast as possible. But after crossing the bridge, the colour and texture of the landscape suddenly penetrate the senses. What is undescribed, even unseen on one side of the border, becomes green and fertile and animated on the home terrain.

At the end of his narrative, Norman reflects on the spirituality of the land. For Norman, who defines himself as a non-religious man, the Rhodesian bush landscape is "God's own country". This idiom, widely used by ex-Rhodesians, signifies a place of belonging, one's native ground, a birthplace, a home and a homeland. And it also implies an earthly paradise. Norman, however, conspicuously stresses the numinous essence of the place.[12] To him, the wilderness expresses the presence and nearness of God. That particular nook in the middle of rural Rhodesia into which he offers driving directions, is "God's bush". It is a place that God at the time of creation "kept and reserved for himself". Norman's intriguing gardening practice, his re-creation of a little spot for God in the middle of mowed lawns and manicured shrubs he otherwise so meticulously attends to, is his unique way of worshipping, of composing a sanctuary and thus commemorating the place of his belonging. By this exceptional practice, Norman demonstrates the essential ambiguity that characterises the settler conceptualisation of landscape; namely the idea that colonial "wide open spaces" call for appropriation and development, the outcome of which is, in the end, its destruction. The dilemma lies in the simultaneous attempt to both preserve the open space, understood as the pure and pristine state of nature and thus valuable as such, and to exploit its natural resources.

11  Messina and Beitbridge are border towns and custom posts between South Africa and Zimbabwe. Beitbridge, linking the two countries, was built in 1927–1929 across the Limpopo River.

12  The spiritualization of land may also be linked to the idea of a promised land; the idea of a chosen people in their God-given land, of divine purpose carved into a geographic territory. This type of conceptualization can be found in much of the literature on Afrikaners in South Africa, as well as in analysis of various diasporic groups. According to Vincent Crapanzano (1986) for example, the Afrikaner history and their occupation of territory in South Africa is narrated in Biblical terms.

## Untangling the bush

How do David's and Norman's stories conform to the classic form of colonial landscape narrative where the 'bush', understood as an untouched natural 'wilderness', is the conceptual core? To explore this question, I will trace the historical layers, temporal complexities and moral meanings that this landscape idea is composed of. How were European, and particularly British, landscape ideas transported to the settler territories? What kinds of a human relationships with the landscape are imagined as virtuous and desirable? How is 'the bush as nature' set in conceptual opposition with culture or society in these moral perceptions of landscape?

David's *country* and Norman's *bush* are cultural categories which are composite of complex temporalities. As such, they are deeply rooted in nature/culture conceptual oppositions in "Western" thinking.[13] Further, they connote distinct elements distinguishable in the concept of "wilderness" within the nature/culture complex. The very idea of wilderness, needless to say, is a cultural construct rather than a precise physical entity. Indeed, as William Cronon writes (1996: 7):

> Far from being the one place on earth that stands apart from humanity, it is quite profoundly a human creation [...]. It is not a pristine sanctuary where the last remnant of an untouched, endangered but still transcendent nature can be [...] encountered [but] a product of that civilization.

As a cultural product, wilderness contains layered traces from distinct historical eras. One may detect hints of pre-Israelite demonology, in which wilderness was considered as the realm beyond the reach of God (Coetzee 1988: 49). Likewise, one may observe elements of Judaeo-Christian thinking, where wilderness was seen as a safe retreat, a place of contemplation and purification, and a place where one's true being could be discovered (ibid.). In ancient Greek and Roman thought wilderness was, along with the garden and the city, considered one of the "archetypal landscapes" (Cosgrove 1993: 297–298). These three landscape categories – wilderness, garden and city – imply a moral narrative suggesting an intensifying human interference with nature; an idea which may also be recognized in David's and Norman's ways of moral juxtaposition of the bush with the town.

It has been suggested by many writers that fear was the strongest element in European attitudes to wilderness until the 19th century (e.g. Short 1991: xvi). In fairy tales and folklore, demons and dangers lurked in the forests and mountains. Wilderness was frightening both because of the creatures who dwelled there, and because of the effects it could have on individuals

---

13 Andre Gingrich argues that the potentially all-encompassing character of the nature/culture dichotomy in Western conceptualization is historically grounded in "secularized monotheistic legacy" (2014: 111). The differentiation of nature and culture rests on a tripartite hierarchy between "God, humans and 'the rest of Creation' in its organic and non-organic forms" (ibid.: 112).

exposed to its influence. However, in Britain, by the early 19th century, fear had been replaced by a romantic vision; wilderness had become an ennobled symbol of lost innocence. The idealised past in this imaginary was spatially situated in the countryside – and loosely dated somewhere in the early 18th century – and not in uninhabited wilderness. According to Jean and John Comaroff (1991: 71–73), the disappearing yeomanry became the mythical embodiment of a traditional lifestyle, and the most tragic symptom of the era was the scarring of the notion of England-as-garden. In actuality, however, the image of England-as-garden – with its neatly walled or hedged fields – was a consequence of the enclosure movement, the privatisation of the commons and the commodification of agriculture, which had preceded and enabled industrialisation and consequently caused the death of the yeomanry. Thus, the longed-for imaginary past merged two different historical periods: the so-called typical English scene of a tidy, geometric patchwork of green fields and one tilled mainly by yeoman households (ibid.: 322 n. 33; Miller 1995: 94). In these nostalgic views, the city had become the moral equivalent of the medieval forest, populated as it was by demons.

Reverie for the mythical wilderness/countryside was accompanied by a keen interest in outdoor life – both very much upper and middle class passions in Britain.[14] This enthusiasm was actualised, for example, in the birth of various rambling movements as well as natural history societies. In the words of David Evans (1992: 31), the lone "sportsman-naturalist-collector" became paradigmatic of the 19th century. Such interests further bloomed and prospered in the colonies. Scientific ideas became deeply embedded in imperial rule, shaping the conceptualisation of landscape, as well as ideas and practices of environmental conservation (Grove 1995; Griffiths and Robin 1997; Beinart and Hughes 2007). Thus, a complex mixture of landscape ideas – wilderness as a pristine place of purification, countryside as a rural idyll, Victorian wilderness movements, scientific and conservational pursuits – were all carried out and reshaped on imperial frontiers. Significantly, what these distinctive preoccupations demonstrate is that there was no singular "European landscape imaginary" transported to the colonies and imposed upon the occupied terrains. Instead, the imaginary stems from various historical roots, and mixes and merges complex and seemingly contradictory ideas and temporalities.

WIDE OPEN COUNTRY?

At the time of the colonial occupation, the wide-open spaces of the frontier were interpreted, by and large, as 'free land' for the colonisers. According to Thompson and Lamar, the most important aspect of frontier land was

14  Indeed, Short refers to the reinforcement of the Country ethic as "Balmorality" (1991: 74). However, he notes that the beginning of the 20th century also saw the emergence of different wilderness and rambling movements in Britain, some of which were explicitly socialist. They encouraged the opening up of the countryside for the benefit of the urban workers; the beauty of nature was seen as an encouragement to a simpler life and higher thinking (ibid.: 77).

its implication of ownership. "Free land [...] not only inspired aggressive expansion into indigenous areas for social and psychological reasons, it perpetuated hierarchical concepts of society and fostered forced labour systems on the so-called free frontiers of both North America and Southern Africa" (1981: 30). Jay Vest (1987: 310) analyses the utilitarian foundations of Western land use ideals – and thus the "European imperialist ethos" – and argues that they are built on John Locke's pre-societal natural right and individualised ownership theory. For instance, for the Puritans, the occupation of land in America was justified by their concept of *vacuum domicilium* – a notion that a place is without human habitation or civilisation and thus 'lonely' or 'desolate'. Lands such as these were seen as instrumentally valuable, worthy in what they could offer. Fusing Locke's theory with a Puritan reading of Genesis 1:28,[15] the pioneers refused to see Native Americans as human. On the colonial African continent, similar examples are legion. For instance, W. H. Brown, in his pioneering account *On the South African Frontier* (1899, cit. Palmer 1977: 16), writes:

> With the Bantu, removal does not entail the same degree of hardship that we contemplate in the dispossession of land in civilized communities. The natives do not hold the soil in the same sense of ownership. To them the earth is as free as the air and the water [...]. The occupancy of any given plot of ground is but temporary.

The fact that the land was *not* devoid of human involvement at the pioneers' arrival is obvious; neither can its "occupancy" be termed as "temporary". However, neither was this the exclusive way that landscape was depicted in the early European explorers and travellers' accounts. These characteristically included detailed descriptions of local political systems, natural landmarks, and seasonal variations (Beinart 1998). In fact, the 'empty land' appears to be a result of much narrative effort; it emerged through a historical process in which descriptive accounts gave way to the gradual hollowing out of the landscape as colonial control was instilled and strengthened, with the effect of rooting the pioneers' belonging in the soil. Thus, in the piecemeal transformation and solidification of the travellers' story into the pioneer origin narrative, natural features as well as traces of human involvement in the landscape, were shifted to the background. This created a blank space in which the core action – the colonial 'opening up' of the country – could be played out (Uusihakala 2008: 86–90). That the landscape has remained narratively empty since the frontier days, is again the result of substantial cultural work; it has included selectivity, dismissal and disregard (McIntosh 2016). In David Hughes' words, the settler colonials have had to "imagine the natives away" (2010: xii). It has also meant overlooking and dismissing the fact of severe land segregation; the land could appear wide open and

---

15 "God blessed them and said to them, 'Be fruitful and increase in number; fill the earth and subdue it. Rule over the fish of the sea and the birds of the air and over every living creature that moves on the ground.'"

empty because the Africans were displaced and settled in Native Reserves and subsequent Tribal Trust Lands.[16]

Very little of these struggles has penetrated the canonical colonial narratives, which remain resolutely stories of emptiness. Their central motif has been the depiction of wide open spaces as something that suggest opportunity and prosperity looming in the future. Interestingly, the potential futures were very often perceived and articulated by stressing the delightful resemblance and familiarity – the Europeanness – of the landscape, rather than its novelty or exoticism. For example, Errol Trzebinski, a popular historian of white Kenyans, muses on how early pioneers encountered the Kenyan highland wilderness: "The views that lay before them encompassed forest, lake, thicketed valley and green, moist grass where cattle might graze, evoking memories of a summer's day in Europe" (1991: 28). This landscape vision presents a curious blend of nostalgia, which is not just *retrospective* in that it longs for the familiar European surroundings of a bygone era, but also *prospective* (Boym 2001). In its political projection, it envisages, through the evocation of memory, a future that is homespun and familiar.

Elaine and Richard, an elderly couple I became acquainted with in South Africa, reminisced about Rhodesia with deep longing. Their memory narrative plays on a comparison between colonial Rhodesia as open country and the 'stitched up' land in South Africa. For them the Rhodesian open country was a democratic (as regarded the whites) wide-open space of opportunity. As a hobby, the couple used to prospect for minerals and gems in Rhodesia.

> Elaine: I think even on the mining side we were different. [Compared to South Africa.] Up there anybody could go and get a license to prospect. And all the land belonged to the state.

> Richard: What you did, you got a license [...] and you could go on anybody's land, subject to a written notice, registered, and send it to the farmer and you could prospect on his land for a month. Certain places you couldn't go, like into his *mielie*[17] crops and dip tanks and things like that, and obviously you went to see him first to get on good terms. And if you found something, [there was] a rigorous sort of pegging procedure, and then you registered it and you had to develop it or pay a penalty at the end of year [...] It was wild country. The thing was that *you felt as though the country belonged to you. It was my country.*

> Elaine: The difference [is, that in South Africa] every bit of what have you, they've got a value. Either it belongs to the farmer, the mineral rights, or it belongs to a mining company. And it's all *stitched up*. There is no *open country* as such. No. That you could go along and just help yourself.

---

16  To give one example, Donald S. Moore's (2005) study in the Eastern Highlands of Zimbabwe is an example of colonial politics of displacement and dispossession. Moore shows how colonial evictions displaced families from their ancestral lands and how the postcolonial authorities have subsequently turned those lands into resettlement schemes.

17  *Mielie* (Afrikaans) is maize or corn on the cob.

The open country in opposition to the South African stitched-up one is thus conceived of as one of limitless potential, where "you could go along and help yourself". The wildness Richard emphasises has to be interpreted from this perspective of potential, for the landscape he remembers and represents was hardly untouched. Instead, it was a land regulated by racially segregated social order and ownership; it belonged either to the colonial state or to private, white, farmers. The state regulated prospecting by controlling and registering the prospectors and requiring the development of claims. The way Richard recasts the land also dots it with human engagement; the *mielie* fields and the dip tanks on the farmer's property speak of a structured and nurtured farmland. Moreover, the landscape is intertwined with social relationships; to be able to help oneself to the offerings of the land required social interaction: one needed to be on good terms with the farmer who owned the plot. However, irrespective of these obvious elements of domestication in the landscape, the country is presented as wild. In addition to opportunity, the limitlessness of space evokes a sense of possession, a feeling that "the country belonged to you". Thus, the pioneering values of enterprise, freedom, and opportunity are time and again narratively carved into the concept of 'open country'.

Again, the picture is more complicated. In some accounts, 'emptiness' was not considered as an opportunity in a purely positive sense. A land without development and control could also implicate danger and maliciousness. Felix, one of my interlocutors in his fifties, called this "the *bundu* aspect". He connected the idea of dominating the environment to that of dominating the society. He spoke of Rhodesian politics being guided by an analogy of the way in which the physical environment was encountered:

> You were told that you were a cut above in a way. We were Lords of our creation in a sense. It's a dominating thing. The sort of *bundu* aspect. Unless you dominate the environment, it's gonna come at you. The sort of *bundu* aspect. It's around you.

Felix' *bundu aspect*, the idea that the white relationship with land was analogous with their position in the colonial social hierarchy – that both land and people needed to be controlled or they would "come at you" – indicates how deeply ideas of nature are tied to moral and political concerns. Thus, in a subtle way, Felix's contemplation integrates political conflict and struggle into the landscape.

## The bush as a moral guide

> I wish to speak a word for Nature, for absolute freedom and wildness, as contrasted with a freedom and culture merely civil – to regard man as an inhabitant, or a part and parcel of Nature, rather than a member of society (*The Portable Thoreau* 1947: 592).

Felix's *bundu aspect* exemplifies the way people's relationship with nature can be understood to reflect their relationship with the society; in his

227

version, both nature and society are potential sources of danger and malice. A more common, but equally politically charged, understanding among the ex-Rhodesians was formed along the more classic line of nature/ culture dichotomy. In this narrative pattern, the bush (or country) is set in an antagonistic relationship with town (or plantation), and the former acquires moral superiority. For instance, Stuart, a retired engineer in his 60s, articulates this in the following way:

> I would love to live in the bush where there are no houses at all. I love the *bush*. I go back as often as I can. [...] It is just being on your own. With the animals and the trees and just nature. You know a lot of people love *towns*. They can't live without a town. I can live without a town quite easily. [...] I take my boat, I go fishing. But it's not even the fishing. Fishing is an excuse. You sit there and you hold a fishing rod and you just look into the bush and everything else and it's just so relaxing!

In David, Norman and Stuart's nature vs. society polarisation, the bush is idealised as pure and innocent and valued above the society. David "never much cared for the *society*". He made do with it, but he really "loved the actual *country* itself". The place that calls Norman is "just pure God's *bush*" and "not this stupid *plantation*". Stuart, as well, could easily "live without a town". In this sense, their *country* and *bush* connote to those long-established ideas in European wilderness thinking in which wilderness is regarded as intrinsically precious and morally pure, rather than valuable in the sense of what it could be made into.

These conceptual dichotomies are also reflected and employed in more recent wilderness thinking in contemporary Zimbabwe. According to William Wolmer (2007: 142), the wilderness vision in which conservation and development programmes are rooted has two facets. On the one hand the lowveld landscape is seen as "disease-ridden, barren and fearful landscape that must be battled and tamed to become productive". On the other hand, wilderness is regarded as a "pristine and glorious piece of national heritage that must be preserved or rehabilitated." Although both of these facets of wilderness may be present, the latter view has, in recent years, become hegemonic.

The trend can be observed in my ethnographic examples as well. While Richard's and Elaine's open country is very much the pioneering frontier land of opportunity, for David, Norman, and Stuart, the wilderness is meaningful in itself: it is valued for what is perceived as its unspoiled and pure essence, rather than its productive potentiality. For Stuart, the bush is not as much a localisable place as it is for Norman. Stuart goes 'back to the bush' as often as he can, although the bush he goes back to is not always the same. Knowledge of particular locales that Stuart has previously encountered may be considered as setting up "structures of expectation and feeling", as Christopher Tilley proposes (1996: 162). These "structures of expectation and feeling" affect the way the bush, wherever it may be located, is encountered and categorised. Thus, the bush may be conceived of as not so much a particular place as it is a morally evaluated affective experience of landscape.

The structure of expectation relates not only to the way landscape is experienced but also to the way in which it is narratively construed. What is significant in David's and Norman's recollections is that while the stories appear to be situated in the classic settler landscape narrative which builds on the nature vs. society dichotomy, neither of them factually erases people, their engagements, built structures, or beliefs from the landscape. Whereas the familiarised colonial genre sets up historically structured frames, conceptual oppositions, and particular idioms with which the experienced landscape may be represented, David's and Norman's detailed reminiscences complicate the prevailing image of white postcolonial nostalgia. Their narratives do not unfold simply as stories of an empty land; nor do they suggest a postcolonial ambiguity of belonging (cf. Hughes 2010). Both men clearly sense that the landscapes they reflect upon are their spiritual homes. The emptiness, wildness and infinite quality they perceive in the landscape emerge as a moral commentary highlighting the essential sanctity of the place.

## Affect and temporality in postcolonial nostalgia

I have suggested that the ex-Rhodesian recollections of homeland landscapes – characterised by purity and emptiness and their separation from the society – are more complex than the conventional dichotomies of anthropological analysis suggest. As such they create an illuminating site for examining some key elements in white postcolonial nostalgia. What makes nostalgia a particular form of remembering is its affective dimension (Keightley and Pickering 2012: 116). In David's and Norman's narratives the emphasised affect combines an intimate sense of belonging and an intense yearning for the homeplace with the felt potentiality and virtue of that place. This is powerfully expressed in the idea that the remembered landscape is animated, capable of intention and action, and has a power to speak. The landscape is presented as tying the persons recalling it into a mutual relationship: the landscape calls back, haunts, lures and enchants those recalling it.

In Keith Basso's analysis such an animation of places is set in motion by the thoughts and feelings of persons who attend to them. Animation is linked to the fact that self-consciously attended-to familiar places are experienced as inherently meaningful, and their value is considered to emanate from "the form and arrangement of their observable characteristics" (1996: 55). In David's and Norman's descriptions, these characteristics are the wild and undomesticated, thus spiritual and mystical, elements they observe in the landscape. Further, actively sensed places are more than mere points in physical space. They possess a unique capacity for triggering acts of moral evaluation and self-reflection, as well as engendering a deeply felt connectedness. The recollection of places may take one across periods of time – the places may "evoke memories of who one used to be and thoughts about who one might become" (Basso 1996: 56).

Basso's last point suggests that actively sensed and affectively recalled places evoke reflections of oneself through time revealing relationships that exist between past, present and future. In nostalgic narratives, the homeland landscape becomes the site in which the converging of *space of experience* and the *horizon of expectation* can be observed. These concepts with which the past and the future are coordinated are, according to Reinhart Koselleck, both metahistorical and historically particular. He writes: "Every human being and every human community has a space of experience out of which one acts, in which past things are present or can be remembered, and, on the other, one always acts with reference to specific horizons of expectation" (2002: 111). Ricoeur (2004: 443; *pace* Heidegger) links these temporal horizons to the pairing of "return" and "anticipation", which in my mind captures pointedly the temporality of nostalgia – reaching both retrospectively to the past as well as prospectively towards the future – in relation to remembered landscapes.

Reflexively, nostalgic remembering can then be critically turned to what is lacking in the present and what is anticipated and hoped for in the future. Thus, according to Rebecca Bryant (2008: 404) nostalgic visions of lost place imply a homeland that is not absent but rather apocalyptic, a homeland yet to be realized. Bryant further suggests that nostalgia appears to emerge with a break represented by a lost dream: "Whether this is the dream of the immigrant who longs for a country that has changed in her absence, a dream of capitalism whose collapse results in post-Soviet nostalgia, or the dream of modernity whose alienation leads to a longing for some imagined former *Gemeinschaft*, nostalgia seems to be predicted on collapsed hope. Nostalgia then may be said to represent a type of everyday disenchantment" (2014: 155).

In David's and Norman's nostalgic narratives the temporal dimensions of past and future meet in the homeland landscape, the recollection of which calls for intense reflection on one's life trajectory. David's remembering of the site of his home and the surrounding magical mountains, and his sense that the place wills for his return, urges him to consider his life "as having gone a circle". In this nostalgic temporality, his future return will take him back to beginning, to the place which has "gone unchanged". David's homeplace offers itself as his future that might be "an endpoint rather than a lost beginning" (Bryant 2014: 160). Norman, for his part, shows that the return in body might not be necessary to hold the remembered homeplace – a place of redemption and renewal (Stewart 1996: 5) – close by. His inimitable engagement with the hallowed homeland landscape, his transportation and re-rooting of a metonymic piece of "God's own country" into a foreign soil, demonstrates by a creative nostalgic act of renewal, what nostalgia does and enables.

## Conclusion

This article has explored the complex ways in which the idea of empty land is embedded in the nostalgic postcolonial recollections of homeland among white former Rhodesians in South Africa. It has drawn out intricate historical layers, which underpin this culturally construed idea. It has further sketched how relationships with landscapes of memory are formed from a spatiotemporal distance, where exclusion from the place becomes an intrinsic element defining the human/landscape relationship. Although the two main narratives I have focused on may well be located in a familiar genre of settler narratives of empty, wide open spaces, in actuality the landscapes that David and Norman portray, are much more complex. While the two men describe the landscape they long for as pure and primeval, they do not erase its social and cultural layeredness. Thus, more than a lived reality or a literal space, the 'emptiness' of landscape, I argue, is a narrative and perceptual frame of expectation, and a moral commentary about ideal relationship between people and their landscapes. Further, instead of a classic settler colonial understanding of landscape as opportunity and possession valued for its productive potentiality, the landscape that David and Norman present is cherished for what is perceived as its authenticity, purity and sanctity. It is portrayed as a spiritual home and an intrinsic place of belonging.

As a particular mode of remembering, nostalgia captures closely some central elements in postcolonial human/landscape relationships, one of which is their affectability and intimacy. The particular places and locations tied into meaningful and intimate relationships are sites in which history appears to be condensed in ways that intertwine personal life experience with immutable natural presence. In the two examples, these are also places which are considered potent, powerful and intentional. It is quite evident that not all places speak or call for an affective mutual relationship. According to Basso (1996) only places "of focused thought and emotion" may be given the power to speak. Through a relationship of interanimation with places, their value is further increased. Such places are uplifted from the mundane. They are coated with a numinous essence – a sense that they are capable of emitting moral messages.

By closely examining diasporic homeland narratives, I have considered moral landscape commentaries and practices of return and renewal as elements of a nostalgic process in which a particular spatiotemporal relationship between persons and places of deep belonging are being created. However, not all narratives of the past are nostalgic. What characterises nostalgia as a particular mode of remembering is its reaching back to moments before and beyond conflict. Distinguished by their remoteness and wildness, the homeland landscapes discussed in this paper offer an example of such temporalisation and moral appraisal: the places recalled are set over and above social upheavals and political struggles. In this respect the remembered landscape is distinctly shaded by dismissal, denial and forgetting, and characterised by a mode of moral consciousness, which might be termed as structural oblivion (McIntosh 2016: 10–11). 'Empty land' emerges as a paradigm of such oblivion embedded in the landscape. The oblivion further relates to a specific temporal position – nostalgia is not necessarily about longing to return, it is a particular, selective way of narrating the past from the diffuse elements it is composed of.

# References

Alexander, Jocelyn 2006. *The Unsettled Land: State-making and the politics of land in Zimbabwe 1893–2003*. Oxford: James Currey.

Angé, Olivia and David Berliner 2015. Introduction: Anthropology of nostalgia – anthropology as nostalgia. In Olivia Angé and David Berliner (eds), *Anthropology and Nostalgia*. New York: Berghahn.

Basso, Keith 1996. Wisdom Sits in Places: Notes on a Western Apache landscape. In Steven Feld and Keith Basso (eds), *Senses of Place*. Santa Fe: School of American Research Press.

Basu, Paul 2004. My Own Island Home: The Orkney homecoming. *Journal of Material Culture* 9 (1): 27–42.

Beinart, William 1998. Men, Science, Travel and Nature in the Eighteenth and Nineteenth-century Cape. *Journal of Southern African Studies* 24 (4): 775–799.

Beinart, William and Lotte Hughes 2007. *Environment and Empire*. Oxford: Oxford University Press.

Berdahl, Daphne 2010. *On the Social Life of Postsocialism: Memory, consumption, Germany*. Bloomington: Indiana University Press.

Bissell, William Cunningham 2005. Engaging Colonial Nostalgia. *Cultural Anthropology* 20 (2): 215–248.

Bissell, William Cunningham 2015. Afterword. In Olivia Angé and David Berliner (eds), *Anthropology and Nostalgia*. New York: Berghahn.

Boyer, Dominic 2006. Ostalgie and the Politics of the Future in Eastern Germany. *Public Culture* 18 (2): 361–381.

Boym, Svetlana 2001. *The Future of Nostalgia*. New York: Basic Books.

Brubaker, Rogers 2005. The "Diaspora" Diaspora. *Ethnic and Racial Studies* 28 (1): 1–19.

Bryant, Rebecca 2008. Writing the Catastrophe: Nostalgia and its histories in Cyprus. *Journal of Modern Greek Studies* 26 (2): 399–422.

Bryant, Rebecca 2014. Nostalgia and the Discovery of Loss: Essentializing the Turkish Cypriot past. In Olivia Angé and David Berliner (eds), *Anthropology and Nostalgia*. New York: Berghahn.

Chennels, Anthony 1996. Rhodesian Discourse, Rhodesian Novels and the Zimbabwe Liberation War. In Ngwabi Bhebe and Terence Ranger (eds), *Society in Zimbabwe's Liberation War*. Oxford: James Currey.

Coetzee, J. M. 1988. *White Writing: On the culture of letters in South Africa*. New Haven: Yale University Press.

Cohen, Robin 1999 [1997] *Global Diasporas: An introduction*. London: UCL Press.

Comaroff, Jean and John Comaroff 1991. *Of Revelation and Revolution: Christianity, colonialism, and consciousness in South Africa*. Chicago: University of Chicago Press.

Cosgrove, Denis 1993. Landscapes and Myths: Gods and humans. In Barbara Bender (ed.), *Landscape: Politics and perspectives*. Providence: Berg.

Crapanzano, Vincent 1986. *Waiting: The whites of South Africa*. London: Paladin Grafton Books.

Cronon, William 1996. The Trouble with Wilderness or, Getting Back to the Wrong Nature. *Environmental History* 1 (1): 7–28.

Dominy, Michèle 2001. *Calling the Station Home: Place and identity in New Zealand's High Country*. Lanham: Rowman & Littlefield Publishers.

Eaton, W. G. 1996. *A Chronicle of Modern Sunlight: The story of what happened to the Rhodesians*. Rohnert Park: Inno Vision.

Evans, David 1992. *A History of Nature Conservation in Britain*. London: Routledge.

Fox, Graham 2012. Race, Power and Polemic: Whiteness in the anthropology of Africa. *Totem: The University of Western Ontario Journal of Anthropology* 20 (1), article 10.

Gingrich, Andre 2014. Establishing a 'Third Space'?: Anthropology and the potentials of transcending a great divide. In Kirsten Hastrup (ed.), *Anthropology and Nature*. New York: Routledge.

Godwin, Peter and Ian Hancock 1999 [1993]. *Rhodesians Never Die: The impact of war and political change on white Rhodesia, c. 1970–1980*. Harare: Baobab Books.

Gressier, Catie 2015. *At Home in the Okavango: White Batswana narratives of emplacement and belonging*. New York: Berghahn Books.

Griffiths, Tom and Libby Robin (eds) 1997. *Ecology and Empire: Environmental history of settler societies*. Edinburgh: Keele University Press.

Grove, Richard 1995. *Green Imperialism: Colonial expansion, tropical island Edens and the origins of environmentalism, 1600–1860*. Cambridge: Cambridge University Press.

Hammar, Amanda 2010. Ambivalent Mobilities: Zimbabwean commercial farmers in Mozambique. *Journal of Southern African Studies* 36 (2): 395–416.

Hughes, David McDermott 2010. *Whiteness in Zimbabwe: Race, landscape and the problem of belonging*. New York: Palgrave MacMillan.

Huxley, Elspeth 1981 [1962]. *The Mottled Lizard*. Harmondsworth: Penguin Books.

Huxley, Elspeth 1982 [1959]. *The Flame Trees of Thika*. England: Penguin Books.

Huxley, Elspeth 1987 [1985]. *Out in the Midday Sun*. England: Penguin Books.

Ingold, Tim 1993. The Temporality of the Landscape. *World Archaeology* 25 (2): 152–174.

Ingold, Tim 2011. *Being Alive: Essays on movement, knowledge and description*. London: Routledge.

Keightley, Emily and Michael Pickering 2012. *The Mnemonic Imagination: Remembering as a creative practice*. London: Palgrave Macmillan.

Koselleck, Reinhart 2002. *The Practice of Conceptual History: Timing history, spacing concepts*. Stanford: Stanford University Press.

Lessing, Doris 1973 [1952]. *Martha Quest*. Frogmore: Panther.

Lessing, Doris 1979 [1973]. *Collected African Stories: Volume one*. London: Triad/Panther Books.

McIntosh, Janet 2016. *Unsettled: Denial and belonging among white Kenyans*. University of California Press.

Miller, Simon 1995. Land, Landscape and the Question of Culture: English urban hegemony and research needs. *Journal of Historical Sociology* 8 (1): 94–107.

Moore, Donald S. 2005. *Suffering for Territory: Race, place and power in Zimbabwe*. Durham: Duke University Press.

Moyo, Sam 2011. Three Decades of Agrarian Reform in Zimbabwe. *The Journal of Peasant Studies* 38 (3): 493–531.

Mupira, Paul 2003. The Case of Nyanga Cultural Landscape, N. E. Zimbabwe. A paper presented at *ICOMOS 14th General Assembly: Place – memory – meaning: preserving intangible values in monuments and sites*. Victoria Falls, Zimbabwe October 27–31, 2003. http://www.international.icomos.org/victoriafalls2003/papers/B2%20-%20 4%20-%20Mupira.pdf <accessed 14 November 2016>.

Palmer, Robin 1977. *Land and Racial Domination in Rhodesia*. London: Heinemann.

Pilossof, Rory 2012. *Unbearable Whiteness of Being: Farmers' voices from Zimbabwe*. Harare: Weaver Press.

*Portable Thoreau* 1947. C. Bode (ed.) New York: The Viking Press.

Ricoeur, Paul 2004. *Memory, History, Forgetting*. Chicago: University of Chicago Press.

Rutherford, Blair 2017. *Farm Labor Struggles in Zimbabwe: The ground of politics*. Bloomington: Indiana University Press.

Short, John Rennie 1991. *Imagined Country: Environment, culture and society*. London: Routledge.

Smith, Andrea 2003. Place Replaced: Colonial nostalgia and pied-noir nilgrimages to Malta. *Cultural Anthropology* 18 (3): 329–364.

Steyn, Melissa 2012. The Ignorance Contract: Recollections of apartheid childhoods and the construction of epistemologies of ignorance. *Identities: Global Studies of Culture and Power* 19 (1): 8–25.

Stewart, Kathleen 1996. *A Space on the Side of the Road: Cultural poetics in an "other" America*. Princeton: Princeton University Press.

Thompson, Leonard and Howard Lamar 1981. The North American and Southern African Frontiers. In H. Lamar and L. Thompson (eds), *The Frontier in History: North America and Southern Africa compared*. New Haven: Yale University Press.

Tilley, Christopher 1996. The Power of Rocks: Topography and monument construction on Bodmin Moor. *World Archaeology* 28 (2): 161–176.

Trzebinski, Errol 1991 [1985]. *The Kenya Pioneers: The frontiersmen of an adopted land*. London: Mandarin.

Turner, Victor and Edith Turner 1978. *Image and Pilgrimage in Christian Culture: Anthropological perspectives*. Chicago: University of Chicago Press.

Vest, Jay 1987. The Philosophical Significance of Wilderness Solitude. *Environmental Ethics* 9 (4): 303–330.

Werbner, Pnina 2000. The Materiality of Diaspora – Between aesthetic and "real" politics. *Diaspora* 9 (1): 5–20.

Wolmer, William 2007. *From Wilderness Vision to Farm Invasions: Conservation and development in Zimbabwe's south-east lowveld*. Oxford: James Currey.

Philippe Descola

# Landscape as transfiguration: Edward Westermarck memorial lecture, October 2015[1]

It is customary, when asked to deliver a named lecture, to begin with a few words of praise for the person whose memory the lecture series pays homage to, in the present case Professor Edward Westermarck. However, although I did read bits and pieces of the *History of Human Marriage* (1891) when I began to study anthropology and, more recently, the very informative book edited by David Shankland (2014) on Westermarck, I am ashamed to confess that none of the main topics of interest of this most illustrious anthropological ancestor – systems of marriage, the origin of the family and the theory of morality – figures prominently on my research agenda. However, I do favour the comparatist approach that Westermarck advocated all his life, that is, the testing of anthropological hypotheses by checking their explanatory value and scope against empirical evidence, an endeavour which tends to fade away nowadays in favour of what one may call 'ethnographism', that is, unwarranted small-scale inductive generalizations out of very narrow case studies. In this lecture, I will in fact attempt to combine both anthropology as a hypothetico-deductive method and ethnography as an interpretive one to test a new approach to, and definition of, the concept of landscape and to look at its purchase on an ethnographic case, to wit the Amazonian Achuar of the Ecuadorian rainforest with whom I spent some of the most interesting years of my life, but to whom I had not turned back for quite a while. By doing so, I hope to honour another great Finnish anthropologist, Rafael Karsten, himself a student and unruly disciple of Westermarck whom he succeeded in the chair of moral and social philosophy at the University of Helsinki, a noteworthy Americanist and a remarkable pioneer in the ethnology of the Jivaroan tribes I myself studied some 60 years later.

Back to the anthropological question, then: What is a landscape? And more precisely: how are we to define a landscape if we wish to extend the concept beyond the few cultures who have created representations of sites, whether in images or in writing? Do we only find a perception of the

1 This lecture was originally published in *Suomen Antropologi: Journal of the Finnish Anthropological Society* 41 (1): 3–14. It is reprinted with the permission of the author and publisher.

landscape in the civilizations where a tradition of depicting it has flourished, or may we use that concept in an anthropologically productive way by detaching it from its aesthetic background? To these classical questions there are two main lines of answers, none of which is really satisfying. The first kind of answers could be called 'extensionist' because they extend the field of meaning of the original concept (to the point where it has little bearing anymore with its specialized definition) as it was construed in Europe from the Renaissance onwards as a pictorial or literary representation of a piece of land. The extensions may operate in different manners. The most common in the social sciences consider landscape as what results from human labour on the environment – open fields in Medieval Europe or terraced slopes in Luzon, in the Andes or in Provence – an objective phenomenon, then, which can be studied everywhere by following the way opened up by human geography ever since Alexander von Humboldt set to this discipline, which he largely created, the mission of studying what he called "the progressive habitability of the earth".[2] This meaning of landscape, widely adopted by historians, archaeologists and anthropologists, retains nothing of interest from the initial denotation of the word and imposes moreover a dualist conception of the environment – a physical substratum socialized by human actions – which hardly corresponds to the manner in which most non-modern civilizations conceptualize the places where they dwell. Another, even more trivial, form of universalization of the notion of landscape is the one which takes the term in its loosest meaning, as the space cognitively and emotionally apprehended by a human subject. And since every human develops a subjective apprehension of space forged by a combination of personal tastes, biographical particulars and cultural upbringing, it results that they are as many experiences of landscape as there are individuals, so that one cannot say much about landscape in general. These manners of breaking with the conventional meaning of landscape are not very productive, either because they do not respect the originality of the notion as it developed initially in Europe, or, on the contrary, because they do not respect the peculiarities of the non-European societies to which they are applied.

By contrast, the other approach to landscape could be called comprehensive in that it densifies the comprehension of the concept instead of extending it. It revolves around the idea of the landscape as a representation of a piece of land seen by a viewer which was put forth by historians of art such as Kenneth Clark (1949) and Ernst Gombrich (1953), who both emphasized the exceptionality of this pictorial genre. The comprehensive approach is particularly developed in France among some geographers and philosophers. It requires that a set of strict criteria be satisfied before one can qualify anything as a landscape or a landscaping scheme: notably the existence of a word, or words, that can be translated as landscape, of literary creations celebrating the beauties of nature, of pictures that have the representation of a piece of land as an exclusive theme, and of pleasure gardens which manifest the desire to emulate aesthetically a pleasurable environment (see,

2   In a letter to Friedrich Schiller (quoted in Minguet 1969: 77).

e.g., Berque 1995; 2008; Roger 1997). I do agree that we need explicit clues in this matter, since no one has access otherwise to the sensible world of others: how am I to know that my Achuar neighbour, with whom I am watching the sand bars emerging from an Amazonian river against the background of a stormy sky, does perceive in what he sees the kind of landscape that filters my own vision, informed as it is by a long familiarity with landscape paintings of different traditions? However, by fixing *a priori* criteria, this reasonable attitude has the disadvantage of closing the enquiry before it even began: one will certainly be in a position to recognize the predefined criteria, but will one be able to detect a landscaping intention or pattern in the laying out and the use of a site if these criteria are not present?

This is why I chose to embrace a third approach. It is predicated on the idea that, if one wants to exploit the most interesting feature of what the notion of landscape referred to initially, one has to associate this notion less with constituted objects – pictures, gardens, laid out environments – than with the very process by which these objects are constituted into landscapes, a process which may be defined as a transfiguration. When applied to a site, a transfiguration is a deliberate change of appearance at the end of which this site becomes the global sign of something other than what it was globally before it was transfigured, revealing and actualizing in the process some features that it contained potentially. A landscape is above all an object intentionally produced or fashioned by humans so that, among a diversity of other possible uses – utilitarian, recreational, religious – it may function *also* as an iconic sign standing for something else, to wit a portion of a real or imaginary space. Acknowledging this difference between the materials of the composition – vegetation, relief, water, buildings – and the outcome that it produces – whether a garden or a picture – does not imply at all either that this transfiguration leads to an aesthetization – that is, the quest for a result that pleases the senses – or that it presupposes a marked divide between a physical substratum existing beyond all representation and a cultural poïésis that would give it an *a posteriori* meaning. To produce a landscape, this transfiguration should satisfy three conditions: first, the result of the operation must be deliberately sought after, not be the fortuitous result of an action conducted for another end; second, this operation must not be exclusively utilitarian, that is, aiming at the laying out or the technical improvement of a productive, defensive or dwelling site; and finally, at the end of the operation there must exist a clear conscience on the part of those who have undertaken it of a difference in nature between the elements they had at their disposal initially and their metamorphosis into what we will conventionally define as a landscape. Note that neither an aesthetization nor a great divide between nature and culture are requested here. Transfiguration can present itself under two modalities: one is direct, the transfiguration *in situ*, that is, the laying out of a portion of environment, most commonly under the form of a garden; the other is indirect, the transfiguration *in visu*, and it expresses itself in figurative codes conditioning the representation of landscapes – in pictures or scale models, for instance – structuring, therefore, the perceptual schemes conditioning the manner in which a piece of land will be seen.

How are we to detect traces of this process of transfiguration where neither landscape painting nor pleasure gardens are to be found? To do that, it is necessary to expand the scope both of the transfiguration *in visu*, so as to include in it other forms of iconic representation of the world than those that can be recognized in conventional landscape painting, and of the transfiguration *in situ* so as to include in it forms of creation of ecosystems which do not follow the standards of the art of pleasure gardens, whether European or Far-Eastern. I will only deal in this lecture with the latter aspect. A lead seems particularly promising for renewing the scope of the transfiguration *in situ*: the meanings attached to subsistence gardens. While it can be readily admitted that pleasure gardens constitute a legitimate expression of an *in situ* transfiguration which leads up to more or less extensive forms of landscaping, there is a tendency to consider subsistence gardens as having no other function than utilitarian. It is far from being the case and this is what I would like to show with examples of Amazonian gardens.

Like many tropical gardens of polyculture elsewhere, Amazonian gardens combine two characteristic features which provide a fertile ground for processes of transfiguration. On the one hand they are swiddens, that is, they render patently visible the relationship between cultivated vegetation and the forest cover which it replaces, a relationship which plays on the variations of scale between the two domains and on complex modulations of the articulation between what is spontaneous and what is controlled. On the other hand, Amazonian gardens usually allow for the coexistence in the same plot of a great number of species and varieties, in such a way that each plant requires individualized treatment. Let us look first at the latter feature. In the case of the polyculture of cultigens propagated by vegetative multiplication, gardening labour appears as an enterprise of pairing and associating singularized vegetal individuals, the assemblage of which must form a harmonious collective. Contrary to the heroic image of the cultivator of cereals, tropical gardeners are composers who marry plants whose cohabitation they favour. This personalized relation derives notably from the fact that the majority of cultivated plants in tropical swiddens are roots that are reproduced vegetatively, that is, clones which are perpetuated thanks to the individual operation of propagation by cuttings realized by humans. The descent of each plant in a line of genetically identical organisms is thus realized through a continuous relationship with a human who actualizes it periodically. Let us now go back to the first feature of tropical gardens, that is, the fact that they appear at first glance as the substitution of a spontaneous vegetal cover by a vegetal cover controlled by humans. In fact, the relation between the forest and the garden is more complex than what appears to a non-informed observer as the conquest of a natural space by the agrarian civilization. Such an opposition between the wild and the domesticated makes no sense in tropical swidden horticulture for two complementary reasons. First, because the equatorial rain forest has been profoundly affected by human action in the course of millennia so that it is partly anthropogenic: horticulture and sylviculture complete each other as much in the techniques they use as in the results obtained. Second, because the garden reproduces at a smaller scale the multi-layered structure of the forest, a stratification which diminishes the destructive effects of solar radiation and bleaching on generally poor soils. Thus, the distinction between the polycultural swidden and the forest in which it was cleared is far from clear cut, on the one hand because the forest can be seen as a macro-garden, on the other hand because the garden can be seen as a micro-forest.

For lack of time, I cannot enter here into the technical discussion of these two propositions which have triggered in the past decades a number of controversies. I will restrict myself to the two following statements. First, concerning the notion that the forest can be seen as a macro-garden. All the studies in ethnoecology carried out in Amazonia in the course of the past 30 years, including mine, have brought to light different types, often combined, of intentional manipulations by the Amerindians of sylvan species of fruit trees and palms: in the gardens themselves, in the fallows and the former sites of habitat, and in a peripheral area of one or two hours walk around the settlements sites.[3] This configuration, common to all native Amazonia, and aptly christened "swidden-fallow agroforestry" by William Denevan and Christine Padoch (1987), is now widely accepted by the scientific community. It constitutes a more likely alternative for defining the anthropisation of the Amazonian rainforest than the claim occasionally put forth by certain researchers that there exist completely anthropogenic forests which have been planted and managed intentionally by Amerindians. As to the proposition that the tropical garden of polyculture imitates the forest from a triple point of view – systemic, structural and functional – an idea initially put forth by Clifford Geertz (1963) and which has also been hotly discussed, two remarks can be made.[4] First, that it is unlikely that the populations whose gardens obviously reproduce certain features of the rainforest have attempted to copy deliberately a generalized ecosystem of which they would fully understand the mechanisms and the benefits so as to transpose them to their horticultural system. In fact, Geertz himself never claimed that tropical swidden gardeners had had the intention to reproduce in their gardens the main ecosystemic characteristics of the forest to which he had drawn attention: the high degree of specific diversity, the stratified structure of the vegetation and the internal recycling of nutrients. All that one can say in his wake is that there exists a structural continuum between the forest and the garden since both function according to similar ecological principles. This continuum is due to the fact that in the course of the several millennia during which tropical horticulturists have domesticated the main cultigens, they have little by little perfected techniques of plant management which did not differ in their principles from those they used in the manipulation of sylvan resources, notably the selective maintenance of certain plants of which they favoured the growth under forest cover. Swidden horticulture and agroforestry are thus two sides of the same process of plant manipulation. This is why, rather than asking oneself if tropical gardens

3   Among pioneering works on this topic in Amazonia, see Balée (1989), Descola (1994), Frickel (1978), Harris (1971), Hödl & Gasché (1981).

4   In 1983 a special issue of *Human Ecology* 11 (1) was devoted to discussing Geertz's thesis.

imitate the forest or not, it seems more interesting to consider the relations of analogy explicitly detected and stated by Amerindians between these two ecosystems. Due to lack of time I will only take a few examples starting with that of the Achuar.

Among the Achuar there is little doubt that the forest is perceived and treated as a large garden and that the gardens are planted in such a way as to look like miniature forests in their disposition, their composition and their structure. Let us consider the first point. If the forest takes, in the eyes of the Achuar, the appearance of a large plantation it is not because they cultivate it themselves as a garden, but because they are fully aware that their properly horticultural activities – notably the transplantation of approximately 40 species of sylvan plants into their gardens – have a long-term effect on the phytosociology of the forest in the areas that have been regularly cleared for gardens. The Achuar practice a pioneer horticulture, that is, they do not open new swiddens in recent fallows, but rather in ancient secondary forests which may have been cleared three or four generations ago and which they precisely identify as such by the abundance in them of useful sylvan species. In view of the very low human density and of the very scattered habitat, the influence of this long-term anthropisation on the forest remains limited, although sufficient to be perceived by a population who is attentive to the distinctive features of the forest that it exploits as much for its food (approximately 50 species are consumed) as for a variety of other uses (pharmacopeia, tools and weapons, firewood, timber) and where the memory of the abandoned sites of habitat is retained over a few decades. Within a radius of approximately 10 kilometres from a house, the forest can be likened to a vast orchard which women and children visit at all times for gathering excursions, for collecting palm grubs or for poison fishing in the brooks and small lakes. It is a domain which is known intimately, where each palm and tree bearing edible fruits is periodically visited during the season. But inasmuch as this anthropisation of the forest, although visible, is not the product of a planned action, the Achuar only recognize it, as it were, in the second degree: the forest has indeed been planted intentionally, but by a spirit. This spirit answers to the name of Shakaim and his main task is to guide men in the labour of clearing gardens. Shakaim is conceived as the husband or the brother of Nunkui, the female spirit who watches over gardens; while Nunkui rules cultivated plants, Shakaim is the gardener of the sylvan plants. As the curator of the forest vegetation, Shakaim visits men during their dreams and signals to them the best sites for opening new gardens since he is in the best position to know where the land is fertile, where the plants he cares for thrive best.

Due to the fact that it is planted and maintained by a spirit, the forest is no more a wild domain in the eyes of the Achuar than their garden is. This is why it is not difficult for them to consider this vegetal continuum from one pole or from the other, and also to see in their gardens miniature forests, that is, plantations similar to those of Shakaim, but of which they have the care and the responsibility. The resemblance is obvious: as much from the point of view of the diversity and of the intermingling of species – they use over 60 cultigens distributed in 130 varieties – as from the point of view of the stratified structure of the vegetation. The analogies between the two ecosystems are clearly visible, especially because species of sylvan origin are transplanted into the gardens while plants formerly acclimatized in the gardens also subsist in the forest in very ancient fallows that are almost undistinguishable from climax vegetation. It would thus be absurd to take the contrast between the garden and the forest as an opposition between the wild and the domesticated; when the Achuar clear and plant a swidden they replace the plantations of a spirit imitating a garden by human plantations imitating the forest. In fact, both the obvious pleasure that the Achuar derive from multiplying the number of cultigens and cultivars in their gardens and the desire to maintain in them the greatest possible quantity of sylvan species is less the product of a utilitarian imperative than the symptom of a pronounced attraction for vegetal diversity which can be likened to a kind of aesthetic satisfaction in the collection of plants, a common enough disposition among gardeners in other parts of the world. In sum, the vegetal diversity of Achuar gardens, probably one of the highest in the Amazon basin, is not strictly functional and one may consider that it falls within the ambit of a desire to emulate at another scale the floristic diversity of the forest.

The Achuar see cultivated plants as persons endowed with an interiority to whom admonitions and exhortations can be addressed and with whom one can communicate in dreams and by the medium of spells. These vegetal persons live in families, cooperate and enter into conflicts, so that the garden constitutes a micro-society in the literal sense, a collective of leafy people with whom humans must live on good terms. The plants of the garden are under the jurisdiction of a female spirit, Nunkui, who created them initially, and it is only with her agreement that humans can deal with them and always on a temporary basis. An origin myth relates that after she had first created the cultivated plants, the spirit Nunkui became displeased with the behaviour of humans and made the plants vanish. The modalities of the disappearance of plants diverge according to the variants of this myth among the various Jivaroan groups. In a Shuar version collected by Michael Harner (1972: 70–76), the cultivated plants are swallowed up by the ground, at the same time as the trails opened in the forest. In other Shuar and Aguaruna variants, cultivated plants are transformed into sylvan plants; an Aguaruna variant collected by Brent Berlin (1977) is remarkable from this point of view as it lists precisely the sylvan counterparts of the 22 cultigens mentioned. In Achuar variants of the myth, the cultivated plants do not disappear but their size diminishes by successive stages to the point of becoming minuscule. Whether their destiny is to disappear completely, to transform into sylvan plants or to become diminutive, the plants cultivated by the various Jivaroan groups are always under the threat of the curse of Nunkui. The mode of reappearance of plants after the initial catastrophe is not very explicit. In Achuar glosses, an elusive reference is made to the compassion of Nunkui, who resolves to give back to humans a few seeds and cuttings so that they may plant gardens again. But this act of kindness is coupled with a corollary requirement: humans will now have to work hard to maintain this vegetal inheritance transmitted from generation to generation. Described in a myth,

241

the fading of cultivated plants is an event which, according to the Achuar, can happen again today. The experience of abandoned gardens gives it an empirical foundation which reinforces the teachings of the myth. For the main cultigens disappear rapidly in the fallows, overcome by the secondary vegetation and by the transplanted sylvan species, a phenomenon well-known to the Achuar who return regularly to the recent fallows to collect fruits. The progressive disappearance of the plants cultivated by humans and their replacement by the plants cultivated by Shakaim are for them a common experience which happens to confirm the possibility of the inaugural catastrophe related in the Nunkui myth.

What are the consequences of this mythical genesis from the point of view of the garden as a landscape? There is no doubt that the Achuar garden can be viewed as a landscape since it figures in miniature a forest which is similar to the one which surrounds it, and is thus in that sense a transfiguration *in situ*, not so much of a piece of land as of a type of ecosystem. But it is a landscape of a particular kind, since the components of this miniature forest – the plants the use of which Nunkui granted to the humans – are under the constant threat of becoming sylvan again, as in the Aguaruna variant of the myth, by changing into their sylvan doubles. The landscape is thus permanently under the threat of disappearing, that is, of reverting to the referent of which it is the iconic sign; it is always on the verge of losing, with its function of sign, its character as a landscape, by merging with what it is meant to figure. Far from expressing an opposition between nature and culture, the contrast between the garden and the forest takes the guise of a relation, threatened by confusion, between a representation and what it represents; a relation of transfiguration *in situ* indeed, but always reversible. In that sense one can speak of a metamorphic landscape, which fits well with the nature of representation in an animist ontology such as that of the Achuar. For the characteristic of an animist ontology is that it allows metamorphosis, that is, the switch between the point of view of the internal subjectivity of beings and the point of view of their corporeal form. The garden, a space cultivated by humans thanks to the plants of the Nunkui spirit, is an image of the forest, a space cultivated by the spirit Shakaim, who sees in turn the gardens of humans as a forest encroaching on his plantations. Metamorphosis is thus here a game of perspectives: the garden which becomes a forest again in the eyes of the Achuar when it turns into a fallow is, in the eyes of the spirits, a forest which reverts to being a garden.

But there is more. In principle, the garden is a space of consanguinity, and for a number of reasons. First, because it is at the core of the domestic space of each household in which, due to certain properties of the Dravidian kinship system common in Amazonia, the relations of affinity are erased in favour of relations of consanguinity: the house and the garden are ideally consanguine spaces. Second, because the garden is a female space and the manipulation of the kinship terminology and of the system of behaviour results in an association of women with consanguine sociality. Last, because the plants cultivated by women are seen as their children and the Achuar consider motherhood as the consanguine relation par excellence. However, the most common and ubiquitous child-plant in the garden, manioc, is also the most dangerous since it reputedly sucks the blood of humans through its leaves. Manioc thus expresses a predatory disposition which is characteristic not of the sphere of consanguinity proper to women, but rather of the relations of ideal affinity that the men maintain in the forest with other men, during war, and with game animals on the occasion of hunting. Besides, by sucking the blood of human children, the manioc plants merely take revenge for the treatment that their human mothers impose on them, since women feed their human children with manioc gruel. This reciprocal devouring of human and vegetal children renders the consanguinity of the garden truly paradoxical. Now it is this paradox which is expressed in the garden as landscape, that is, the fact that the miniature image of the forest that it offers is under the permanent threat of disappearing and thus of merging with what it is supposed to figure. For, as a sign, the garden is indeed a material object created and maintained by women, that is, pertaining to domestic consanguinity; but it is also, via the ubiquitous cannibal manioc, contaminated by the values of predatory affinity which reign in the forest that it figures. The garden is thus both fully an iconic representation of a space, the forest, and, at least under certain aspects, a real actualization of this space.

Let us now turn more briefly to the meanings attached to gardens in tribal groups of the Amazonian Northwest, more particularly among the Yukuna, the Makuna and the Miraña.[5] As among the Achuar, cultivated plants were created there by mythical heroes and they disappeared once before being again accessible and existing in the form of persons, defined as consanguines of the women who take care of them. Among the Yukuna and the Makuna, the mythical genesis of cultivated plants provides the model of their disposition in the garden which moreover reproduces the spatial layout of the *maloca*, the collective house. The latter is organized according to a series of contrasts between male and female (according to the east-west axis), between affines and consanguines, between elder and younger (according to various declinations of the north-south axis), and between ceremonial and domestic spaces opposing the centre to the periphery. The garden is structured according to the same categories: a male front part and a female back part, a ritualized centre and a profane periphery. Moreover, myths associate coca to a bone, a male element, so that one can see the garden as a human or animal body: in the centre the coca plants form the skeleton, surrounded by the manioc bushes which symbolize the flesh and the blood. In their actual composition, Yukuna and Makuna gardens thus reflect at the same time the mythical operations which constituted them and the organization of social relations in the *maloca*.

The Miraña also plant coca in the centre of the plot in parallel rows, the plant being assimilated to the backbone of the garden, which confirms the symbolism of the skeleton associated with the coca. Furthermore, the Miraña say that each cultivated plant is guarded by one or two masters who watch over it, most of them being 'punishing' spirits – generally biting or

5   For the Yukuna see van der Hammen (1992); for the Makuna see Cayón (2002); for the Miraña see Karadimas (2005).

243

stinging insects – who castigate humans by sending them diseases if they behave badly in the gardens. Inasmuch as the Miraña garden is a vast metamorphosis of the body of the demiurge, one understands that the latter wishes to retaliate if the plants which he generated are being manhandled, by entrusting this mission to the master spirits of each species: the parallelism is obvious between the garden seen by humans as the body of the creator hero and the human body seen by the creator hero as a sort of garden in which he can let lose his ravaging pests. Lastly, among the Miraña as among the Yukuna and the Makuna, it is imperative to negotiate permission to clear a garden with the spirits of the forest, a task entrusted to the shaman of the local group: for all the elements of the world, all beings, all sites have a master with whom one has to reckon with when one undertakes any activity. Clearing a garden is to encroach on the domain of the spirits who control the sylvan flora, a very risky enterprise and one that can only be undertaken with their consent. Among the Miraña, the parallel with the Achuar is even more obvious; as Dimitri Karadimas (2005: 341) writes "the forest is in fact but a 'plantation' under the responsibility of a master". *De facto*, the deep forest is a dangerous space, under the jurisdiction of predatory spirits who protect the animals and the trees from which they derive their food and who hunt humans: it can be seen as the garden of animals and some cultivated species are indeed considered as humanized variants of sylvan plants proceeding from the garden of the animals. In sum, when the Miraña clear a swidden in the forest, they destroy part of the garden of animals and it is to placate them that they offer coca to their masters.

It is obvious that in these four Amazonian societies, the garden is always a transfiguration: whether of the forest, of the body of the demiurge or of a microcosmic house conceived as an organism. In all these cases, the relation between the garden and the forest, or between the cultivated plants and the sylvan plants, is not expressed in the form of an opposition between nature and culture, or between the wild and the domesticated, but rather in the form of a series of metamorphoses in which forest transforms into garden, garden transforms into forest, persons transform into plants, divine bodies transform into gardens, human bodies are treated as plants, animals reveal themselves as plants; in short, a permanent movement back-and-forth between macrocosm and microcosm, between types of environment and between ontological categories, a movement which provides an insight into the richness of the conceptions that Amazonian populations have developed to describe and interpret the interactions between biotic communities.

Can one speak here of landscape? If one means by that the transfiguration of a site laid out in such a way that it constitutes an iconic sign of a reality which is distinct from its patent function, then there is no doubt that these Amerindian gardens are landscapes. The idea of transfiguration is manifest in all cases. Among the Achuar and the Miraña, one can note moreover a narrowing of the gap between the sign and the referent which converts the garden into a very ambiguous landscape. For the Achuar, the plantation of a spirit imitating a garden is replaced by human plantations imitating the forest, but these plantations are under the constant threat of disappearing if the gardeners displease the spirit of the garden, a disappearance which will happen in the end anyway when the garden is abandoned and when the distinction between the image and what it represents disappears. The garden will then have lost its function as a landscape since it will have become again a true forest. In the Miraña case, the plantations of spirits imitating the garden are replaced by human plantations stemming from the body of another spirit, but those who plant them are under the constant threat of seeing their body treated as a garden by the delegates of the spirit, that is, of being dismembered and cut down by diseases following the example of the body of the demiurge. Here again, ambiguity takes over: the initial transfiguration carries the cost of seeing humans transfiguring themselves against their will, with the results that it is the producers of signs who are themselves threatened with becoming signs of what they had figured by creating their gardens.

*

The subtle forms of landscape that native populations of Amazonia have managed to create in their gardens offer a conceptual yield far more interesting than what the anthropologists and the archaeologists usually call a landscape, in the loose sense of a subjectively apprehended and anthropogenic ecosystem. And since the type of transfiguration *in situ* that these gardens realize can equally be detected in other subsistence gardens in other parts of the world where there exists no tradition of literary or pictorial representation of landscapes, particularly in Melanesia and in certain regions of South East Asia, the field of comparative investigation that this perspective opens up seems particularly promising. Proceeding in such a way is also a means of being faithful to the general project of symmetrisation which I see as one of the missions entrusted to anthropology. By symmetrisation I mean the effort to render compatible and treat on an equal footing the cultural features of the observer and those of the observed, so as to escape the situation where the point of view of the analyst doing the comparison encompasses the point of view of the members of the societies that are being compared, or at least sets a convenient point of reference for its evaluation. Why could treating landscape as a transfiguration be construed as a symmetrisation? Because the analytic point of view is not given here *ab initio*, either as the product of a supposedly universal disposition of human nature – the capacity of humans to apprehend a place subjectively or their ability to leave a mark on it – or as the template provided by a Eurocentric concept. The point of view results from the never ending operation by means of which cultural features, norms, institutions, systems of signs, are constituted as variants of one another within a set. The set is here composed of the various man-made ecosystems that fall within the definition of a transfiguration *in situ*, that is, the deliberate conversion of a piece of land into a global iconic sign which highlights some features of the site previously not emphasized. In this perspective, Amazonian gardens are not landscapes because they resemble European pleasure gardens or Japanese gardens, but rather because Amazonian gardens, European gardens and Japanese gardens are variants of one another within a broader group of transformation which includes

245

also a number of other variants elsewhere, each one of them constituting a particular expression of the process of transfiguration which is constitutive of a landscape.

# References

Balée, William 1989. The Culture of Amazonian Forests. In D. A. Posey and W. Balée (eds), *Resource Management in Amazonia: Indigenous and Folk Strategies*. Bronx, New York: The New York Botanical Garden.

Berlin, Brent 1977. *Bases empíricas de la cosmologia aguaruna jibaro, Amazonas, Peru*. Studies in Aguaruna Jivaro Ethnobiology, Report n°3. Berkeley: University of California.

Berque, Augustin 1995. *Les raisons du paysage: de la Chine antique aux environnements de synthèse*. Paris: Hazan.

Berque, Augustin 2008. *La pensée paysagère*. Collection Crossborders. Paris: Archibooks.

Cayón, Luis 2002. *En las aguas de Yuruparí: Cosmología y chamanismo Makuna*. Bogotá: Ediciones Uniandes.

Clark, Kenneth 1949. *Landscape into Art*. London: John Murray Publishers.

Denevan, William M. and Christine Padoch (eds) 1987. *Swiden-Fallow Agroforestry in the Peruvian Amazon*. Bronx, New York: New York Botanical Garden.

Descola, Philippe 1994. *In the Society of Nature: A native ecology in Amazonia*. Translated by Nora Scott. Cambridge Studies in Social and Cultural Anthropology. Cambridge: Cambridge University Press.

Frickel, Protásio 1978. Areas de arboricultura pré-agrícola na Amazônia: Notas preliminares. *Revista Antropológica* 31 (1): 45–52.

Geertz, Clifford 1963. *Agricultural Involution: The Process of Ecological Change in Indonesia*. Berkeley and Los Angeles: University of California Press.

Gombrich, Ernst 1953. Renaissance artistic theory and the development of landscape painting. *Gazette des Beaux-Arts* 41: 335–360.

Harner, Michael J. 1972. *The Jívaro: People of the Sacred Waterfalls*. Garden City (New York): Doubleday / Natural History Press.

Harris, David 1971. The ecology of swidden cultivation in the Upper Orinoco rainforest, Venezuela. *The Geographical Review* 61 (4): 475–495.

Hödl, Walter and Jürg Gasché 1981. Die Secoya Indianer und deren Landbaumethoden (Rio Yubineto, Peru). *Sitzungsberichte der Gesellschaft Naturforschender Freunde zu Berlin* 20-21: 73-96.

Karadimas, Dimitri 2005. *La raison du corps: Idéologie du corps et représentations de l'environnement chez les Miraña d'Amazonie colombienne*. Langues et sociétés d'Amérique traditionnelle. Louvain-Paris: Editions Peeters.

Minguet, Charles 1969. *Alexandre de Humboldt, historien et géographe de l'Amérique espagnole*. Paris: François Maspero.

Roger, Alain 1997. *Court traité du paysage*. Bibliothèque des sciences humaines. Paris: Gallimard.

Shankland, David (ed.) 2014. *Westermarck*. Canon Pyon: Kingston Publishing.

van der Hammen, Maria Clara 1992. *El manejo del mundo: Naturaleza y sociedad entre los Yukuna de la Amazonia colombiana*. Estudios en la Amazonia Colombiana. Bogotá: TROPENBOS.

Westermarck, Edward 1891. *The History of Human Marriage*. London: MacMillan.

Tuomas Tammisto
https://orcid.org/0000-0001-9767-7832

# Making temporal environments: Work, places and history in the Mengen landscape

## Introduction

For the Mengen living in the Wide Bay area of New Britain Island, Papua New Guinea, landscape is an important materialisation of personal and group histories. People see in the landscape traces of each other's productive activities, namely 'work' as the Mengen understand it. Work, as activity that creates and maintains valued social relations, is at the basis of Mengen conceptions of relatedness. Conversely, all activity that produces and maintains valued social relations, is classed as 'work' and hence work is a key source of value for the Mengen. Care and nurture, expressed especially in acts of giving and feeding, are important, if not the most important, forms of work (Tammisto 2018: 11, 54; see also Fajans 1997). Food and gardens are central media through which these relations are acted out, as well as key expressions of value (e.g. Turner 2008: 47, 53; Stasch 2009: 14, 19–20). The socially productive activities of people also leave visible traces on the environment. Thus, in the course of their social life, people make places (see also M. Scott 2007: 167, 213).

The near environment of the Wide Bay Mengen villages is a patchwork of gardens, fallows and secondary forest. What to an outsider looks like undifferentiated forest is, for those living there, an environment made by, and speaking of, human activities. These places constitute the Mengen landscape, which is "the world as it is known to those who dwell therein, who inhabit its places and journey along the paths connecting them", and "a pattern of activities 'collapsed' into an array of features", to borrow Tim Ingold's definition (2000: 193, 198). Abandoned villages are visible to the attentive onlooker in the shape of domestic trees planted by former inhabitants, although the sites had returned to primary forest. Even old and more distant forests are full of signs of past and present activity: paths, old burial sites, places where people have gathered house materials and so forth. These signs of work are 'memories' of people, bringing to mind the persons associated with them. The semiotic aspects of the landscape come together in the Mengen term for landscape, *glanpapa*, translated to me as "how things draw themselves out clearly when you look at them".[1] Here Philippe Descola's definition of landscape as "transfiguration", the deliberate re-shaping of a site so that it can also function as a sign (2016: 5), is helpful, because it focuses on placemaking and the semiotic qualities of the landscape – which the Mengen themselves emphasise.

All social relations are spatial, they happen in space and co-produce spaces, as Jason Moore notes (2015:11). Thus, places which constitute spaces and landscapes, are also inherently political. Places are, as Margaret Rodman puts it, "politicized, culturally relative, historically specific, local and multiple constructions" (1992: 641). This means that different forms of value production create different kinds of places and different forms of politics are enacted in different ways in and through the places they create.

In this paper I examine how the Mengen make their landscape, how time and place intersect in it and how places become one of the concrete media through which the Mengen relate to each other (see Munn 1992: 17; Stasch 2009: 19–20). I start by focusing on how the Mengen organise their horticulture in time by following the cycles of particular trees thus dividing the year into several seasons during which different gardening tasks are done. This is a concrete example of the temporality of the Mengen landscape. It shows how ecological temporalities, such as the growth of certain trees and food plants, intersect or converge with human temporal trajectories (see also Stasch 2003: 369, 381). Following that, I show how people not only coordinate their activities by observing a temporal landscape, but through their gardening activities they also create it. Places created in the course of people's lives are important historical markers and indices of people's relations with each other and the land.

As Mengen social relations, histories and values are intimately intertwined with the gardens, forests and land – in short the lived environment – I ask how Mengen forms of politics are enacted through and expressed in the landscape. I examine how engaging with land and placemaking can also be contested acts, and how places in the landscape become contested sites with respect to landholding. Furthermore, intensified natural resource extraction not only connects the Mengen in new ways to a global market economy, it reshapes questions of landholding, and very concretely speaking, it changes the political landscape of the Mengen.

## The Mengen tree calendar

The tropical climate of Wide Bay is most notably divided into two main seasons of about equal length, the dry and the rainy. The Mengen call the dry and rainy seasons *kae koureta* ('only sun [*kae*]') and *windfa* respectively. The seasons are most strongly associated with their extreme periods, namely November to January for the sunny season and June to August for the rainy

---

1 The term may very well be a neologism. Nonetheless, it illustrates well the visual aspects of the Mengen landscape. (Mengen [M]: *gel*: to see, to look; *pa*: to draw, to write.)

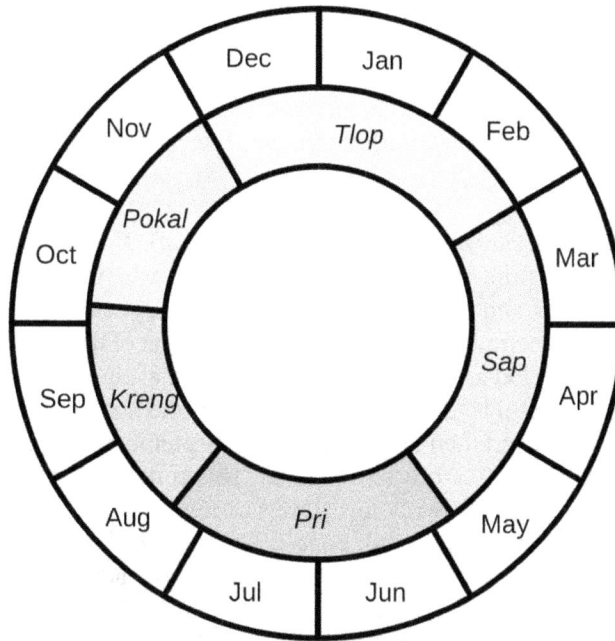

*Figure 1. The index tree phase.*

season. The intermediary times are characterised by more or less gradual shifts from one extreme to another. The seasons dominate activities in as much planting is not possible during the height of the rainy season, and the rough seas caused by the strong winds of the period make traveling by boat difficult – and dangerous. However, there is no major shift in activities of dwelling corresponding with the contrast of seasons (Panoff 1969: 154).

The two seasons provide the most general division of time, but the Mengen conception of seasons is much more sophisticated. Specific gardening activities are performed according to the so-called tree or village calendar (Tok Pisin [TP]: *kalender bilong ples*), in which the yearly cycle is represented according to the flowering and leaf phases of five index trees (see Figure 1). (The notion of "index tree" is Michel Panoff's (1969: 156), who documented this calendar in use in the 1960s among the Mengen of Jacquinot and Waterfall Bay.) By "index" I refer to a semiotic relation where the signifier and signified are physically connected or occur at the same time (Parmentier 1994: 4). In this case, the flowering of a specific tree occurs at the same time as a specific season and hence the former is an index of the latter. Similarly, in this paper I use the term 'icon' to refer to a sign that has a formal resemblance with the thing signified (Parmentier 1994: 4, 6).

During my fieldwork, the Wide Bay Mengen coordinated their gardening work according to this schedule, having systematised their calendar in the early 2000s so that it could be taught in elementary schools. This was part of a national education reform initiative in which elementary schools began teaching in local languages. In this version, the phases of the index trees were adjusted in terms of Western calendar months, which are more generally used for reckoning time. However, people follow the index tree phases in their day-to-day gardening work and speak about their work in terms of them – in Wide Bay Mengen this is known as *vekmein* (*vek*: tree, *mein*: phase, 'round'). For example, people often explained to me that a garden being cleared was to be planted with taro of the *sap*, one of the index trees, or that during another tree, *pri*, the yam harvest would begin, and so on.

- *Tlop* (*Euodia elleryana*; also *Melicope elleryana*): The phases of the *tlop* tree index the time roughly between December, when its distinctive red flowers appear, and February. The height of the dry season, occurring in January, is sometimes called *tlop maengngan* (heat of the *tlop*), while the end of this period around February is *tlop kan*, as the seed (*kan*) of the *tlop* is clearly visible. During the flowering of the *tlop* lesser and greater yam is planted and then harvested around September–October. Later in December–January taro is also planted. This constitutes a 'slow' season for the taro, which is ready for harvest around October and lasts until December. Yearly festivals (M: *pnaeis*, TP: *kastom*, also *lukara*) are held during the season of *tlop* as the main food taro is ready for harvest.
- *Sap* (*Alphitonia marcocarpa*): *Sap* is used as an index for the period lasting from March to April, with *sap lvun* (the leaf of *sap*) referring more specifically to April. The sap phase is still part of the dry season although characterised by light rains. During *sap* taro is planted, to be ready for harvesting around October–November. Taro planted during *sap* is often transplanted from yam gardens planted during December–January (*tlop*).
- *Pri* (*Erythrina indica*): the start of the *pri* phase was identified to me differently by people, either starting in May or June, but in most accounts *pri* is associated with June and July, which could also be referred to as *pri chu chumtan* (*pri* is leafless). The rainy season starts at this time. Both taro and yam can be planted at the beginning of *pri* although it is regarded as a 'minor' season for both. The taro-planting season of *pri* usually merges with *sap*. Yam planted during the *kreng* phase in September starts to ripen and is ready to harvest. During the height of the rainy season there is usually no planting.
- *Kreng* (*Pterocarpus indicus*): *Kreng mukmguang* means that the *kreng* starts to flower and 'leads' other trees, which flower later. This occurs by the turn of August–September, when rains are easing off. The season of *kreng* continues to October when the rainy season is over and the weather is 'good', that is, moving towards the dry season. *Kreng* is the main season for planting yam. Yam gardens are readied during August and September and seed yam is brought from the *kreng* gardens of the previous year. Yam planted during *kreng* ripens around June–July (see *pri*). The annual ceremonies are usually held in January when taro is harvested, but they can also be held in September–October when yam is harvested and distributed as the gift. Sometimes minor prestations are made with yam at this time, anticipating the actual ceremonies held in December–January, during which taro is given. In this case, the prestations are 'shadows' (M: *koun*, shadow, spirit, image, reflection) of the ceremonies proper to come.

- *Pokal* (*Albizzia falcataria*): The *pokal* tree flowers during November when the dry season is well under way. While identified as one of the index trees, many people with whom I spoke tended to leave *pokal* out of their accounts and merged the season with *kreng* and *tlop*. *Pokal* is a time for planting yam and taro and clearing gardens for the yam and taro seasons of *tlop*.

The division of the year into *vekmein* constitutes a sophisticated way of dividing the principal meteorological seasons into distinct phases for the planting and harvesting of the main food plants. My interlocutors did not know how the system had evolved, nor were there any accounts of its emergence, but it is clear that it is based on very careful observation of trees, their relation to the growth of food plants and the yearly cycle. It is just one example of the impressive knowledge the rural Mengen have of their environment. People noted that if the 'tree calendar' is observed carefully – and nothing unusual such as droughts occur – food would be abundant throughout the year. As soon as a garden is planted, clearing new ones for the next season or crop should get underway, as the clearing and fencing of gardens can take considerable time – usually at least a month.

Besides the tree calendar, people use plants more widely to conceptualise time. When I interviewed a man in his 70s on the history of a village, he used the growth of coconut palms to recall how, for many years, the villagers hid in the forest during World War II:

> The war started and we fled into the forest. I think we must have been something like three years in the forest, because when we came back, the coconut palms were ready to carry fruit.

While trees and plants are a way of counting the flow of time and conceptualising seasons, they also serve as metaphors for history for the Mengen (Panoff 1969: 164). Like the growth of a tree, history was seen by the Jacquinot Bay Mengen as progressive, and events, such as branching, as irreversible (Panoff 1969: 164). This conception also applies to the histories of clans which were called vines and vine-branches in the vernacular. This kind of "botanic metaphor [...] that combine[s] notions of growth and succession", as James Fox (1996a: 8) observes, is common among the Austronesian peoples to which the Mengen also belong. The index cycles of the index trees, visible to the skilled observer in the landscape, were used by the Mengen to conceptualise time and organise gardening.

## Gardening and place making

Besides this yearly cycle as indexed by trees and connected to the practices and work of the Mengen, there are other temporal features worth considering in the Mengen landscape. Gardening and dwelling practices, such the establishment of settlements and burial sites or the gathering of building materials and food stuff from the forest, as active engagements with the environment, create places that are visible in the Mengen landscape. People leave their gardens to fallow after one harvest, and the environment near the Wide Bay Mengen villages is thus a patchwork of differently aged fallow-forests. Along with gardens and fallows, there are also abandoned villages, burial sites and other signs of people's productive activities that have created a multi-layered landscape. The Mengen term for landscape *glanpapa*, which a Mengen man translated to me as how things draw themselves out as one looks at them, focuses on the abundance of different signs that constitute the landscape.

Here it is helpful to draw on Philippe Descola's proposal (2016: 5, 11–12) for a stricter definition of landscape, understood as transfiguration, namely the deliberate changing of the appearance of a site. In order to be a 'landscape', transfiguration should satisfy three conditions: the result of the activity must be deliberately sought after, the activity should not be exclusively utilitarian, and at the end of the activity, people should recognise the change in appearance of the site (Descola 2016: 5). Moreover, a landscape formed by transfiguration, whether by modification of the site itself or through its pictorial representation, can function as a sign standing for something else (Descola 2016: 5). The signs of productive activity that make up the Mengen landscape, stand for a variety of social relations. This is especially pronounced in Mengen gardens and in the succession between gardens and fallows.

There are several temporal trajectories in Mengen gardens. The food plants require weeding and pruning at different times and stages of growth. The time-span of a given garden is largely determined by the main food plant and how it matures for harvesting. After harvest, people leave gardens to fallow, and by doing so create an ever-changing landscape of gardens and fallows in different stages of maturation. For example, when a yam garden matures, the taro planted in it are uprooted and transplanted into newly cleared gardens. Like the *vekmein*, which seamlessly merge into each other, there is no absolute distinction between a mature and an abandoned garden, instead, letting the garden become fallow is a gradual process. This effect is made even more pronounced by the way the Mengen never plant a garden with only one crop, and different foods mature at different times and are thus harvested at different periods. Final harvesting takes place as fences start to deteriorate and species associated with bush fallow begin to take over a garden.

The importance of horticulture is evident in the forest terminology of the Wide Bay Mengen. The general term for forest, *gurlon*, covers both primary and secondary forest of different kinds. *Gurlon* however, is divided into four terms referring to forests of distinct types and ages:

1. *papli*: this encompasses mature gardens, gardens left fallow and secondary forest that begins to grow in abandoned gardens. *Papli* is recognised as a former gardening area. No new gardens can be cleared at this stage.

2. *mlap*: secondary forest growing in abandoned gardens. *Mlap* is distinguished from *papli* by the size and type of trees. Certain tree species

start to grow in size and thus overwhelm species typical to immediate secondary growth or *papli*. In contrast to *papli*, *mlap* starts to resemble 'real forest' and trees grow into substantial specimens. *Mlap is* still recognised as former garden where traces of human work, such as tree stumps and axe marks, are visible. *Papli* becomes *mlap* in about seven to twenty years, depending on various factors that influence the growth of trees. At this stage new gardens can be cleared. There is no rule about how many years are needed before *mlap* can be cleared for gardens, it depends on the size of the trees, which in turn varies from area to area. To my knowledge, fallows younger than five years should not be cleared.

3. *lom*: primary forest. *Lom is* not regarded as former garden, but some of my interlocutors noted that if left unused for a "very long time", *mlap* will turn into *lom*. The *lom is* distinguished from *papli* and *mlap* through the type and size of the trees: these are of different species and considerably bigger than in a secondary forest. Traces of work, such as gathered plants, but also trails (*gue*), abandoned villages (*knau*) distinguished by domestic plants or earth oven stones, and burial sites (*o*), are visible in the forest.

4. *lom son*: the definitions for this category are somewhat vague, but it refers to forest growing on mountain ranges, where vegetation is poorer due to less fertile land and not much fauna. In some definitions *lom son is* distinguished from other types of forest as characterised by a lack of (visible?) human action. One person noted that if people were to start using this kind of forest, it would change into *lom*. Another considered the main distinction to be the different flora. The distance from the everyday environment of people is also a factor. Some people noted that *lom son* are the "blue ranges" visible far away (as opposed to the more proximate forest characterized by different shades of green).[2] The counterpart of *lom son* – in the opposite direction, namely toward the sea – is *mail son*, the far away ocean – characterised similarly by another shade of blue.

As is evident in this forest terminology, the Mengen emphasise 'work' and its visibility in the environment. The two terms for secondary forest refer to gardening areas and are directly linked to horticulture, as these types of environments would not exist without human action. The terms *ngur* (garden), *papli* and *mlap* are partly overlapping and on a continuum. A garden where harvesting has started may be called *papli*, while a secondary forest ready to be cleared again (*mlap*) can be also referred to as somebody's *papli*. People thus emphasise that fallows are always *somebody's* fallows. In contrast, secondary forest that had been logged, but not cultivated, is not *papli* or *mlap*, but called *tlanglis* (M: *tlang*: to fell, *lis*: to decompose), forest cleared for no apparent reason (TP: *katim bus nating*). While *lom* is not an anthropogenic forest type, it incorporates a wide range of visible human action. However, in terms of horticulture *lom* is 'empty' and whoever clears a garden in it retained further rights to cultivate the area.

Botanists' classification and description of the forests near Toimtop village overlap with Mengen classification. Pius Piskaut and Phille Daur

---

2   Note that in Mengen 'green' and 'blue' are referred to with the same word.

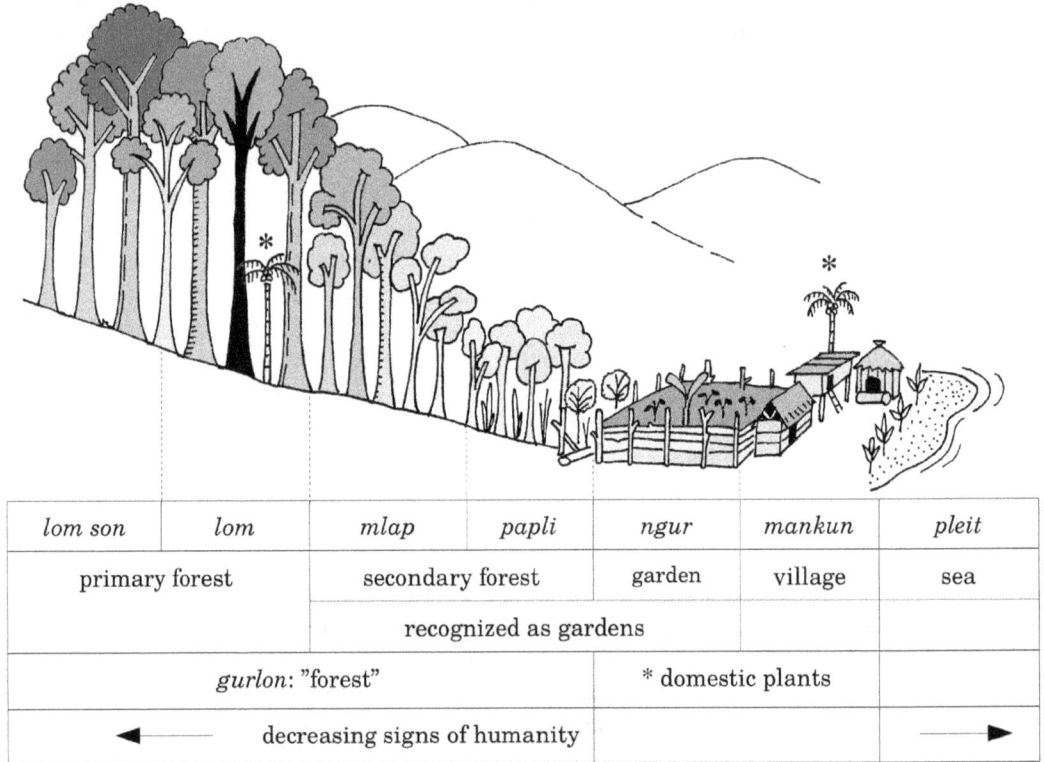

| lom son | lom | mlap | papli | ngur | mankun | pleit |
|---------|-----|------|-------|------|--------|-------|
| primary forest | | secondary forest | | garden | village | sea |
| | | recognized as gardens | | | | |
| gurlon: "forest" | | | | * domestic plants | | |
| ◄———— decreasing signs of humanity | | | | | ————► | |

Figure 2. Schematic representation of Mengen forest terminology.

(2007: 21) distinguish between early secondary forest with tree heights of up to 10 m, and advanced secondary forest with the canopy layer at 20–25 m and trees occasionally as high as 30 m. In primary forest the canopy layer is generally at 20–30 m with trees occasionally as high as 40 m (Piskaut and Daur 2007: 20). Botanists divide the primary forest into three types: upper and lower lowland hill forests (at elevations of up to 220 m asl) and *Dillenia* (230–400 m asl) and Mixed *Castanopsis* forests (400 m asl and upwards) that grow on ridge tops with shallow and nutrient-poor brown forest soils (Piskaut and Daur 2007: 20).

Taking the village as a starting point, the fallow succession and the different types of forests can be schematically represented in relation to time and the gradual diminishing of signs of human presence (see Figure 2). The village and the surrounding gardens are the most evidently human areas. As the gardens start to become fallow, signs of human activity decrease. In the primary forest (to which the fallows return if left uncleared), signs of human presence decrease: the forest itself is not anthropogenic in the same way as secondary forest, but domestic trees, oven stones from abandoned village sites and so on provide evidence of past usage. Finally, the far-away forest, the *lom son*, is characterized by the absence of human signs. In this sense the gradient of human presence is also temporal. The *papli* is young bush which, over time, grows into more robust secondary forest and finally

254

back into *lom*, primary forest, a temporal gradient that is connected to signs of human presence and the social relationships they index (Thomas Strong 2008; personal communication).

The villages and gardens index contemporary and present social relations, whereas older fallows and abandoned villages highlight past relations. These semiotic aspects of the different types of forest are also iconic, in as much the diversity in age of forests is iconic of the diversity of social relations of different ages. Similarly, Mengen gardens are indices of their users and important food plants are indices of the women who tend them, while the diversity of plants in a single garden is an icon of the diversity of social relations through which the women have acquired the different plants (for more details, see Tammisto 2018: 41–43). Thus the Mengen landscape, and its elements, can function not only as iconic signs, as Descola (2016: 5) notes, but also as indices. The signs of people's socially productive activities, or work, in the landscape materialise personal histories (also Maschio 1994: 180; Kirsch 2006: 189). These places evoke memories of the people who, through their activities, created them, and are thus not just about recollecting past activities; remembering other people often has a strong emotional component. As a Mengen woman in her 50s told me:

> A grandfather of mine, once we were clearing a garden on an abandoned village, he sat down and cried. It's bush now! But people still know this area. [...] And he said he recalled his mothers and uncles from the past, because when I felled that tree, a *rin*[3], it smelled. [...] He asked me: "Do you smell that? They planted it in front of the men's house." And he said to me, "you go and plant that garden". And once I had done it, I [...] gave him a piece of shell money, a pig and a heap of food. And another one I gave to an old grandmother of mine. I compensated the two like that. I made the two cry, made them worry and think back, because in the past they lived there, then the government came and we came down [to the coast] and now we go back to work our gardens there.

The quote brings up several important issues. First, while the visual aspects of places are central in the epistemology of the Mengen, other senses are also important. While Descola's (2016) definition of landscape focusing on placemaking and signification is helpful, landscape is not only experienced through sight. Here the smell of the tree functions as a sign as well. In this story, the smell of the *rin*, a domestic plant and an index of people's activities, triggers a memory of the abandoned village, the men's house and the people who lived there. A young man told me how he had gone to look for an abandoned village that his grandmother had told him about. Knowing its approximate location, he finally found the village because of the scent of the domestic plants. This points to another important way in which the places in themselves are not the whole story, so to speak; their full social significance unfolds only when people know the area and its history. This knowledge is passed on both by visiting the places and through narration – in these

---

3   The *rin* (*Euodia anisodora*) is a fragrant plant often planted in villages, because it has ritualistic uses and because of its aesthetic and decorative properties. In time the shrub grows into a tree.

two cases by the elders telling younger relatives about abandoned hamlets, where they were located and who lived there. This intertwining of places and history is common for Austronesian societies (see Fox 1997b): for the Rauto of New Britain, the recitation of place names and the stories connected to them are a social history (Maschio 1994: 182), and this is also the case for the Mengen.

Thomas Maschio (1994: 181) notes that among the Rauto the trees people plant could be called memorials, as indeed is the case among the Mengen. Signs of people's productive activities, such as trees, are called *rnagil* (M: *gil*, to know) and were points of active remembering – to paraphrase Debbora Battaglia (1990: 10). When I was preparing to leave Wide Bay, a friend of mine suggested that I plant a fruit tree, people could remember me by it. In the extract above, the woman says that she "compensated" her elders for making them cry and "worry". (The Tok Pisin idiom *wari* means here sorrowful, nostalgic longing [see also Maschio 1994]). "Compensation" does not imply that the woman had done wrong. On the contrary, her grandfather had approved her family's clearing the garden on the site of the abandoned village (which was, moreover, located on land that claimed by their clan). Rather, it was an acknowledgment of their sorrow and the work of past people.

Finally, the quote shows how in pursuit of control and "legibility" (J. Scott 1998), the colonial government encouraged and ordered people to leave their dispersed inland hamlets and move to the coast and main trail routes. As a Mengen man told me:

> The government wanted people only along the roads [main trails]. They didn't like to go around the bush looking for people. [...] People had to be along the roads at the time they were to be given work or checked that they live in an orderly fashion. [The patrol officer] would only walk along a road. Climbing mountains and such was too much hard work.

This process took place gradually, and people continued to move between their inland settlements and coastal villages, coming down to the coast for church and the government-appointed communal work day on Monday before returning inland. In some cases, people who had already permanently settled to the coast, returned to their inland hamlets to perform their children's initiations on their own clan land. I was told that the last inland villages were abandoned in the 1970s. The history of colonialism and state formation is also inscribed in the landscape as roads established by the colonial government, abandoned settlements in the forest as well as copra plantations that the mission and colonial governments established in Wide Bay and New Britain (Tammisto 2018: 129–134). As Maxine Dennis notes (1981: 219), plantations in New Guinea were not only economic projects, but also ways of occupation and pacification that supplemented the work of the colonial government. Like concentrating people into villages, they were a spatialised form of governance.

The Wide Bay Mengen were not dispossessed of their lands – they still communally own them under Papua New Guinea law (Lakau 1997) – nor did colonial policies break people's links with the land and landscape. People remember past settlements that materialise histories of land use and relations to the land, discussed more in depth below. Similarly, at the time of my fieldwork, some people in the southern Wide Bay Mengen areas had resettled old inland villages as new roads had been established in the course of logging operations starting in the 1990s (see Tammisto 2018: 84–89). Along with re-establishing links to the land, this resettlement was most probably also a way of enforcing claims to land in disputes over ownership that had arisen in consequence of the logging. As these examples show, people's relationship with the socially meaningful landscape and its scattered places of significance, is not static. On the contrary, it is one of active engagement. In the above example, an abandoned village was cleared for a garden and the appearance of the place was transformed. Still later, after the harvest, the garden was left to fallow and turn into forest again. With the ceremonial gift prestation, those who had cleared the garden publicly acknowledged relatives' emotional and historical ties to the place. This also meant upholding the memory of the site as a past village.

The productive activities of people root them in the land and leave a testimony of their lives in the landscape. This is an inevitable result of Mengen social life, but like all social life, it has also its tensions. Rootedness is not only about emotional and historical connection for the Mengen, it is also about claims of various kinds. Because of this, people occasionally hope that others would make their presence visible on the land they themselves coveted. As Simon Harrison (2004: 147) has noted for the Avatip of the Sepik area, sometimes the landscape remembers too much. In a society where knowledge of the past is a value whose circulation should be controlled and carefully restricted, people do not want the landscape to remember more than they do (Harrison 2004: 147). Because of this, people sometimes also deliberately seek to erase the traces of others. In the following section, I turn more closely to these questions of placed histories and land-holding as well as their relation to Mengen politics.

## Placed histories and relating to the land

Along with the histories of individual persons, inscribed in the Mengen landscape are important categories such as the autochthonous clan and the land-using group. Landownership among the Wide Bay Mengen is vested in exogamic matrilineal clans, which are associated with their places of origin (also Panoff 1970: 177). This cosmological link between the people and the land, however, does not translate into a clear-cut local community. Both members of the land-owning clan and those who actually inhabit the land become emplaced by the work performed in villages and gardens. Few people live on their own clan land, and thus land-use is conceptualised as a reciprocal relation between clans, much like intermarriages or ceremonial gifts. This is a common dynamic in the Austronesian matrilineal societies of Melanesia (e.g. Panoff 1970: 177, 194; M. Scott 2007: 223; Eves 2011: 353; Martin 2013: 31, 37). The autonomy of the landowning clan and socially productive relations between clans are also two central values. Pursuing these produces both a productive contradiction in Mengen society that accounts for the dynamism of Mengen landowning practices and Mengen political life generally. The two categories, land-owners and users, have their spatial equivalents, namely origin-places and abandoned villages.

According to Mengen clan histories, the apical ancestress of each clan autonomously emerged in a specific area, often from a plant or a topographical feature. The clan names refer either to the environmental element from which the ancestress was said to have emerged or the circumstances of her emergence. The landscape is scattered with such origin places (M: *plangpun*, *plang*: to emerge, *pun*: root). The clans claim land areas both on the basis of this mythical precedence and first settlement into a vacant territory, as is common in Austronesian societies (Fox 1996b: 9; M. Scott 2007: 7). Among the Arosi of the Solomon Islands, who have very similar notions of lineage emergence and relations, the pre-social emergence of the ancestress forms the basis of landownership. Yet, because of clan exogamy, no lineage can live alone on its land. Therefore, real social existence is only achieved when lineages intermarry and dwell together on the land (M. Scott 2007: 223; also Eves 2011: 359). This is also the case in Mengen clan histories: the apical ancestress meets a man from a different clan (both are often named), they start having children and start to inhabit the land. So in order for real social life to be achieved, the clan has to 'bring' others to their land (M. Scott 2007: 223). For the Arosi there are two ways of relating to the land, what he terms utopic and topogonic (M. Scott 2007: 201–202).

The "non-placed" or utopic refers to the separate emergence of the various lineage ancestress in areas which are devoid of others and "non-placed". The topogonic relation is based on place making and dwelling (M. Scott 2007: 201–202); one Mengen elder referred to uninhabited land before the emergence of the ancestress as "land nothing" (TP: *graun nating*). Through place making activities, both the original lineage and people from other lineages are rooted in the land (M. Scott 2007: 225). The Mengen have distinct spatial categories for the two ways of connecting people to the land. The place of origin only refers to the clan that had emerged from it, whereas villages, gardens and abandoned settlements create links between the land and all its long-standing inhabitants and their progeny. As a Mengen man noted, "[o]nce you have cleared gardens, made kastom and buried your dead, your blood is in the land". These two spatial categories are an important part of Mengen conceptions of history (Panoff 1969: 163).

Each clan has its own history which recounts its emergence, movement and intermarriages. Those I was told followed a similar pattern: they begin by describing how the apical ancestress emerges from the *plangpun* in an area devoid of other people. She resides alone on the land until she meets a man from a clan of the opposing moiety who has ventured into the area while hunting or because he had seen smoke from the woman's fire and was inquisitive. The two inquire about each other's marriage status in a roundabout way and, realising that both are single, they pair up. After this, the clan histories list the children of the apical ancestress and whom they marry, in other words they become genealogies listing the members of the matriline. The histories also recount where the apical pair and later generations moved, the villages they founded, the locations of their gardens and so on. (See Michael Scott [2007: 74, 190] on very similar lineage histories of the Arosi of Solomon Islands.) In other words, the clan histories are also listings of places, or topogenies, which are a common Austronesian "means for the ordering and transmission of social knowledge" (Fox 1997a: 8). When attached to specific locations in an inhabited landscape, topogenies are "a projected externalization of memories that can be lived in as well as thought about" (Fox 1997a: 8). In the Mengen case, the topogenies are closely intertwined with genealogies (see also Fox 1997a: 13).

The relationship between the autonomy of the landowning clan and the socially productive inter-relations between the clans is a 'productive contradiction', because as values they are in constant tension. On the other hand, they also presuppose each other. In order for the exogamous clan to reproduce, its members have to marry people from other clans and share its land with them. So in order to pursue one value, one must pursue the other, but emphasising one too much can have "negative value" potentials (Munn 1992: 12) in respect to the other. For example, as Michael Scott notes (2007: 245–46) in the case of the Arosi, if the landowning lineage emphasizes too much its ownership of the land, it risks making other lineage members feel unwelcome. By 'productive contradiction', I do not mean that the relation is one of conflict, but rather a central dynamic within the Mengen society that accounts for much of the dynamism in communal life. Like with other similar value antinomies in Melanesia (for example Robbins 2006: 192–93, 195–96), socially successful action has to strike a balance between the two opposing and complementary values. Among the Mengen this is especially pronounced in matters relating to land use.

Questions of land use and ownership rose to the fore with large-scale logging which began in Wide Bay in the early 1990s like in many other rural areas of Papua New Guinea (Tammisto 2018: 84–89; also Bell 2015). Malaysian logging companies saw PNG as a frontier of unused resources, while both the government of PNG and many rural communities hoped that logging would bring in income, infrastructure and services (Filer 1998; Tammisto 2018: 87). As under PNG law local communities own their lands, they had to be consulted before the logging operations could start (see for example Lattas 2011 on wrong-doings by loggers). So too among the Wide Bay Mengen. When logging was first proposed to the Mengen, many communities started discussing if and how it should be allowed. As noted, landownership is vested in the matrilineal clans, which owned distinct areas, but user rights to land are more widely spread and hence actual Mengen communities are always multi-clan polities, to borrow Scott's expression (2007: 33, 247). The logging proposal sometimes created disputes over who should decide on logging and how benefits should be shared among landowners and land users for instance.

Likewise, not all of the Mengen supported logging, but some feared that large-scale logging would hamper swidden horticulture and destroy important parts of the landscape, while others saw logging and the use of forests as a means of establishing productive relations with outsiders.

259

Likewise, even among those who agreed on allowing logging, the distribution of compensations and decision-making power created tensions. People debated whether compensations should be held by the clan on whose land actual logging took place or whether the money should be distributed between all community members. This reflects the 'productive contradiction' between the values of clan autonomy and inter-clan relations. For example, some members of the clan on whose land logging took place, decided to distribute the logging royalties among all the clans involved in the landowner company, but wanted auxiliary payments from the loggers for clan members only. The idea was to emphasise their status as landowners.

Meanwhile men who were active in logging, initially sought to present the operations as community projects involving all clans in the given communities. Interestingly, the landowner companies that represented the local population and acted as contractual partners with foreign loggers, were named after abandoned villages. In doing this, the men sought to emphasise the communal aspects of logging, as abandoned villages in the landscape are signs of inter-clan relations and of long-standing histories of shared land-use by the different clans. In disputes over the ownership of land, clan histories and particularly topogeny, or recitations of places, is used also as evidence of landownership. Basing their claims on place of origin and on villages founded by their ancestors, the disputing clans seek to point out their long-standing relations with the land. Thus the above mentioned re-settlement of abandoned settlements was a way to reinforce claims to the land. These are examples of how the Mengen use the semiotic aspects of the landscape as signs of claims to the land. The forest and the places in it became with logging a new object of contest over who owns it, who decides its use and what is done with it, as well as a media through which these contests were acted out.

## Conclusions

Time, history and social relations are thoroughly emplaced in the gardens and forests of Wide Bay. The places, both mythical and those made through human action constitute the Wide Bay Mengen landscape, in which human and ecological temporalities intertwine and converge. To refer back to Jason Moore (2015: 11), all social relation are spatial inasmuch they develop in through space and actively co-produce it in the process. Moreover, this means that 'humans' and 'the environment' or 'society' and 'nature', are not distinct entities, but form what Moore calls a double-internality (2015: 13, 25, 36), a dialectical relation in which human activity unfolds in and through nature and vice versa. However, different forms of activity and different forms of value production make different environments (Rodman 1992: 641; Moore 2015: 44–45).

In the Mengen case, forests and the land are not only, or even foremost, conceptualised as resources. Rather, the landscape is thoroughly social and it tells of past and present activity. It is both a product of human activity, as forests around the villages are anthropogenic fallows regarded as gardens, and the mythical origin of Mengen clans. As a testimony of human activity, the landscape is also thoroughly political: the origin places, abandoned villages and gardens speak of histories and legitimate land use and ownership in the present. A garden is not only a trace of important livelihood practices, it tells the Mengen about relationships between a landowning clan and its affines, as well as about relations between them. And like all pursuits of value have their tensions, so it is with the Mengen. What I have argued is that these are enacted through the landscape. The clearing of gardens or planting of trees is not only about making a living, in certain contexts, both can be highly political acts establishing links to land and making claims to it.

Composed of signs of human activity, the Mengen landscape is semiotically dense. To escape both a narrow definition of landscape as a pictorial representation, and a broad conception of it as an experienced environment (e.g. Ingold 2000: 198), Descola defines landscape as the deliberate change of appearance, or transfiguration, of a site (2016: 4–5). The proposal for a cross-culturally sensitive, but analytically precise definition (Descola 2016: 3) is useful here, because it focuses on placemaking and its possible semiotic functions. The Mengen are particularly sensitive to placemaking and emphasise the semiotic aspect of the landscape in their own definition of landscape as how things draw themselves out to the onlooker. The places that form the Mengen landscape are often results of transfiguration and typically results of dwelling practices. As I noted above, while the Mengen emphasise visual aspects, places are experienced more holistically. Other sensory experiences, such as the smell of a domestic tree, can and do function as indexical signs of people and social relations. Adding to Descola's definition, I note that transfiguration can be experienced with many senses. This means we should be sensitive to how people experience their lived environment.

The Mengen landscape is and has been formed through the relations between the Mengen and various actors, such as colonial governments, missions and foreign companies. Logging roads, copra and cocoa plantings and such are signs of these, often highly unequal, relationships (e.g. Bell 2015). Large-scale oil palm projects currently underway over the east coast of New Britain loom also at the fringes of the Mengen landscape. These projects promise income, employment and services (Tammisto 2018). However, they threaten radical changes in the landscape and the livelihood practices that form it. Despite these, the Wide Bay Mengen have managed to retain control over their lands and the landscape, to keep them infused with their history and to ensure Mengen pursuits of value remain meaningful.

## Acknowledgement

I wish to thank Eeva Berglund, Timo Kallinen and Anu Lounela as well as the two anonymous reviewers for their insightful comments. This article is based on a total of 18 moths of fieldwork I conducted in Wide Bay in 2007, 2011–12 and 2014, funded by a one year grant from the University of Helsinki and the Academy of Finland (grant 253680). I also want to thank

Henni Alava, Timo Kaartinen, Jenni Mölkänen, Sonal Makhija, Liina-Maija Quist and Heikki Wilenius, who have commented on various parts of this paper. Finally, my research would not have been possible had not the Wide Bay Mengen allowed me to live with them and opened up their lives for me. It is thus to them that I owe my deepest gratitude.

# References

Battaglia, Debbora 1990. *On the Bones of the Serpent: Person, Memory, and Mortality in Sabarl Island Society*. Chicago: University of Chicago Press.

Bell, Joshua 2015. The Structural Violence of Resource Extraction in the Purari Delta. In Joshua Bell, Paige West and Colin Filer (eds), *Tropical Forests Of Oceania: Anthropological Perspectives*. Canberra: ANU Press.

Dennis, Maxine 1981. Plantations. In Donald Denoon and Catherine Snowden (eds), *A Time to Plant and a Time to Uproot: A History of Agriculture in Papua New Guinea*. [Papua New Guinea]: Institute of Papua New Guinea Studies.

Descola, Philippe 2016. Landscape as Transfiguration: Edward Westermarck Memorial Lecture, October 2015. *Suomen Antropologi: Journal of the Finnish Anthropological Society* 41 (1): 3–14.

Eves, Richard 2011. Puzzling Over Matrilineal Land Tenure and Development in New Ireland, Papua New Guinea. *Pacific Studies* 34 (2): 350–373.

Fajans, Jane 1997. *They Make Themselves: Work and Play Among the Baining of Papua New Guinea*. Chicago: Chicago University Press.

Filer, Colin with Nikhil Sekhran 1998. *Loggers, Donors and Resource Owners*. London: IIED.

Foster, Robert 1995. *Social Reproduction and History in Melanesia: Mortuary Ritual, Gift Exchange, and Custom in the Tanga Islands*. Cambridge: Cambridge University Press.

Fox, James 1996a. Introduction. In James Fox and Clifford Sather (eds), *Origins, Ancestry and Alliance: Explorations in Austronesian Ethnography*. Canberra: Australian National University.

Fox, James 1996b. The Transformation of Progenitor Lines or Origin: Patterns of Precedence in Eastern Indonesia. In James Fox and Clifford Sather (eds), *Origins, Ancestry and Alliance: Explorations in Austronesian Ethnography*. Canberra: Australian National University.

Fox, James 1997a. Place and landscape in comparative Austronesian perspective. In James Fox (ed.), *The Poetic Power of Place: Comparative Perspectives on Austronesian Ideas of Locality*. Canberra: Australian National University.

Fox, James (ed.) 1997b. *The Poetic Power of Place Comparative Perspectives on Austronesian Ideas of Locality*. Canberra: ANU Press.

Graeber, David 2001. *Toward An Anthropological Theory of Value: The False Coin of Our Own Dreams*. New York: Palgrave Macmillan.

Harrison, Simon 2004. Forgetful and memorious landscapes. *Social Anthropology* 12 (2): 135–151.

Ingold, Tim 2000. *Perception of the Environment: Essays in Livelihood, Dwelling and Skill*. London: Routledge.

Kirsch, Stuart 2006. *Reverse Anthropology: Indigenous Analysis of Social and Environmental Relations in New Guinea*. Stanford: Stanford University Press.

Laufer, Carl 1955. Aus Geschichte und Religion der Sulka. *Anthropos* 50 (1–3): 32–64.

Martin, Keir 2013. *The Death of the Big Men and the Rise of the Big Shots: Custom and Conflict in East New Britain*. New York: Berghahn Books.

Maschio, Thomas 1994. *To Remember The Faces Of The Dead: The Plentitude Of Memory In Southwestern New Britain*. Madison: University of Wisconsin Press.

Moore, Jason 2015 *Capitalism in the Web of Life: Ecology and the Accumulation of Capital*. New York: Verso.

Munn, Nancy 1992. *The Fame of Gawa: A Symbolic Study of Value Transformation in a Massim Society*. New edition edition. Durham: Duke University Press Books.

Panoff, Michel 1969. The Notion of Time Among the Maenge People of New Britain. *Ethnology* 8 (2): 154–166.

Panoff, Michel 1970. Land Tenure among the Maenge of New Britain. *Oceania* 40 (3): 177–194.

Parmentier, Richard 1994. Signs in Society: Studies in Semiotic Anthropology. Bloomington: Indiana University Press.

Piskaut, Pius and Phille Daur 2007. Plants and Ethnobotany. In Andrew Mack, Maureen Ewai and Janine Watson (eds), *A Biological Survery of a Lowland Rainforest Site in East New Britain Province, Papua New Guinea*. Unpublished document.

Rascher, P. Matthäus 1904. Die Sulka: Ein Beitrag zur Ethnographie von NeuPommern. *Archiv für Anthropologie* 29: 209–235.

Robbins, Joel 2004. *Becoming Sinners: Christianity and Moral Torment in a Papua New Guinea Society*. Berkeley: University of California Press.

Rodman, Margaret 1992. Empowering Place: Multilocality and Multivocality. *American Anthropologist* 94 (3): 640–656.

Scott, James 1998. *Seeing Like a State: How Certain Schemes to Improve the Human Condition Have Failed*. New Haven: Yale University Press.

Scott, Michael 2007. *The Severed Snake: Matrilineages, Making Place, and a Melanesian Christianity in Southeast Solomon Islands*. Durham: Carolina Academic Press.

Slotta, James 2014. Revelations of the World: Transnationalism and the Politics of Perception in Papua New Guinea. *American Anthropologist* 116 (3): 626–642.

Stasch, Rupert 2003. The semiotics of world-making in Korowai feast longhouses. *Language & Communication* 23 (3–4): 359–383.

Stasch, Rupert 2009. *Society of Others: Kinship and Mourning in a West Papuan Place*. Berkeley: University of California Press.

Tammisto, Tuomas 2018. *New Actors, Old Landscapes: The Making of a Frontier Place in Papua New Guinea*. PhD thesis. Helsinki: Unigrafia.

Turner, Terence 2008. Marxian Value Theory: An Anthropological Perspective. *Anthropological Theory* 8 (1): 43–56.

Jason M. Brown

# Worlds and worldviews: Resource management, re-enchantment and landscape

"This world is but a canvas to our imagination."
– Henry David Thoreau (1867)

"Human beings do not, in their movements, inscribe their life histories upon the surface of nature as do writers upon the page; rather, these histories are woven, along with the life-cycles of plants and animals, into the texture of the surface itself."
– Tim Ingold (2000)

## Introduction

At a recent anthropology conference in Vancouver, British Columbia, I saw Squamish archaeologist Rudy Reimer give a talk on the relationship between local obsidian deposits and the place names and history of the Squamish Nation.[1] After giving the geological history of the region, he told the story of how Thunderbird, a supernatural being in the Squamish world, could shoot lightning out of its eyes. Obsidian, a precious resource to pre-European contact Squamish peoples, was created where the lightning from Thunderbird's eyes hit the ground. Professor Reimer presented his talk and summarised the correlation between obsidian sources, Squamish place names and history. At the end of the talk, a young man raised his hand and asked, "You don't believe that obsidian was caused by a Thunderbird though, that is just a metaphor, right?" The archaeologist didn't miss a beat and responded, "It is not a metaphor. I understand what science says about where obsidian comes from geologically. But the Thunderbird is real, its existence is just very difficult to prove empirically. I am OK dwelling in two worlds."

It was this question of two worlds that intrigued me. I was familiar with the places Professor Reimer referred to in his talk: Black Tusk and The Lions, two prominent peaks in the Metro Vancouver Area, were renamed by Europeans. They were originally called Ch'ich'iyúy Elxwíkn (The Twin Sisters) and T'ak̲t'ak̲ mu'yin tl'a in7in'a'xe7en (the landing place of the Thunderbird) and form an integral part of the Squamish landscape. The young man who

---

1 The Squamish Nation is a First Nations Community whose traditional and unceded territory is located in what is today called Vancouver, British Columbia.

raised his hand did what most North Americans of European descent do when presented with two narratives explaining a given phenomenon: 1) we seek to decipher which is 'true', and 2) we interpret them based on our own ontological categories. For the young man who raised his hand, one story was true and one was false, and clearly the one referring to chemical reactions, geological epochs and tectonic upheavals was true because it appealed to Western scientific knowledge about nature, the material basis of the world that can be measured, quantified and explained using instrumentation and reason (Tarnas 1993). The other narrative, about Thunderbird, was clearly a metaphorical etiology that explained *why* there was obsidian where there was. It belonged to the black box of subjective opinion, where any value, idea, story or myth could be projected onto the *real* world (Ingold 2000: 191).

This lost-in-translation kind of moment, though familiar from the life experiences of many indigenous peoples, is common enough in institutional settings as well. Corporations, governments and natural resource managers continue to start conversations with indigenous peoples based on the assumption that they have something called a 'worldview' rather than dwell in something like a 'world.' By this I mean that they take for granted a bifurcated world of facts and values, culture and nature. Consequently, Western resource managers and extractive industries tend to assume from the beginning that Western science is the only legitimate interpreter of the domain of 'nature' and that any 'cultural values' that indigenous peoples bring to these conversations will be listened to, praised and considered, but never fully believed (Povinelli 1995; Descola 1996; Nadasdy 2007). Issues of difference are to be interpreted epistemologically, not ontologically.

This 'multi-cultural' or 'multi-stakeholder' approach ensures that resource management regimes or extractive industries remain bifurcated between natural and cultural understandings with indigenous worlds relegated to a layer superimposed on top of the natural landscape, rather than being woven through it (Ingold 2000). Mining, pipeline, logging, development and hydroelectric projects in British Columbia for example, must all go through a rigorous environmental assessment process that, legally at least, requires developers to consult with indigenous peoples on whose traditional territories developments are being proposed. Yet, time and time again, in countless places across the globe, indigenous objections to development projects are ignored, passed over or violently suppressed. The most recent example in British Columbia is the proposed Site C Hydro Electric dam that would flood 9,300 hectares of traditional indigenous territory. In addition, Justin Trudeau's Liberal Party government approved the expansion of the Kinder Morgan Trans-Mountain Pipeline which runs through the Burrard Inlet. This is the traditional and unceded territory of the Tsleil Waututh People, and expanding the pipeline would increase oil tanker traffic in the Burrard inlet from 5 tankers per month to 35.[2]

---

2   The Tsleil Waututh have been vocal opponents of the project and recently published their own Environmental Assessment of the proposed liquefied natural gas pipeline. It is available at: https://twnsacredtrust.ca/ Accessed Nov. 22, 2018.

This ontological misreading has real-world implications. Anthropologist Elizabeth Povinelli argues that "[t]he very act of representing such conceptions of the world as beliefs – rather than as 'methods for ascertaining truth' – necessarily reinforces the state's monopoly over the terms of debate and the criteria for assessing value and justice" (Povinelli 1995: 506). This can lead to situations where resource managers cherry pick from indigenous ontologies by referring to them as 'traditional ecological knowledge' rather than science, treating their insights as something that might add to a cultural understanding of a given project, but not challenge fundamental ontological assumptions about the nature of the resource in question. Watch words such as 'symbol', 'cultural construction', 'metaphor' and 'intangible values' pervade these literatures, serving to confine indigenous ontologies into the category of human subjectivity, as valid as any other experience of the landscape in question, but not objectively true within the realm of quantifiable science.

More recently, Paul Nadasdy has argued quite pointedly that social science has been complicit in the power imbalance that results from these ontological impasses. By this he does not mean that resource management institutions are getting the descriptions wrong, they are actually delegitimising indigenous worlds by translating them into Western ontological categories that are routinely used in landscape management institutions or economic enterprises (Nadasdy 1999; Nadasdy 2007). This has real world consequences for indigenous peoples, because, as he writes, anthropologists often "provide government officials with the very models they use to justify the delegitimiation of indigenous knowledge and the extension of the state's authority over aboriginal peoples" (Nadasdy 2007: 26). In the case of indigenous hunters from Northern Canada who claim that deer and caribou routinely give themselves to hunters, Nadasdy writes: "In short, we must acknowledge that they are not just cultural constructions and accept instead the possibility that they may be actually (as well as metaphorically) valid. For the most part, we have refused to do this" (Nadasdy 2007: 26).

In this chapter, I attempt to shed light on this ontological impasse by using Philippe Descola's ontological typology to argue that the worlds of resource management institutions frequently mistranslate the worlds of indigenous peoples. Because the 'naturalist' ontology of these institutions tends to frame the world in terms of subjective human values and natural objects, indigenous ontologies that do not experience the landscape in this way, are often misread as culturally constructed subjective worldviews or cultural landscapes, and are then projected onto the physical landscape in question. The bulk of the essay is concerned with demonstrating how a diversity of literatures, even those sympathetic to indigenous ontologies, have made similar errors in translation. I then propose a possible way forward through a reading of Bruno Latour's political ecology, Eduardo Kohn's anthropology of life beyond the human, and the pioneering (yet ancient) work of Indigenous Science. I assert that these literatures provide crucial theoretical tools for building bridges beyond the inherently Western language of symbol, value, traditional knowledge and worldview, so that the social sciences and resource management institutions can better engage with

Table 1. Philippe Descola's Ontological Schema (adapted from Descola 2013).

|  | Beings dissimilar in Physicality | Beings similar in Physicality |
|---|---|---|
| **Beings similar in Interiority** | Animism | Totemism |
| **Beings dissimilar in Interiority** | Analogism | Naturalism |

indigenous peoples on their own terms without being required to adopt their ontologies.[3]

## Lost in translation: Misreading indigenous ontology

In his book *Beyond Nature and Culture*, anthropologist Philippe Descola outlines a schema for four ontologies, broadly applicable to the way human beings interact with and create landscapes. Descola criticises anthropology for assuming its role to be that of describing the cultural constructions of other approaches to a world that remains universally divided between subjects and objects, culture and nature, etc.; interpreting the semiotics of a *cultural* landscape read as text, rather than as a way of being in the world (see Geertz 1977). Descola suggests that importing this generally Western ontology into its work, anthropology has misread the diverse array of indigenous approaches to their worlds.

Descola schematises human ontology along two spectrums of continuity and two of discontinuity in physicality and interiority based on how a given culture relates to the rest of the world (Table 1). This schema includes both human and non-human entities and encapsulates the whole of a bio-cultural landscape.

The peoples living under the ontological assumptions of what is generally described as 'Western civilization', mainly Europe and North America with their colonies and scientific and economic institutions, dwell in a 'naturalist' or some might say 'modernist' ontology (see Tarnas 1993). Along these two spectrums of continuity and discontinuity, the average college educated North American of European descent has come to live in a world where humans and non-humans share similarity in physicality (we are made out of the same biological stuff), but humans and non-humans differ radically in interiority (humans possess will, reason, intelligence and consciousness, while animals and plants possess only awareness, instinct, biological drive, etc.).[4] These bedrock assumptions, particularly regarding the perceived

---

3  This theoretical work is only supplementary to the political mobilization and institutional reforms that must continue to push for co- and full management by indigenous peoples to lands they claim as traditional.

4  This is of course a general description, and is changing especially among environmentalists, but this is the general notion of what constitutes the difference between humans and non-humans.

differences between human consciousness and the physical world, routinely take for granted the idea that sciences such as ecology, biology and chemistry are the legitimate interpreters of the natural landscape, while the humanities, anthropology and other social sciences are the interpreters of the *cultural* landscape (see Tarnas 1993; Worster 1994; Merchant 2003).

On the other hand, Descola describes the ontology of Amazonian peoples with whom he works as largely being either animistic or totemistic. Based on his ontological schema, animists experience the world as made up of different physicalities but similar interiorities (similar subjectivities or cultures, with different physical forms). Thus aspects of the landscape such as birds, jaguars or monkeys act out of similar cultural forms, the need to eat, hunt, cook, sleep, marry, have fun, etc. but exist in distinctly different physical forms from human beings with whom they share this common culture.

This approach is also well translated by Eduardo Viveiros de Castro in his 1998 article "Cosmological Deixis and Amerindian Perspectivism". Viveiros de Castro describes 'perspectivism', as 'multi-naturalism' (as opposed to multi-culturalism) because it views the landscape as similar in cultural formation, yet distinct in physicality. He writes:

> (Multi)cultural relativism supposes a diversity of subjective and partial representations, each striving to grasp an external and unified nature, which remains perfectly indifferent to those representations. Amerindian thought proposes the opposite: a representational of phenomenological unity which is purely pronominal or deictic, indifferently applied to a radically objective diversity. One single 'culture,' multiple 'natures' – perspectivism is multinaturalist, for a perspective is not a representation (Viveiros de Castro 1998: 478).

Thus, "what to us is blood, is maize beer to the jaguar; what to the souls of the dead is a rotting corpse, to us is soaking manioc; what we see as a muddy waterhole, the tapirs see as a great ceremonial house" (Viveiros de Castro 1998: 479). While the Western biologist or landscape ecologist might feel comfortable assuming that 'nature' is everywhere the same, and that 'cultures' differ as they come in contact and make meaning with the landscape, for Amazonian peoples who work with Viveiros de Castro and Descola, the world is experienced as a 'meshwork' to use Tim Ingold's phrase, of personhoods and relationship.[5]

Totemistic ontology, similar and in some cases overlapping with animism, sees both interiority between humans and non-humans as continuous, and experiences physicality as inherently similar.[6] So for example, totemic

---

5   Of course Western people are not exempt from anthropomorphisms of pets, cars, computers, institutions, etc. (see Sahlins 2014). However, for our purposes, in the context of resource management, these assumptions can be said to hold quite strongly.

6   There is not an exclusive difference between animistic and totemistic ontologies, and they sometimes blend. But for our purposes they can be seen as unique approaches to landscape.

cultures of the Pacific NorthWest of North America, such as the Squamish discussed above, depending on the clan, are descended directly from wolves, ravens, coyote, whales or cougars (Thom 2005). Kinship and lineage are seen as continuous between both the cultural and physical aspects of these totems, and totem poles both ancient and modern, tell the stories associated with these complex lineages (Mawani 2004).

Analogism is then the opposite of totemism, and can be viewed as a kind hierarchical animism, wherein there exists radical discontinuity of both physicality and interiority between humans and non-humans, as exists in the totems of the Manambu People of Papua New Guinea who employ competing images from indigenous or colonial cultures to integrate traditional totems with a particular clan's claims to political dominance (Sahlins 2014).

With these basic typologies, Descola's work exemplifies what many are calling an ontological shift within anthropology. This shift moves from an emphasis on epistemology to one of ontology, from knowledge to ways of being, from reading a rich cultural text to mapping a way of life. In what follows, I will retrace the steps of several important literatures relevant to this question of misreading the indigenous world, and then propose a way to bridge these two worlds.

### ETHNOGRAPHIC ACCOUNTS

Within the ethnographic accounts of the world's rich cultural heritage, ethnographers of Western background have tended to make sense of their research subjects' ontologies in terms of their own. This has resulted, in many cases, in ethnography assuming that the landscape is a physically neutral space with what are equated to be subjective beliefs imposed upon it. For example, Edward Tylor's now famous coining of the term *animism*, which is undergoing a revival in anthropological and environmental literatures, was first a description for what was assumed to be the *false* belief by his subjects that the non-human world possessed the kind of personhood that humans possess (see Bird-David 1999; Harvey 2006).

However, as anthropology became more reflexive, it began to articulate a more culturally relative approach that embedded these approaches within a given cultural context. Inevitably however, even with the wealth of knowledge and understanding we have gained from ethnography, some of these accounts have misread or mistranslated indigenous understandings of their worlds. For example in Nancy Munn's study of Australian Aboriginal dreaming, she insists that Aboriginal peoples are *translating* objects into subjects by constructing physical settings as the abodes of human persons or ancestors (Munn 1984; in Harvey 2006: 73).

And, yet, even more recent ethnographies have not caught the error. For example, despite her defense of Mi'kmaq understandings of sacred landscape in the face of appropriation by the spiritual ecology movement, anthropologist Anne-Christine Hornborg calls the Mi'kmaq concept of a Mother Earth a 'metaphor' (Hornborg 2008: 156). Julie Cruikshank's study of the social lives of glaciers in the Yukon Territory and Alaska, which has been widely praised for incorporating Athapaskan and Tlingit worlds into climate science modeling, invokes the subjectivist stance when she writes that "glaciers *seem to be invested* with moral dimensions that illuminate social values and consequences of breaching them" (my emphasis, Cruikshank 2005: 68). And Nicholas Peterson (2011) insists that all the recent hype about a so-called "Sentient Landscape," referring to the so-called "New Animism," goes too far in occupying an animist ontology. Peterson insists that at least for the Warlpiri of Australia, they simply employ a "rich *metaphorical* ontology" that ritually mediates their subjective relationship to the *natural* world, rather than representing a fundamental ontological break with the categories of subject and object as developed in the Western academy. And lastly, anthropologist Chie Sakakibara characterises the Iñupiat of Arctic Alaska as holding the "*belief* that humans and animals physically and spiritually constitute one another; that the soul, thoughts, and behaviors of animals and people interpenetrate in the collaboration of life" (Sakakibara 2010: 1007).

There are of course many more examples we could draw upon, but all this is to illustrate that even anthropology, a discipline that at least in contemporary times frames itself as an ally of indigenous peoples (Scheper-Hughes 1995), has fallen into the trap of mistaking ontology for epistemology.

### Environmental values

The literature on environmental values is diverse, but generally seeks to describe the contours of how and why certain groups of people value specific features of the landscape from national parks to proposed wilderness areas, to peri-urban or urban green space (Zube et al. 1982; Taylor et al. 1987; Daniel 2001). In addition, environmental valuation has been used to assign an economic value to nontangible or nonmarket aspects of the environment (Kalof and Satterfield 2005).

In ontological terms, the literature on environmental values can be said to focus on the cognitive process of meaning making, that assumes a uniformly physical landscape, understood differently by different cultural or stakeholder groups. So again, while resource management institutions have made great strides in listening to indigenous perspectives, these perspectives are often embedded among many others that may not share the same ontological understandings of a given landscape.

For example, Garibaldi and Turner (2004) coin the term "cultural keystone species" to talk about the way that indigenous people value certain aspects of a given environment. This concept is borrowed from the keystone species concept in ecology, coined in 1960s by Robert Paine, who observed the importance of ochre starfish in the tidal pools of the Pacific Ocean. Thus the cultural keystone species is to the ecological keystone species as the ethnosphere is to the biosphere (Garibaldi and Turner 2004). The authors seek to emphasise a lesser known *understanding* of the world, but do so by drawing equivalences between two domains within the naturalist ontological categories. Thus keystone species such as wild rice, red laver seaweed, Western red cedar, bison, wapato and tobacco can vary over temporal, spatial and social scales, and they are a "metaphorical parallel with ecological keystone species" (Garibaldi and Turner 2004). In other words, not quite as real as ecological keystone species.

This assumption within the cognitive approach, that we live in a semiotically neutral 'nature', made sense of by predominantly cognitive 'culture', is where Environmental Values disadvantages indigenous peoples. In Peter Ashley's 2007 study, the author describes the types of spiritual values held by different user groups of a wilderness area in Tasmania. His content analysis shows similarities between managers and civilians in terms of feelings of joy and peace when hiking, but differences between the two groups in terms of whether they cited specifically religious or spiritual experiences while hiking. Ashley frames his study with the pervasive frustration at the seeming variability of spiritual values: "wilderness is whatever people think it is, the '*terra incognita*' of people's minds" (emphasis in the original, Ashley 2007: 59), thus setting up any ontological differences as simply epistemological ones, to be listened to and accommodated, but not necessarily believed.

This notion that landscape value is in the eye of the beholder is repeated by Ellen Lee in the 2000 edition of *Parks Journal*: "The same area of land can be looked upon as several different versions of cultural landscape depending on the cultural or disciplinary filters and values of the person who is doing the looking" (Lee 2000: 3). And this is certainly how Thomas Greider and Loraine Garkovich (1994) frame landscape when they write "[t]he open field is the same physical thing, but it carries multiple *symbolic* meanings that emanate from the values by which people define themselves" (my emphasis, Greider and Garkovich 1994: 1).

TRADITIONAL ECOLOGICAL KNOWLEDGE (TEK)
Concomitant to the environmental values literature has been a focus on what is called 'traditional ecological knowledge', or TEK, which refers to "all types of knowledge about the environment derived from experience and traditions of a particular group of people" (Usher 2000). Nicolas Houde (2007) suggests that aspects of traditional ecological knowledge each in turn address differences in factual knowledge, or types and names of species in the environment: management systems, or ways of managing a given resource; past and current uses of a landscape unique to a given people or place; ethics and values, culture and identity, cosmology (referred to as a worldview).

While indigenous knowledge is being collected in unprecedented quantities with respect to landscaper management decisions, and First Nations communities in Canada have made much progress with co-management arrangements legal challenges to colonial land title arrangements, (Houde 2007); final decisions continue to ignore claims to indigenous values and worlds, and knowledge is used selectively. These decisions rest once again on the ontological assumptions of Western world.

If TEK is viewed as a "knowledge-practice-belief complex" (Butler et al. 2012), then that knowledge can simply co-exist with other knowledge about a given landscape. For example, when Becker et al. (2008) outline the struggles between Thunderbird and Whale in which earthquakes and tsunami-like effects occur, they are quick to remind us that these stories are "likely to be abstract tales of an actual event" (Becker et al. 2008: 492). The authors' main argument being that even if they are not real, worldviews can be useful as

271

"cross-culturally appealing and effective ways of delivering contemporary messages" (Becker et al. 2008: 490). This notion of the stakeholder assumes diverse cultural values of a unified physical landscape. Diverse knowledges are permitted provided they fit within the ontological assumptions of the knowledge keepers of the physical landscape: ecologies, managers, biologists etc. (Houde 2007). This epistemological stance in TEK is well critiqued by Descola who writes:

> If every culture is considered as a specific system of meanings arbitrarily coding an unproblematic natural world, which everywhere possesses all the features that our own culture attributes to it, then not only does the very cause of the nature-culture(s) division remain unquestioned, but, declarations to the contrary notwithstanding, there can be no escape from the epistemological privilege granted to western culture, the only one whose definition of nature serves as the implicit measuring rod for all others (Descola 1996: 84).

While I agree that efforts to recognise value in non-commodity aspects of life, and non-Western science are steps in the right direction, and that they have given many indigenous peoples the vocabulary and tools they need to protect certain aspects of their traditional territories, resource management institutions and agencies continue, willfully or not, to mistranslate actual experiences of the landscape. Julie Cruikshank identifies how this has created a kind of double exclusion:

> Codified as TEK, and engulfed by frameworks of North American management science, local knowledge shifts its shape. Sentient and social spaces are thus transformed to measurable commodities called 'lands' and 'resources'. Indigenous peoples then face double exclusion, initially by colonial processes that expropriate land, and ultimately by neo-colonial discourses that appropriate and reformulate their ideas (Cruikshank 2005: 259).

I am not here to fault the vast literature that seeks to re-value indigenous wisdom and knowledge, but simply point it towards some of these potential weaknesses. The literature on traditional ecological knowledge has made great strides in giving voice to indigenous approaches to resource management and values. However, it has sometimes fallen into the trap of too quickly assuming false equivalences between indigenous ontologies and North American or European ones as they play out on the landscape.

## SPIRITUAL ECOLOGY

Whereas environmental values reproduces the approach to landscape that sees culture as a subjective layer projected onto the neutral landscape, spiritual ecology, a recent descendent of Deep Ecology, imagines that there is an original 'sacred' cultural landscape to which Western civilization must return. This makes spiritual ecology's goal of 're-enchanting' the landscape susceptible to romanticising indigenous ontologies, and misreading concepts such as animism, reciprocity and interconnection.

Historian Lynn White, Jr. argued in his famous 1967 essay, that a combination of Christianity and European science 'dis-enchanted' the landscape of its spiritual power and agency, which was then more readily viewed as a collection of resources and objects to be put to use for human wellbeing and wealth generation (White 1967). Post-secular environmental writers in recent decades have argued that one important strategy of the environmental movement then should be to re-instill or re-invest the landscape with some semblance of the 'sacred.' For scholars of specific religious traditions, this involves the 'retrieval' (see Tucker and Grim 2001: 16) of environmentally friendly doctrines, teachings or traditions. For others it simply means, returning to assumed indigenous notion that land is 'sacred'. Sufi activist Llewellyn Vaughan Lee frames spiritual ecology in terms of an ethical push to reimagine this enchanted world: "The world is t not a problem to be solved; it is a living being to which we belong" (Vaughan Lee 2012: 1). Eliciting Ralph Waldo Emerson's World Soul, and climatologist James Lovelock's Gaia, the world is an interconnected sacred entity of which we are only a part. Thus solutions to the ecological crisis should start not with policy and technology, but with cultural transformation and re-valuing of landscape as sacred community.

Antecedent to this emerging approach was Norwegian philosopher Arne Naess, who coined the term Deep Ecology to argue that the West did not only need better laws or technology, but a fundamental shift in our perception of the world and our relationship to it (Naess 1973; Taylor 2001). While Deep Ecology often takes a more philosophical and political approach (see Deval and Sessions 1985), spiritual ecology focuses on the connections between the human soul and the landscape, while seeking to emphasise the sacredness of the landscape (Vaughan Lee 2012; Sponsel 2012).

However, proponents of this literature are often guilty of appealing to an essentialised 'Native Wisdom' as foil for Western destructive dualisms. This appeal often frames indigenous worlds as *inherently* relational, harmonious, and respectful of ecological systems. The 'Harmony with Nature' narrative will be familiar to most, as it has a long history rooted in the literary trope of the innocent 'Noble Savage', or, 'Ecological Indian' whose primal state was one of peace, harmony and simplicity (see Kretch III 1999; Mann 2005).

However, looking to indigenous traditions as foil to Western under-standings often results in simplistic and cherry-picked appeals to actual indigenous landscapes. In *The Sacred Balance*, environmental activist David Suzuki praises indigenous wisdom as a kind of sacred original knowledge (Suzuki 1997) which should be revered along with scientific knowledge. Anthropologist Leslie Sponsel (2012) describes animism as an "enchanted" worldview and global indigenous peoples as our "original Spiritual Ecologists" who naturally embody and model the interconnected worldview and ethic activists seek to promote and shepherd us towards. Anthropologist David Abram, in his *Spell of the Sensuous* (1996) seeks to use ethnographic detail to describe the ways that literacy may have divorced the West from a deeply rooted experience of the world, which he believes must now be restored. He writes, contrary to Western assumptions about the world, "[t]he world and I reciprocate one another. The landscape as I directly experience it is hardly a determinate object; it is an ambiguous realm that responds to my emotions and calls forth feelings from me in turn" (Abrams 1996: 33). We must, he argues, return to our original view of a relational and reciprocal approach to landscape if we are to avoid the coming ecological crisis.

The problem is not that Western people are beginning to realise that the world is interconnected, but that while many indigenous peoples certainly describe their world in reciprocal terms, that reciprocity is not always harmonious, and certainly does not represent some kind of primordial harmony. For example, Northern hunters need to obey strict protocols in order to merit game giving themselves to the hunter (Nadasdy 2007). In NorthWestern North America, glaciers are temperamental beings that require Athapaskan and Tlingit people to keep certain taboos in their presence such as cooking with grease, or making fun of another person. There are predators, demons, dark spirits, malevolent entities and evil in these worlds. Highlighting or even celebrating indigenous worlds as a kind of primal worldview to which we can return, puts us in danger of romanticising indigenous peoples when they perform this interconnectivity and patronising them when they do not (Hornborg 2013).

## Sacred natural sites

With the increased interest within spiritual ecology in sacred aspects of landscape, there has also been a move to educate resource and protected area managers of these so-called 'unseen' non-material landscapes that indigenous peoples inhabit. Recent years have seen a significant increase in publications on connections between biodiversity conservation and sacred sites, under the banner of 'sacred natural sites'. Independent researcher Bas Verschuuren defines a sacred natural site as an "area of land or water having special spiritual significance to people and communities" (Verschuuren 2010: 1) and the literature suggests that SNS are the world's first protected areas. Unfortunately, *all three of these words*, sacred, natural and sites, import Western ontological assumptions along lines discussed in this chapter. For many indigenous peoples, so-called Sacred Natural Sites are not sacred, natural or sited.

Sacred in its Western linguistic context means separate, set apart derived from the temple precincts of Judaism and Roman and Greek cult worship (Glacken 1976: 13). In indigenous cultures ranging from Central South and North America, Sub-Saharan Africa and Oceania, New Zealand and Australia however, sacredness, holiness or the spiritual are integrated into everyday space and places such as the home, hearth, garden and orchard. The SNS literature tends to focus primarily on sites that reproduce a similar character to Western views of the sacred as separate. Sacred groves, temple complexes, mountains, monasteries and bodies of water all harmonise with notions of conservation or religious separation normally attributed to sacred precincts. But as social scientist Fikret Berkes points out, "many rural and indigenous peoples do not make a distinction between the biological, economic, and social objectives of conservation, as scientists often do, but tend to regard these aspects as interrelated" (Berkes 2009: 20).

In addition, nature as a separate domain of reality (from culture) can be seen as part of Descola's naturalist ontology. Buttressed by Western views of nature/culture as irreconcilable, traditional practices such as hunting, gathering and swidden have been characterised as threatening and destructive. Where indigenous peoples are not forcibly removed, tension often exists between protected area and resource managers and traditional or indigenous peoples. For example, in Highland Guatemala, traditional forest management, swidden and firewood collection has recently come into conflict with the centralised state forestry institute who seeks to standardise and systematise forestry along Western scientific lines (Brown et al. 2013).

Another tendency in SNS is to focus on discrete sites. Verschuuren et al. (2010) acknowledge that 'site' is vague, broad enough to denote a single rock or an entire region. However, the SNS literature is filled with case studies that focus on discrete locales that once again fall with the dichotomies discussed here. As Anne-Christine Hornborg states, "[a] holy place is for the Christian a place that differs from the profane places. But applied to the North American Natives' traditional way of viewing places, the concept of 'holy' might […] include the whole country" (Hornborg 2008: 162).[7]

It is not that resource managers should continue to ignore intangible values associated with the precincts within their care, but rather that this care should be in full consultation with the relevant peoples. Better yet, practices should move towards autonomous management schemes so that indigenous values are not repeatedly assumed to conform to Western notions of what constitutes sacred, natural, or sites. In the concluding section, I will point towards positive developments in the social science and ecology literatures that might act as tools for better translations between the worlds. These diverse sources are not meant to be taken as a systematic prescription, but as sign posts along the way towards ontological reconciliation.

## Building bridges between worlds

I have argued that the approaches outlined above continue to import aspects of the 'modernist' or as Descola calls it the 'naturalist' ontology into resource and landscape management schemes involving indigenous peoples. This basic framing of the world sees nature as everywhere the same and human culture and subjectivity as a spectrum of difference that makes meaning with the physical landscape. Because in many regions of the world especially North America, resource management institutions are rooted in Western science, this ongoing habit has had onto-political consequences for the identities, territories and the very fabric of being for many indigenous peoples. This is not to denigrate the sciences, but only put them in perspective of their own cultural milieu.

One might ask if perhaps a solution is for colonial and settler societies to learn to dwell inside whichever indigenous world they find themselves working. As the spiritual ecologist approach suggests, must we then all adopt a more enchanted or animistic view of the world, even if it contradicts

---

7   I do not necessarily agree with Hornborg's characterisation of Christianity as holding this rigid duality between sacred and profane, but nonetheless the quotation illustrates my primary point regarding indigenous notions of sacredness.

our scientific approach? An approach in which settler societies are asked to simply adopt the worlds of indigenous peoples comes with its own problems, questions and drawbacks, and denies that Western peoples possess a legitimate ontology to begin with. Rather, in dialogue with what indigenous peoples are actually asking for, what I propose is needed are better *bridges* between the worlds, so that translations between them, though inadequate, can improve.

PHENOMENOLOGY OF LANDSCAPE

First, it is of utmost importance that land and resource managers realise that understanding indigenous worlds is not necessarily the same thing as understanding worldviews. The ontological turn in anthropology has seen a shift towards a more phenomenological approach to landscape. Central among these proposals has been Tim Ingold's collection of writings which elaborate on Martin Heidegger's work on dwelling. Ingold begins by critiquing the assumed metaphorical nature of using kinship terms like 'mother' or 'ancestor' in relation to the sustenance-providing forest of the Mbuti Pygmies. He states, "[p]arenting is not a construction that is projected onto acts of this kind, it rather subsists in them, in the nurture and affection bestowed by adults on their offspring" (Ingold 2000, 45). Repeating what many indigenous peoples must be tired of saying: "Organisms are not just *like* persons, they are persons" (Ingold 2000: 51).

In this approach, the landscape is part of an 'unfolding process' within which humans and other organisms participate, not a dualism of different *kinds* of beings or domains. Taking Gregory Bateson's *Ecology of Mind* a step further, Ingold argues that we don't construct a worldview in the mind, and then use it to make sense of the world, we exist as a body-mind that participates in the lifeworld (Ingold 2000: 14). Responding to Denis Cosgrove's 1988 statement that "a landscape is a cultural image," Ingold counters that landscape is not a "picture in the imagination, surveyed by the mind's eye", but, "through living in it, the landscape becomes a part of us, just as we are a part of [...] a landscape each component enfolds within its essence the totality of its relations with each and every other" (Ingold 2000: 191). This means that stories, myths and legends are not layers that cloak the landscape, but technologies in the task of opening it to the dwellers, indigenous or not. Rather than seeing values as a layer or filter through which one sees 'reality', landscape is more of a parallel reality, existing side by side with our own.

By allowing indigenous peoples to define the categories and terms of their landscapes, we acknowledge that the world is alive with objective qualities and affordances. The knowledge associated with a place is not just projected onto it, it is co-produced by the act of dwelling, something many indigenous peoples have been practicing over many thousands of years.

ACTOR NETWORK THEORY/NEW MATERIALISM

In addition, it is important that notions of agency, action, intention and personhood be addressed. Rather than embracing particular animist ontologies that often carry concomitant spiritual implications, some philosophers are moving towardss a kind of 're-*animation*' of the physical landscape through what is being called actor network theory or the new materialism.

Prominent in this approach is French philosopher of science Bruno Latour, who argues that the naturalist approach to the world has divided the academy into those concerned with facts and those concerned with values; e.g., "[t]hat's a question for the theologians", or "[t]he facts speak for themselves" (Latour 2004: 68). For Latour, this artifice does not actually exist in the real world, even for Western peoples, who are rarely scientific about their daily lives, and who attribute personality to cars, corporation and household pets. Thus, for Latour we must do nothing less than abandon the constructed dualist ontology of naturalism. He proposes that in fact, we live in a *Collective*, an assemblage of humans, non-humans and ideas that has always been mixed up (we have never really *been* modern).

Latour is not a social constructivist who sees the mind as a *terra incognita*, where all meaning-making takes place within cognitive processes, reproducing the familiar dualism discussed above. Rather, Latour and others suggest we need to abandon nature as a domain of reality, and take seriously the ways *things* (humans or non-humans) speak and act in the world beyond conventional categories of subject and object (Latour 2004). Latour suggests, that in an era of climate change where institutions, laws, climates, organisms, technology, people, GMOs, etc. all mix freely, this distinction, and the power that comes with being able to speak on behalf of 'facts', is not only undemocratic, but is hindering our ability to solve problems and work towards the common good (Latour 2004). To speak of 'Society' and 'Nature' as separate domains of reality is making less and less sense.

Latour wishes to see us acknowledge that there is not a "science of things" and a "politics of subjects," but "a political ecology of collectives consisting of humans and non-humans" which shifts matters of fact to *matters of concern* (Latour 2004: 61). This *Parliamentary* social ethic turns Immanuel Kant's Kingdom of Ends (humans) on its head, a move that Latour calls a "Revolt of the Means," in which the earth, and non-humans demand to be taken into account (Latour 2004: 155–156).

But Latour does not call for a post-modern hyper-subjectivism. Rather, Latour suggests we replace (capitalised) 'Science' and its dualist ontology, with 'the sciences.' The *sciences* he argues, rather than describing an objective world in one camp, and describing meaning and value in another are tasked with redistributing speech and the capacity to be a social actor between humans and non-humans (Latour 2004). The sciences do this by advancing 'propositions'; or, associations of humans and non-humans that may be well or poorly articulated members of the Collective, all aimed at creating a Good Common World (Latour 2004: 83–87). However, in doing away with the old distinction between facts and values, Latour proposes a *new bicameralism*: taking into account, or ensuring propositions have not left any voices (human or non-human) out. So, in the case of a pipeline or hydroelectric dam, utility companies, consumers, salmon, indigenous peoples, endangered newts, the climate, should all have representation in a given suit of alternatives.

Next he proposes Putting in Order, or, determining the effects of the propositions on the habits of others (Latour 2004: 105–109). What impact will a given proposition have on the lives of those deemed part of the Collective? In other words, how does a given extractive project or management prescription fit in the ontology in question, and how will it affect the beings in that ontological landscape? Whereas contemporary resource management projects consider a suite of social, economic and biological factors, what Latour and many indigenous peoples, are calling for, is greater attention to those beings that fall outside the Western definition of a person, but that constitute the very fabric of many indigenous landscapes, or as Latour might say, Collectives.

Thus the sciences should be seen as distinct for from Science, which includes a tendency towards a hegemonic ideology of Nature. Thus, the sciences should include the humanities, and begin to distribute their tasks not along an axis from discovering natural facts to deciphering subjective values, but in terms of identifying all the actors involved in a given scenario and working towards a way to better live together. This would of course require taking non-humans like salmon, climates, mountains and those who propose to speak for them, more seriously.

What about indigenous claims that cannot be verified using conventional empirical methods such as the existence of Thunderbird, or whether a deer or caribou can give itself to Northern Hunters as many Inuit claim? While Latour has been praised for shedding light on the myriad ways that things act in the world, on the hybridity of subject-object distinction, he stops short of endorsing volition to the non-human world. Certainly the deer, like the hunter, is an actor in a complex web of relations. But when it comes to the question of animal or glacial will, many in the West jump ship.

Philosopher Jane Bennett's approach, akin to Latour's, is helpful in this regard. Bennet suggests that unlike traditional philosophical notions of the self as an autonomous will contained within the person, "causality is more emergent than efficient, more fractal than linear. Instead of an effect obedient to a determinant, one finds circuits in which effect and cause alternate position and redound on each other" (Bennett 2009: 33). So while the Western scientist might fail to see a deer as having the cognitive capacity, let alone Darwinian incentive, to allow themselves to be killed by a hunter, the story told by the hunter, can be embedded in this wider net of agencies, networks and emergence that neither forces Western scientists to dwell in the world of the indigenous hunter, nor relegates their experience to the realm of metaphor, symbol or value.

ANTHROPOLOGY OF LIFE

Within the 'naturalist' ontology it is assumed that semiosis, or making meaning of the world, was strictly a human affair. But as the ethnography of Eduardo Kohn shows, this is no longer supported by the evidence. For the Runa of the Ecuadorian rainforest, Kohn argues that non-humans can not only be described as persons who "act", as in ANT, but as selves that represent other selves.

Kohn uses Charles Peirce's semiotics, which differentiates between iconic, indexical and symbolic signs to show that all living things, in fact life itself, make use of representation in order to live. While Kohn argues with biologist

Terrance Deacon (1998) that *symbolic* signs (such as alphabets) are a human phenomenon, iconic and indexical signs are pervasive in the non-human world. Kohn states: "Life is constitutively semiotic. That is, life is, through and through, the product of sign processes. What differentiates life from the inanimate physical world is that life-forms represent the world in some way or another, and these representations are intrinsic to their being. What we share with non-human living creatures, then, is not our embodiment, as certain strains of phenomenological approaches would hold, but the fact that we all live with and through signs [...] signs make us what we are" (Kohn 2013: 9).

For example, a jaguar will not attack someone who is sleeping on their belly because they are more recognisable as human, rather than prey. When hunting with his informants, Kohn observed that monkeys, trees and humans all make use of semiotics to interact with the world in a very real way. Semiosis, meaning-making, is always embodied and always entangled (Kohn 2013: 5). Iconic signs participate in some way with what the sign points to. For example, when a hunter makes a monkey call, the word itself sounds like the call of the monkey. In indexical signs, the sign points to some other meaning. For example, when the hunter cuts down the tree to flush a monkey, the sound of the crashing tree is indexical to the monkey of possible danger that must then be interpreted by the monkey's previous experiences to determine her course of action.

Selfhood, even personhood, then, is not a projection of human meaning, but the locus of that accumulated experience. It represents a very real relationality between organisms that demands taking all forms of life seriously. Far from being natural objects discerned and made meaning with by human subjects, all of life seeks to represent its surroundings in ways that are analogous at least in the iconic and indexical modes, to human perception. Kohn's trans-human ethnography, like Latour's parliamentary sciences, is a starting place for Western recognition of non-human semiosis, and the embodied nature of meaning-making that transcends the supposed exclusive subjectivity of human persons.

## INDIGENOUS SCIENCE

In addition to these philosophical and social science approaches, many indigenous peoples are working to reframe resource management and science according to their needs. In his co-authored paper, Kyle Powys Whyte of the Citizen Potawatomi Nation in Oklahoma, USA, insists that what is referred to as traditional ecological knowledge (TEK) is and always has been, indigenous science. Each indigenous world develops knowledge systems that are directed towards livelihoods and community wellbeing. Whyte et al. suggest that these indigenous sciences start with a respect for protocol. By protocol, the authors mean "attitudes about how to approach the world" (Whyte et al. 2016: 2).

In contrast to what the authors call 'sustainability science', which continues to frame the world largely within the naturalist ontology of objects managed by enlightened subjects that are moving towardss a "resource-circulating society" with lower impact on people and ecosystems, indigenous science dwells in a world that is made up of "complex *genealogical* relations" (my emphasis, Whyte et al. 2016: 2). For Whyte et al., indigenous science proceeds on the assumption that

> Humans [are] respectful partners or younger siblings in relationships of reciprocal responsibilities within interconnected communities of relatives inclusive of humans, non-human beings (i.e. plants, animals, etc.), locales (i.e. sacred and spiritual places, etc.) and collectives (i.e. prairies, watersheds, etc.) (Whyte et al. 2016: 26).

No trace of metaphorical language here. Indigenous science protocol then does not imagine that scientists are "somehow separate or epistemically privileged in relation to the many human and non-human relatives" (Whyte et al. 2016: 6).

Thus, Indigenous Science is concerned with 'taking into account' based on the world within which the scientist finds herself, and proposing a protocol for social comportment based on tradition, custom, contemporary necessity, and the wider societal context. This does not exclude the insights of biology, ecology or other Western knowledge systems, but begins with the ontology of the given people involved and their approach to the landscape. For example, the Little Band of Ottawa Indians developed a Lake Sturgeon (Nmé) that begins with the protocol of "Baamaadziwin," or, "living in a good and respectful way." This approach might be translated as stewardship, but the concept goes beyond mere prudent management of a resource. The tribe has implemented a sturgeon restoration project because the Sturgeon is an integral part of clan identity.

## Conclusion

Social science and anthropology have misread indigenous landscapes as being something of a cultural layer atop an objective nature populated with material or biological objects and resource management institutions have consistently acted from a place of ontological hegemony. Criticism from within its own ranks by Descola, Ingold, Povinelli, Nadasdy and many others, have begun to close the gap between these worlds, resulting in a greater emphasis on the ontological rather than the epistemological aspects of landscape perception.

If, as Bruno Latour claims, the West has never been 'modern', then indigenous peoples have never been 'traditional.' It seems that we do not live in *entirely* different worlds, and approaches such as Actor Network Theory, phenomenology of landscape, Kohn's semiotics, and Indigenous Science, though not necessary commensurate, are showing that the distinct ontologies of the worlds can be bridged and translated. Tim Ingold reminds us that we are in fact part of the world as experienced through our own embodiment. Eduardo Kohn provides evidence that semiosis is essential to life itself, and not simply a unique characteristic of human cognitive processes. Both Whyte et al. (2016) and Bruno Latour show that the sciences, rather than being an adversary of indigenous worlds, are the tools the West must use to *socialise* 'Nature', by which I mean take its various constituents seriously as actors or persons within the broader landscape.

Thus, whether we are talking about living in the collective, a meshwork, lifeworld, an assemblage, or world, Jane Bennett makes the ethical implications of a world made up of many worlds clear:

> The ethical aim becomes to distribute value more generously, to bodies as such. Such a newfound attentiveness to matter and its powers will not solve the problem of human exploitation or oppression, but it can inspire a greater sense of the extent to which all bodies are kin in the sense of inextricably enmeshed in a dense network of relations. And in a knotted world of vibrant matter, to harm one section of the web may very well be to harm oneself. Such an enlightened or expanded notion of self-interest is good for humans (Bennett 2009: 13).

Even if we do not dwell in a particular mode of that world, by building bridges between the worlds, rather than walls, we can more easily navigate between them. And, paradoxically, the best way towards creating this world of many worlds, is for the West to embrace the reality that there is only one.

# References

Abrams, David 1996. *The Spell of the Sensuous: Perception and Language in the More-than-human World.* New York: Pantheon Books.

Ashley, Peter 2007. Toward an Understanding and Definition of Wilderness Spirituality. *Australian Geographer* 38 (1): 53–69.

Becker, Julia, David Johnston, Heather Lazrus, George Crawford, and Dave Nelson 2008. Use of Traditional Knowledge in Emergency Management for Tsunami Hazard: A Case Study from Washington State, USA. *Disaster Prevention and Management: An International Journal* 17 (4): 488–502.

Bennett, Jane 2009. *Vibrant Matter: A Political Ecology of Things.* Durham: Duke University Press.

Berkes, Fikret 1999. *Sacred Ecology.* Florence: Taylor & Francis.

Berkes, Fikret 2009. Community Conserved Areas: Policy Issues in Historic and Contemporary Context. *Conservation Letters* 2 (1): 20–25.

Bird-David, Nurit 1999. "Animism" Revisited: Personhood, Environment, and Relational Epistemology. *Current Anthropology* 40 (S1): S67–S91.

Brown, Jason M., John P. Hawkins, James H. McDonald and Walter Randolph Adams 2013. 'They do not know how to take care of the forest': Analyzing State Sponsored "Decentralization" of Forest Management in Santa Catarina Ixtahuacán. In John P. Hawkins, James H. McDonald and Walter Randolph Adams (eds), *Crisis of Governance in Maya Guatemala: Indigenous Responses to a Failing State.* Norman: University of Oklahoma Press.

Butler, James R. A., Alifereti Tawake, Tim Skewes, Lavenia Tawake and Vic McGrath 2012. Integrating Traditional Ecological Knowledge and Fisheries Management in the Torres Strait, Australia: The Catalytic Role of Turtles and Dugong as Cultural Keystone Species. *Ecology and Society* 17 (4): 34.

Cosgrove, Denis and Stephen Daniels 1989. *The Iconography of Landscape.* New York: Cambridge University Press.

Cruikshank, Julie 2005. *Do Glaciers Listen? Local Knowledge, Colonial Encounters, and Social Imagination.* Vancouver: UBC Press.

Daniel, Terry C. 2001. Whither Scenic Beauty? Visual Landscape Quality Assessment in the 21st Century. *Landscape and Urban Planning* 54 (1): 267–281.

Deacon, Terrance W. 1998. *The Symbolic Species: The Co-evolution of Language and the Brain.* New York: WW Norton & Company.

Devall, Bill and George Sessions 1985. *Deep Ecology: Living as if Nature Mattered.* Layton: Gibbs M. Smith, Inc.

Descola, Philippe 1996. Constructing Natures: Symbolic Ecology and Social Practice. In Philippe Descola and Gísli Pálsson (eds), 1996, *Nature and Society: Anthropological Perspectives.* New York: Routledge.

Descola, Philippe 2013. *Beyond Culture and Nature.* Chicago: University of Chicago Press.

Garibaldi, Ann and Nancy Turner 2004. Cultural Keystone Species: Implications for Ecological Conservation and Restoration. *Ecology and Society* 9 (3): 1.

Geertz, Clifford 1977. *The Interpretation of Culture.* New York: Basic Books Classics.

Glacken, Clarence J. 1973. *Traces on the Rhodian Shore: Nature and Culture in Western Thought from Ancient Times to the end of the Eighteenth Century.* Oakland: University of California Press.

Greider, Thomas and Loraine Garkovich 1994. Landscapes: The Social Construction of Nature and Environment. *Rural Sociology* 59 (4): 578–605.

Harvey, Graham 2006. *Animism: Respecting the Living World.* Kent Town: Wakefield Press.

Hornborg, Anne-Christine 2008. *Mi'kmaq Landscapes.* Burlington: Ashgate Publishing.

Houde, Nicolas 2007. The Six Faces of Traditional Ecological Knowledge: Challenges and Opportunities for Canadian Co-management Arrangements. *Ecology and Society* 12 (2): 34.

Ingold, Tim 2000. *The Perception of the Environment: Essays on Livelihood, Dwelling and Skill.* London: Routledge.

Kalof, Linda and Terre Satterfield (eds) 2005. *The Earthscan Reader in Environmental Values.* London: Earthscan/James & James.

Kohn, Eduardo 2013. *How Forests Think: Toward an Anthropology beyond the Human.* Berkeley: University of California Press.

Krech III, Shepherd 2000. *The Ecological Indian: Myth and History.* New York: WW Norton & Company.

Latour, Bruno 1993. *We Have Never Been Modern.* Cambridge: Harvard University Press.

Latour, Bruno 2004. *Politics of Nature: How to Bring the Sciences into Democracy.* Cambridge: Harvard University Press.

Lee, Ellen. 2000. Cultural Connection to the Landscape – A Canadian Example. *Parks* 10:2.

Lewis, John L. and Stephen Sheppard 2005. Ancient Values, New Challenges: Indigenous Spiritual Perceptions of Landscapes and Forest Management. *Society and Natural Resources* 18 (10): 907–920.

Mann, Charles C. 2005. *1491: New Revelations of the Americas before Columbus.* New York: Alfred A. Knopf Inc.

Mawani, Renisa 2004. From Colonialism to Multiculturalism? Totem Poles, Tourism and National Identity in Vancouver's Stanley Park. *ARIEL: A Review of International English Literature* 35 (1–2): 31–57.

Merchant, Carolyn 2003. *Reinventing Eden.* New York: Routledge.

Nadasdy, Paul 1999. The Politics of TEK: Power and the "Integration" of Knowledge. *Arctic Anthropology* 36 (1–2): 1–18.

Nadasdy, Paul 2007. The Gift in the Animal: The Ontology of Hunting and Human–animal Sociality. *American Ethnologist* 34 (1): 25–43.

Naess, Arne 1973. The Shallow and the Deep, Long-range Ecology Movement: A Summary. *Inquiry: An Interdisciplinary Journal of Philosophy* 16 (1–4): 95–100.

Peterson, Nicolas 2011. Is the Aboriginal Landscape Sentient? Animism, the New Animism and the Warlpiri. *Oceania* 81 (2): 167–179.

Povinelli, Elizabeth A. 1995. Do Rocks Listen? *American Anthropologist* 97 (3): 505–518.

Sahlins, Marshall 2014. On the Ontological Scheme of Beyond Nature and Culture. *HAU: Journal of Ethnographic Theory* 4 (1): 281–290.

Sakakibara, Chie 2010. 'Kiavallakkikput Agviq (Into the Whaling Cycle): Cetaceousness and Climate Change among the Inupiat of Arctic Alaska. *Annals of the Association of American Geographers* 100 (4): 1003–1012.

Scheper-Hughes, Nancy 1995. The Primacy of the Ethical: Propositions for a Militant Anthropology. *Current Anthropology* 36 (3): 409–440.

Sponsel, Leslie E. 2012. *Spiritual Ecology: A Quiet Revolution*. Santa Barbara: ABC-CLIO.

Suzuki, David 1997. *The Sacred Balance: Rediscovering our Place in Nature*. Vancouver: Douglas & McIntyre.

Tarnas, Richard 1993. *The Passion of the Western Mind: Understanding the Ideas That Have Shaped Our World View*. New York: Ballantine Books.

Taylor, Jonathan G., Ervin H. Zube and James L. Sell 1987. Landscape Assessment and Perception Research Methods. In Robert B. Bechtel, Robert W. Marans and William Michaelson (eds), *Methods in Environment and Behavioral Research*. New York: Van Nostrand Reinhold.

Taylor, Bron 2001. Earth and Nature-based Spirituality (Part I): From Deep Ecology to Radical Environmentalism. *Religion* 31 (2): 175–193.

Thoreau, Henry David 1867. A Week on the Concord and Merrimack Rivers. *The Works of Henry David Thoreau*. Amazon Digital Services LLC.

Thom, Brian David 2005. *Coast Salish Senses of Place: Dwelling, Meaning, Power, Property and Territory in the Coast Salish World*. Master's Thesis, McGill University.

Tucker, Mary Evelyn and John Grim 2001. Religion and Ecology: Can the Climate Change? *Daedalus,* Fall 2001.

Usher, Peter J. 2000. Traditional Ecological Knowledge in Environmental Assessment and Management. *Arctic* 53 (2): 183–193.

Vaughan Lee, Llewellyn 2013. *Spiritual Ecology: The Cry of the Earth*. Point Reyes: The Golden Sufi Center.

Verschuuren, Bas, Robert Wild, Jeffrey Mcneely and Gonzalo Oviedo 2010. *Sacred Natural Sites: Conserving Nature and Culture*. London: Earthscan.

Viveiros de Castro, Eduardo 1998. Cosmological Deixis and Amerindian Perspectivism. *The Journal of the Royal Anthropological Institute* 4 (3): 469–488.

White, Lynn 1967. The Historical Roots of our Ecological Crisis. *Science* 155: 1203–1207.

Whyte, Kyle Powys, Joseph P. Brewer II and Jay T. Johnson 2016. Weaving Indigenous Science, Protocols and Sustainability Science. *Sustainability Science* 11 (1): 25–32.

Worster, Donald 1994. *Nature's Economy: A History of Ecological Ideas*. New York: Cambridge University Press.

Zube, Ervin H., James L. Sell, and Jonathan G. Taylor 1982. Landscape Perception: Research, Application and Theory. *Landscape Planning* 9 (1): 1–33.

# List of Contributors

**Eeva Berglund** (ⓘ https://orcid.org/0000-0003-0269-562X) teaches and writes on issues to do with society and the environment, particularly on grassroots urbanism, environmental social movements and transformations in notions of expertise, whilst occasionally participating in, and persistently trying to better understand, activism. She has a doctorate in social anthropology from the University of Cambridge, and an MSc in planning from University College, London. She is currently Adjunct professor of environmental policy, Department of Design at Aalto University. The book about Helsinki that she co-edited with her colleague Cindy Kohtala, *Changing Helsinki? 11 Views on a City Unfolding* was published in 2015 by Nemo publishers.

**Jason M. Brown**, PhD is a Sessional Lecturer with the Department of Humanities and the Faculty of Environment at Simon Fraser University in Burnaby, Canada. He is also a Joint Research Associate with the Faculty of Forestry and W. Maurice Young Centre for Applied Ethics at the University of British Columbia in Vancouver. Jason has an eclectic background with degrees in anthropology, forestry, theology and environmental studies. He recently published an essay on the spiritual ecology of the LDS Sacred Grove for the *Journal for the Study of Religion, Nature and Culture*. His research interests include the phenomenology of place and landscape, the ethics of forestry, and religion and public lands in North America.

**Philippe Descola** initially specialised in the ethnology of Amazonia under the supervision of Claude Lévi-Strauss, focusing on how native societies relate to their environment. He has published extensively on his field research with the Achuar of Ecuador and on the comparative analysis of the relations between humans and nonhumans, including images. He is Professor of Anthropology at the Collège de France and a Director of Studies at the École des Hautes Études en Sciences Sociales, Paris. Among his books in English are *In the Society of Nature, The Spears of Twilight, Beyond Nature and Culture* and *The Ecology of Others*. He is a fellow of the British Academy and a foreign member of the American Academy of Arts and Sciences.

**Jasmin Immonen** holds a PhD in social anthropology from Goldsmiths, University of London. She writes about issues related to development, citizenship, diversity politics and the grey economy in the context of Peru. The focus in her writing is in the gaps that emerge in policies, and she is especially interested in new claims that arise with neoliberal policies, and the implication of these for policy and practice.

**Tiina Järvi** (⊙ https://orcid.org/0000-0002-3508-9389) is a doctoral student finalising her dissertation in social anthropology at Tampere University. Her dissertation research examines the future aspirations of Palestinian refugees living in refugee camps in Jordan, Lebanon and occupied West Bank, and particularly contemplates the question of how these hopes have been moulded by conditions created by more than 70 years of exile. Järvi is interested in the material, social and political consequences of Israel's settler colonial nation building, and her areas of expertise include anthropology of the future, Israel/Palestine, Lebanon, and refugees and displacement.

**Timo Kallinen** (⊙ https://orcid.org/0000-0001-7916-6203) is Professor of Comparative Religion at the University of Eastern Finland and a Docent of Social and Cultural Anthropology at the University of Helsinki. His research interests include religion, ritual and secularism, but he has also published on topics related to environmental, economic and legal anthropology. His recent book, *Divine Rulers in a Secular State* (2016), was the culmination of a project looking at the transformation of sacred chiefship/kingship in Ghana and seeking better to understand processes of secularisation in Africa and elsewhere in the Global South.

**Anu Lounela** (⊙ https://orcid.org/0000-0002-8903-1983) is an anthropologist and university researcher in Social and Cultural Anthropology and Development Studies, University of Helsinki. Her PhD, *Contesting Forests and Power: Dispute Violence and Negotiation in Central Java* (2009), demonstrated how forest land disputes relate to the struggles over power and state formation. Currently her research examines state formation and water-related vulnerabilities in Kalimantan, Indonesia. Her research interests include environment, nature-people relations, values, dispute, state formation, climate change, swamp forests and water, and her ethnographic focus is on Indonesia, specifically the islands of Java and Borneo.

**Morgan Moffitt** is a PhD candidate in the Department of Anthropology at the University of Alberta in Edmonton, Canada. She carried out the research for this project from 2014 to 2016, including ethnographic fieldwork while living in the community of Tulít'a in 2015. She has taught as an Instructor at Aurora College and edited a book of Elders' Stories for the Sahtu Divisional Education Council. She currently lives and works in Yellowknife, Northwest Territories.

**Jenni Mölkänen** is a PhD candidate in Social and Cultural Anthropology at the University of Helsinki. She is finalising her thesis exploring environmental conservation and land use processes in rural northeast Madagascar, with a special interest in the perspective of the Tsimihety rice and vanilla cultivators. Currently, she is working in the multidisciplinary ALL-YOUTH research consortium where she is focusing on how Finnish youth envision sustainability and wellbeing.

**Joonas Plaan** is a Lecturer of Anthropology in Tallinn University. Currently, he is writing his PhD dissertation, studying how climate change affects inshore fisheries in Newfoundland, Canada. Joonas has done fieldwork among the fishing communities in Kihnu Island, Estonia and Bay de Verde peninsula, Newfoundland. He is an active member in the international research group Too Big To Ignore that focuses on global issues in small-scale fisheries, and he is one of the authors of small-scale fisheries guidelines in Newfoundland and Labrador. His wider research interests revolve around human-environment interactions, encompassing environmental anthropology, political ecology, environmental history, and landscape studies.

**Cristiano Tallè** has long been involved in fieldwork in Mexico, at the *Ikoots* indigenous community of San Mateo del Mar (Oaxaca). His main research interests concern indigenous schooling, socio-environmental conflicts and indigenous rights in Latin America. He is the author, among other things, of *Sentieri di parole: Lingua, paesaggio e senso del luogo in una comunità indigena di pescatori nel Messico del sud* (2016) (Paths of words: Language, landscape and sense of place in an indigenous fishing community in southern Mexico). He teaches Cultural Anthropology and Ethno-linguistics at the University of Naples "L'Orientale", where carries out his research activity.

**Tuomas Tammisto** (● https://orcid.org/0000-0001-9767-7832) is a socio-cultural anthropologist interested in human-environmental relations, tropical land use and agriculture. He completed his PhD at the University of Helsinki on how the Mengen living in the rural Pomio District in Papua New Guinea reproduce their society and their lived environment by engaging in swidden horticulture, logging, wage labour on plantations and community conservation. Currently, he is working as a post-doc researcher at the University of Helsinki exploring the intersection between the commodification of nature, value production and state-formation on the oil-palm frontier of Papua New Guinea.

**Anna Tsing** (⬥ http://orcid.org/0000-0002-0411-959X) is a professor of anthropology at the University of California, Santa Cruz. Between 2013 and 2018, she co-directed Aarhus University Research on the Anthropocene (AURA), a programme in which anthropologists and ecologists worked together to describe the Anthropocene. Some products of that programme include the special section of *Journal of Ethnobiology* (vol 38, 2018) "Feral Dynamics of Post-Industrial Ruin," and the co-edited collection *Arts of Living on a Damaged Planet* (University of Minnesota Press 2017). The related digital collection/archive/game *Feral Atlas: The More-than-Human-Anthropocene* is forthcoming.

**Katja Uusihakala** (⬥ https://orcid.org/0000-0001-6432-6323) is an Academy of Finland Research Fellow who works in Social and Cultural Anthropology at the University of Helsinki. Her current research project, *Children as an "Imperial Investment": British Child Migration to Colonial Southern Rhodesia,* examines British post-war child migration to colonial Rhodesia. The research examines the fragmentedness of memory, silence and silencing, remembering and relatedness, as well as questions of migration, education and socialisation connected to building white colonial citizens. Previous research focussed on the study of colonial and postcolonial settler communities in Eastern and Southern Africa, particularly looking at identity politics and social memory practices.

**Francesco Zanotelli** (⬥ https://orcid.org/0000-0003-4257-4275) has a PhD in Social Anthropology (Turin University), and is currently Associate Professor at the University of Messina. He has published extensively on debt and moral economy in neoliberal Mexico, and on kinship, work, migration and welfare in Italy. He is the author of *Santo Dinero* (latest ed. 2012), and he is co-editor, with Simonetta Grilli, of the book *Scelte di famiglia* (2010). At present, his research deals with the interactions between the environmental turn in the global economy and its interaction with indigenous ontologies and politics, with a special focus on Oaxaca, Mexico.

# Abstract

## Dwelling in Political Landscapes: Contemporary Anthropological Perspectives

Edited by Anu Lounela, Eeva Berglund and Timo Kallinen

People all over the globe are experiencing unprecedented and often hazardous situations as environments change at speeds never before experienced. This edited collection proposes that anthropological perspectives on landscape have great potential to address the resulting conundrums. The contributions build particularly on phenomenological, structuralist and multispecies approaches to environmental perception and experience, but they also argue for incorporating political power into analysis alongside dwelling, cosmology and everyday practice. The book's 13 ethnographically rich chapters explore how the material and the conceptual are entangled in and as landscapes, but it also looks at how these processes unfold at many scales in time and space, involving different actors with different powers. Thus it reaches towards new methodologies and new ways of using anthropology to engage with the sense of crisis concerning environment, movements of people, climate change and other planetary transformations.

*Dwelling in political landscapes: contemporary anthropological perspectives* builds substantially upon anthropological work by Tim Ingold and others, which emphasises the ongoing and open-ended, yet historically conditioned ways in which humans and nonhumans produce the environments they inhabit. In such work, landscapes are understood as the medium and outcome of meaningful life activities, where humans, like other animals, dwell. This means that landscapes are neither social/cultural nor natural, but socio-natural. Protesting against and moving on from the proverbial dualisms of modern, Western and maybe capitalist thought, is only the first step in renewing anthropology's methodology for the current epoch, however. The contributions ask how seemingly disconnected temporal, representational, economic and other systemic dynamics fold back on lived experience that are materialised in landscapes.

Foremost through studying how socially valued landscapes become irreversibly disturbed, commodified or subjected to wilful markings or erasures, the book explores a number of approaches to how landscapes are entangled in the ways people gather and organise themselves. These processes have material as well as conceptual dimensions that anthropological analysis typically attends to. Developing such thinking in the context of studies of landscape specifically, several chapters draw from the work of Anna Tsing, who writes in this book about a case from Denmark. Mindful of troubling changes in Earth Systems, they nevertheless argue from empirics, using anthropological and interdisciplinary sources. In this way the authors show that processes of landscape change are always both habitual *and* laden with choices. That is, landscape change is political.

Undoubtedly, landscape politics is bound up not just in how nature has been imagined, but in long histories of consumption. Today, an alarming quest for raw materials and energy is changing both political and geological formations. Meanwhile dominant socio-political aspirations mean the exploitation of staggering volumes of cheap resources like fossil fuels in order to sustain economic processes that are as taken-for-granted as they are unsustainable. Like anthropology generally, this book attends to the contextual details buried in such planetary-scale pictures, whether in typically place-based ways of being human, or in the conditions and value systems reproduced through processes, for example resource extraction, that we usually think of as global.

Building on traditional anthropological strengths, many authors consider the details of how the past is brought into the present – or erased from it – in material flows and sensory awareness, as well as in narratives that are explicitly linked to particular landscapes. Colonial identity formation and the different ways that it links with how landscape is viewed and managed (for instance for resource development for a global market), whether in Southern Africa, Israel/Palestine, the Canadian arctic or Indonesia, is a particularly striking example of how to talk about landscape is also to talk about past, present and future. And as the idea that we inhabit the Anthropocene becomes commonplace, questions of the future have pushed their way into anthropology too, so that like Anna Tsing in this book, the discipline can meaningfully discuss the current era as one of disavowed ruins as well as of poorly understood multispecies relations. Even if new landscape approaches in anthropology explicitly acknowledge the many difficult legacies that the past 500 years of Western hegemony has bequeathed, careful ethnography also highlights complex, often multispecies and multi-sited and temporally nonlinear, processes of new landscape formation.

The interdisciplinary ethos of the book is also manifest in how it builds on previous work not just in anthropology, but also in the history of art and geography. Several authors pick up powerful critiques of representational conventions typical of Euro-American, and particularly colonial, administrations, but which also have historical roots in landscape painting. The authors remind us that, whether for business or pleasure, European visual techniques detached the human observer from the surroundings. Through ethnographic examples, they show the practical problems that arise through time, when such representational systems persist in discounting or devaluing entities and processes of no interest to this colonising gaze. Late capitalism and post-colonialism have been even more destructive, for instance in Indonesia where forests have been disturbed over decades by successive but different waves of resource extraction. Similar dynamics are shown to apply in very varied settings: on an island community in the Baltic whose seascape has been managed to serve the shifting needs of distant powers, in Madagascar where ecotourism has left its traces in local lives, or in Mexico where the colonising force has a disturbingly "green" character in the shape of contested renewable energy (windmills). Like technology more generally, visual technologies and techniques usually associated with colonialism, mapping for example, thus remain important dimensions of anthropological work on landscapes, but in always open ways. For instance, the chapters discuss how they have been adopted and adapted by various colonised and marginalised groups for their own purposes.

To think of landscape as historical and produced across multiple scales, does not mean ignoring its sensuous qualities let alone its often significant role in cosmological systems and other strongly felt and meaningful knowledge. On the contrary, the analyses in the collection attend to the ways people's movements through the landscape produce it as a material and conceptual resource. And in dealing with landscapes of very different kinds, from the Highlands of Papua New Guinea or the gardens-turned-forest and back again in the Amazon, as Philippe Descola's chapter does, to the paradigmatically urban experience of frenetic construction, the book makes important connections between the very visions that the modernist imagination once separated, between the forward-looking city and the supposedly backward hinterlands. The book documents disruption and disturbance that connect even as they disconnect.

# Index

## Studia Fennica Ethnologica

**Memories of My Town**
*The Identities of Town Dwellers
and Their Places in Three
Finnish Towns*
Edited by Anna-Maria Åström,
Pirjo Korkiakangas &
Pia Olsson
Studia Fennica Ethnologica 8
2004

**Passages Westward**
Edited by Maria Lähteenmäki
& Hanna Snellman
Studia Fennica Ethnologica 9
2006

**Defining Self**
*Essays on emergent identities
in Russia Seventeenth to
Nineteenth Centuries*
Edited by Michael Branch
Studia Fennica Ethnologica 10
2009

**Touching Things**
*Ethnological Aspects of Modern
Material Culture*
Edited by Pirjo Korkiakangas,
Tiina-Riitta Lappi &
Heli Niskanen
Studia Fennica Ethnologica 11
2008

**Gendered Rural Spaces**
Edited by Pia Olsson &
Helena Ruotsala
Studia Fennica Ethnologica 12
2009

Laura Stark
**The Limits of Patriarchy**
*How Female Networks of
Pilfering and Gossip Sparked the
First Debates on Rural Gender
Rights in the 19th-century
Finnish-Language Press*
Studia Fennica Ethnologica 13
2011

**Where is the Field?**
*The Experience of Migration
Viewed through the Prism of
Ethnographic Fieldwork*
Edited by Laura Hirvi &
Hanna Snellman
Studia Fennica Ethnologica 14
2012

Laura Hirvi
**Identities in Practice**
*A Trans-Atlantic Ethnography of
Sikh Immigrants in Finland and
in California*
Studia Fennica Ethnologica 15
2013

Eerika Koskinen-Koivisto
**Her Own Worth**
*Negotiations of Subjectivity in
the Life Narrative of a Female
Labourer*
Studia Fennica Ethnologica 16
2014

## Studia Fennica Folkloristica

Venla Sykäri
**Words as Events**
*Cretan Mantinádes in
Performance and Composition*
Studia Fennica Folkloristica 18
2011

**Hidden Rituals and Public
Performances**
*Traditions and Belonging among
the Post-Soviet Khanty, Komi
and Udmurts*
Edited by Anna-Leena Siikala
& Oleg Ulyashev
Studia Fennica Folkloristica 19
2011

**Mythic Discourses**
*Studies in Uralic Traditions*
Edited by Frog, Anna-Leena
Siikala & Eila Stepanova
Studia Fennica Folkloristica 20
2012

Cornelius Hasselblatt
**Kalevipoeg Studies**
*The Creation and Reception of
an Epic*
Studia Fennica Folkloristica 21
2016

**Genre – Text – Interpretation**
*Multidisciplinary Perspectives on
Folklore and Beyond*
Edited by Kaarina Koski, Frog &
Ulla Savolainen
Studia Fennica Folkloristica 22
2016

**Storied and Supernatural
Places**
*Studies in Spatial and Social
Dimensions of Folklore and Sagas*
Edited by Ülo Valk & Daniel
Sävborg
Studia Fennica Folkloristica 23
2018

**Oral Tradition and Book
Culture**
Edited by Pertti Anttonen,
Cecilia af Forselles and
Kirsti Salmi-Niklander
Studia Fennica Folkloristica 24
2018

www.ingramcontent.com/pod-product-compliance
Lightning Source LLC
Chambersburg PA
CBHW081736270326
41932CB00020B/3296